# Con

C000319980

## Tasmania

| | |
|---|---|
| Tasmania Key Map & Distance Chart | 48 |
| Hobart CBD | 49 |
| Hobart Region | 50 |
| Southern Tasmania | 52 |
| Northern Tasmania | 54 |
| Launceston Region | 56 |

## Queensland

| | |
|---|---|
| Queensland Key Map & Distance Chart | 1 |
| Brisbane CBD | 2 |
| Brisbane Throughroads | 3 |
| Brisbane Region | 4 |
| South-East Queensland | 6 |
| Central-East Queensland | 8 |
| North Queensland | 10 |
| Outback Queensland | 12 |
| South-West Queensland | 14 |
| Cape York | 16 |

## South Australia

| | |
|---|---|
| South Australia Key Map & Distance Chart | 57 |
| Adelaide CBD | 58 |
| Adelaide Throughroads | 59 |
| Adelaide Region | 60 |
| Fleurieu Peninsula | 61 |
| South-East South Australia | 62 |
| Central-East South Australia | 64 |
| North-East South Australia | 66 |
| Western South Australia | 68 |

## New South Wales

| | |
|---|---|
| New South Wales Key Map & Distance Chart | 17 |
| Sydney CBD | 18 |
| Sydney Throughroads | 19 |
| Sydney Region | 20 |
| Central-East New South Wales | 22 |
| North-East New South Wales | 24 |
| North-West New South Wales | 26 |
| South-West New South Wales | 28 |
| South-East New South Wales | 30 |
| Canberra CBD (Australian Capital Territory) | 32 |

## Western Australia

| | |
|---|---|
| Western Australia Key Map & Distance Chart | 69 |
| Perth CBD | 70 |
| Perth Throughroads | 71 |
| Perth Region | 72 |
| South-West Western Australia | 74 |
| Central-West Western Australia | 76 |
| North Western Australia | 78 |
| The Kimberley | 80 |
| The Pilbara | 82 |
| South-East Western Australia | 83 |

## Victoria

| | |
|---|---|
| Victoria Key Map & Distance Chart | 33 |
| Melbourne CBD | 34 |
| Melbourne Throughroads | 35 |
| Melbourne Region | 36 |
| South-West Victoria | 38 |
| North-West Victoria | 40 |
| North-East Victoria | 42 |
| Gippsland Region | 44 |
| South-East Victoria | 46 |

## Northern Territory

| | |
|---|---|
| Northern Territory Key Map, Distance Chart & Darwin City | 84 |
| Darwin Region | 85 |
| The Top End | 86 |
| Central Northern Territory | 88 |
| Southern Northern Territory | 90 |
| Index | 92 |
| Quick-Find Distance Chart (Inside back cover) | |

# Legend

| | | |
|---|---|---|
| **Freeway/Divided Highway** | ════════ | Autobahn / Autostrasse<br>Autoroute / route rapide à chaussées séparées<br>Autostrada / superstrada |
| **Freeway – future** | ‑‑‑‑‑‑ | Autobahn – im Bau<br>Autoroute – en construction<br>Autostrada – in costruzione |
| **Major Highway – sealed / unsealed** | ━━━━ ━ ━ ━ | Durchgangsstrasse – befestigt / unbefestigt<br>Route principale – revêtue / non revêtue<br>Strada di grande comunicazione – pavimentata / non pavimentata |
| **Metroad** | ═⟨3⟩═ | Metroad |
| **Main Road – sealed / unsealed** | ━━━━ ━ ━ ━ ━ | Hauptstrasse – befestigt / unbefestigt<br>Route de communication – revêtue / non revêtue<br>Strada principale – pavimentata / non pavimentata |
| **Minor Road – sealed / unsealed** | ──── ─ ─ ─ | Sonstige Strasse – befestigt / unbefestigt<br>Autre route revêtue / non revêtue<br>Altra strada – pavimentata / non pavimentata |
| **Track, four-wheel drive only** | ‑ ‑ ‑ ‑ ‑ ‑ | Piste, nur mit 4-Rad-Antrieb befahrbar<br>Piste, utilisable pour véhicule à 4 roues motrices<br>Pista, praticabile solo con trazione integrale |
| **Walking Track / Trail** | ‑ ‑ ‑ ‑ ‑ ‑ ‑ | Fussweg / Pfad<br>Sentier<br>Sentiero / viottolo |
| **Total Kilometres** | ⋆ 44 ⋆ | Totaldistanz in km<br>Distance totale en km<br>Distanza totale in km |
| **Intermediate Kilometres** | ⌐ 20 ⌐ 24 ⌐ | Teildistanz<br>Distance partielle<br>Distanza parziale |
| **National Route Number / National Highway Number** | ⟨32⟩ A1 | Nationale Strassennummer / Nationale Durchgangsstrassen-Nummer<br>Numéro de route nationale / de route rapide<br>Numero della strada nazionale / Numero della strada di grande comunicazione |
| **State Route Number** | ⟨82⟩ B400 | Staats – Strassennummer<br>Numéro de route d'Etat<br>Nùmero della strada dello stato |
| **Railway – in use / disused** | ━━━━ ━ ━ ━ | Eisenbahn – in Betrieb / stillgelegt<br>Chemin de fer – en service / abandonné<br>Ferrovia – in esercizio / interrotto |
| **Lake or Reservoir** | ⬭ | See oder Reservoir<br>Lac ou réservoir<br>Lago o lago artificiale |
| **Intermittent or Salt Lake** | ⬭ | Periodischer oder Salzwassersee<br>Lac périodique ou d'eau salée<br>Lago periodico o salato |
| **National Park, Reserve** | ▬ | Nationalpark, Reservat<br>Parc national, réserve<br>Parco nazionale, riserva |
| **Regional Reserve** | ▬ | Regionalreservat<br>Réserve régionale<br>Riserva regionale |
| **Conservation, Protected Area** | ▬ | Schutzgebiet<br>Zone protégée<br>Regione protetta |
| **Aboriginal Land** | ▬ | Aborigines – Gebiet<br>Région d'aborigènes<br>Regione d'aborigeni |
| **City or Major Town** | Gawler • | Gross – oder wichtige Stadt<br>Ville importante<br>Città grande o importante |
| **Town or Community** | Skipton • | Stadt oder Gemeinde<br>Ville ou commune<br>Città o comunità |
| **Homestead** | 'Plumbago' ▪ | Gehöft<br>Ferme<br>Masseria |
| **Tourist Point of Interest** | Lookout • | Touristische Sehenswürdigkeit<br>Curiosité touristique<br>Curiosità turistica |
| **Rest Area with Toilet / Water Tank** | ⊼ | Rastplatz mit Toilette oder Wassertank<br>Aire de repos avec toilettes ou citerne d'eau<br>Area di riposo con gabinetto o serbatoio d'acqua |
| **Tourist Route** | 204 | Touristenstrasse<br>Route touristique<br>Strada turistica |
| **Airport** | ✈ | Flughafen<br>Aéroport<br>Aeroporto |
| **Mountain / Hill** | + Mt Brown | Berg / Hügel<br>Montagne / colline<br>Monte / colle |
| **State border** | ━ ・ ━ | Staatsgrenze<br>Frontière d'Etat<br>Confine dello stato |

# Queensland

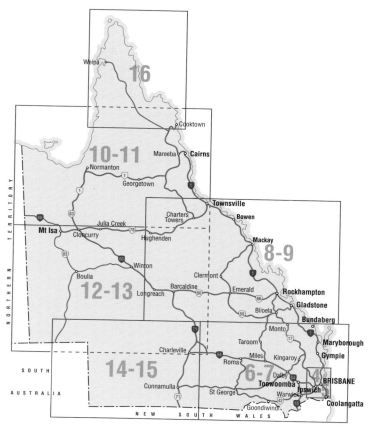

## Distance Chart

| | Brisbane | | | | | | | | | | | | | |
|---|---|---|---|---|---|---|---|---|---|---|---|---|---|---|
| **Bundaberg** | 361 | | | | | | | | | | | | | |
| **Cairns** | 1399 | 1712 | | | | | | | | | | | | |
| **Cape York** | 1038 | 2437 | 2750 | | | | | | | | | | | |
| **Charleville** | 2659 | 1621 | 918 | 744 | | | | | | | | | | |
| **Goondiwindi** | 624 | 2750 | 1712 | 591 | 350 | | | | | | | | | |
| **Longreach** | 1052 | 509 | 2150 | 1112 | 995 | 1172 | | | | | | | | |
| **Mackay** | 785 | 981 | 1038 | 1781 | 743 | 656 | 969 | | | | | | | |
| **Mount Isa** | 1240 | 636 | 1688 | 1145 | 2278 | 1240 | 1631 | 1808 | | | | | | |
| **Rockhampton** | 1309 | 334 | 673 | 647 | 833 | 2115 | 1077 | 322 | 635 | | | | | |
| **Roma** | 568 | 1329 | 773 | 693 | 359 | 265 | 2391 | 1353 | 653 | 479 | | | | |
| **Toowoomba** | 351 | 639 | 1680 | 973 | 1044 | 222 | 616 | 2754 | 1716 | 412 | 128 | | | |
| **Townsville** | 1355 | 1004 | 728 | 891 | 394 | 763 | 1363 | 1272 | 1387 | 349 | 1050 | 1363 | | |
| **Winton** | 587 | 1220 | 869 | 849 | 460 | 963 | 176 | 1228 | 685 | 1829 | 791 | 1171 | 1348 | |

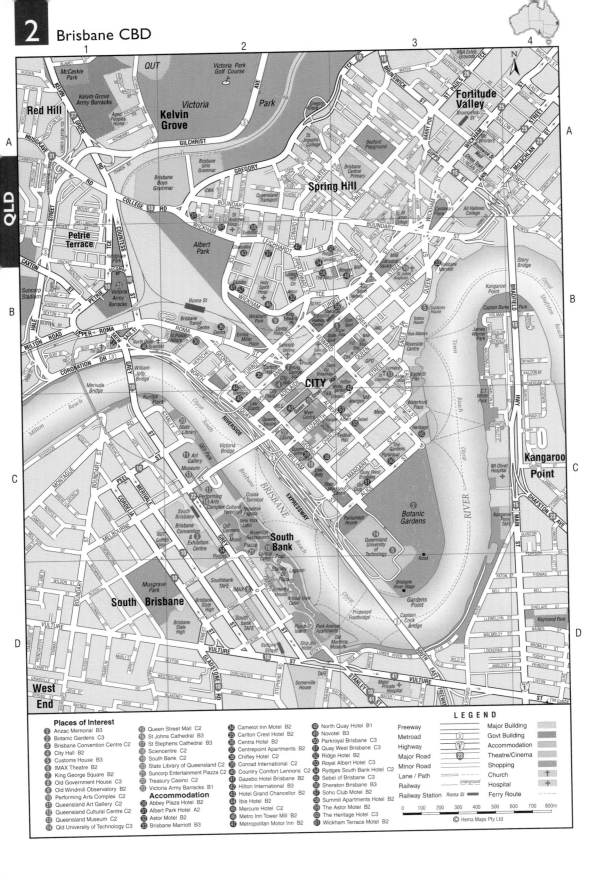

**Places of Interest**
1. Anzac Memorial B3
2. Botanic Gardens C3
3. Brisbane Convention Centre C2
4. City Hall B2
5. Customs House B3
6. IMAX Theatre B2
7. King George Square B2
8. Old Government House C3
9. Old Windmill Observatory B2
10. Performing Arts Complex C2
11. Queensland Art Gallery C2
12. Queensland Cultural Centre C2
13. Queensland Museum C2
14. Qld University of Technology C3
15. Queen Street Mall C2
16. St Johns Cathedral B3
17. St Stephens Cathedral B3
18. Sciencentre C2
19. South Bank C2
20. State Library of Queensland C2
21. Suncorp Entertainment Piazza C2
22. Treasury Casino C2
23. Victoria Army Barracks B1

**Accommodation**
30. Abbey Plaza Hotel B2
31. Albert Park Hotel A2
32. Astor Motel B2
33. Brisbane Marriott B3
34. Camelot Inn Motel B2
35. Carlton Crest Hotel B2
36. Centra Hotel B2
37. Centrepoint Apartments B2
38. Chifley Hotel C2
39. Conrad International C2
40. Country Comfort Lennons C2
41. Gazebo Hotel Brisbane B2
42. Hilton International B3
43. Hotel Grand Chancellor B2
44. Ibis Hotel C2
45. Mercure Hotel C2
46. Metro Inn Tower Mill B2
47. Metropolitan Motor Inn B2
48. North Quay Hotel B1
49. Novotel B3
50. Parkroyal Brisbane C3
51. Quay West Brisbane C3
52. Ridge Hotel B2
53. Royal Albert Hotel C3
54. Rydges South Bank Hotel C2
55. Sebel of Brisbane C3
56. Sheraton Brisbane B3
57. Soho Club Motel B2
58. Summit Apartments Hotel B2
59. The Astor Motel B2
60. The Heritage Hotel B3
61. Wickham Terrace Motel B2

**LEGEND**

| | |
|---|---|
| Freeway | Major Building |
| Metroad | Govt Building |
| Highway | Accommodation |
| Major Road | Theatre/Cinema |
| Minor Road | Shopping |
| Lane / Path | Church |
| Railway | Hospital |
| Railway Station | Ferry Route |

0  100  200  300  400  500  600  700  800m

© Hema Maps Pty Ltd

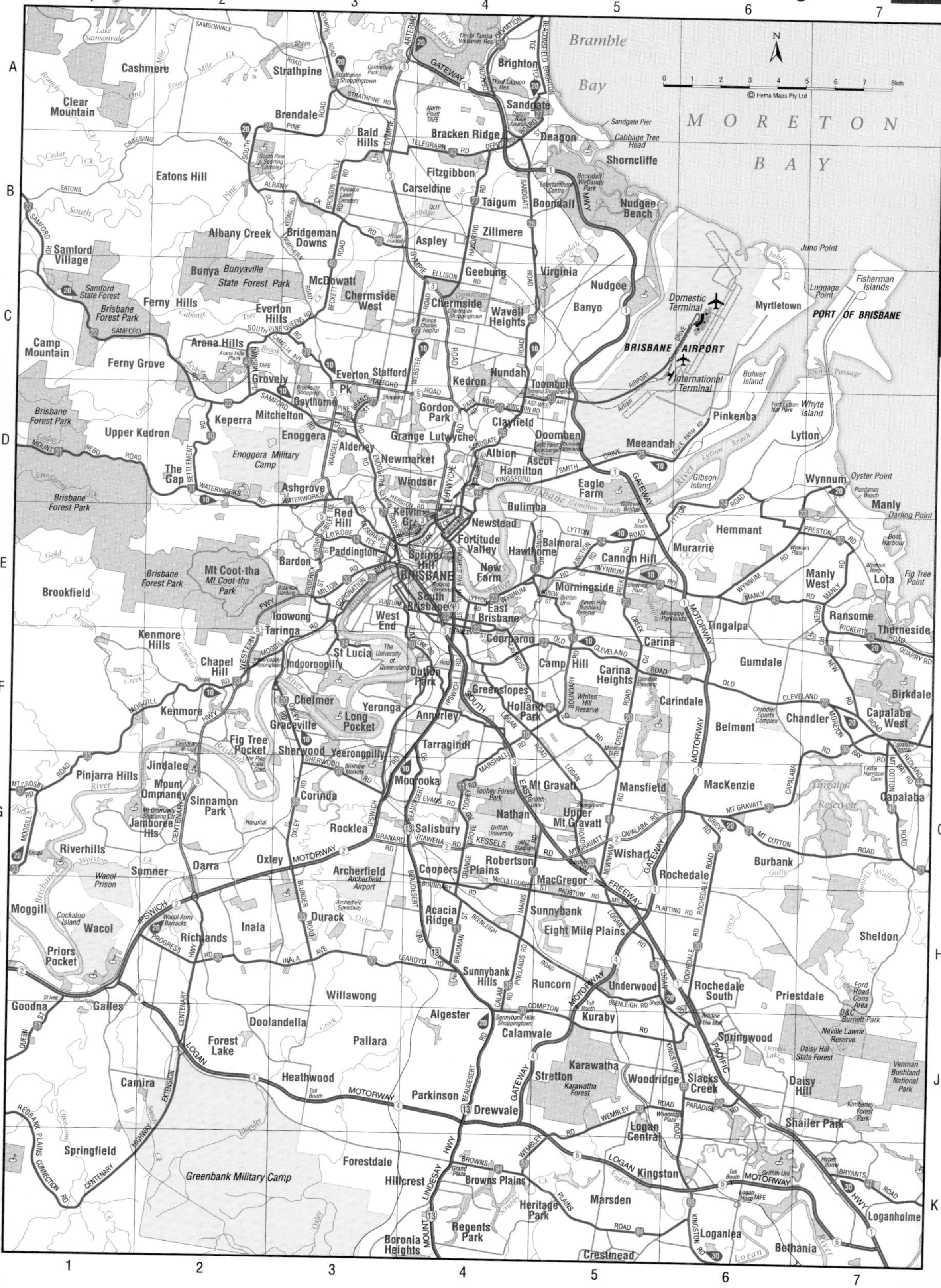

Bramble Bay
MORETON BAY
Hema Maps Pty Ltd
0 1 2 3 4 5 6 7 8km
Cashmere
Clear Mountain
Strathpine
Brendale
Bald Hills
Bracken Ridge
Brighton
Sandgate
Deagon
Shorncliffe
Eatons Hill
Fitzgibbon
Carseldine
Taigum
Boondall
Nudgee Beach
Albany Creek
Bridgeman Downs
Aspley
Zillmere
Samford Village
Bunya
Bunyaville State Forest Park
McDowall
Geebung
Virginia
Nudgee
Samford State Forest
Brisbane Forest Park
Ferny Hills
Everton Hills
Chermside West
Chermside
Wavell Heights
Banyo
Domestic Terminal
Myrtletown
PORT OF BRISBANE
Fisherman Islands
Luggage Point
Juno Point
Camp Mountain
Arana Hills
Ferny Grove
BRISBANE AIRPORT
International Terminal
Grovely
Everton Pk
Stafford
Kedron
Nundah
Toombul
Bulwer Island
Whyte Island
Pinkenba
Mitchelton
Gaythorne
Gordon Park
Clayfield
Lytton
Upper Kedron
Keperra
Enoggera
Alderley
Grange
Lutwyche
Doomben
Meeandah
Enoggera Military Camp
Newmarket
Albion
Ascot
Hamilton
The Gap
Windsor
Eagle Farm
Gibson Island
Wynnum
Manly
Ashgrove
Red Hill
Kelvin Grove
Newstead
Bulimba
Hemmant
Paddington
Spring Hill
Fortitude Valley
Hawthorne
Balmoral
Cannon Hill
Murarrie
Lota
Bardon
Mt Coot-tha
Mt Coot-tha Park
BRISBANE
New Farm
Morningside
Manly West
Brookfield
Milton
South Brisbane
East Brisbane
Toowong
Taringa
West End
Ransome
Thorneside
Tingalpa
Kenmore Hills
St Lucia
Coorparoo
Carina
Camp Hill
Gumdale
Chapel Hill
Indooroopilly
Dutton Park
Carina Heights
Birkdale
Kenmore
Chelmer
Greenslopes
Carindale
Yeronga
Holland Park
Chandler
Capalaba West
Graceville
Long Pocket
Annerley
Belmont
Fig Tree Pocket
Tarragindi
Sherwood
Yeerongpilly
Jindalee
Pinjarra Hills
Moorooka
Mt Gravatt
Mansfield
MacKenzie
Capalaba
Mount Ommaney
Corinda
Sinnamon Park
Nathan
Upper Mt Gravatt
Jamboree Hts
Rocklea
Salisbury
Riverhills
Oxley
Wishart
Burbank
Sumner
Darra
Archerfield
Coopers Plains
Robertson
MacGregor
Rochedale
Wacol Prison
Moggill
Wacol
Durack
Acacia Ridge
Sunnybank
Richlands
Inala
Eight Mile Plains
Sheldon
Priors Pocket
Sunnybank Hills
Runcorn
Underwood
Rochedale South
Priestdale
Goodna
Gailes
Willawong
Algester
Kuraby
Doolandella
Calamvale
Springwood
Forest Lake
Pallara
Daisy Hill State Forest
Camira
Heathwood
Stretton
Karawatha
Woodridge
Slacks Creek
Daisy Hill
Venman Bushland National Park
Parkinson
Drewvale
Shailer Park
Springfield
Logan Central
Greenbank Military Camp
Forestdale
Hillcrest
Browns Plains
Kingston
Marsden
Heritage Park
Loganholme
Boronia Heights
Regents Park
Crestmead
Loganlea
Bethania

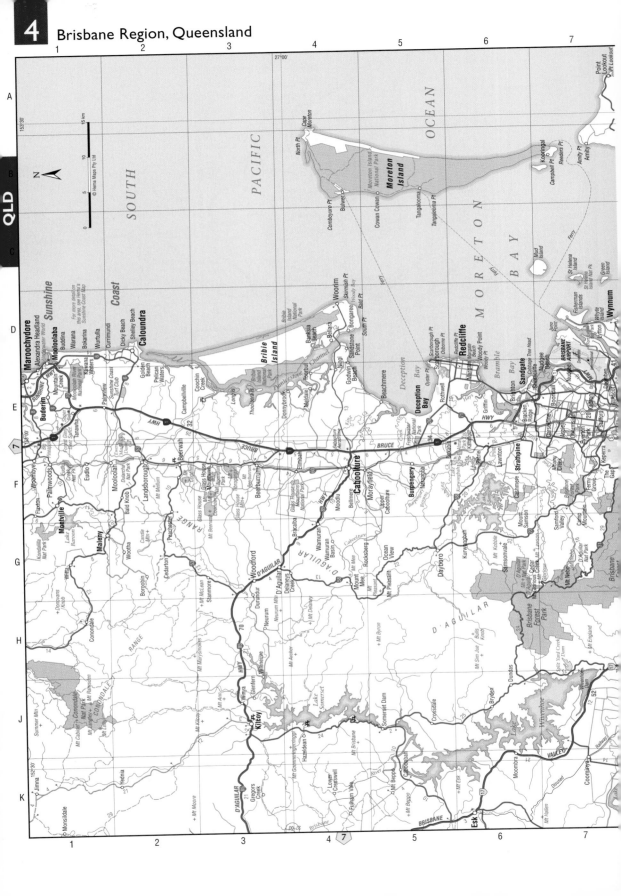

QLD

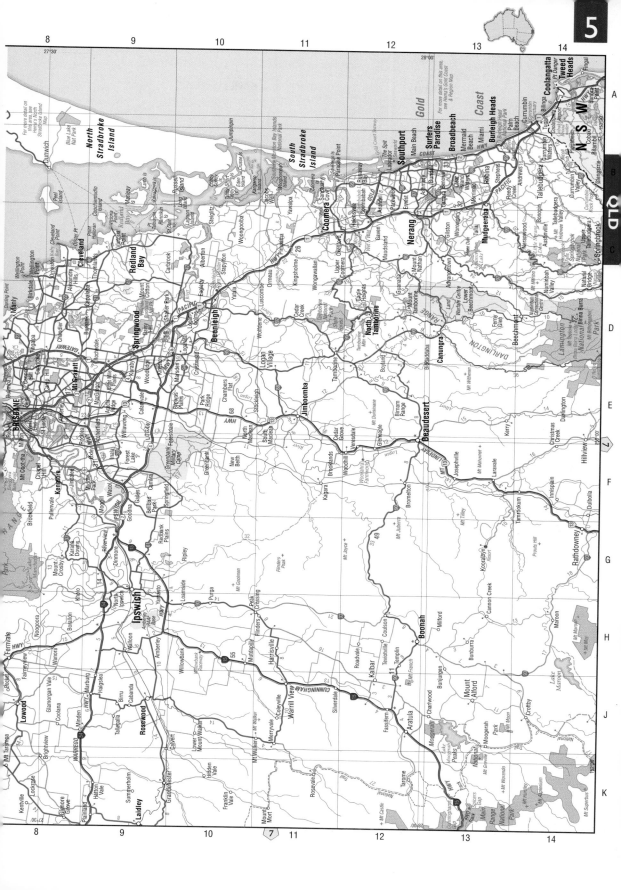

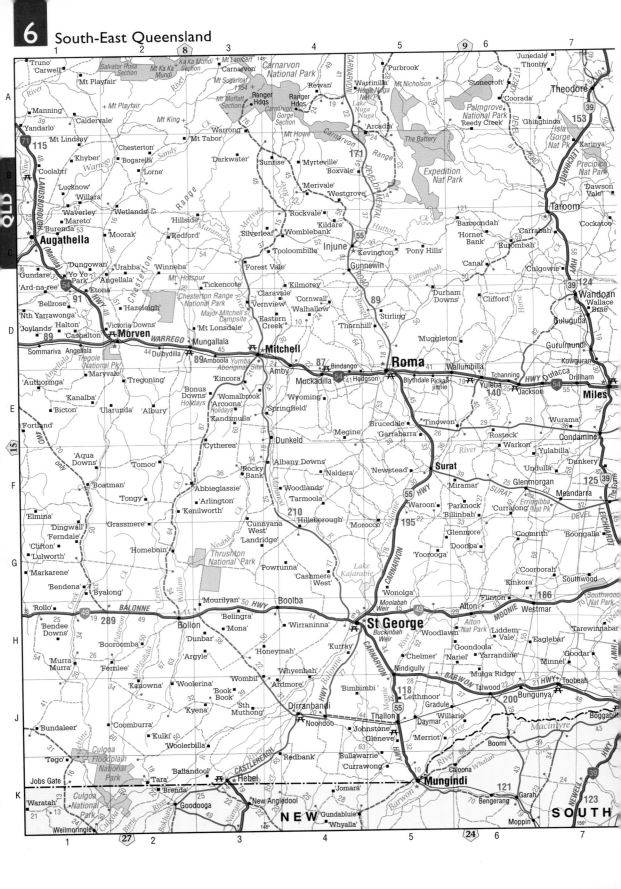

HERVEY BAY MARINE PARK

Sandy Cape

© Hema Maps Pty Ltd

0 50km

N

QLD

SOUTH

PACIFIC

OCEAN

**Major towns and cities:**

'Kurrajong' · Cania Gorge NP · Moonford · Kalpowar · Mungungo · Bancroft · Miara · Moore Park · Burnett Heads · Bargara · Coral Coast

'Glandore' · Monto · Mulgildie · Three Moon · Yandaran · Avondale · Monduran Dam · South Kolan · Bullyard · **Bundaberg** · Elliott Heads · Buxtonville · Burrum Coast

Camboon · Rawbelle · 'Barram' · Abercorn · Gin Gin · Wallaville · Goodnight Scrub NP · Goodwood · Burrum Heads · **Hervey Bay** · Woody Is · Fraser Island

'Glencoe' · 'Tireen' · Cynthia · Ceratodus · 'Kerwee' · Mount Perry · Booyal · Cordalba · Isis · Woodgate · **Childers** · Howard · Torbanlea · Kingfisher Bay

Cracow · Eidsvold · Wuruma Dam · 'Rosslyn' · Dallarnil · Aramara · Maryborough · Maaroom · Boonooroo · Poona · Eurong

'Fairyland' · 'Calrossie' · 'Redbank' · Widbury · Binjour · Byrnestown · Coalstoun Lakes · Biggenden · Brooweena · Mungar · Tiaro · Bauple · Mt Bauple Nat Park

**Mundubbera** · Dykehead · **Gayndah** · Ban Ban Springs · Mt Walsh National Park · Theebine · Tin Can Bay · Inskip Point · Rainbow Beach

'Hawkwood' · Auburn River National Park · Boogooramunya · Windera · Tansey · Kilkivan · Woolooga · Glenwood · Gunalda · Double Island Point · Cherry Venture

'Mt Misery' · 'Auburn' · Mt Saul · Brovinia · Boondooma Dam · Proston · Goomeri · Manyung · **Gympie** · Kin Kin · Cooran · Pomona · Tewantin · Noosa Heads

'Glenrowan' · 'Durah' · Monogorilby · Lake Boondooma · Hivesville · Wondai · Goomeri · Glastonbury · Kin Kin · Cooroy · Eumundi · Noosa Nat Park

Barakula · 'Fairyland' · Durong South · Boondooma · Tingoora · Cherbourg · Manumbar · Amamoor · Kandanga · Imbil · Brooloo · Cooroy · Coolum Beach

Goombi · Baking Board · 'Pinedale' · Boonarga · **Kingaroy** · Memerambi · Wooroolin · Elgin Vale · Yednia · Conondale · Kenilworth · Yandina · **Nambour** · **Maroochydore**

Columboola · **Chinchilla** · Brigalow · Warra · Kumbia · Goodger · **Nanango** · Jimna · Mapleton · Montville · Mooloolaba

Kogan · Jandowae · Cooranga North · Bunya Mtns Nat Pk · Yarraman · Linville · Conondale · Maleny · Landsborough · Coast · **Caloundra**

South Tara Glen · Macalister · Jimbour · Pirrinuan · Bell · Kaimkillenbun · Wutul · Cooyar · Blackbutt · Moore · Harlin · Woodford · Beerwah · Glass Hse Mtns · Bribie Is Nat Park

Goranba · Daandine · Quinalow · Peranga · Acland · Toogoolawah · Somerset Dam · Kilcoy · Warnuran · Beerburrum · Bribie Island · Bongaree

Cabawin · **Dalby** · Kulpi · Haden · Crows Nest · Esk · Samsonvale · Dayboro · Strathpine · Deception Bay · **Redcliffe** · Tangalooma · Moreton Island

Tullagrie · Kumbarilla · Bowenville · Jondaryan · Goombungee · Meringandan · Hampton · Coominya · Lowood · Petrie · Samford · **BRISBANE** · Amity · Point Lookout

Weranga · Gulera · Oakey · Aubigny · Murphys Ck · Helidon · Marburg · **IPSWICH** · Capalaba · Dunwich · Blue Lake Nat Park

'Halliford' · Cecil Plains · **TOOWOOMBA** · Gatton · Laidley · Rosewood · **Logan** · Redland Bay · North Stradbroke Island

'Waar Waar' · 'New Dunmore' · Brookstead · Camboya · Pittsworth · Greenmount · Nobby · Clifton · **Beenleigh** · Jimboomba · Tamborine · South Stradbroke Island · Coomera

Moonie · 'Allawah' · Millmerran · Leyburn · Allora · Aratula · Boonah · Kalbar · **Nerang** · **Southport** · **Surfers Paradise** · Gold Coast

'Trevanna Downs' · 'Wyaga' · Karara · Hendon · Main Range Nat Park · Rathdowney · Beaudesert · Canungra · Mudgeeraba · Broadbeach · Burleigh Heads

Bendidee Nat Park · Inglewood · Whetstone · Cobba-da-mana · Mt Burrabaranga · **Warwick** · Killarney · Binna Burra · Springbrook · **Coolangatta** · **Tweed Heads**

Gibnbell · Yelarbon · Pikedale · Coolmunda Dam · Woodenbong · Urbenville · Mt Warning · Uki · **Murwillumbah** · Pottsville · Kingscliff

Kurumbul · Limevale · **Stanthorpe** · Sundown Nat Park · Toonumbar Nat Park · Wiangaree · Kunghur · Mooball

North Star · **Texas** · Silver Spur · Boonoo Boonoo Nat Park · Richmond Range Nat Park · Ettrick · Nimbin · **Brunswick Heads** · Cape Byron · **Byron Bay**

Yallaroi · Bonshaw · Glenlyon Dam · Wallangarra · Mummulgum · Bonalbo · **Kyogle** · Bangalow · Lennox Head

**WALES** · **Tenterfield** · Alice · Bruxner Hwy · **Casino** · **Lismore** · Coraki · **Ballina** · Broadwater · Evans Head · Whiporie · Woodburn · Broadwater Nat Park

# Central-East Queensland

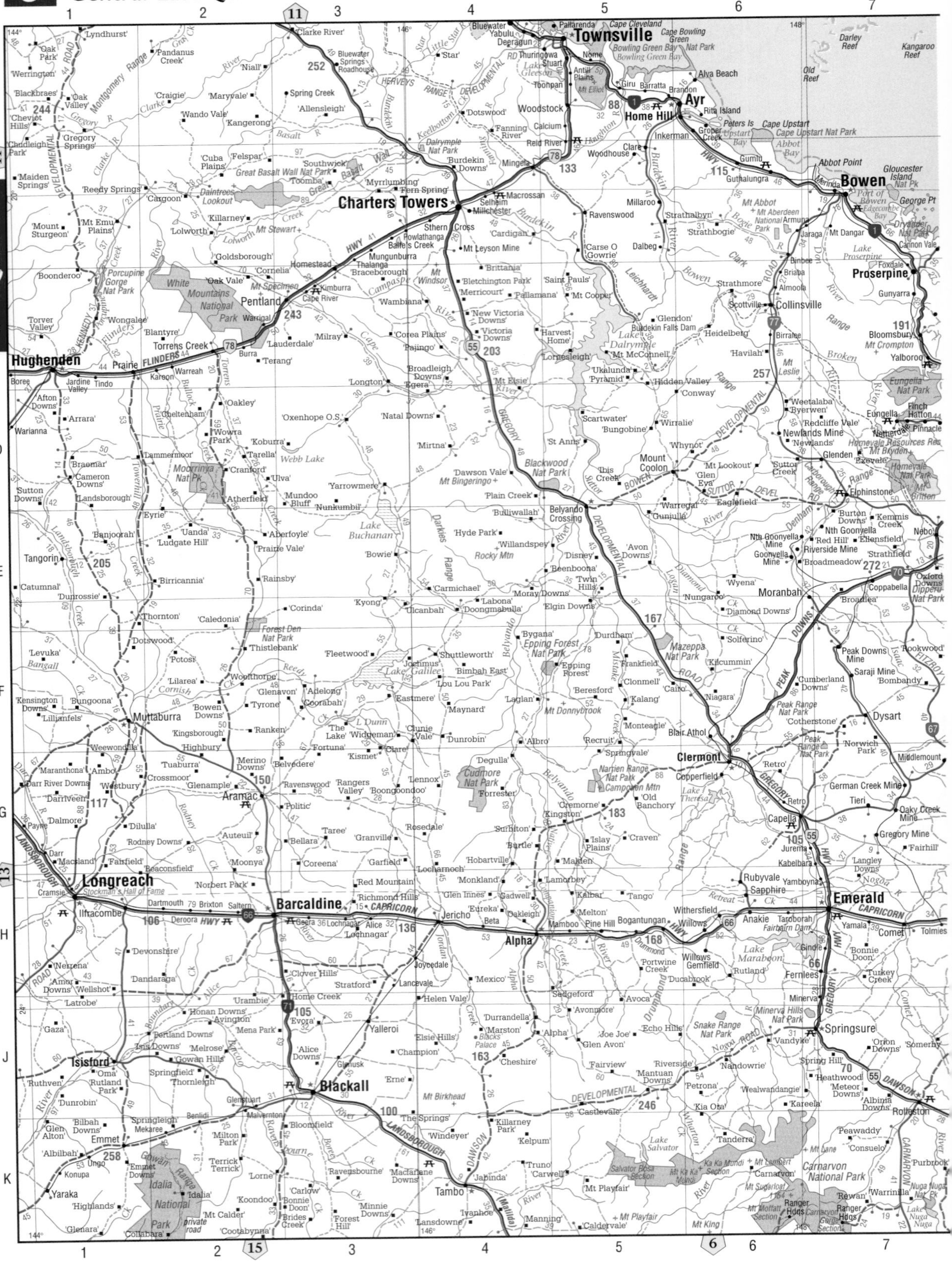

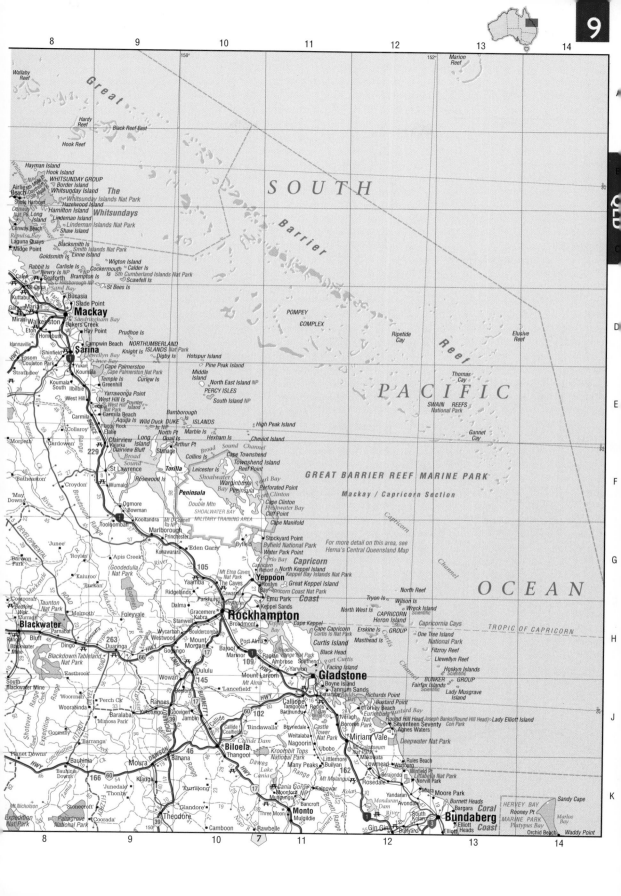

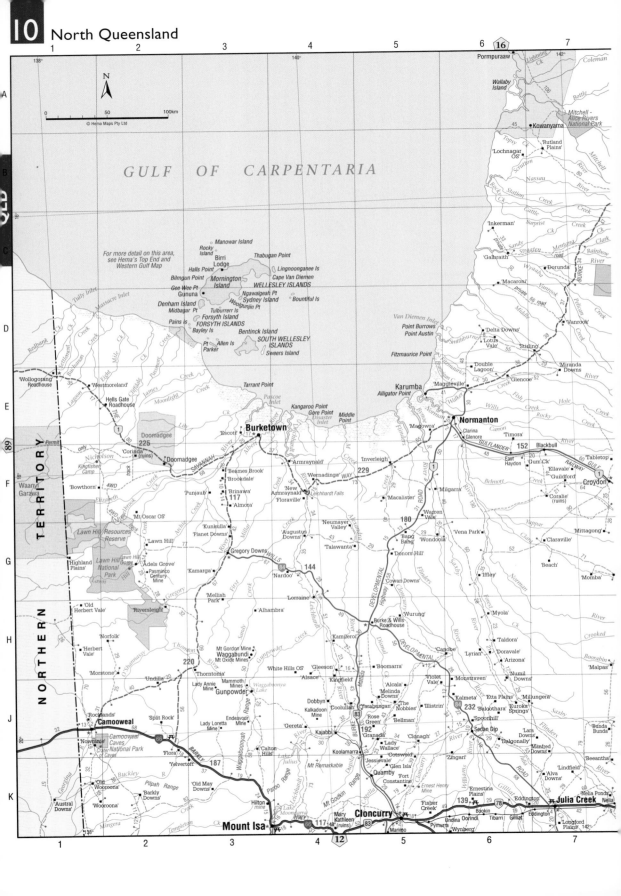

GULF OF CARPENTARIA

For more detail on this area,
see Hema's Top End and
Western Gulf Map

0    50    100km
© Hema Maps Pty Ltd

**NORTHERN TERRITORY**

Manowar Island
Rocky Island
Birri Lodge
Halls Point
Bilmgun Point
Gee Wee Pt
Gununa
Mornington Island
Denham Island
Midbagar Pt
Pains Is
Bayley Is
Pt Allen Is
Parker

WELLESLEY ISLANDS
Thabugan Point
Lingnoonganee Is
Cape Van Diemen
Ngawalgeah Pt
Sydney Island
Woolgunjin Pt
Tulburrer Is
Forsyth Island
FORSYTH ISLANDS
Bentinck Island
SOUTH WELLESLEY ISLANDS
Sweers Island
Bountiful Is

Van Diemen Inlet
Point Burrows
Point Austin

Fitzmaurice Point

Pormpuraaw
Wallaby Island
Mitchell - Alice Rivers National Park
Kowanyama
'Lochnagar OS'
'Rutland Plains'
'Inkerman'
'Galbraith'
'Dorunda'
Macaroni
private 86 road
'Vanrook'
'Delta Downs'
'Lotus Vale'
Stirling
Miranda Downs
'Double Lagoon'
Glencoe

'Wollogorang Roadhouse'
'Westmoreland'
Hells Gate Roadhouse
Tarrant Point
Kangaroo Point
Gore Point
Disaster Inlet
Middle Point

Karumba
Alligator Point
'Maggieville'
Normanton
Clarina
Glenore
GULFLANDER
'Magowra'
'Timora'
152  Blackbull
Tabletop
East Haydon
'Gum' Ck
'Ellavale'
'Guildford'
Croydon

Doomadgee
225
'Corinda' (ruins)
Doomadgee
'Escott'
Burketown
'Armraynald'
'Inverleigh'
'Beames Brook'
Brookdale'
'Brinawa'
117
'Almora'
New Armraynald'
'Floraville'
Leichhardt Falls
'Wernandinga'
229
'Macalister'
'Milgarra'
'Coralie' (ruins)

Punjaub'
'Mt Oscar OS'
'Kunkulla'
'Planet Downs'
'Augustus Downs'
'Neumayer Valley'
'Warren Vale'
180
'Vena Park'
'Claraville'
Mittagong'

Lawn Hill Resources Reserve
Lawn Hill National Park
'Highland Plains'
Pasminco Century Mine
'Adels Grove'
'Kamarga'
Gregory Downs
144
'Nardoo'
'Wondoola'
'Bang Bang'
Donors Hill
'Iffley'
'Beach'
'Momba'

'Old Herbert Vale'
'Riversleigh'
'Mellish Park'
Lorraine
Cowan Downs
'Myola'
Taldora'
'Doravale'
Boorabin

'Herbert Vale'
'Norfolk'
220
Mt Gordon Mine
Waggabundi
Mt Oxide Mines
'Alhambra'
Burke & Wills Roadhouse
'Wurung'
'Kamileroi'
'Canobe'
'Lyrian'
'Arizona'
'Malpas'

'Morstone'
Undilla
Thorntoma
White Hills OS
'Gleeson'
'Alsace'
16
'Boomarra'
'Monstraven'
Numil Downs

Lady Annie Mine
Mammoth Mines
Gunpowder
Kingfield
'Alcala'
'Melinda Downs'
The Nobbies'
Illistrin'
Kalmeta
'Etta Plains'
Millungera'
Euroka Springs'

'Rocklands'
Endeavour Mine
Dobbyn
Kalkadoon Mine
'Yarabungan'
'Rose Green'
'Bellman'
Spoorhill'
Sedan Dip
Lars Dally'
'Bunda Bunda'

Camooweal
'Nowranie'
Camooweal Caves
Crade National Park of Caves
'Split Rock'
Lady Loretta Mine
'Gereta'
Kajabbi
183
Granada
'Clonagh'
Dalgonally'
Beeantha'

'Flora'
'Yelvertoft'
187
'Calton Hills'
Koolamarra
'Lady Wallace'
Cotswold'
Quamby
'Lindfield'
'Alva Downs'

'Old Wooroona'
'Barkly Downs'
'Old May Downs'
Hilton mine
Mt Remarkable
Jessievale'
'Glen Isla'
Fort Constantine'
Ernest Henry Mine
'Ernestina Plains'
139
Bookin
78
Eddington
Julia Creek
Nelia Ponds
Nelia

'Austral Downs'
'Wooroona'
Mount Isa
HWY
117
Mary Kathleen (ruins)
Cloncurry
83
Marimo
Pymurra
Undina Oorindi
Tibarri Gilliat
'Wynberg'
Longford Plains
12
'Fisher Creek'
192
Quamby
Sedan Dip
Zingari'
Manfred Downs

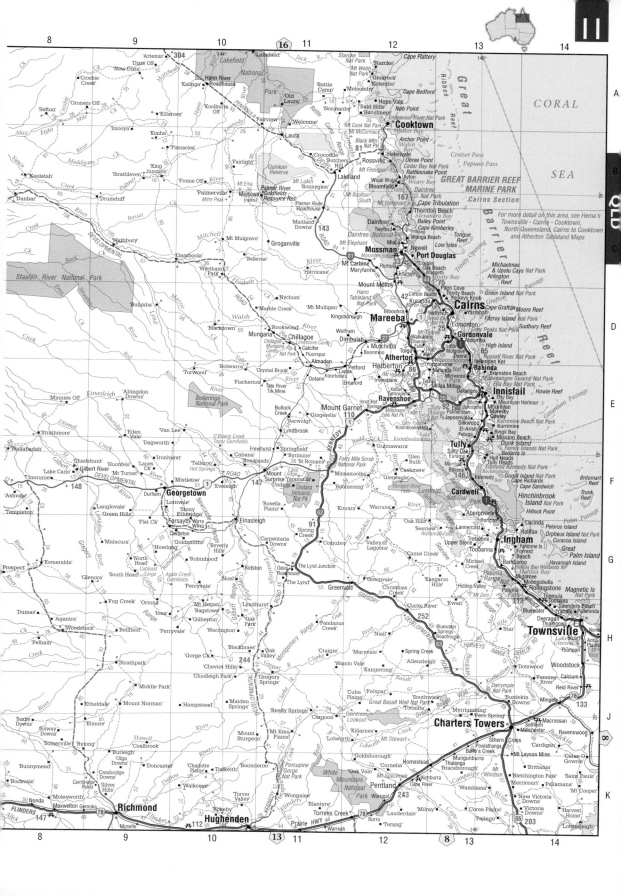

QLD

NORTHERN TERRITORY

SOUTH AUSTRALIA

Simpson Desert

Simpson Desert National Park

TROPIC OF CAPRICORN

**Major towns:** Mount Isa, Cloncurry, Julia Creek, McKinlay, Kynuna (Roadhouse), Middleton, Boulia, Bedourie, Birdsville, Betoota, Duchess, Dajarra, Urandangi

Alnetye Aboriginal Land

Astrelba Downs National Park

Diamantina Gates 'Diamantina Lakes' National Park

For more detail on this area, see Hema's Queensland's Outback Map

Poeppel Corner

Haddon Corner

Simpson Desert Conservation Park

FRENCH LINE

QAA LINE

WAA LINE

Tropic of Capricorn

© Hema Maps Pty Ltd

0 ... 50

N

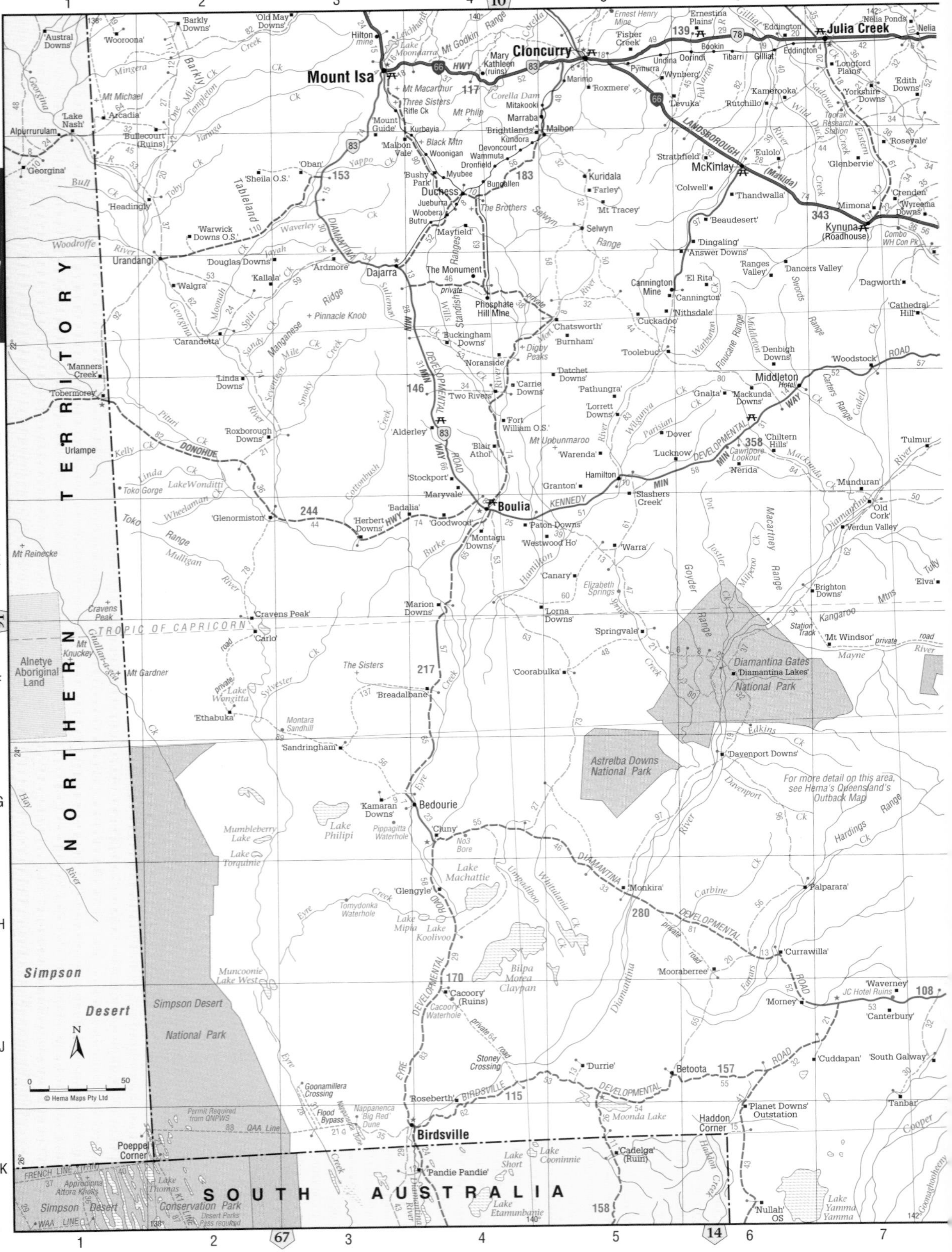

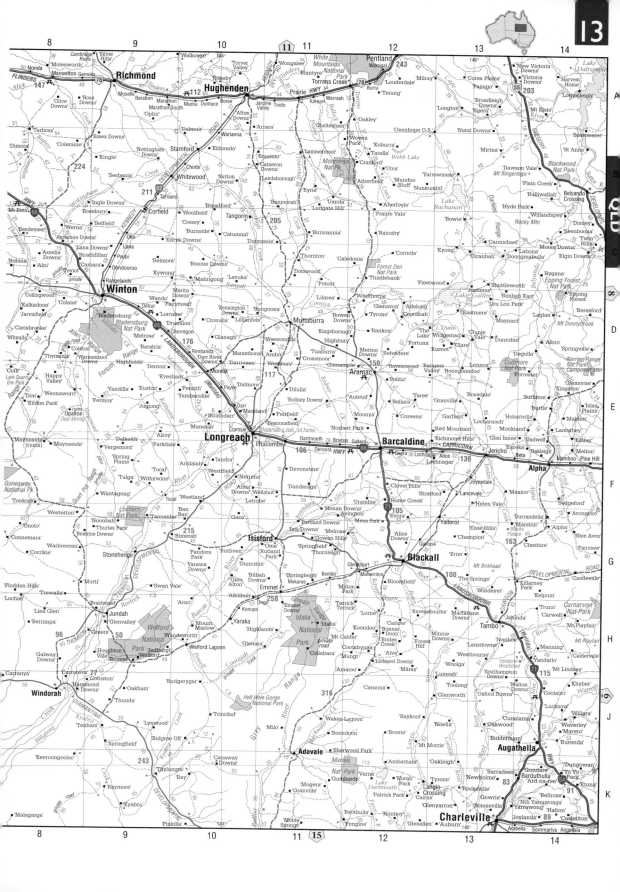

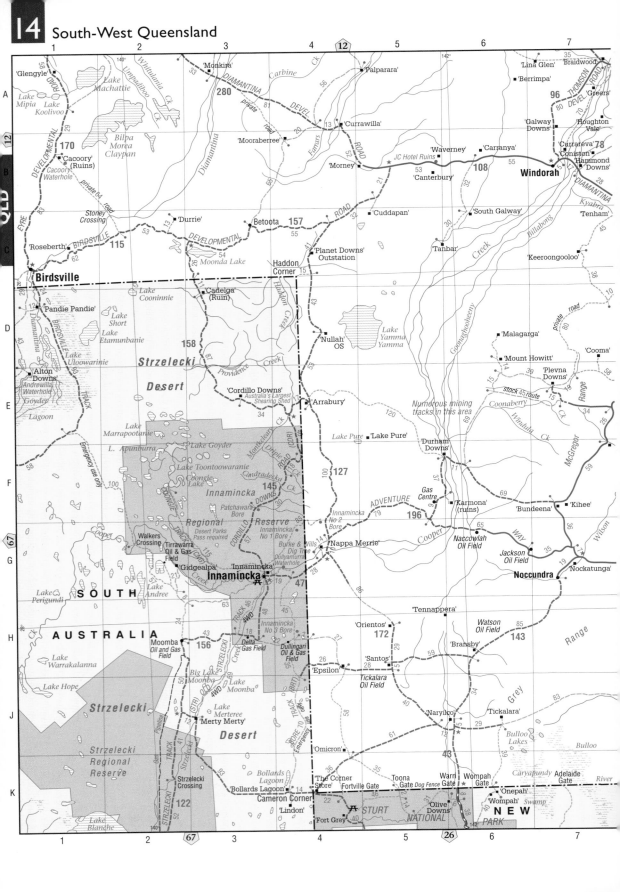

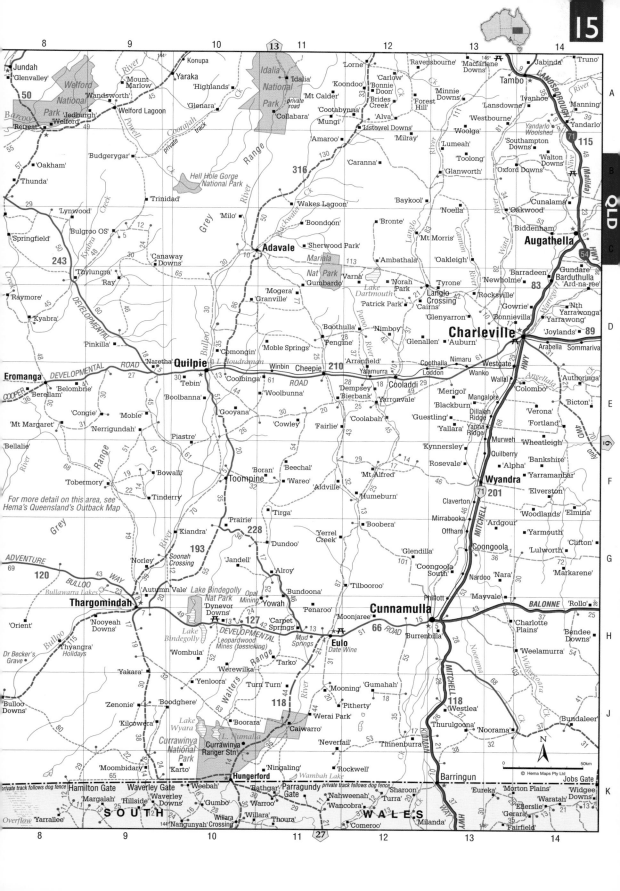

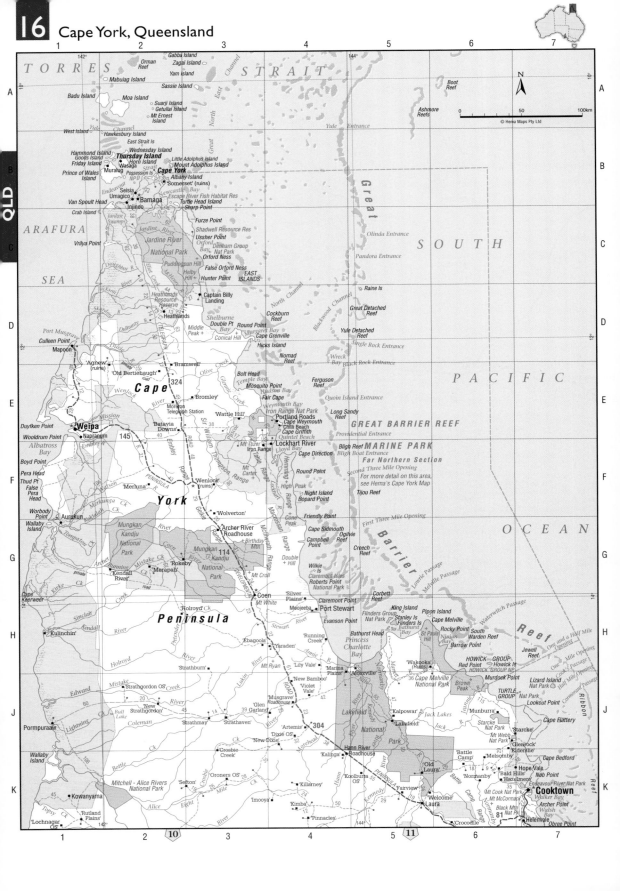

# New South Wales

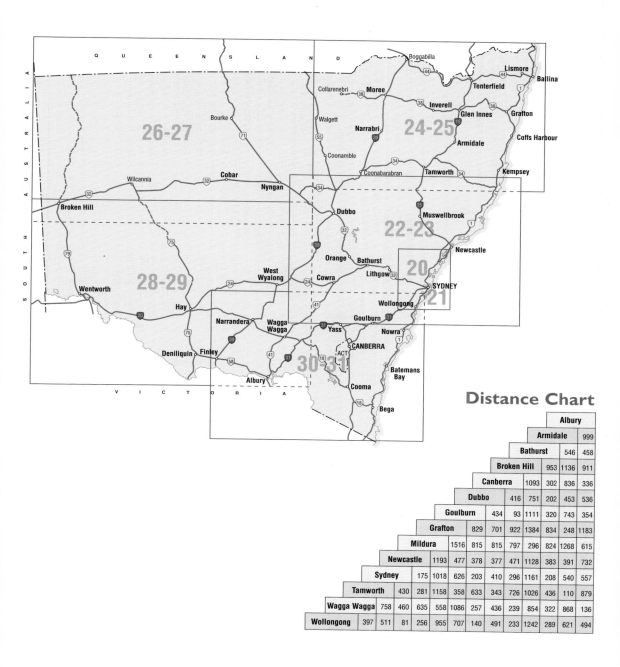

## Distance Chart

| | Albury |
|---|---|
| **Armidale** | 999 |
| **Bathurst** 546 | 458 |
| **Broken Hill** 953 1136 | 911 |
| **Canberra** 1093 302 836 | 336 |
| **Dubbo** 416 751 202 453 | 536 |
| **Goulburn** 434 93 1111 320 743 | 354 |
| **Grafton** 829 701 922 1384 834 248 | 1183 |
| **Mildura** 1516 815 815 797 296 824 1268 | 615 |
| **Newcastle** 1193 477 378 377 471 1128 383 391 | 732 |
| **Sydney** 175 1018 626 203 410 296 1161 208 540 | 557 |
| **Tamworth** 430 281 1158 358 633 343 726 1026 436 110 | 879 |
| **Wagga Wagga** 758 460 635 558 1086 257 436 239 854 322 868 | 136 |
| **Wollongong** 397 511 81 256 955 707 140 491 233 1242 289 621 | 494 |

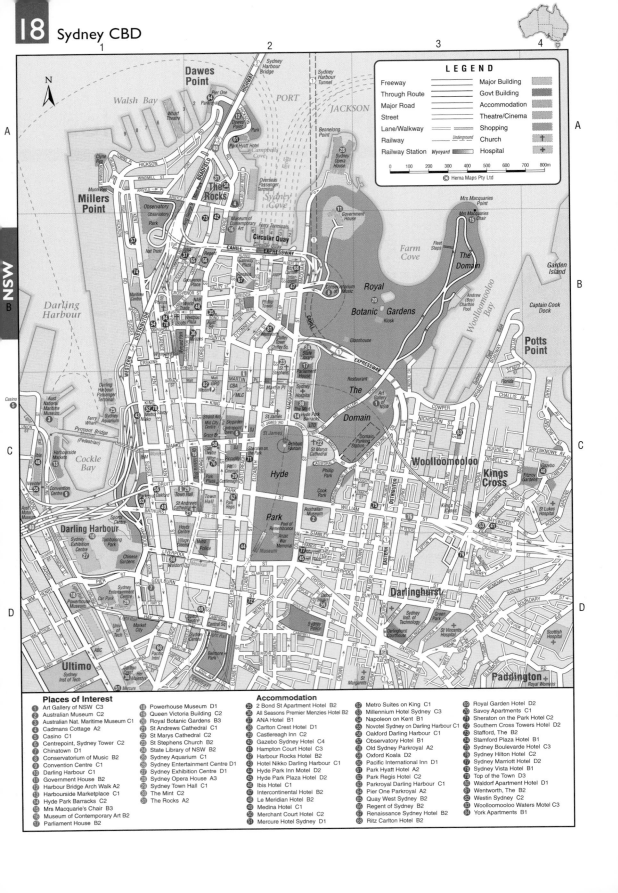

## LEGEND

| | | | |
|---|---|---|---|
| Freeway | | Major Building | |
| Through Route | | Govt Building | |
| Major Road | | Accommodation | |
| Street | | Theatre/Cinema | |
| Lane/Walkway | | Shopping | |
| Railway | Underground | Church | † |
| Railway Station | Wynyard | Hospital | + |

0 100 200 300 400 500 600 700 800m

© Hema Maps Pty Ltd

## Places of Interest

1  Art Gallery of NSW  C3
2  Australian Museum  C2
3  Australian Nat. Maritime Museum C1
4  Cadmans Cottage  A2
5  Casino  C1
6  Centrepoint, Sydney Tower  C2
7  Chinatown  D1
8  Conservatorium of Music  B2
9  Convention Centre  C1
10  Darling Harbour  C1
11  Government House  B2
12  Harbour Bridge Arch Walk  A2
13  Harbourside Marketplace  C1
14  Hyde Park Barracks  C2
15  Mrs Macquarie's Chair  B3
16  Museum of Contemporary Art  B2
17  Parliament House  B2
18  Powerhouse Museum  D1
19  Queen Victoria Building  C2
20  Royal Botanic Gardens  B3
21  St Andrews Cathedral  C1
22  St Marys Cathedral  C2
23  St Stephens Church  B2
24  State Library of NSW  B2
25  Sydney Aquarium  C1
26  Sydney Entertainment Centre  D1
27  Sydney Exhibition Centre  D1
28  Sydney Opera House  A3
29  Sydney Town Hall  C1
30  The Mint  C2
31  The Rocks  A2

## Accommodation

35  2 Bond St Apartment Hotel  B2
36  All Seasons Premier Menzies Hotel B2
37  ANA Hotel  B1
38  Carlton Crest Hotel  D1
39  Castlereagh Inn  C2
40  Gazebo Sydney Hotel  C4
41  Hampton Court Hotel  C3
42  Harbour Rocks Hotel  B2
43  Hotel Nikko Darling Harbour  C1
44  Hyde Park Inn Motel  D2
45  Hyde Park Plaza Hotel  D2
46  Ibis Hotel  C1
47  Intercontinental Hotel  B2
48  Le Meridian Hotel  B2
49  Medina Hotel  C1
50  Merchant Court Hotel  C2
51  Mercure Hotel Sydney  D1
52  Metro Suites on King  C1
53  Millennium Hotel Sydney  C3
54  Napoleon on Kent  B1
55  Novotel Sydney on Darling Harbour C1
56  Oakford Darling Harbour  C1
57  Observatory Hotel  B1
58  Old Sydney Parkroyal  A2
59  Oxford Koala  D2
60  Pacific International Inn  D1
61  Park Hyatt Hotel  A2
62  Park Regis Hotel  C2
63  Parkroyal Darling Harbour  C1
64  Pier One Parkroyal  A2
65  Quay West Sydney  B2
66  Regent of Sydney  B2
67  Renaissance Sydney Hotel  B2
68  Ritz Carlton Hotel  B2
69  Royal Garden Hotel  D2
70  Savoy Apartments  C1
71  Sheraton on the Park Hotel  C2
72  Southern Cross Towers Hotel  D2
73  Stafford, The  B2
74  Stamford Plaza Hotel  B1
75  Sydney Boulevarde Hotel  C3
76  Sydney Hilton Hotel  C2
77  Sydney Marriott Hotel  D2
78  Sydney Vista Hotel  B1
79  Top of the Town  D3
80  Waldorf Apartment Hotel  D1
81  Wentworth, The  B2
82  Westin Sydney  C2
83  Woolloomooloo Waters Motel  C3
84  York Apartments  B1

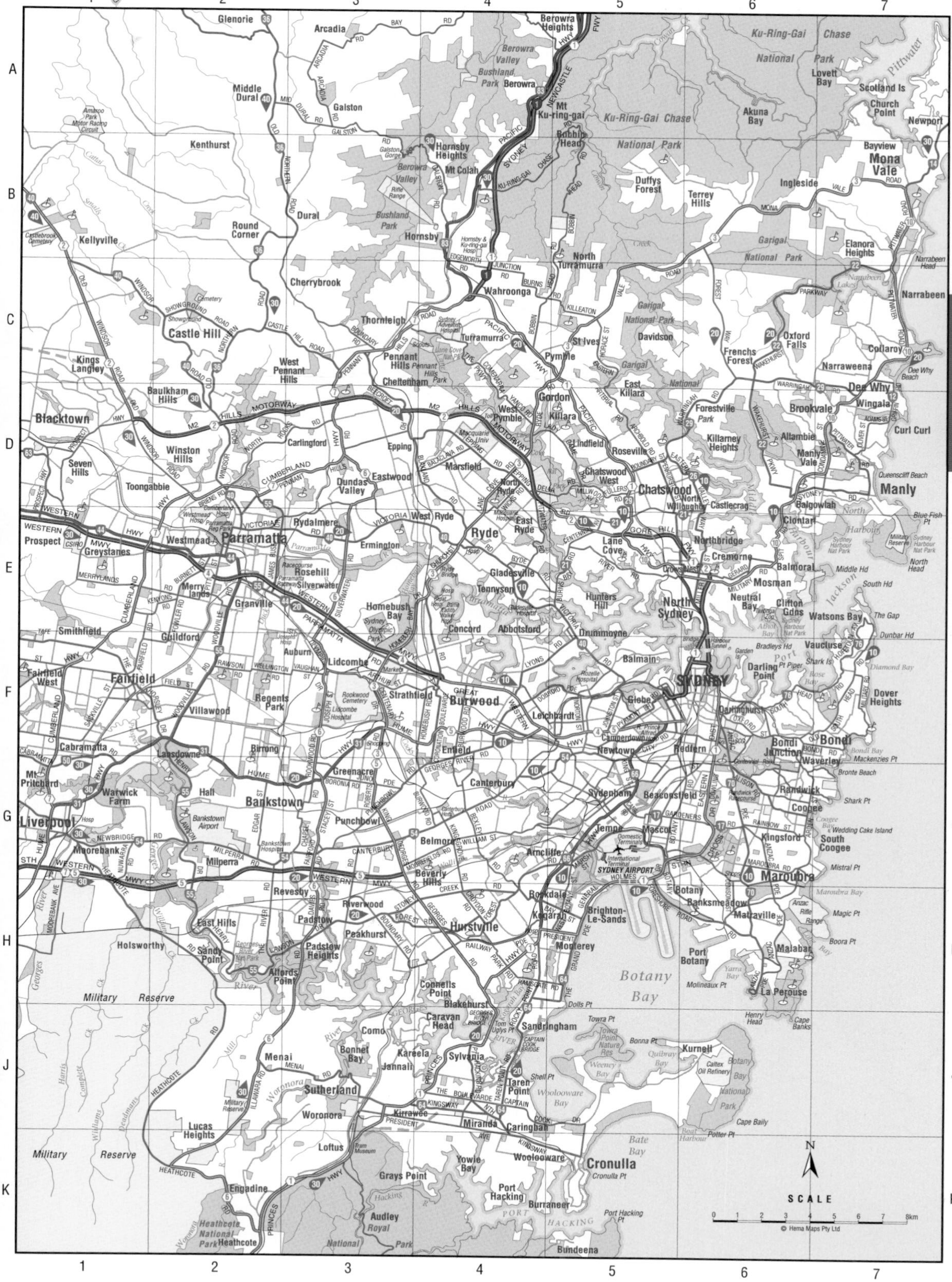

**NSW**

Grid columns: 1 2 3 4 5 6 7
Grid rows: A B C D E F G H J K

Selected place names (map labels):

Glenorie, Arcadia, Berowra Heights, Ku-Ring-Gai Chase, Lovett Bay, Scotland Is, Church Point, Newport, Middle Dural, Galston, Hornsby Heights, Mt Ku-ring-gai, Berowra, Bobbin Head, Akuna Bay, Bayview, Mona Vale, Kenthurst, Mt Colah, Ku-Ring-Gai Chase National Park, Duffys Forest, Terrey Hills, Ingleside, Narrabeen Head, Kellyville, Round Corner, Dural, Hornsby, Bushland Park, North Turramurra, Garigal National Park, Elanora Heights, Narrabeen, Cherrybrook, Wahroonga, Thornleigh, Turramurra, St Ives, Davidson, Frenchs Forest, Oxford Falls, Collaroy, Castle Hill, West Pennant Hills, Pennant Hills, Cheltenham, Pymble, Garigal, Narraweena, Dee Why, Kings Langley, Baulkham Hills, Gordon, Killara, East Killara, Forestville Park, Killarney Heights, Allambie, Brookvale, Wingala, Curl Curl, Blacktown, Winston Hills, Carlingford, Epping, Marsfield, West Pymble, Lindfield, Roseville, Chatswood West, Chatswood, Castlecrag, Manly Vale, Manly, Seven Hills, Toongabbie, Dundas Valley, Eastwood, North Ryde, Willoughby, Balgowlah, Clontarf, Prospect, Greystanes, Westmead, Parramatta, Rydalmere, Ermington, West Ryde, Ryde, East Ryde, Lane Cove, Northbridge, Cremorne, Mosman, North Head, Merrylands, Rosehill, Silverwater, Homebush Bay, Gladesville, Tennyson, Hunters Hill, North Sydney, Neutral Bay, Clifton Gdns, Balmoral, Watsons Bay, Smithfield, Guildford, Auburn, Lidcombe, Concord, Abbotsford, Drummoyne, Balmain, SYDNEY, Darling Point, Vaucluse, Dover Heights, Fairfield West, Fairfield, Regents Park, Strathfield, Burwood, Leichhardt, Glebe, Bondi Junction, Bondi, Waverley, Villawood, Enfield, Newtown, Redfern, Randwick, Coogee, Cabramatta, Greenacre, Canterbury, Sydenham, Beaconsfield, Mt Pritchard, Warwick Farm, Bankstown, Punchbowl, Belmore, Tempe, Mascot, Kingsford, South Coogee, Liverpool, Moorebank, Bankstown Airport, Beverly Hills, Arncliffe, Sydney Airport, Botany, Banksmeadow, Matraville, Milperra, Revesby, Padstow, Riverwood, Peakhurst, Hurstville, Rockdale, Kogarah, Brighton-Le-Sands, Port Botany, Malabar, La Perouse, East Hills, Sandy Point, Padstow Heights, Connells Point, Blakehurst, Monterey, Holsworthy, Alfords Point, Caravan Head, Sandringham, Botany Bay, Kurnell, Menai, Como, Bonnet Bay, Kareela, Jannali, Sylvania, Taren Point, Woolooware Bay, Caltex Oil Refinery, Sutherland, Woronora, Kirrawee, Miranda, Caringbah, Cape Banks, Lucas Heights, Loftus, Yowie Bay, Woolooware, Cronulla, Cape Baily, Engadine, Grays Point, Port Hacking, Burraneer, Bundeena, Heathcote National Park, Audley, Royal National Park

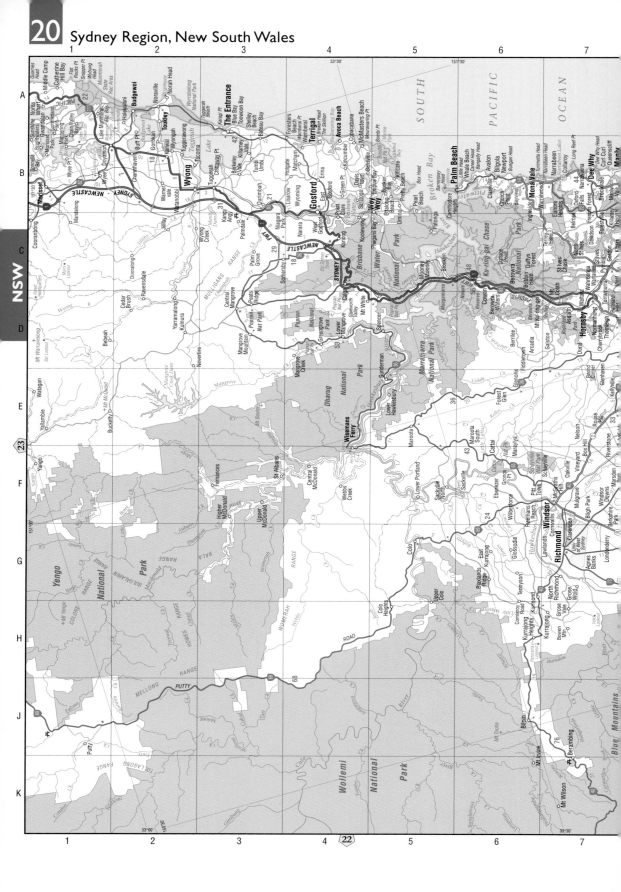

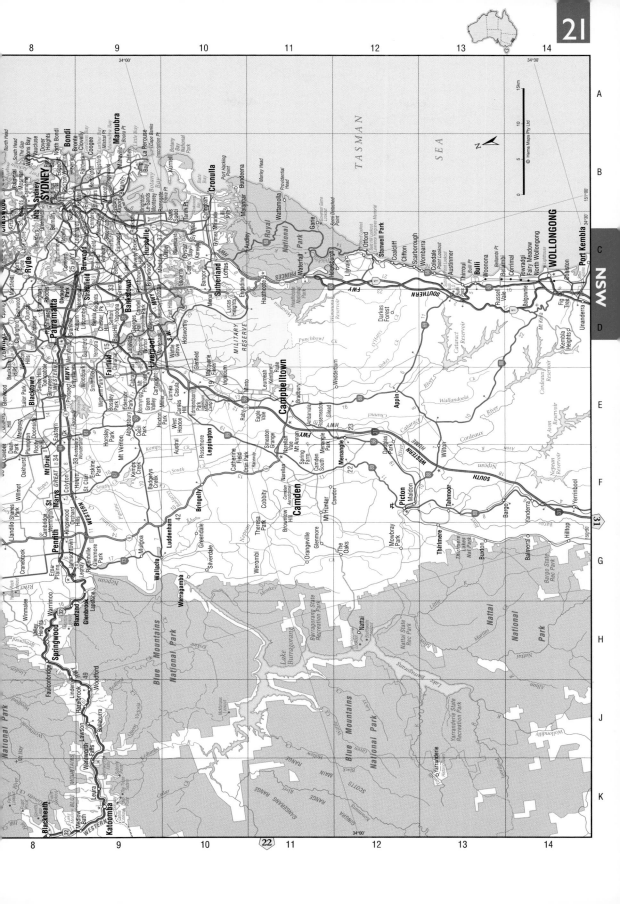

# Central-East New South Wales

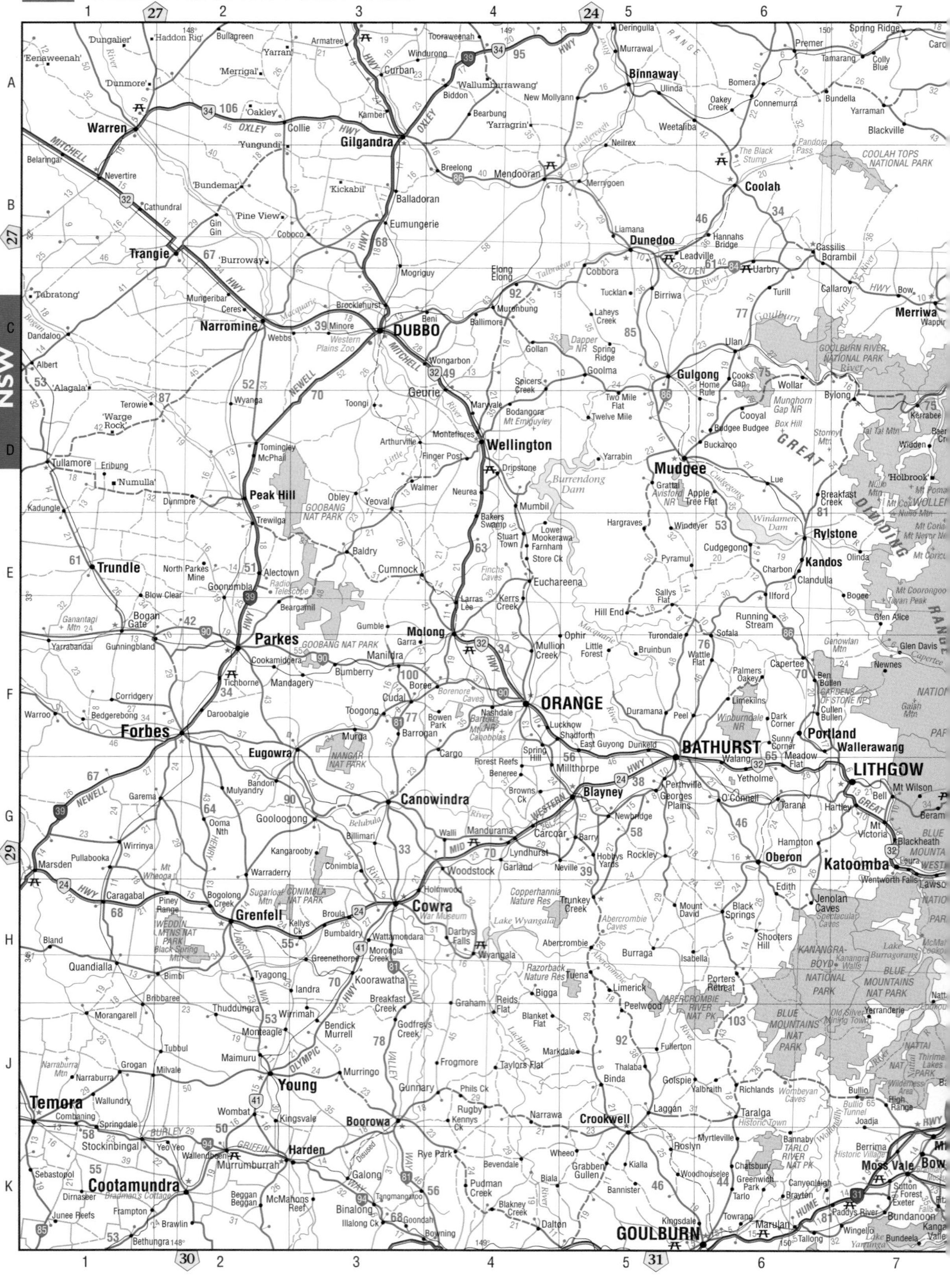

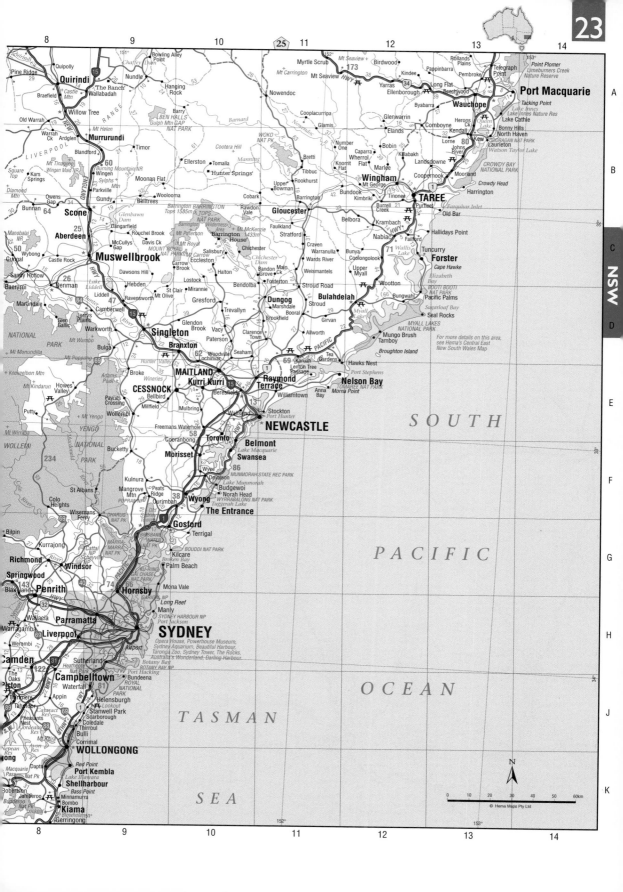

NSW

Q · U · E · E · N · S

'Whyenbah' · 'Ardmore' · 'Bimbimbi' · Nindigully · 'Nariel' · 'Mulga Ridge' · 'Minnel' · Bendidee Nat Park · Commonl · 85

BARWON · Bungunya · HWY · Toobeah · CUNNINGHAM 90

200 · Talwood · 22 · 21

Noondoo · Gradule · Goondiwindi · Gibbtell · 90

Dirranbandi · 20 · Thallon · Daymar · 'Willarie' · Boggabilla · Kurumbul · Yelarbon · 44

'Johnstone' · 'Merriot' · Macintyre River · 'Osterley' · North Star · 116 · Yetman

'Redbank' · 'Gleneve' · 'Bullawarrie' · Caloona · Boomi · Whalan Creek · 'Kiga' · BRUXNER

'Currawong' · Mungindi · Neeworra · Weemelah · Garah · 'Mt Mitchell' · Mt Russell · Yallaroi · Coolatai · Wallangra

Glendalough Gate · 'Jomara' · Bengerang · Moppin · Croppa Creek · 'Mt Pleasant' · 95

'Whyalla' · Gundablouie · 'Gingham' · Ashley · Crooble · Milguy

'Wongalee' · 'Currigundi' · Camurra · Moree · 121 · 123 · 'Myall Park' · Balfours Peak · Graman

'Banarway' · 'Wantoona' · Pallamallawa · Biniguy · Gravesend Mtn · Hadleigh · Gragin Peak

Dunumbral · 'Manchester' · Bullaran · 141 · GWYDIR HWY · Tycannah · Gravesend · WARIALDA · Koloona

Warrinilla · Collarenebri · Telleraga · 'Courallie' · Gravesend · 80 · Mount Russell · Mt Jerrybang

'Heathfield' · 'Lourney' · Pokataroo · 'Poison Gate' · 'Moomin' · Waah Waah Ck · Slaughterhouse · Pinnacle · DELUNGRA · 63 · Little Plain

'Dungalear' · 74 · Merrywinebone · Gurley · Cap & Bonnet · Mt Rodd · Elcombe

'Bairnkine' · Rowena · 128 · 'Thalaba' · Millie · 98 · Terry Hie Hie · BINGARA

'Eumanbah' · Wiminda · Pian Creek · Bellata · Coffin Hill · 103 · Dinoga · Keera

Cryon · Nowley · Doreen · Haystack Mtn · Mt Waa · Caroda · Upper Bingara

WALGETT · KAMILAROI · Bugilbone · Burren Junction · 'Boolcarrol' · Grattai Mtn · Grattai Wilderness Area · Rocky Creek · Mt Drummond

'River View' · 'Towrie' · Cubbaroo · Merah North · 'Myall Vale' · Edgeroi · Castle Top Mtn · Upper Horton · Gull Ck

Goangra · Namoi River · 'Bugilbone' · Wee Waa · Culgoora · Nandewar Wilderness Area · MT KAPUTAR · Trevallyn' · Cobbadah · 'Barlow'

101 · 'Drilldool' · Australia Telescope · 98 · Mt Kaputar · Rusten Wilderness Area · 'Rocky Glen' · The Furnace

'Beanbah' · Bungle Gully · Milchomi · Pilliga · Cuttabri · 'Yarrie Lake' · Narrabri West · NARRABRI · Derian Mtn · 95 · Woods Reef · BARRABA

Combogolong · Annual Picnic Races · 'Cubbo' · Lucky Flat · Turrawan · 'Myall Vale' · Mt Byar · Crow + Mtn · Crow Mountain · Warrabah Nat Park

117 · 'Wingadee' · Gwabegar · 13 · Baan Baa · Waterloo + Pinnacle · Goonbri Mtn · 'Hobden' · Split Rock Dam · Upper Manilla

'Gunyillah' · 76 · 118 · Mt Lowry · 

'Billeroy' · 'Mayfield' · Merebene · Kenebri · 96 · BOGGABRI · 37 · MANILLA · Halls Creek

'Edale' · Gilgooma · 'Urawilkey' · Pilliga Nature Reserve · Mt + Binalong · Kelvin · Moonaran · Mundowey

'Narraway' · Nebea · Teridgerie · Emerald Hill · Lake Keepit · Carroll Gap · Somerton · 95 · Attunga

Taloon · COONAMBLE · BARADINE · 'Borah' · Goohl · GUNNEDAH · Carroll · 75 · 34 · Moore Creek

Combara · 'Goorianawah' · Wittenbra · 45 · Rocky Glen · OXLEY · Mullaley · King Jack Mtn · Curlewis · 'Allawah' · TAMWORTH Country Music Capital · Nemingha

'Budgeon' · 'Brigalow' · Bugaldie · Yearinan · 105 · Garrawilla · Nea · Piallaway · Duri

Merri Merri · 98 · 'Mt Tenandra' · Warrumbungle · 'Gummin Gummin' · Siding Spring Observatory · Mt Nombi · Breeza · CURRABUBULA

'Bourbah' · Gular · WARRUMBUNGLE NATIONAL PARK · Warkton · COONABARABRAN · Ulamambri · 'Currajong' · Tambar Springs · Spring Ridge · 'Ashgrove' · Goonoo Goonoo

Pine Clump · Tooraweenah · Purlewaugh · 'Long Ridge' · WERRIS CREEK · 74

Bullagreen · Armatree · Windurong · Deringulla · RANGE · Premer · Caroona · Quipolly

'Merrigal' · Curban · 95 · Murrawal · Bomera · Tamarang · Colly Blue · Pine Ridge · QUIRINDI · 15

'Oakley' · Kamber · Biddon · Bearburg · New Mollyann · 'Wallumburrawang' · BINNAWAY · Ulinda · Oakey Creek · Connemurra · Bundella · Yarraman · Braefield · Wallabadah · 'The Ranch'

OXLEY HWY · Weetalibs · 149° · 150° · 22

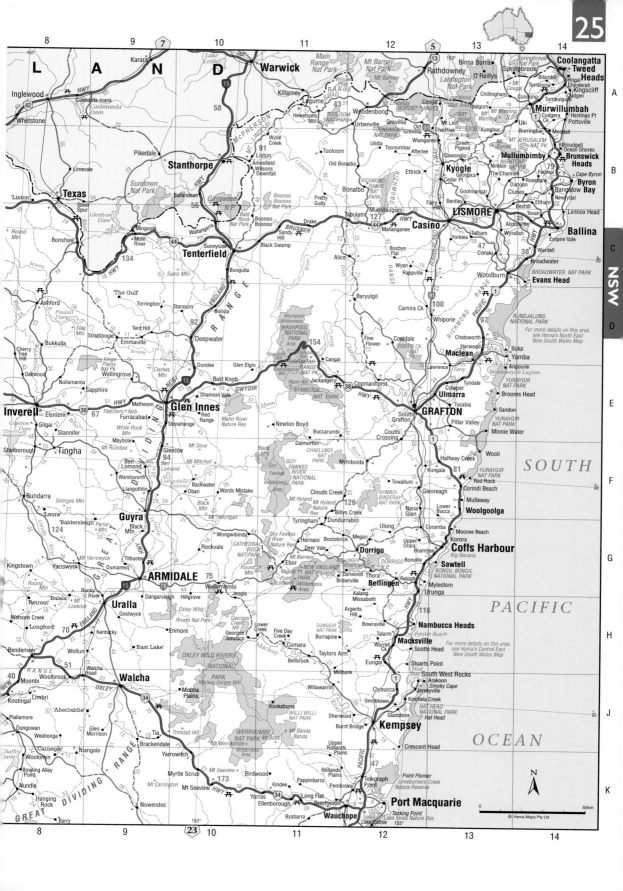

QUEEN... N

NSW

SOUTH AUSTRALIA

**STURT NATIONAL PARK**

**CURRAWINYA NATIONAL PARK**

Hungerford

Tibooburra

Milparinka

Packsaddle Roadhouse

White Cliffs

Wilcannia

BROKEN HILL

Menindee

KINCHEGA NATIONAL PARK

MUTAWINTJI NATIONAL PARK

Nocoleche Nature Reserve

Wanaaring

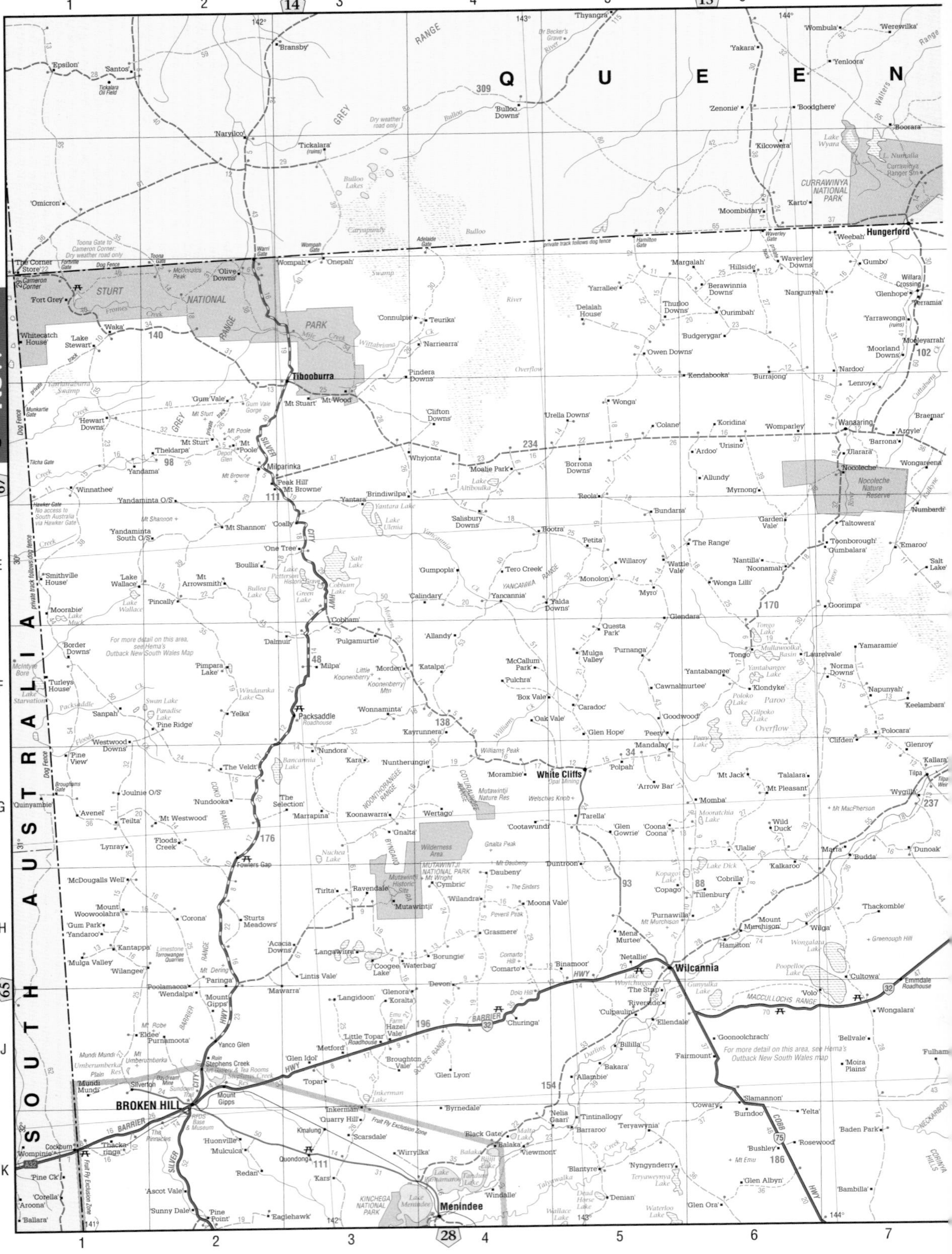

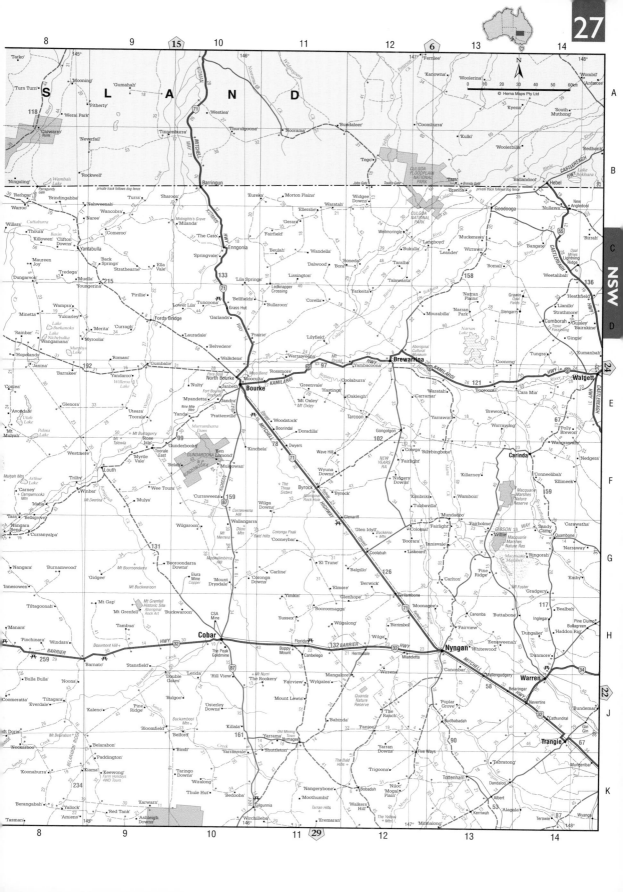

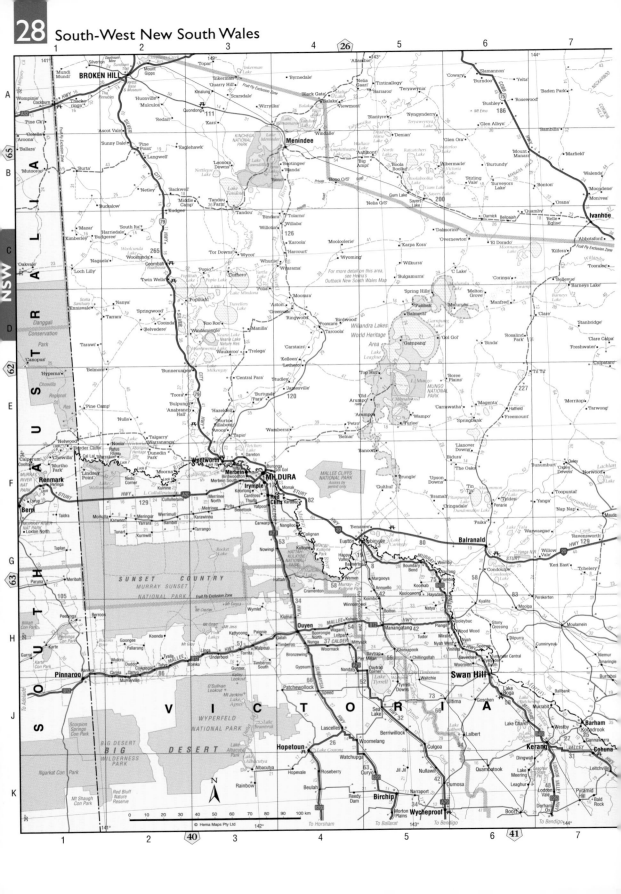

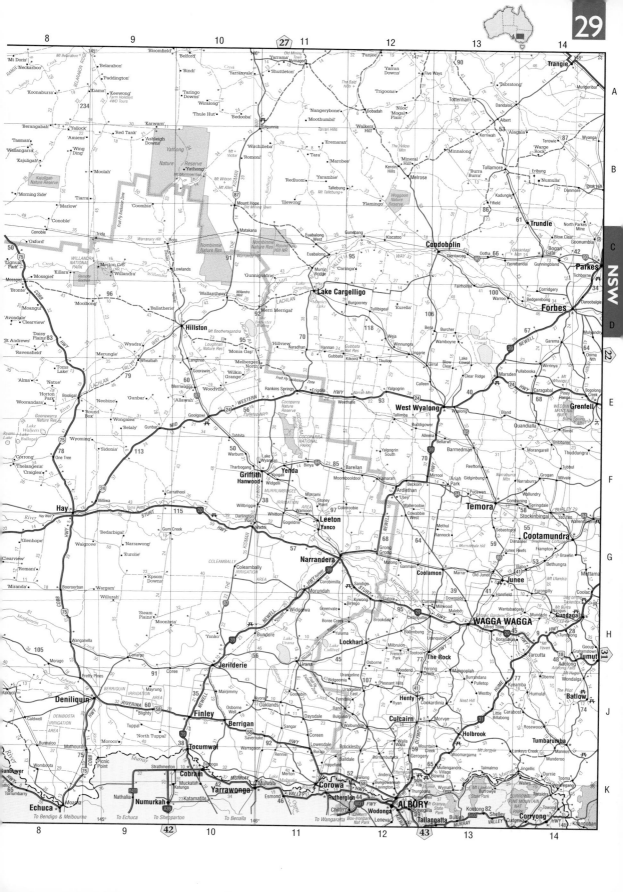

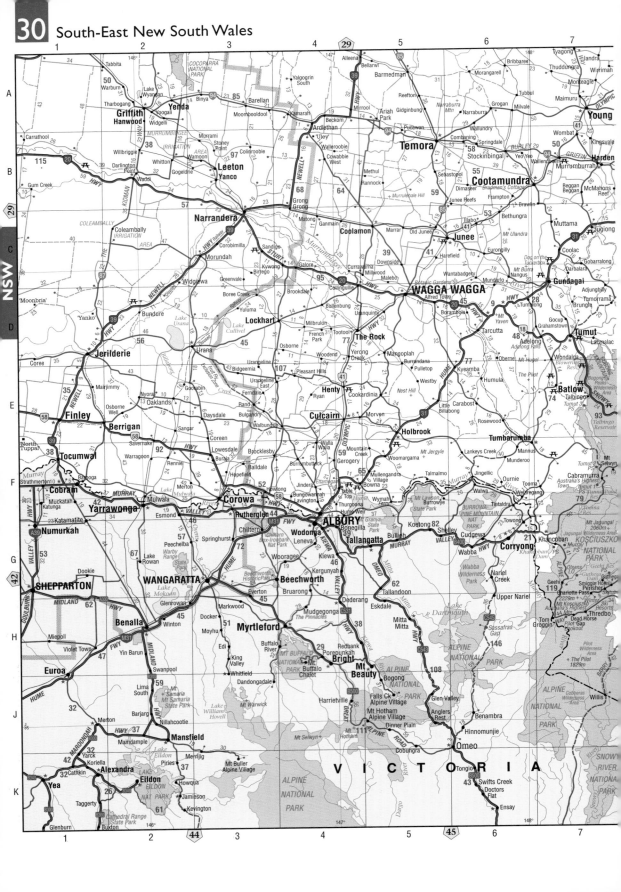

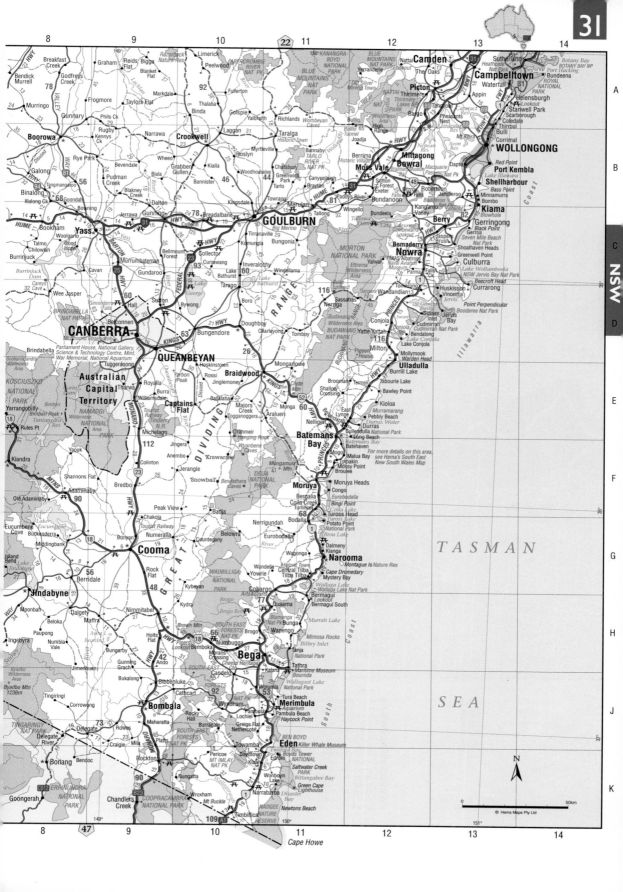

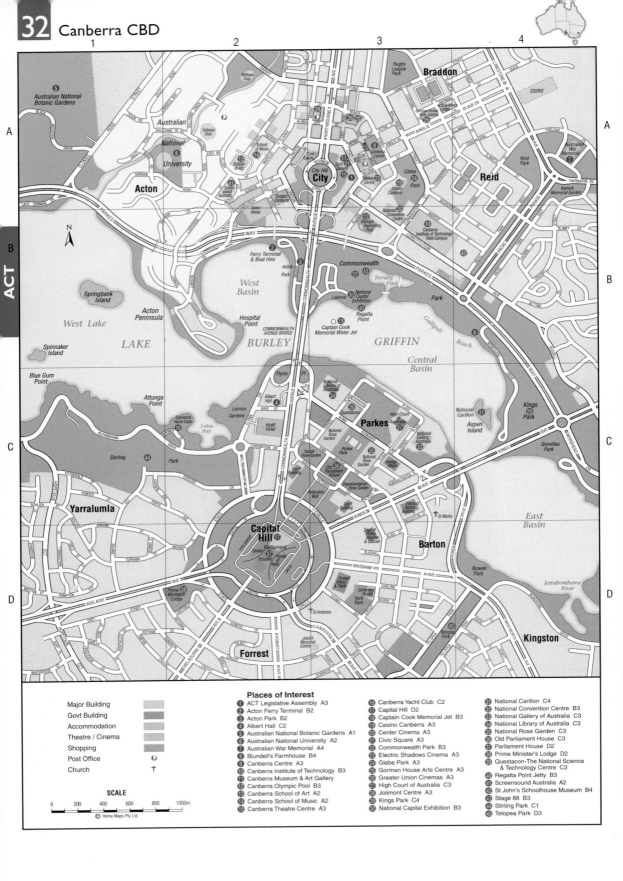

### Places of Interest

1. ACT Legislative Assembly  A3
2. Acton Ferry Terminal  B2
3. Acton Park  B2
4. Albert Hall  C2
5. Australian National Botanic Gardens  A1
6. Australian National University  A2
7. Australian War Memorial  A4
8. Blundell's Farmhouse  B4
9. Canberra Centre  A3
10. Canberra Institute of Technology  B3
11. Canberra Museum & Art Gallery
12. Canberra Olympic Pool  B3
13. Canberra School of Art  A2
14. Canberra School of Music  A2
15. Canberra Theatre Centre  A3

16. Canberra Yacht Club  C2
17. Capital Hill  D2
18. Captain Cook Memorial Jet  B3
19. Casino Canberra  A3
20. Center Cinema  A3
21. Civic Square  A3
22. Commonwealth Park  B3
23. Electric Shadows Cinema  A3
24. Glebe Park  A3
25. Gorman House Arts Centre  A3
26. Greater Union Cinemas  A3
27. High Court of Australia  C3
28. Jolimont Centre  A3
29. Kings Park  C4
30. National Capital Exhibition  B3

31. National Carillon  C4
32. National Convention Centre  B3
33. National Gallery of Australia  C3
34. National Library of Australia  C3
35. National Rose Garden  C3
36. Old Parliament House  C3
37. Parliament House  D2
38. Prime Minister's Lodge  D2
39. Questacon-The National Science
    & Technology Centre  C3
40. Regatta Point Jetty  B3
41. Screensound Australia  A2
42. St John's Schoolhouse Museum  B4
43. Stage 88  B3
44. Stirling Park  C1
45. Telopea Park  D3

### Legend

Major Building
Govt Building
Accommodation
Theatre / Cinema
Shopping
Post Office
Church

SCALE

0    200    400    600    800    1000m

© Hema Maps Pty Ltd

# Victoria

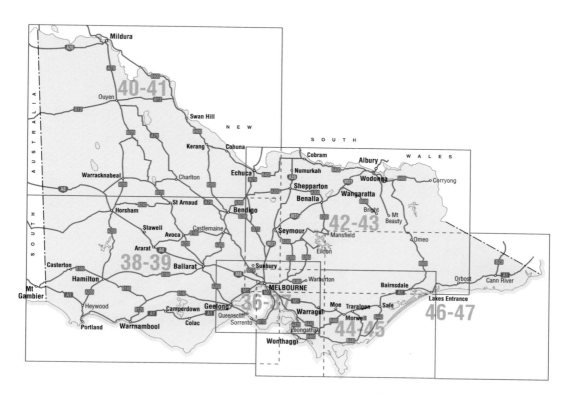

## Distance Chart

| | | | | | | | | | | | | | | Albury |
|---|---|---|---|---|---|---|---|---|---|---|---|---|---|---|
| | | | | | | | | | | | | | **Ballarat** | 385 |
| | | | | | | | | | | | | **Bairnsdale** | 393 | 301 |
| | | | | | | | | | | | **Bendigo** | 429 | 121 | 282 |
| | | | | | | | | | | **Echuca** | 93 | 491 | 214 | 233 |
| | | | | | | | | | **Geelong** | 273 | 180 | 355 | 87 | 388 |
| | | | | | | | | **Hamilton** | 230 | 366 | 273 | 567 | 174 | 555 |
| | | | | | | | **Melbourne** | 286 | 74 | 210 | 148 | 281 | 112 | 314 |
| | | | | | | **Mildura** | 551 | 448 | 547 | 375 | 403 | 832 | 460 | 608 |
| | | | | | **Shepparton** | 446 | 184 | 395 | 258 | 71 | 122 | 406 | 243 | 175 |
| | | | | **Swan Hill** | 225 | 221 | 336 | 348 | 368 | 154 | 188 | 617 | 285 | 387 |
| | | | **Traralgon** | 500 | 349 | 715 | 164 | 450 | 238 | 374 | 312 | 117 | 276 | 418 |
| | | **Wangaratta** | 389 | 328 | 103 | 549 | 242 | 483 | 316 | 174 | 210 | 303 | 313 | 72 |
| | **Warrnambool** | 487 | 425 | 406 | 417 | 548 | 261 | 100 | 187 | 388 | 295 | 542 | 174 | 559 |

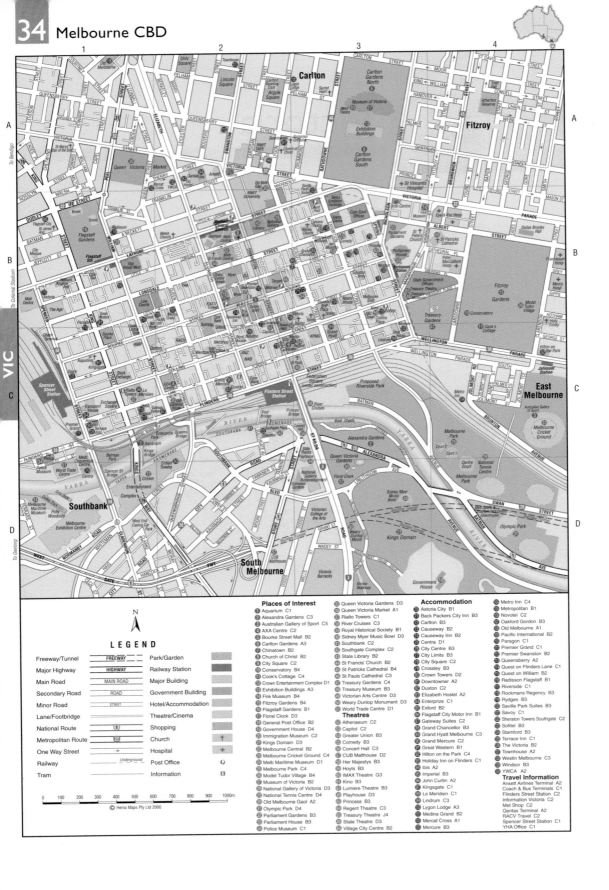

## LEGEND

| | |
|---|---|
| Freeway/Tunnel | FREEWAY |
| Major Highway | HIGHWAY |
| Main Road | MAIN ROAD |
| Secondary Road | ROAD |
| Minor Road | STREET |
| Lane/Footbridge | |
| National Route | 1 |
| Metropolitan Route | 22 |
| One Way Street | ► |
| Railway | Underground |
| Tram | |

| | |
|---|---|
| Park/Garden | |
| Railway Station | |
| Major Building | |
| Government Building | |
| Hotel/Accommodation | |
| Theatre/Cinema | |
| Shopping | |
| Church | † |
| Hospital | + |
| Post Office | |
| Information | |

0  100  200  300  400  500  600  700  800  900  1000m

© Hema Maps Pty Ltd 2000

### Places of Interest
1 Aquarium  C1
2 Alexandra Gardens  C3
3 Australian Gallery of Sport  C5
4 AXA Centre  C2
5 Bourke Street Mall  B2
6 Carlton Gardens  A3
7 Chinatown  B2
8 Church of Christ  B2
9 City Square  C2
10 Conservatory  B4
11 Cook's Cottage  C4
12 Crown Entertainment Complex  D1
13 Exhibition Buildings  A3
14 Fire Museum  B4
15 Fitzroy Gardens  B4
16 Flagstaff Gardens  B1
17 Floral Clock  D3
18 General Post Office  B2
19 Government House  D3
20 Immigration Museum  C2
21 Kings Domain  D3
22 Melbourne Central  B2
23 Melbourne Cricket Ground  C4
24 Melb Maritime Museum  D1
25 Melbourne Park  C4
26 Model Tudor Village  B4
27 Museum of Victoria  B2
28 National Gallery of Victoria  D3
29 National Tennis Centre  D4
30 Old Melbourne Gaol  A2
31 Olympic Park  D4
32 Parliament Gardens  B3
33 Parliament House  B3
34 Police Museum  C1

35 Queen Victoria Gardens  D3
36 Queen Victoria Market  A1
37 Rialto Towers  C1
38 River Cruises  C3
39 Royal Historical Society  B1
40 Sidney Myer Music Bowl  D3
41 Southbank  C2
42 Southgate Complex  C2
43 State Library  B2
44 St Francis' Church  B2
45 St Patricks Cathedral  B4
46 St Pauls Cathedral  C3
47 Treasury Gardens  C3
48 Treasury Museum  C3
49 Victorian Arts Centre  D3
50 Weary Dunlop Monument  D3
51 World Trade Centre  D1

### Theatres
52 Athenaeum  C2
53 Capitol  C2
54 Greater Union  B3
55 Comedy  C2
56 Concert Hall  C3
57 CUB Malthouse  D2
58 Her Majestys  B3
59 Hoyts  B3
60 IMAX Theatre  G3
61 Kino  B3
62 Lumiere Theatre  B3
63 Playhouse  D3
64 Princess  B3
65 Regent Theatre  C3
66 Treasury Theatre  C3
67 State Theatre  D3
68 Village City Centre  B2

### Accommodation
70 Astoria City  B1
71 Back Packers City Inn  B3
72 Carlton  B3
73 Causeway  B2
74 Causeway Inn  B2
75 Centra  D1
76 City Centre  B3
77 City Limits  B3
78 City Square  C2
79 Crossley  B3
80 Crown Towers  D2
81 Downtowner  A2
82 Duxton  C2
83 Elizabeth Hostel  A2
84 Enterprize  C1
85 Exford  B2
86 Flagstaff City Motor Inn  B1
87 Gateway Suites  C2
88 Grand Chancellor  B3
89 Grand Hyatt Melbourne  C3
90 Grand Mercure  C2
91 Great Western  B1
92 Hilton on the Park  C4
93 Holiday Inn on Flinders  C1
94 Ibis  A2
95 Imperial  B3
96 John Curtin  A2
97 Kingsgate  C1
98 Le Meridien  C1
99 Lindrum  C3
100 Lygon Lodge  A3
101 Medina Grand  B3
102 Mercat Cross  B2
103 Mercure  B3

104 Metro Inn  C4
105 Metropolitan  B1
106 Novotel  C2
107 Oaklord Gordon  B3
108 Old Melbourne  A1
109 Pacific International  B2
110 Paragon  C1
111 Premier Grand  C1
112 Premier Swanston  B2
113 Queensberry  A2
114 Quest on Flinders Lane  C1
115 Quest on William  B2
116 Radisson Flagstaff  B1
117 Rockmans Regency  B3
118 Rydges  B3
119 Saville Park Suites  B3
120 Savoy  C1
121 Sheraton Towers Southgate  C2
122 Sofitel  B3
123 Stamford  B3
124 Terrace Inn  C1
125 The Victoria  B2
126 Townhouse  A2
127 Westin Melbourne  C3
128 Windsor  B3
129 YWCA  C1

### Travel Information
Ansett Airlines Terminal  A2
Coach & Bus Terminals  C1
Flinders Street Station  C2
Information Victoria  C1
Met Shop  C2
Qantas Terminal  A2
RACV Travel  C1
Spencer Street Station  C1
YHA Office  C1

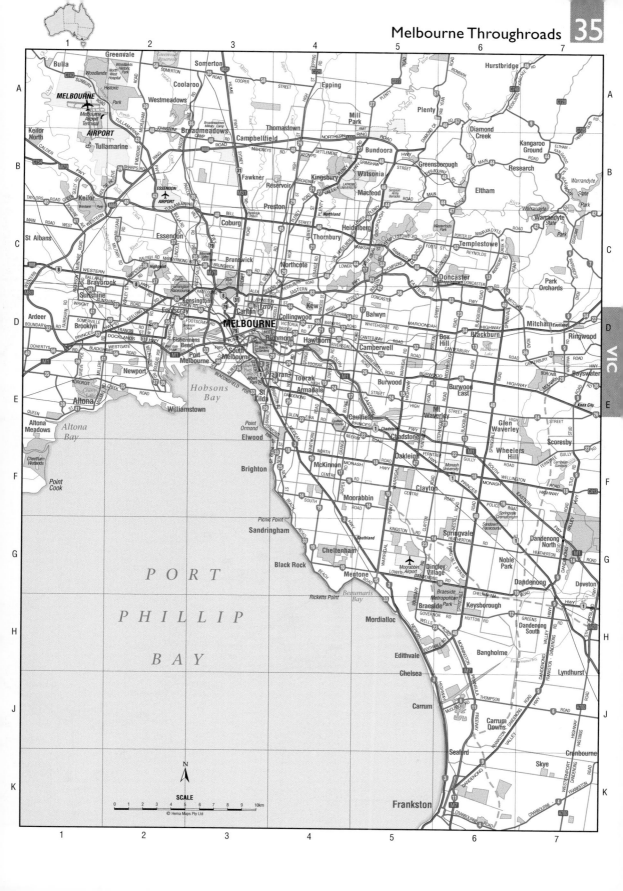

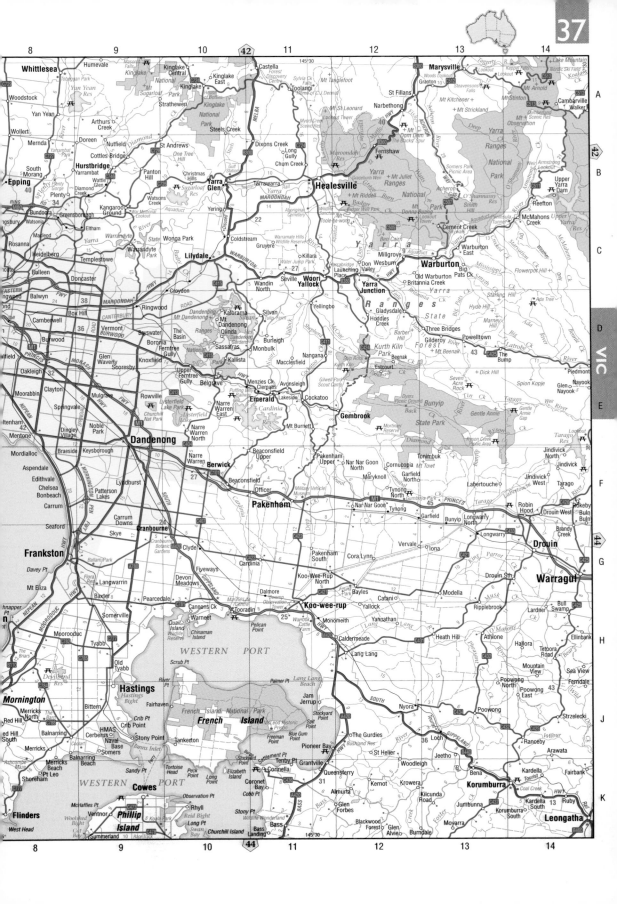

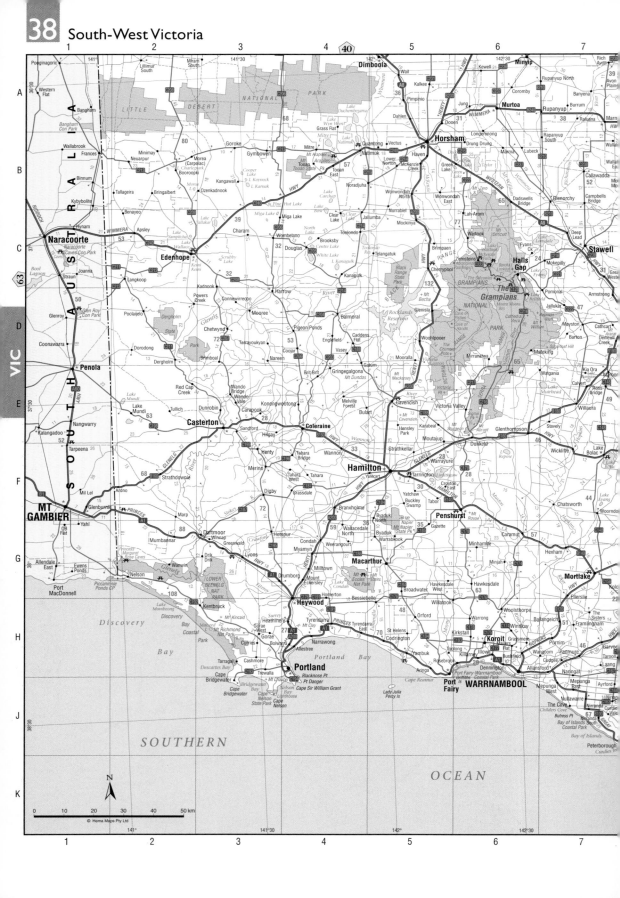

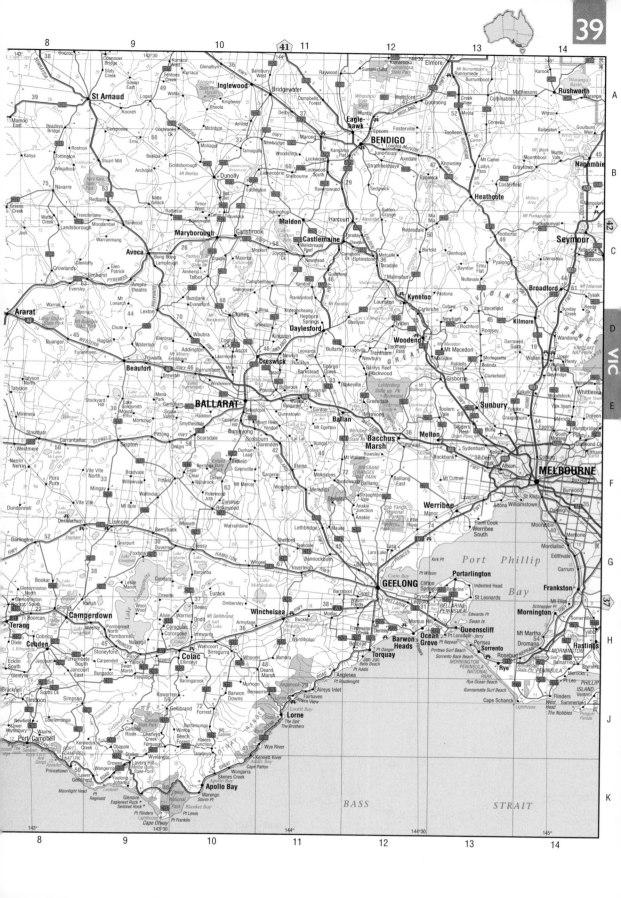

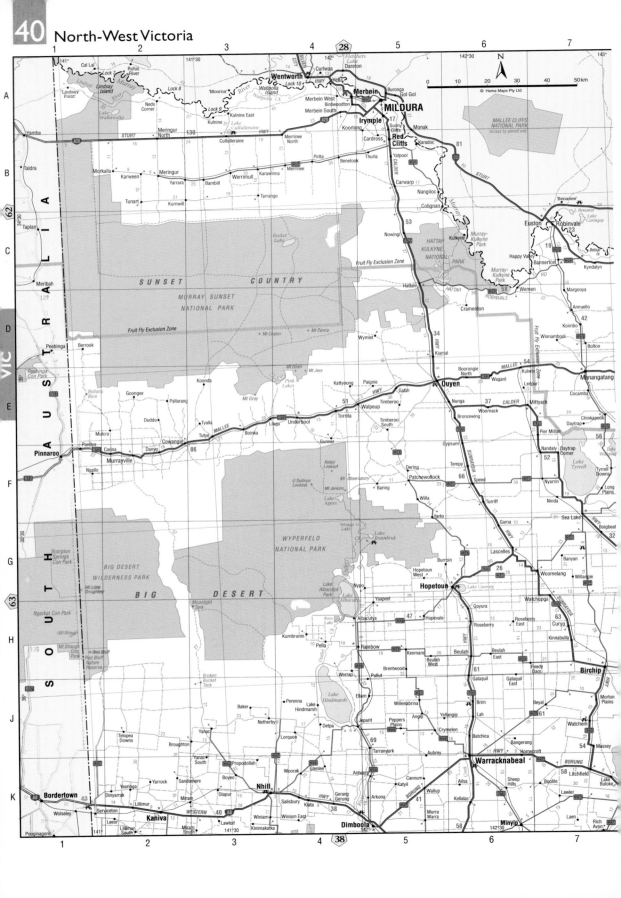

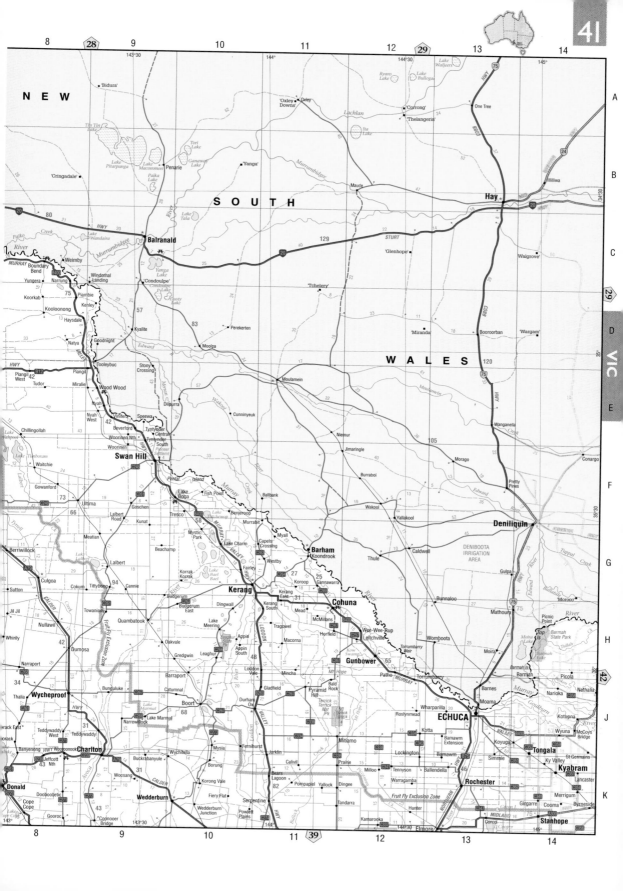

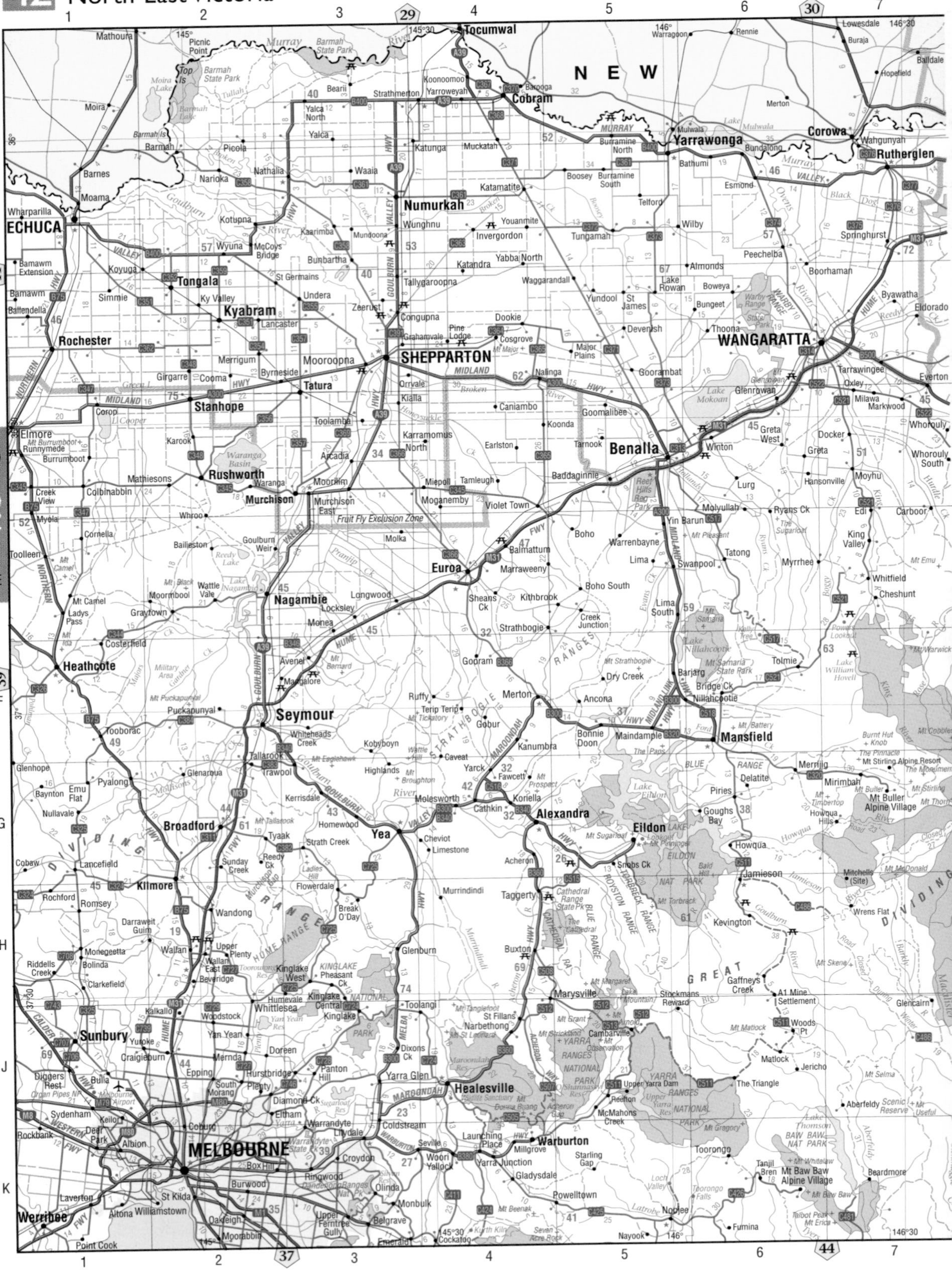

NEW
VIC
Tocumwal
Cobram
Yarrawonga
Corowa
Rutherglen
Mathoura
Picnic Point
Barmah State Park
Moira
Barmah
Picola
Nathalia
Strathmerton
Koonoomoo
Yarroweyah
Katunga
Muckatah
Numurkah
Wunghnu
Waaia
Katamatite
Youanmite
Invergordon
Tungamah
Wilby
Boosey
Burramine South
Burramine North
Mulwala
Bundalong
Bathumi
Esmond
Telford
Peechelba
Springhurst
Lowesdale
Buraja
Balldale
Hopefield
Merton
Wahgunyah
Barnes
Moama
Wharparilla
ECHUCA
Bamawm Extension
Bamawm
Ballendella
Koyuga
Tongala
Kotupna
Wyuna
McCoys Bridge
Kaarimba
Mundoona
Bunbartha
Katandra
Yabba North
Tallygaroopna
Undera
Kyabram
Ky Valley
Lancaster
Simmie
Rochester
St Germains
Zeerust
Congupna
Grahamvale
Pine Lodge
Dookie
Cosgrove
SHEPPARTON
Mooroopna
Merrigum
Byrneside
Girgarre
Cooma
Tatura
Stanhope
Corop
Elmore
Runnymede
Burramboot
Toolamba
Arcadia
Karramomus North
Orrvale
Kialla
Caniambo
Naringa
Koonda
Earlston
Tamleugh
Tarnook
Waggarandall
Yundool
St James
Devenish
Lake Rowan
Almonds
Boweya
Bungeet
Thoona
WANGARATTA
Boorhaman
Byawatha
Eldorado
Tarrawingee
Everton
Oxley
Milawa
Markwood
Major Plains
Goorambat
Glenrowan
Lake Mokoan
Goomalibee
Benalla
Winton
Greta West
Greta
Docker
Whorouly
Whorouly South
Moyhu
Hansonville
Lurg
Baddaginnie
Reef Hills Reg Park
Mathiesons
Rushworth
Waranga Basin
Karook
Waranga
Colbinabbin
Murchison
Moorilim
Murchison East
Miepoll
Moganemby
Violet Town
Fruit Fly Exclusion Zone
Whroo
Creek View
Myola
Cornella
Toolleen
Baillieston
Goulburn Weir
Molka
Euroa
Balmattum
Marraweeny
Boho
Warrenbayne
Yin Barun
Molyullah
Ryans Ck
Edi
Carboor
Lima
Swanpool
Tatong
King Valley
Myrrhee
Whitfield
Cheshunt
Mt Camel
Ladys Pass
Moormbool
Wattle Vale
Nagambie
Graytown
Longwood
Locksley
Monea
Sheans Ck
Kithbrook
Boho South
Creek Junction
Lima South
Strathbogie
Costerfield
Heathcote
Avenel
Mangalore
Gooram
Dry Creek
Lake Nillahcootie
Barjarg
Bridge Ck
Nillahcootie
Tolmie
Lake William Hovell
Ruffy
Terip Terip
Gobur
Merton
Ancona
Bonnie Doon
Maindample
Mansfield
Puckapunyal
Seymour
Whiteheads Creek
Tooborac
Kobyboyn
Caveat
Kanumbra
Glenhope
Glenaroua
Tallarook
Trawool
Highlands
Yarck
Fawcett
Pyalong
Baynton
Emu Flat
Kerrisdale
Molesworth
Cathkin
Koriella
Alexandra
Lake Eildon
Eildon
Goughs Bay
Piries
Delatite
Merrijig
Mirimbah
Mt Buller Alpine Village
Howqua Hills
Howqua
Nullavale
Broadford
Tyaak
Homewood
Yea
Strath Creek
Cheviot
Limestone
Acheron
Snobs Ck
Jamieson
Mitchells (Site)
Cobaw
Lancefield
Sunday Creek
Reedy Ck
Kilmore
Rochford
Romsey
Flowerdale
Murrindindi
Taggerty
Cathedral Range State Pk
Kevington
Wrens Flat
Wandong
Break O'Day
Darraweit Guim
Wallan
Upper Plenty
Wallan East
Glenburn
Buxton
Riddells Creek
Monegeetta
Bolinda
Clarkefield
Kinglake West
Pheasant Ck
Marysville
Stockmans Reward
Gaffneys Creek
A1 Mine Settlement
Glencairn
Beveridge
Humevale
Kinglake Central
Kinglake
Toolangi
Whittlesea
Kalkallo
Woodstock
Yan Yean
Narbethong
St Fillans
Cambarville
Woods Pt
Sunbury
Yuroke
Craigieburn
Mernda
Doreen
Dixons Ck
Panton Hill
Matlock
Jericho
Diggers Rest
Bulla
Epping
South Morang
Hurstbridge
Plenty
Yarra Glen
Healesville
Upper Yarra Dam
Reefton
McMahons Creek
The Triangle
Aberfeldy
Sydenham
Keilor
Deer Park
Rockbank
Albion
Coburg
Diamond Ck
Eltham
Warrandyte
Lilydale
Coldstream
Launching Place
Warburton
Starling Gap
Toorongo
Tanjil Bren
Mt Baw Baw Alpine Village
Beardmore
MELBOURNE
Box Hill
Croydon
Seville
Woori Yallock
Yarra Junction
Millgrove
Gladysdale
Powelltown
Noojee
Laverton
St Kilda
Burwood
Ringwood
Olinda
Monbulk
Werribee
Altona
Williamstown
Oakleigh
Moorabbin
Upper Ferntree Gully
Belgrave
Emerald
Cockatoo
Nayook
Fumina
Point Cook

**VIC**

Grid columns: 1 2 3 4 **42** 5 6 7 — Rows: A B C D E F G H J K

## Major labels

**MELBOURNE**, Keilor, Albion, St Kilda, Altona, Williamstown, Coburg, Burwood, Box Hill, Ringwood, Croydon, Lilydale, Healesville, Warburton, Marysville, Narbethong, Cambarville

Kalkallo, Yuroke, Craigieburn, Bulla, Epping, Mernda, Doreen, Yan Yean, Whittlesea, Humevale, Kinglake, Kinglake Central, Toolangi, St Fillans, Woodstock, Hurstbridge, Panton Hill, Diamond Ck, Eltham, Plenty, South Morang, Coldstream, Yarra Glen, Dixons Ck, Launching Place, Millgrove, Yarra Junction, Gladysdale, Woori Yallock, Seville, Starling Gap, Powelltown, Noojee

Oakleigh, Moorabbin, Mentone, Mordialloc, Edithvale, Carrum, Dandenong, Lyndhurst, Berwick, Beaconsfield, Pakenham, Nar Nar Goon, Tynong, Garfield, Bunyip, Longwarry, Drouin, Warragul, Buln Buln, Darnum, Yarragon, Trafalgar, MOE, Yallourn, Newborough

Frankston, Cranbourne, Clyde, Koo-wee-rup, Cora Lynn, Bayles, Modella, Ripplebrook, Athlone, Ellinbank, Seaview, Childers

Mt Eliza, Mornington, Mt Martha, Dromana, Rosebud, Rye, Cape Schanck, Flinders, Somerville, Tyabb, Hastings, Stony Pt, Somers, Balnarring, Merricks, Pt Leo, Tankerton, Warneet, Tooradin, Lang Lang, Nyora, Poowong, Loch, Ranceby, Mt Eccles, Wooreen, Strzelecki, Mirboo Nth, Boolarra, Yinnar, Mirboo, Budgeree

Cowes, Ventnor, Rhyll, Newhaven, San Remo, Anderson, Kilcunda, Dalyston, Wonthaggi, Inverloch, Cape Paterson, Almurta, Grantville, Bass, Woolamai, Glen Alvie, Kongwak, Korumburra, Jumbunna, Leongatha, Koonwarra, Meeniyan, Dumbalk, Mardan, Dumbalk North

Kernot, Krowera, Woodleigh, Bena, Tarwin, Stony Creek, Buffalo, Foster, Toora, Port Franklin, Barrys Beach, Fish Ck, Venus Bay, Tarwin Lower, Tarwin Meadows, Waratah Nth, Waratah Bay, Liptrap, Walkerville Nth, Walkerville Sth, Bell Pt, Sandy Pt, Yanakie

Duck Pt, Granite Is, Bennison Is, Glennie Group, Tidal River, Norman Bay, Oberon Bay, Mt Oberon, South West Point, Anser Group, Wattle Is, **Wilsons Promontory National Park**, Tongue Point, Sparkes Lookout

**Port Phillip Bay**, **Western Port Bay**, French Island National Park, FRENCH ISLAND, **BASS**, Bass Strait, Mornington Peninsula National Park, **STRZELECKI RIDGE**, **PENINSULA**, **PHILLIP ISLAND**, Penguin Parade, Pyramid Rock, Cape Woolamai, Bunurong Marine Park, Venus Bay, Anderson Inlet, Corner Inlet, Shallow Inlet, Waratah Bay, Corner Inlet Marine & Coastal Park

**KINGLAKE NATIONAL PARK**, **YARRA RANGES NATIONAL PARK**, **BAW BAW NATIONAL PARK**, Mt Baw Baw Alpine Village, Bunyip State Park, Tarago Res, Moondarra State Park, Yallourn North, Erica, Rawson

Neerim, Neerim South, Jindivick, Rokeby, Labertouche, Nayook, Hill End, Willow Grove, Fumina, Tanjil Bren, Mt Baw Baw, Mt Erica, Talbot Peak, Tyers

A1 Mine Settlement, Woods Pt, Matlock, Jericho, Aberfeldy, The Triangle, Stockmans Reward, Mt Matlock, Lake Thomson, Reefton, McMahons Creek, Upper Yarra Dam, Upper Yarra Res, Toorongo, Mt Gregory

Road numbers: M31, M80, M1, M35, M420, A780, C729, C739, C728, C746, C724, C726, C507, C511, C512, C513, C505, C380, C411, C424, C425, C426, C466, C465, C463, C464, C469, C455, C456, C454, C444, C445, C446, C441, C442, C443, C435, C436, C437, C438, C440, C460, C461, C431, C432, C433, C434, C421, C422, C423, C777, C778, C781, C782, C783, C784, C787, C788, C789, B110, B360, B420, B440, B460

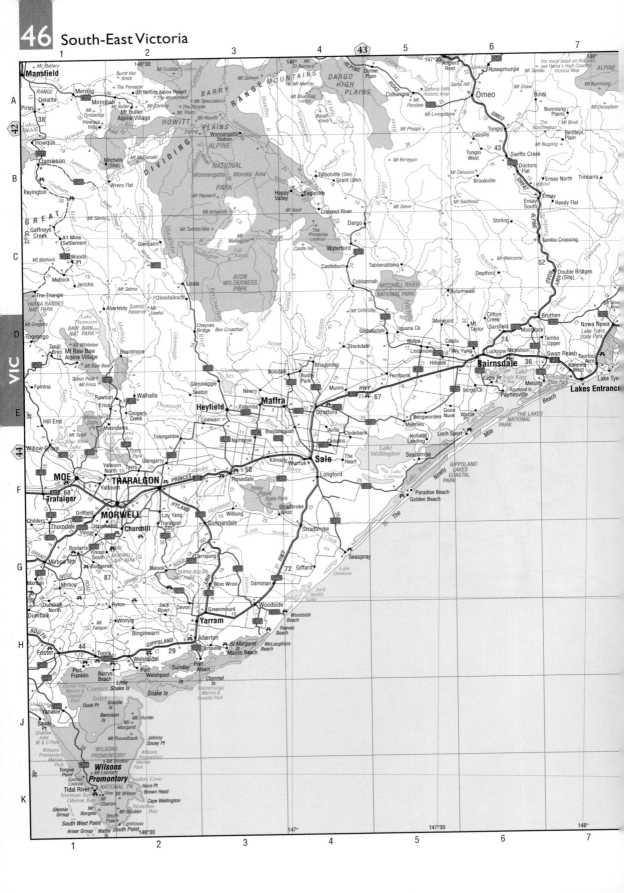

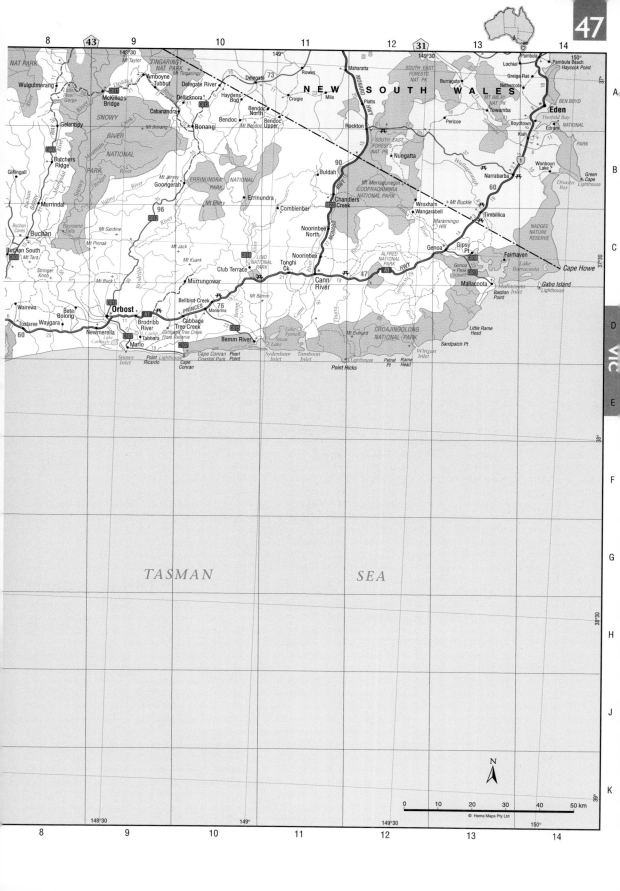

# Tasmania

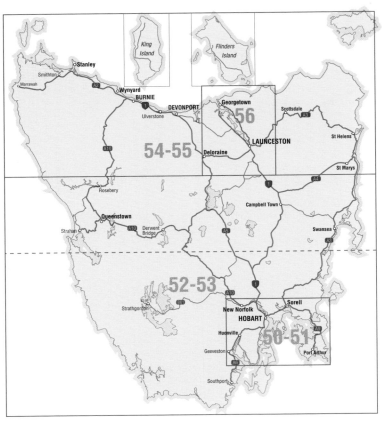

## Distance Chart

| | | | | | | | | | | | Burnie | |
|---|---|---|---|---|---|---|---|---|---|---|---|---|
| | | | | | | | | | | Derwent Bridge | | 226 |
| | | | | | | | | | Devonport | | 175 | 51 |
| | | | | | | | | Hobart | | 254 | 178 | 305 |
| | | | | | | | Launceston | | 203 | 99 | 176 | 150 |
| | | | | | | New Norfolk | | 198 | 37 | 249 | 141 | 300 |
| | | | | | Port Arthur | | 136 | 273 | 99 | 353 | 277 | 404 |
| | | | | Queenstown | | 365 | 229 | 263 | 266 | 202 | 88 | 163 |
| | | | Rosebery | | 54 | 419 | 283 | 209 | 320 | 148 | 142 | 109 |
| | | Sorell | | 346 | 292 | 73 | 63 | 200 | 26 | 280 | 204 | 331 |
| | Southport | | 126 | 420 | 366 | 199 | 137 | 303 | 100 | 354 | 278 | 405 |
| St Helens | | 353 | 227 | 372 | 376 | 300 | 250 | 163 | 253 | 262 | 288 | 313 |
| Stanley | | 392 | 484 | 410 | 181 | 235 | 483 | 379 | 229 | 384 | 130 | 323 | 79 |
| Swansea | 351 | 120 | 233 | 107 | 321 | 349 | 180 | 170 | 141 | 133 | 221 | 261 | 272 |

LEGEND

| | | |
|---|---|---|
| Major Road | **DAVEY STREET** | |
| Route Number | 1 A3 | |
| Street | DUKE STREET | |
| Lane/Walkway | | |
| One Way Street | → | |
| Railway | | |
| Shopping Area | | |
| Church | † | |
| Hospital | + | |
| Park / Reserve | | |
| Information | ℹ | |
| Post Office | ⊙ | |

SCALE

0  200m  400m  600m  800m  1km

© Hema Maps Pty Ltd

## Places of Interest

1. Anglesea Barracks  C2
2. Antarctic Adventure  C2
3. Battery Point Area  D2
4. Bellerive Oval  C4
5. Cat & Fiddle Arcade  C2
6. Designer Makers Tasmania  B1
7. Franklin Square  C2
8. Gas Works Village  C2
9. Harbour Cruises  C2
10. Hobart Town Hall  C2
11. Kelly Steps  C2
12. Maritime Museum  D3
13. Narryna Museum  C2
14. Parliament House  C2
15. Penitentiary Chapel & Courts  C2
16. Royal Tennis Centre  C2
17. Salamanca Market (Saturday)  C2
18. Tasmania Distillery & Museum  C2
19. Tasmanian Museum & Art Gallery  C2
20. Theatre Royal  C2
21. Van Diemens Land Folk Museum  C2
22. Village Cinema Centre  C2
23. Wrest Point Casino  D2

## Services

30. Jewish Synagogue  C2
31. Police Headquarters  C2
⊙. Post Office  C2
32. Qantas  C2
33. RACT  C2
34. Royal Hobart Hospital  C2
35. State Library & Allport Museum  C2
36. St Davids Cathedral  C2
37. St Helens Hospital  C2
38. Tasmanian Visitor Information Centre  C2
39. YHA Office  C2

## Accommodation

40. Blue Hills Motel & Apartments  D2
41. Brooke Street Waterfront Exec Hotel  C2
42. City View Motel  A4
43. Country Comfort Hadleys Hotel  C2
44. Customs House Hotel  C2
45. Davey Place Holiday Town Houses  D1
46. Fountainside Motor Inn  C2
47. Graham Court Holiday Villas  A1
48. Grosvenor Court  D2
49. Hobart Macquarie Motor Inn  C2
50. Hobart Midcity Hotel  C2
51. Hobart Tower Motel  A1
52. Hobart Vista Hotel  C2
53. Hotel Grand Chancellor  C2
54. Lenna of Hobart  C2
55. Macquarie Manor  C2
56. Mayfair Motel  C1
57. Oakford on Elizabeth Pier  C2
58. Pacific Vista Hotel  C1
59. Portsea Terrace  C2
60. Rydges Hobart  B1
61. Salamanca Inn  C2
62. St Ives Motel Apartments  D2
63. The Astor Private Hotel  C2
64. The Lodge on Elizabeth  B1
65. The Old Woolstore  C2
66. Waratah Motor Hotel  C1
67. Woolmers Inn  D2
68. Wrest Point Hotel Casino  D2

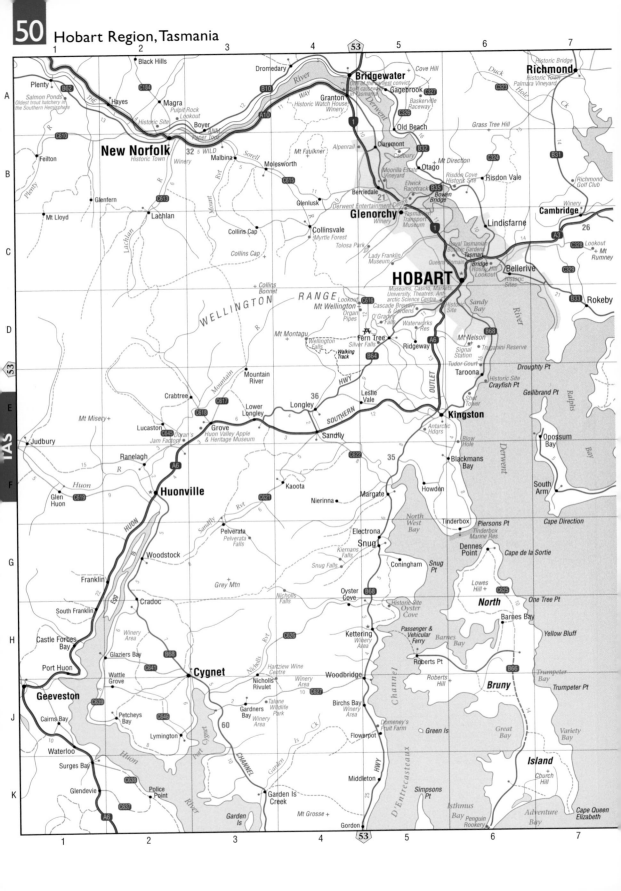

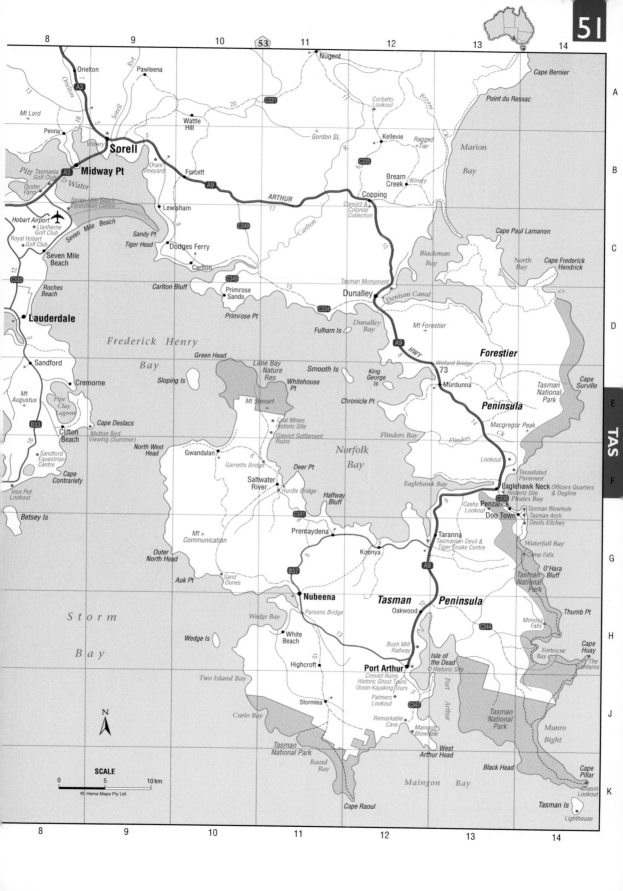

**SCALE**

0        5        10 km

© Hema Maps Pty Ltd

N

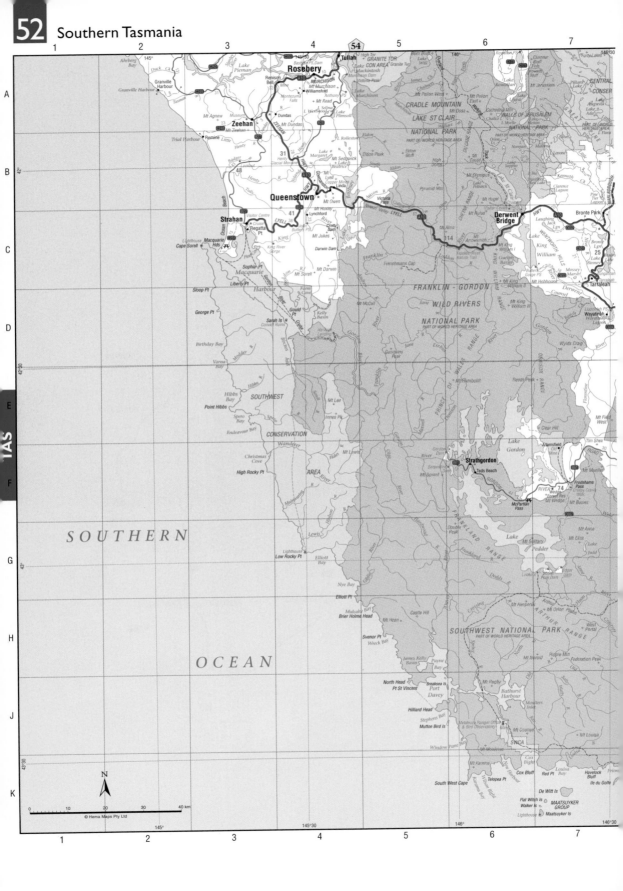

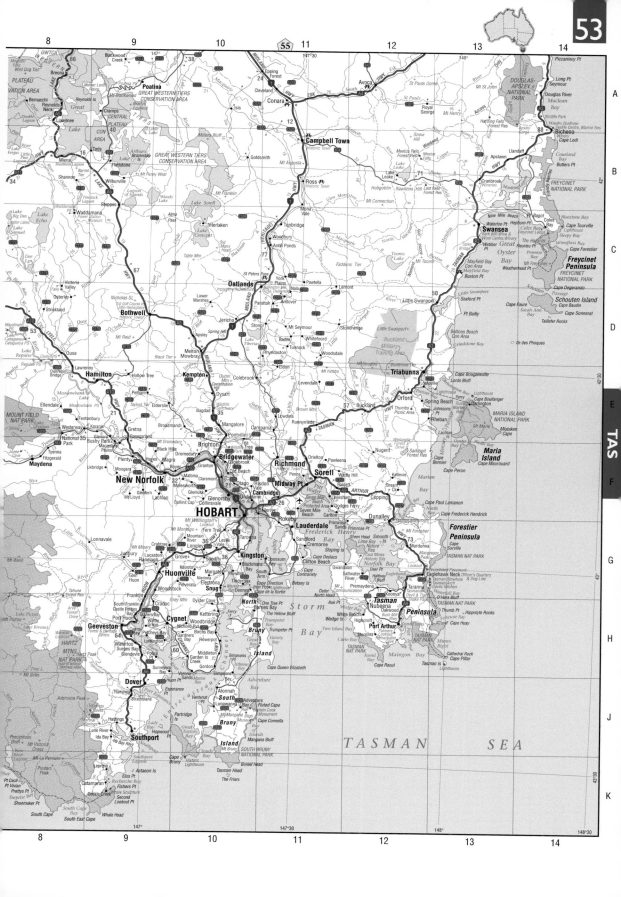

N

0    10    20    30 km

© Hema Maps Pty Ltd

INSET
0    10 km

**BASS    STRAIT**

King Island

**Currie**

**Grassy**

Cape Wickham
Lighthouse
Victoria Cove
Cape Farewell
Disappointment Bay
New Year Is
Christmas Is
Whistler Pt
Phoques Bay
Egg Lagoon
Lake Martha Lavinia
Lavinia Nature Reserve
Yambacoona
Reekara
Tathams Lagoon Wildlife Sanctuary
Cowper Pt
Councillor Island
Elephant Bay
Naracoopa
Loorana
Pegarah
Lymwood
Yarra Creek
Bold Head
Pearshape
Cataraqui Pt
Seal Rocks State Reserve
Surprise Pt
Stokes Pt
Seal Bay

Cape Keraudren
Cape Rochon
Three Hummock Island
Cape Adamson
Cuvier Bay
Hope Is
Hunter Island
Steep Is
Bird Is
Stack Is
Trefoil Is
Woolnorth Pt
Hunter Passage
Walker Island
Robbins Island
Ransonnet Bay
Guyton Pt
Cape Elie
Cape Grim
Woolnorth
Kangaroo Is
Perkins Island
North Pt
West Pt
Highfield Historic Site
Half Moon Bay
Highfield Pt
**Stanley** The Nut
Circular Head
Port Latta
Crayfish Creek
Pebbly Beach
Rocky Cape
Rocky Cape Nat Park
Sisters Beach
Boat Harbour Beach
Bluff Pt
Studland Bay
Montagu
Perkins Bay
Anthony Beach
Sawyer Bay
Black River
Stony Pt
**Smithton**
Mella
Lacrum Dairy Farm
South Forest
Hellyer
Wiltshire
Smokers Banks
Table Cape
Tulip Farm
**Wynyard**
Flowerdale
**Somerset**
**BURNIE**
Green Pt
Arm Bay
**Marrawah**
Redpa
Togari
Christmas Hills
Brittens Swamp
Irishtown
Mengha
Alcomie
Mawbanna
Montumana
Myalla
Moorleah
Preolenna
Lapoinya
Oldina
Calder
Cooee
Heybridge
Howth
Sulphur Creek
**Penguin**
West Pt
Edith Creek
Leah
Nabageena
Roger River
Trowutta
Milkshake Hills Forest Res
Milabena
Meunna
Takone
Yolla
West Ridgley
Ridgley
Upper Stowport
Natone
National Park
**Ulverstone**
Turners Beach
Leith
Don
**DEVONPORT**
Wesley Vale
Roger River West
Tayatea Bridge
Julius River Forest Res
Kanunnah Bridge
Lake Chisholm Forest Res
Takone West
Oonah
Tewkesbury
Highclere
Upper Natone
Riana
South Riana
Abbotsham
Gawler
Spreyton
Eugenana
**Latrobe**
Sassafras
Northdown
Moriarty
Nelson Bay
Couta Rocks
Temma
Hazard Bay
Dawson Bay
Gannet Pt
Ordnance Pt
Hampshire
Loyetea
Preston
Gunns Plains
Central Castra
Sprent
Lower Wilmot
South Nietta
Nietta
Wilmot
West Kentish
**Sheffield**
**Railton**
Nook
Barrington
Lower Barrington
Paradise
Moltema
Kimberley
**ARTHUR PIEMAN CONSERVATION AREA**
Kenneth Bay
Sandy Cape Lighthouse
Johnsons Bay
Mt Norfolk
Mt Bischoff
**Waratah**
Guildford
Savage River
Luina
Mt Cleveland
Talbots Lagoon
Black Bluff
Daisy Dell
Lorinna
Cradle Valley
Cradle Mtn
Mole Creek
**Mole Creek**
Chudleigh
Caveside
Western Creek
**SAVAGE RIVER NATIONAL PARK**
Rupert Pt
Corinna
Pieman River State Reserve
Mt Livingstone
Reece Dam
Granville Harbour
**Rosebery**
Renison Bell
Williamsford
Montezuma Falls
Mt Murchison
**Tullah**
Lake Mackintosh
Lake Rosebery
Lake Plimsoll
Lake Murchison
**CRADLE MOUNTAIN LAKE ST CLAIR NATIONAL PARK**
**WALLS OF JERUSALEM NATIONAL PARK**
**Zeehan**
Dundas
Mt Dundas
Trial Harbour
Remine
Lake Pieman
Lake Selina
**Queenstown**
Mt Lyell
Mt Owen
Mt Huxley
Lynchford
**Strahan**
Macquarie Hds
Cape Sorell Lighthouse
Ocean Beach
Regatta Pt
Sophia Pt
Cape Sorell
Liberty Pt
Macquarie Harbour
King River Gorge
Darwin Dam
Mt Darwin
Mt Sorell
**FRANKLIN-GORDON WILD RIVERS NATIONAL PARK**
**Derwent Bridge**
Bronte Park
Lake St Clair
Mt Olympus
Mt King William I
Tarraleah

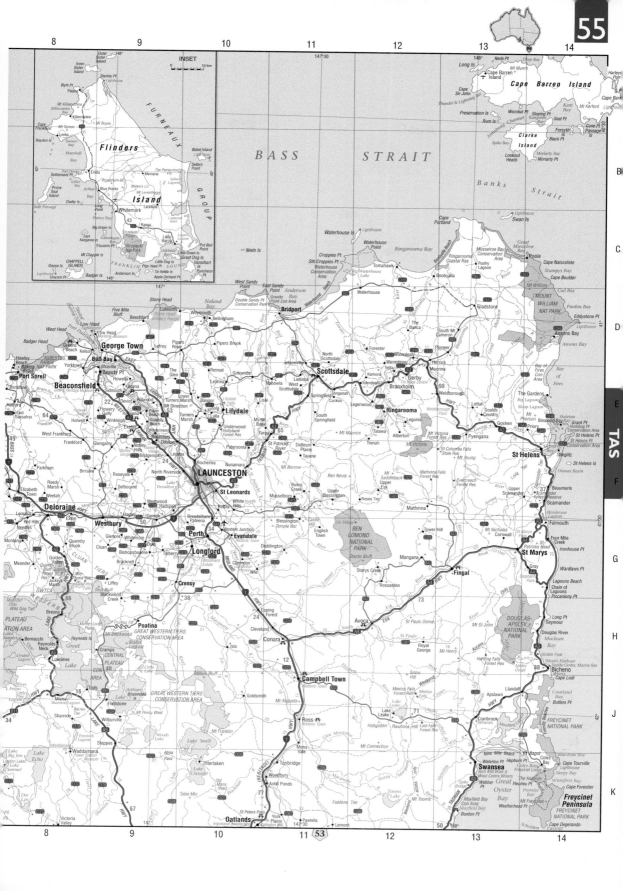

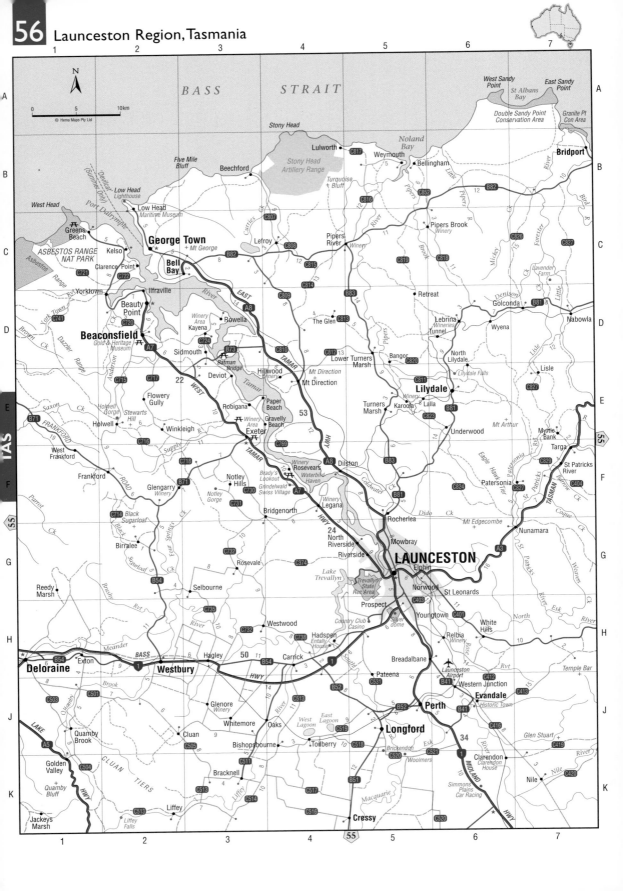

1    2    3    4    5    6    7

**BASS    STRAIT**

West Sandy Point
East Sandy Point
St Albans Bay
Double Sandy Point Conservation Area
Granite Pt Con Area

Stony Head
Noland Bay

A

Lulworth
Weymouth
Bellingham
C817
**Bridport**

Five Mile Bluff
Beechford
Stony Head Artillery Range
Turquoise Bluff

B

0    5    10km
© Hema Maps Pty Ltd

Low Head Lighthouse
Low Head Maritime Museum
Port Dalrymple
Curries Ck
Lefroy
Pipers River Winery
C807
C816
C852
Pipers Brook Winery
B82
C826
C827

C

West Head
Greens Beach
ASBESTOS RANGE NAT PARK
Kelso
Clarence Point
**George Town** + Mt George
B82
C808
C815
C819
C818
Retreat
Golconda
B81
Nabowla
Ilavender Farm

D

York Town
Yorktown
Ilfraville
Beauty Point
**Beaconsfield** Gold & Heritage Museum
Sidmouth
Winery Area
Kayena
Rowella
B73
Batman Bridge
C810
C812
Lower Turners Marsh
Bangor
C820
North Lilydale
Lisle
C827
C721
C722
C741
C720
C724
The Glen
C813

Saxon Ck
Holwell Gorge
Stewarts Hill
Flowery Gully
Deviot
Hillwood Winery
Mt Direction
Mt Direction
Lilydale Falls
**Lilydale**
C811
Lalla
Myrtle Bank
C715
C717
22

E

**TAS**
FRANKFORD
West Frankford
Holwell
Winkleigh
Robigana
Paper Beach
Gravelly Beach
Winery Area
**Exeter**
53
Turners Marsh
Karoola
Underwood
Mt Arthur
Targa
55
B71
C716
C769
B71

F

Frankford
C718
Notley Hills
Brady's Lookout
Roseveans
Waterbird Haven
Dilston
Winery Legana
B83
Patersonia
St Patricks River
C714
Glengarry Winery
Notley Gorge
Grindelwald Swiss Village
A8
C824
C329
C327
C404

Birralee
Black Sugarloaf
Bridgenorth
24
North Riverside
Rocherlea
Mt Edgecombe
Nunamara
C730
C731
C732

G

Reedy Marsh
Selbourne
Rosevale
C374
Riverside
Mowbray
**LAUNCESTON**
Elphin
Norwood
St Leonards
A3
B54
C735

H

Exton
Meander
BASS
Hagley
50
Carrick
Westwood
Hadspen Entally House
Country Club Casino
Silverdome
Prospect
Youngtown
White Hills
Relbia Winery
**Deloraine**
**Westbury**
1
Breadalbane
Launceston Airport
Western Junction
C503
C501
C732
C738
1
C531
B41
C412
C419

J

Quamby Brook
Glenore Winery
Whitemore
Oaks
West Lagoon
East Lagoon
C519
Pateena
B52
**Perth**
**Evandale** Historic Town
Glen Stuart
C505
Cluan
Bishopsbourne
Toiberry
C518
**Longford**
34
Brickendon
Woolmers
Clarendon Clarendon House
Nile
C504
C511
C520
C521
C416
C420

K

Golden Valley
Quamby Bluff
CLUAN TIERS
Bracknell
C513
C514
C517
B51
Simmons Plains Car Racing
MIDLAND HWY
Jackeys Marsh
Liffey
Liffey Falls
C516
**Cressy**
C520

1    2    3    4    55    5    6    7

# South Australia

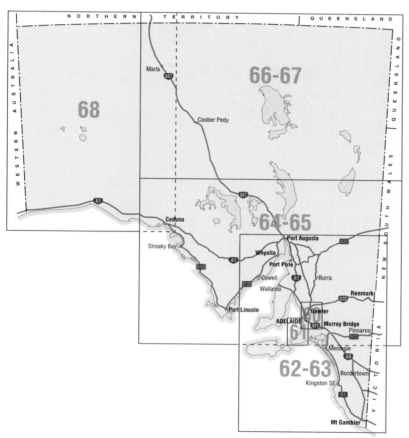

## Distance Chart

| | | | | | | | | | | | | | | Adelaide |
|---|---|---|---|---|---|---|---|---|---|---|---|---|---|---|
| | | | | | | | | | | | | | Alice Springs | 1534 |
| | | | | | | | | | | | | Broken Hill | 1640 | 511 |
| | | | | | | | | | | | Ceduna | 882 | 1688 | 776 |
| | | | | | | | | | | Coober Pedy | 1000 | 952 | 688 | 846 |
| | | | | | | | | | Innamincka | 920 | 1236 | 1094 | 1623 | 1065 |
| | | | | | | | | Leigh Creek | 509 | 485 | 727 | 585 | 1173 | 556 |
| | | | | | | | Mt Gambier | 996 | 1505 | 1286 | 1216 | 951 | 1974 | 440 |
| | | | | | | Oodnadatta | 1481 | 524 | 959 | 195 | 1195 | 1147 | 664 | 1041 |
| | | | | | Port Augusta | 730 | 751 | 262 | 771 | 535 | 465 | 417 | 1223 | 311 |
| | | | | Port Lincoln | 340 | 1070 | 1091 | 602 | 1111 | 875 | 404 | 757 | 1563 | 651 |
| | | | Port Pirie | 432 | 92 | 822 | 667 | 340 | 849 | 627 | 557 | 394 | 1315 | 227 |
| | | Renmark | 323 | 755 | 415 | 1145 | 470 | 590 | 1099 | 950 | 880 | 560 | 1638 | 252 |
| | WA-SA Bdr Village | 1366 | 1043 | 890 | 951 | 1681 | 1702 | 1231 | 1722 | 1486 | 486 | 1368 | 2174 | 1262 |

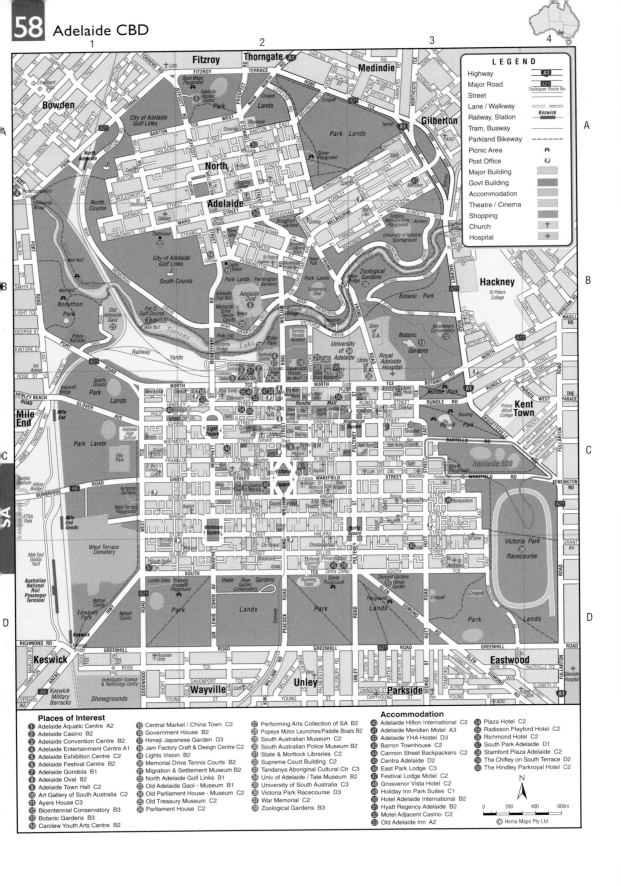

**LEGEND**

| | |
|---|---|
| Highway | A1 |
| Major Road | A21 / Trailblazer Route No. |
| Street | |
| Lane / Walkway | |
| Railway, Station | Keswick |
| Tram, Busway | |
| Parkland Bikeway | – – – |
| Picnic Area | ♣ |
| Post Office | ⓞ |
| Major Building | |
| Govt Building | |
| Accommodation | |
| Theatre / Cinema | |
| Shopping | |
| Church | ✝ |
| Hospital | ✚ |

## Places of Interest

1. Adelaide Aquatic Centre  A2
2. Adelaide Casino  B2
3. Adelaide Convention Centre  B2
4. Adelaide Entertainment Centre  A1
5. Adelaide Exhibition Centre  C2
6. Adelaide Festival Centre  B2
7. Adelaide Gondola  B1
8. Adelaide Oval  B2
9. Adelaide Town Hall  C2
10. Art Gallery of South Australia  C2
11. Ayers House  C3
12. Bicentennial Conservatory  B3
13. Botanic Gardens  B3
14. Carclew Youth Arts Centre  B2
15. Central Market / China Town  C2
16. Government House  B2
17. Himeji Japanese Garden  D3
18. Lights Vision  B2
19. Jam Factory Craft & Design Centre  C2
19. Lights Vision  B2
20. Memorial Drive Tennis Courts  B2
21. Migration & Settlement Museum  B2
22. North Adelaide Golf Links  B1
23. Old Adelaide Gaol - Museum  B1
24. Old Parliament House - Museum  C2
25. Old Treasury Museum  C2
26. Parliament House  C2
27. Performing Arts Collection of SA  B2
28. Popeye Motor Launches/Paddle Boats  B2
29. South Australian Museum  C2
30. South Australian Police Museum  B2
31. State & Mortlock Libraries  C2
32. Supreme Court Building  C2
33. Tandanya Aboriginal Cultural Ctr  C3
34. Univ of Adelaide / Tate Museum  B2
35. University of South Australia  C3
36. Victoria Park Racecourse  D3
37. War Memorial  C2
38. Zoological Gardens  B3

## Accommodation

40. Adelaide Hilton International  C2
41. Adelaide Meridien Motel  A3
42. Adelaide YHA Hostel  D3
43. Barron Townhouse  C2
44. Cannon Street Backpackers  C2
45. Centra Adelaide  D2
46. East Park Lodge  C3
47. Festival Lodge Motel  C2
48. Grosvenor Vista Hotel  C2
49. Holiday Inn Park Suites  C1
50. Hotel Adelaide International  B2
51. Hyatt Regency Adelaide  B2
52. Motel Adjacent Casino  C2
53. Old Adelaide Inn  A2
54. Plaza Hotel  C2
55. Radisson Playford Hotel  C2
56. Richmond Hotel  C2
57. South Park Adelaide  D1
58. Stamford Plaza Adelaide  C2
59. The Chifley on South Terrace  D2
60. The Hindley Parkroyal Hotel  C2

N

0   200   400   600m

© Hema Maps Pty Ltd

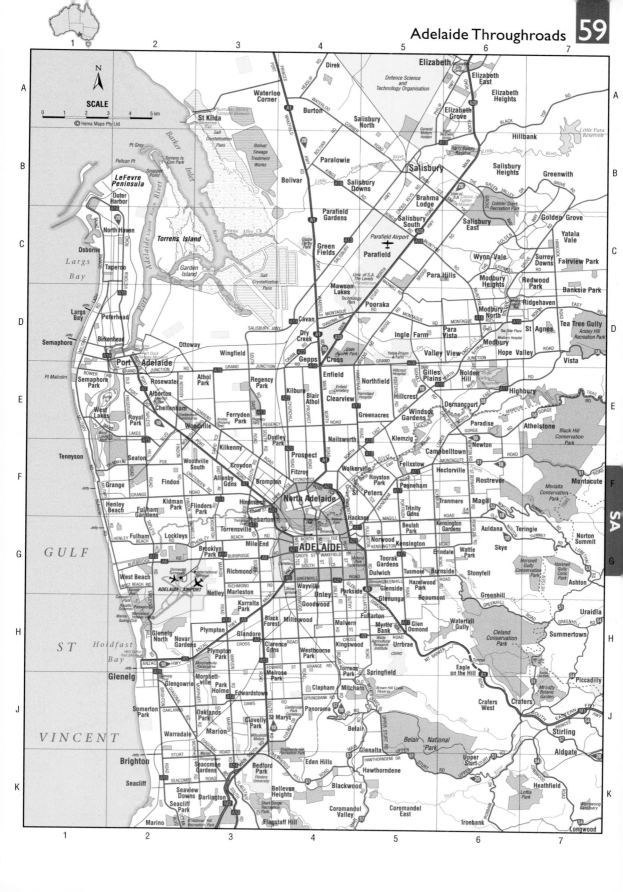

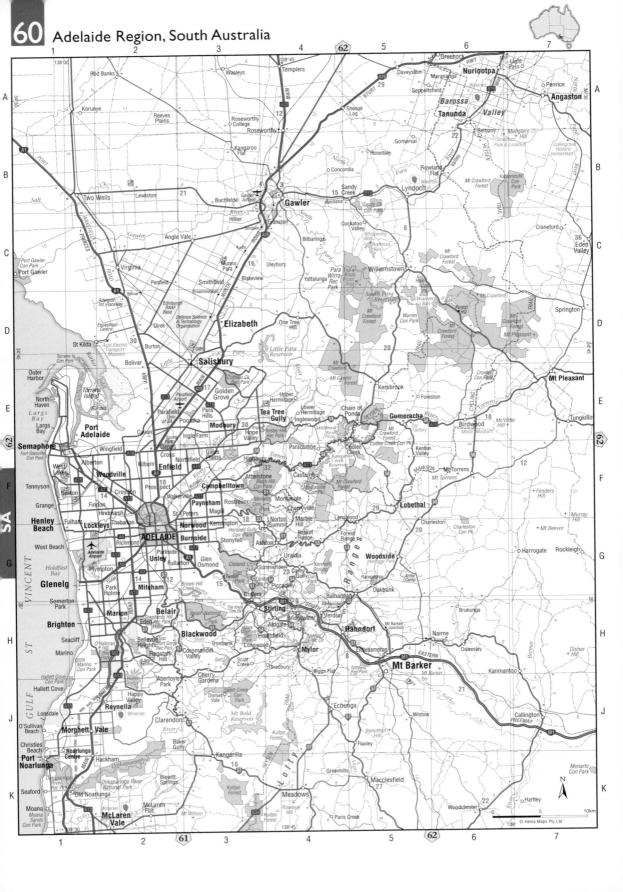

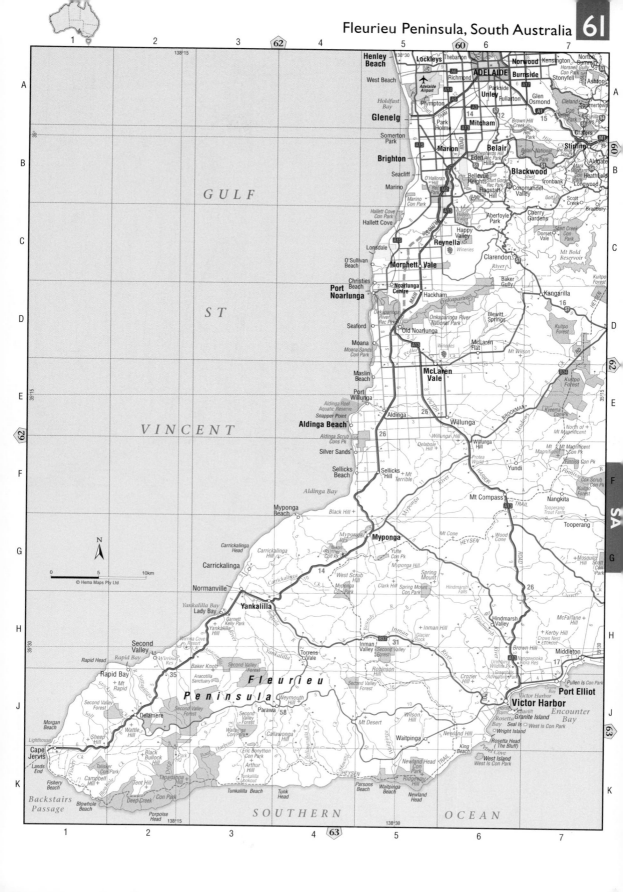

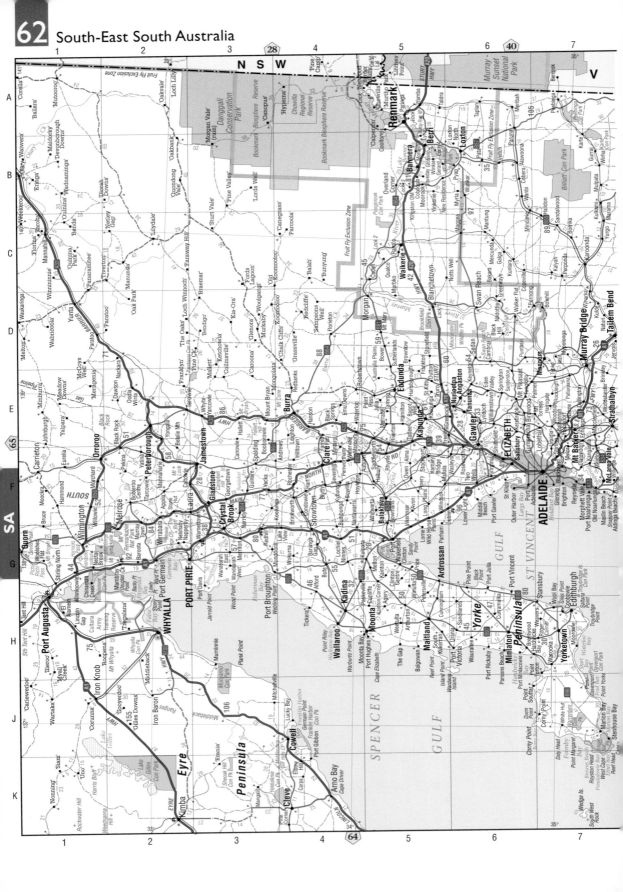

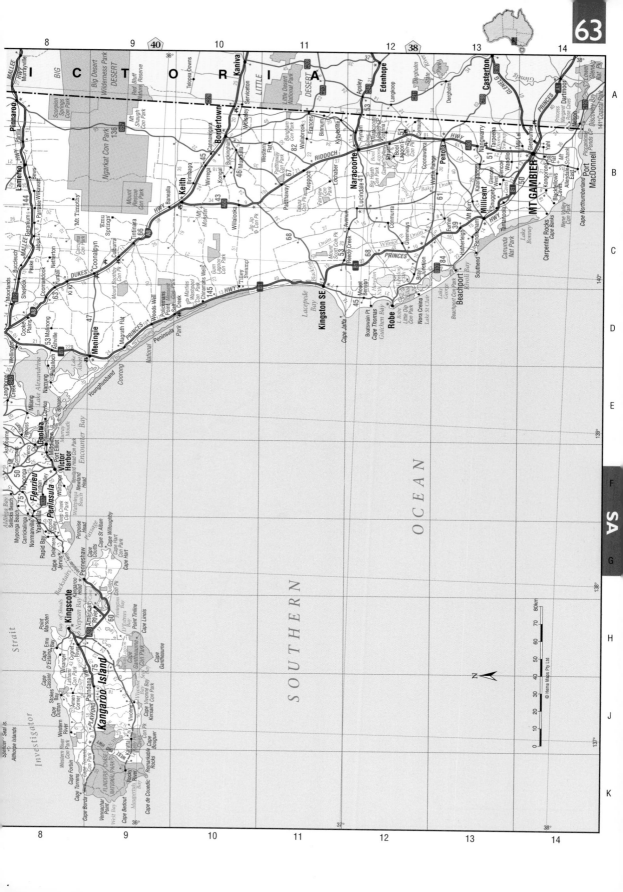

**Southern Ocean**

**Spencer Gulf**

**Investigator**

Major places and features:

Roxby Downs, 'Roxby Downs', Purple Downs, Norris Ridge, 'Koolymilka', Woomera, Pimba, Narlungda, Island Lagoon, Lyons, Malbooma 'Malbooma', Tarcoola, Wilgena, Wigena, Dog Fence, North Well, Ferguson, Kingoonya, Coondambo, Glendambo, Kultanaby, Wirraminna, Mount Vivian, Lake Patricia, Lake Younghusband, Hanson Hill, Lake Harris, Lake Hart, Arcoona

Yellabinna Regional Reserve

For more detail on this area, see Hema's Great Desert Tracks South East Sheet

Goog's Lake, Monuments to Goog & Dinger, Yumbarra Conservation Park, Charoba Tank, Dog Fence, Lone Oak, OTC Earth Station Dishes, Lake Gairdner National Park, Lake Everard, 'Lake Everard', 'Kokatha', 'Yerda', 'Kangaroo Well', Bond Hill, Belt Hill, 'Mahanewo', 'Yalymbo', Lake Finniss, Lake McFarlane

Bookabie, Euria Well, Chading Con Res, Penong (fuel), Kowulka, Kevin, Charra, Moule, Koonibba Community, Koonibba, Ceduna, Denial Bay, Heverard, Mudamuckla, Laura Bay, Karawingi Park, Nunjikompita, Pureba Conservation Park, Numinyah Conservation Res, Koolgera Conservation Reserve, 'Kondoolka', 'Hiltaba', Mt St Mungo, Jumppuppy Hill, Lake Acraman, 'Moonaree', Beacon Hill, Low Hill

Sinclair Is Con Park, Cactus Beach, Point Sinclair, Point Bell, Con Res, Point Bell, Rocky Point, Point Peter, Cape St Peter, Goat Is, St Peter Island, Evans Is, Smoky Bay, Carawa, Wirrulla, Petina, Cungena, Yardea, Thurlga, 'Mount Ive', 'Kolendo', Nukey Bluff, Spring Hill, 'Nonning', 'Siam', 'Uno', Rockwater Hill, Harris Bluff

Nuyts Archipelago Con Park, St Francis Is, Franklin Is, Point Brown, Haslam, Gibson Peninsula, Streaky Bay, Eba Is, Piednippie, Chandada, Poochera, Scrubby Peak, Paney Hill, Mt Fairview, Mt Double, 'Paney', Peterlumbo Hill, 'Buckleboo', Weednanna Hill, Lake Gilles

Cape Bauer, Olive Is CP, Point Westall, Sceale Bay, Minnipa, Yaninee, Pygery, Mt Sturt, Pildappa Rock, Pinkawillinie Conservation Park, Mt Wudinna, Wudinna, Kyancutta, Eyre Peninsula, Buckleboo, Lake Gilles Con Park, Kimba

Cape Blanche, Searcy Bay, Point Labatt, Sealion Colony, Cape Radstock, Venus Bay, Venus Bay Con Pk, Talia, Colley, Port Kenny, Mount Damper, Kulliparu Con Pk, Cocata Con Park, Kopi, Roongawa, Warramboo, Hambidge Con Park, Caralue Bluff, Caralue, Waddikee, Sheoak Hill Con Pk, 'Erania'

Anxious Bay, Walkers Rock, Waldegrave Is Con Park, Cape Finniss, Colton, 'Gum Flat', Mount Wedge, Barwell Con Pk, Darke Peak, Carappee Hill, Mangalo, Darke Peak, Yaldulknie Con Pk, Middlecamp Hills CP

Flinders Island, Ward Is, Investigator Group Con Park, Elliston, Bramfield, 'Kappawanta', Bascombe Well Con Park, Lock, 'Portana', Murdinga, Pine Corner, Rudall, Kielpa, Cleve, Elbow Hill, Port Gibbon, Con Pk, Cowell

Pearson Isles, Talia Caves, Sheringa, 'Oakdale', Tooligie, Tooligie Hill, 'Pine Grove', Hincks Con Park, Verran, Wharminda, Arno Bay, Cape Driver

Waterloo Bay, Sheringa Beach, Cap Is 'n Misery Con Park, Lake Hamilton, Karkoo, Brooker, Mount Hill, Butler Tanks, Ungarra, Port Neill, Cape Hardy

Drummond Point, Mount Hope, 'Yeelanna', Cockaleechie, Brayfield, Lipson, Lipson Cove, Mount Drummond, Rocky Point, Point Sir Isaac, Coffin Bay, Coffin Bay National Pk, Warrow, Coulta, Cummins, Yallunda Flat, Wanilla, Koppio, Tumby Bay, Wincelty Is, Revesby Is, Sir Joseph Banks Group Con Park, Roxby Is, Spilsby Is

Reef Point, Point Whidbey, Avoid Bay, Wangary, Edillilie, White Flat, Green Patch, Louth Bay, Louth Is, Point Boingdarra, Rockhook, Boston Point, Boston Island, Coffin Bay, Kellidie Bay Con Pk, Port Lincoln, Tulka, Lincoln National Park, Shoal Point

Perforated Is, Four Hummocks, Whidbey Isles Con Park, Point Avoid, McLaren Point, Cape Donington, Dangerous Reef, Taylor Is, Thistle Island

Cape Carnot, Liguanea Is, Sleaford Bay, Cape Wiles, West Point, Cape Catastrophe, Williams Is, Observation Point, Waterhouse Point, Wedge Is, South West Rock, Neptune Islands

Corny Point, Berry Bay, Daly Head, Formby Bay, Point Margaret, Browns Beach, Royston Head, Ethel Beach, Pondalowie Bay, West Cape, Marion Bay, Stenhouse Bay, Cape Spencer, Seal Is, Althorpe Islands

Kangaroo Island, Western River Con Park, Cape Forbin, Cape Torrens, Western River

0 50 100 km

© Hema Maps Pty Ltd

N

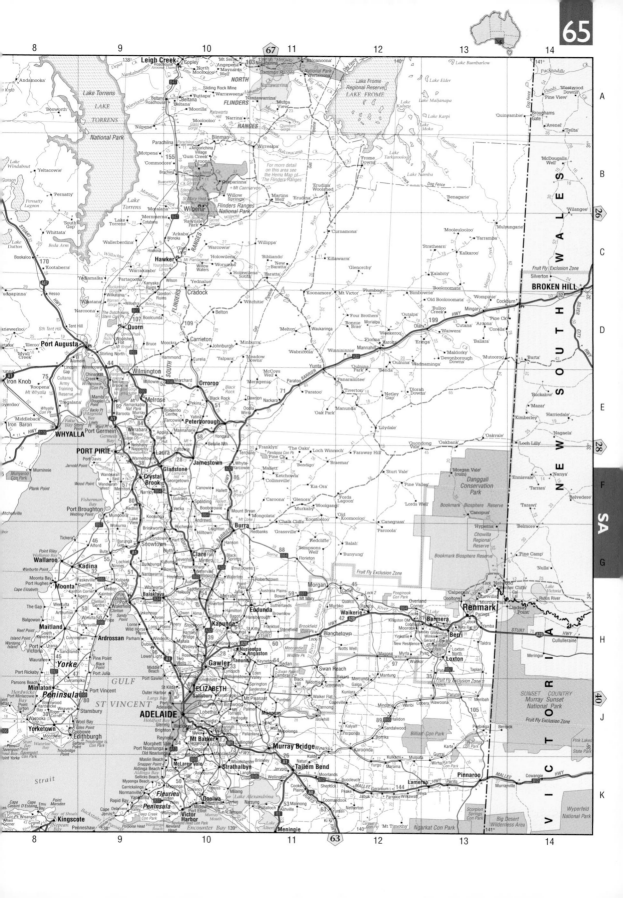

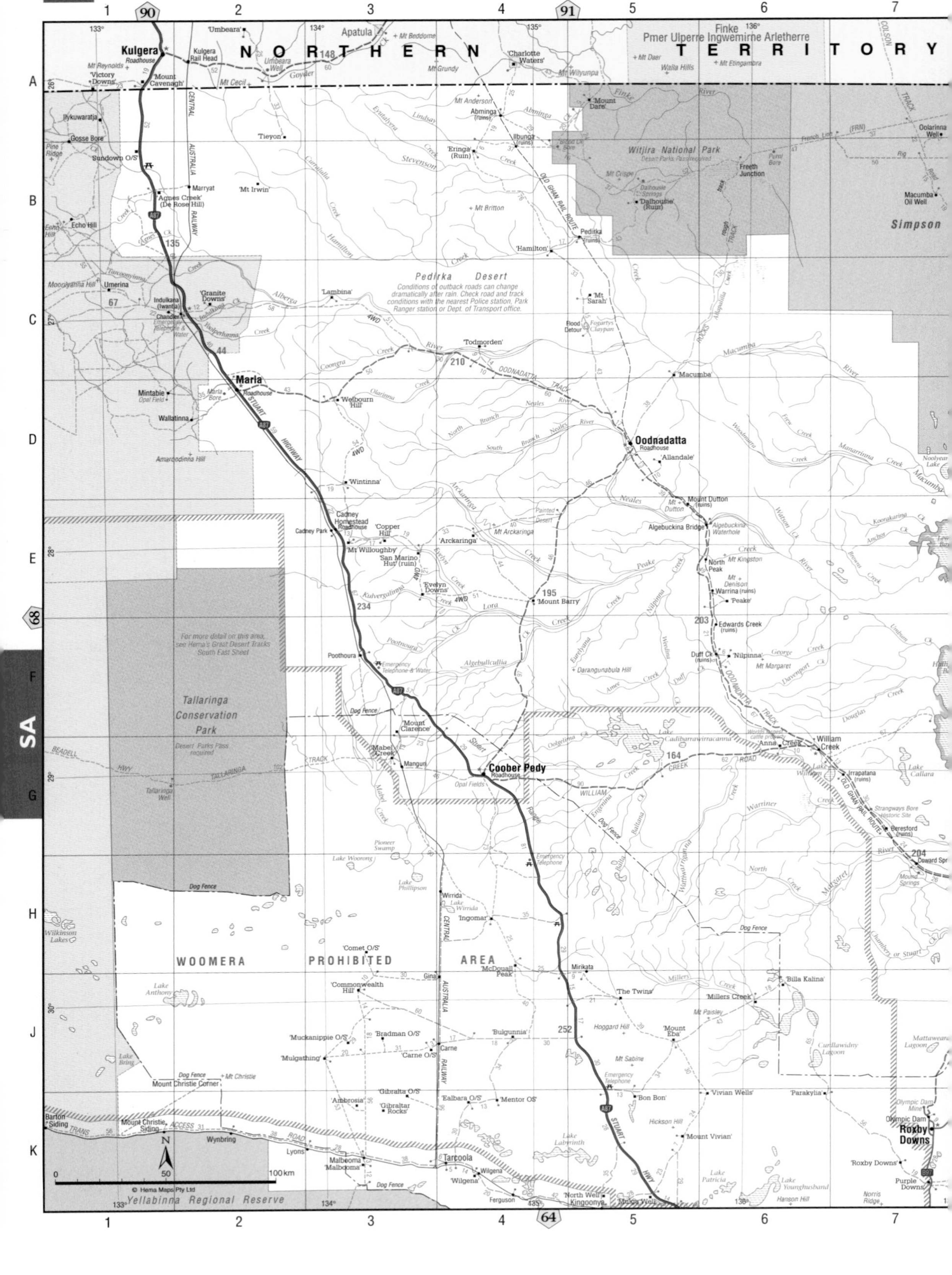

NORTHERN TERRITORY
Kulgera
Roadhouse
Kulgera Rail Head
'Umbeara'
Umbeara Well
Apatula
Mt Beddome
'Charlotte Waters'
Finke
Pmer Ulperre Ingwemirne Arletherre
Mt Daer
Walla Hills
Mt Etingambra
Goyder
Mt Grundy
Mt Wilyunpa
Mt Reynolds
'Victory Downs'
'Mount Cavenagh'
Mt Cecil
'Mount Dare'
Finke River
COLSON TRACK
Oolarinna Well
French Line
Rig
Mt Anderson
Abminga (ruins)
Ilbunga (ruins)
Witjira National Park
Desert Parks Pass required
Mt Crispe
Dalhousie Springs
'Dalhousie' (Ruin)
Freeth Junction
Macumba Oil Well
Simpson
Iiykuwaratja
Gosse Bore
Pine Ridge
Sundown O/S
'Tieyon'
'Eringa' (Ruin)
Stevenson
Lindsay Creek
Marryat
'Agnes Creek' (De Rose Hill)
'Mt Irwin'
Mt Britton
OLD GHAN RAIL ROUTE
CENTRAL AUSTRALIA RAILWAY
Echo Hill
Pedirka (ruins)
'Hamilton'
Hamilton Creek
Moorilyanna Hill
Umerina
Indulkana (Iwantja)
'Granite Downs'
Chandler
Emergency Telephone & Water
Alberga
'Lambina'
Pedirka Desert
Conditions of outback roads can change dramatically after rain. Check road and track conditions with the nearest Police station, Park Ranger station or Dept. of Transport office.
'Mt Sarah'
Flood Detour
Fogartys Claypan
4WD
'Todmorden'
Coongra Creek
ODNADATTA TRACK
Macumba
'Macumba'
Marla
Marla Bore
Roadhouse
Mintabie
Opal Field
Wallatinna
'Welbourn Hill'
Neales River
North Branch
South Branch
STUART HIGHWAY
Oodnadatta
Roadhouse
'Allandale'
Amarooddinna Hill
Woodmurra Creek
Manarrinna Creek
Noolyeana Lake
'Wintinna'
Cadney Homestead
Roadhouse
Cadney Park
'Copper Hill'
Arckaringa
Painted Desert
Mt Arckaringa
'Arckaringa'
Mount Dutton (ruins)
Mt Dutton
Algebuckina Bridge
Algebuckina Waterhole
Koorakarina Ck
Anchor Ck
'Mt Willoughby'
'San Marino Hut' (ruin)
North Peak
Mt Kingston
Peake
Mt Denison
Warrina (ruins)
'Peake'
Kulvergalinna
'Evelyn Downs'
Lora
Mount Barry
For more detail on this area, see Hema's Great Desert Tracks South East Sheet
Poothoura
Pootnoura
Emergency Telephone & Water
Algebullcullia
Edwards Creek (ruins)
Duff Ck (ruins)
'Nilpinna'
Mt Margaret
Davenport Ck
Darangunabula Hill
Tallaringa Conservation Park
Desert Parks Pass required
Dog Fence
'Mount Clarence'
Mabel Creek
Mangun
Coober Pedy
Roadhouse
Opal Fields
Lake Cadibarrawirracanna
'Anna Creek'
William Creek
WILLIAM CREEK ROAD
Lake William
Irrapatana (ruins)
Lake Callara
Strangways Bore Historic Site
Beresford (ruins)
Coward Springs
Mound Springs
BEADELL HWY
TALLARINGA TRACK
Tallaringa Well
Pioneer Swamp
Lake Woorong
Warriner Creek
North Creek
Margaret
Wattiwarriganna
Lake Phillipson
Wirrida
Lake Wirrida
'Ingomar'
Emergency Telephone
Wilkinson Lakes
WOOMERA PROHIBITED AREA
'Comet O/S'
'McDouall Peak'
Mirikata
Gina
'Commonwealth Hill'
'The Twins'
'Millers Creek'
'Billa Kalina'
Millers Creek
Lake Anthony
Mt Paisley
Hoggard Hill
'Mount Eba'
Curdlawidny Lagoon
Mattawearra Lagoon
'Muckanippie O/S'
'Bradman O/S'
'Bulgunnia'
Carne
'Carne O/S'
'Mulgathing'
Lake Bring
Mt Sabine
Chambers or Stuart Ck
Dog Fence
Mt Christie
Mount Christie Corner
'Gibralta O/S'
'Ambrosia'
'Gibraltar Rocks'
'Ealbara O/S'
'Mentor OS'
'Bon Bon'
'Vivian Wells'
'Parakylia'
Olympic Dam Mine
Olympic Dam
Roxby Downs
Barton Siding
Mount Christie Siding
TRANS ACCESS ROAD
Wynbring
Hickson Hill
'Mount Vivian'
Lake Labyrinth
Lyons
Malbooma
'Malbooma'
Tarcoola
Wilgena
'Wilgena'
Lake Patricia
Lake Younghusband
Hanson Hill
'Roxby Downs'
Purple Downs
Norris Ridge
Ferguson
North Well
Kingoonya
Mulga Well
Yellabinna Regional Reserve
0 50 100 km
© Hema Maps Pty Ltd
SA

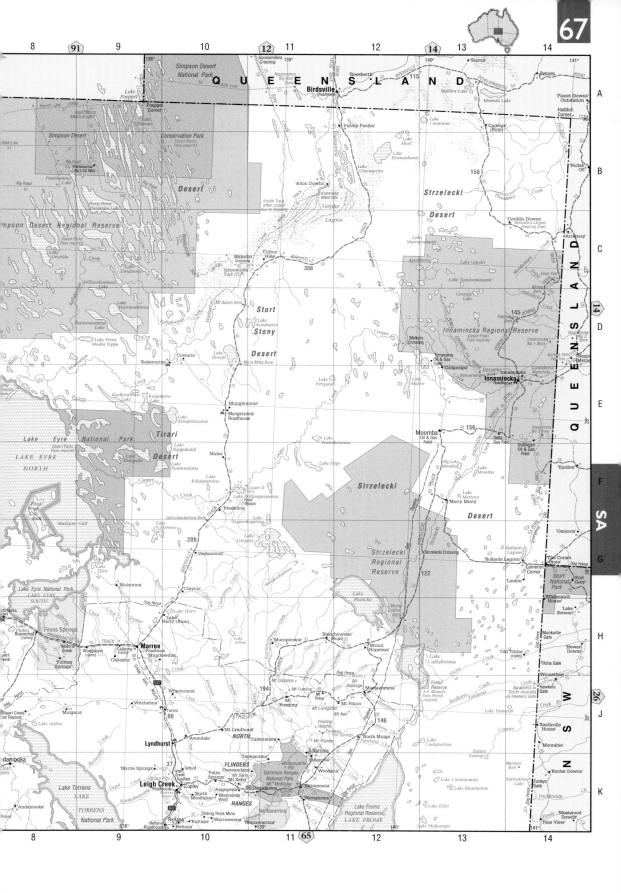

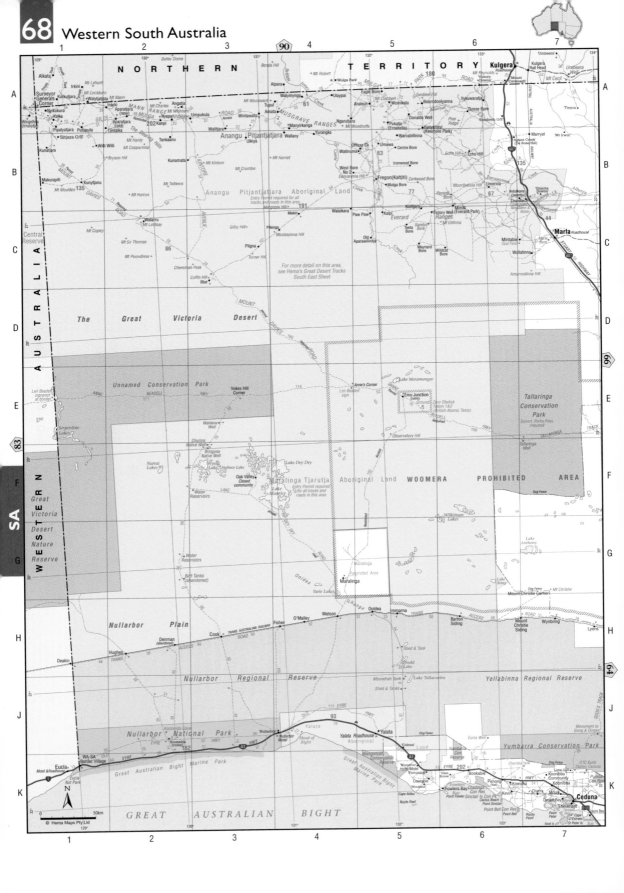

# Western Australia

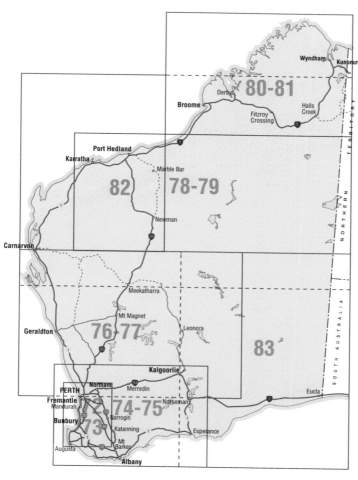

## Distance Chart

| | Albany |
|---|---|
| **Broome** | 2619 |
| **Bunbury** | 2431 | 342 |
| **Carnarvon** | 1086 | 1479 | 1315 |
| **Esperance** | 1624 | 667 | 2846 | 487 |
| **Geraldton** | 1144 | 480 | 606 | 1959 | 835 |
| **Kalgoorlie** | 979 | 392 | 1459 | 774 | 2302 | 879 |
| **Karratha** | 1844 | 1117 | 2261 | 637 | 1723 | 852 | 1952 |
| **Kununurra** | 1823 | 3273 | 2930 | 3817 | 2450 | 3402 | 1039 | 3590 |
| **Mt Magnet** | 2651 | 1222 | 622 | 342 | 1166 | 822 | 751 | 1680 | 939 |
| **Newman** | 616 | 2035 | 606 | 1238 | 958 | 1782 | 974 | 1367 | 1064 | 1555 |
| **Perth** | 1185 | 569 | 3220 | 1541 | 592 | 424 | 720 | 904 | 182 | 2249 | 411 |
| **Port Hedland** | 1636 | 451 | 1067 | 1584 | 239 | 1689 | 1346 | 2233 | 866 | 1818 | 613 | 2006 |
| **WA-SA Bdr Village** | 2864 | 1433 | 2413 | 1797 | 4448 | 2937 | 903 | 1820 | 917 | 2300 | 1584 | 3477 | 1404 |

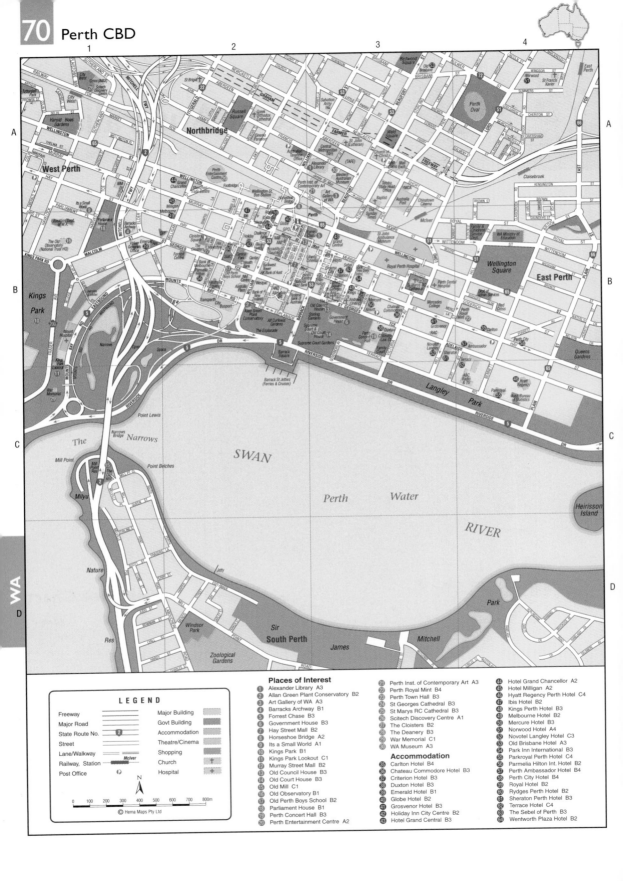

## Places of Interest

1. Alexander Library A3
2. Allan Green Plant Conservatory B2
3. Art Gallery of WA A3
4. Barracks Archway B1
5. Forrest Chase B3
6. Government House B3
7. Hay Street Mall B2
8. Horseshoe Bridge A2
9. Its a Small World A1
10. Kings Park B1
11. Kings Park Lookout C1
12. Murray Street Mall B2
13. Old Council House B3
14. Old Court House B3
15. Old Mill C1
16. Old Observatory B1
17. Old Perth Boys School B2
18. Parliament House B1
19. Perth Concert Hall B3
20. Perth Entertainment Centre A2

21. Perth Inst. of Contemporary Art A3
22. Perth Royal Mint B4
23. Perth Town Hall B3
24. St Georges Cathedral B3
25. St Marys RC Cathedral B3
26. Scitech Discovery Centre A1
27. The Cloisters B2
28. The Deanery B3
29. War Memorial C1
30. WA Museum A3

## Accommodation

35. Carlton Hotel B4
36. Chateau Commodore Hotel B3
37. Criterion Hotel B3
38. Duxton Hotel B3
39. Emerald Hotel B1
40. Globe Hotel B2
41. Grosvenor Hotel B3
42. Holiday Inn City Centre B2
43. Hotel Grand Central B3

44. Hotel Grand Chancellor A2
45. Hotel Milligan A2
46. Hyatt Regency Perth Hotel C4
47. Ibis Hotel B2
48. Kings Perth Hotel B3
49. Melbourne Hotel B2
50. Mercure Hotel B3
51. Norwood Hotel A4
52. Novotel Langley Hotel C3
53. Old Brisbane Hotel A3
54. Park Inn International B3
55. Parkroyal Perth Hotel C4
56. Parmelia Hilton Int. Hotel B2
57. Perth Ambassador Hotel B4
58. Perth City Hotel B4
59. Royal Hotel B2
60. Rydges Perth Hotel B2
61. Sheraton Perth Hotel B3
62. Terrace Hotel C4
63. The Sebel of Perth B3
64. Wentworth Plaza Hotel B2

## LEGEND

Freeway
Major Road
State Route No.
Street
Lane/Walkway
Railway, Station
Post Office

Major Building
Govt Building
Accommodation
Theatre/Cinema
Shopping
Church
Hospital

0 100 200 300 400 500 600 700 800m

© Hema Maps Pty Ltd

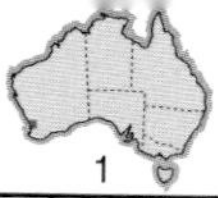

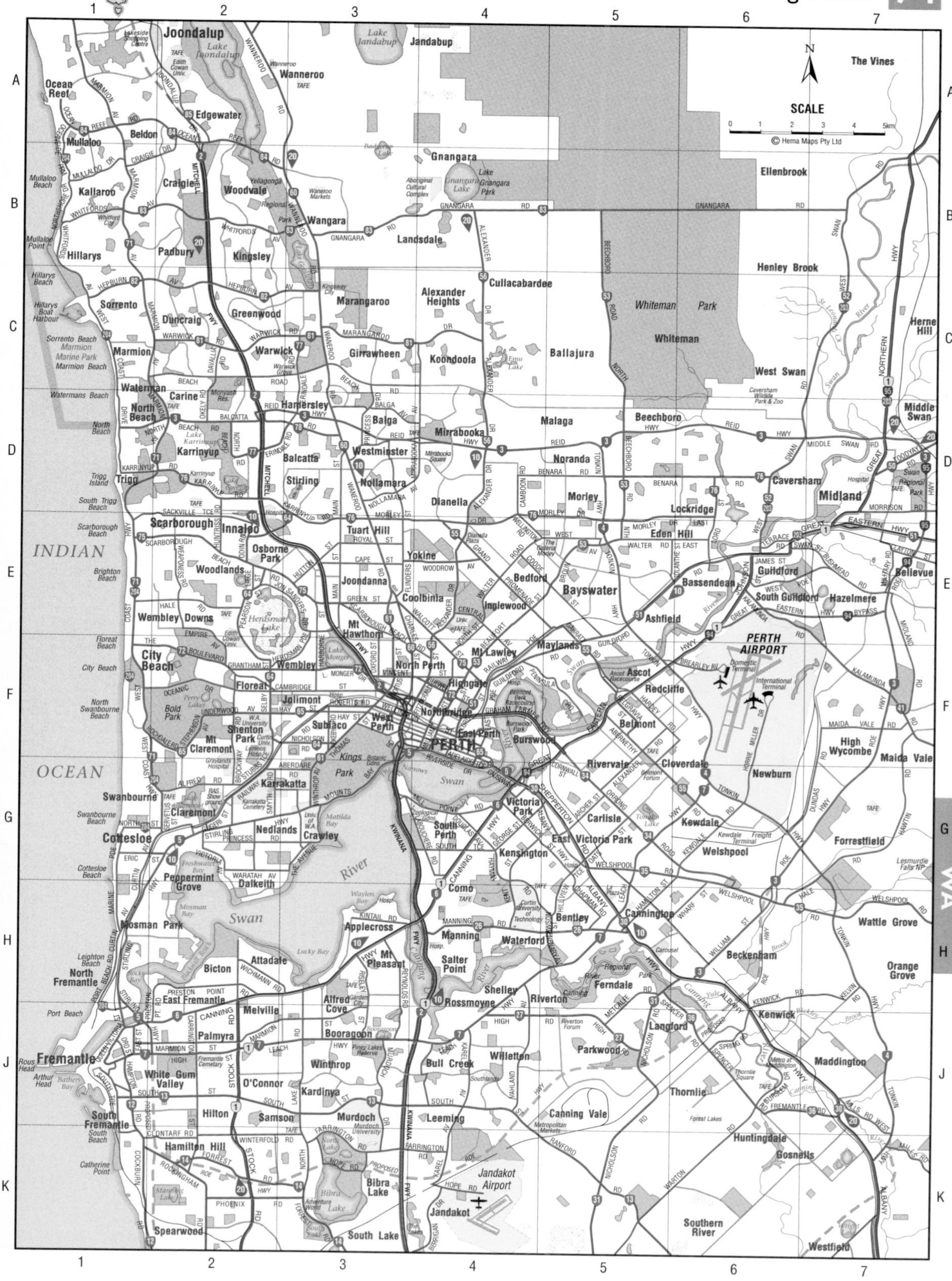

SCALE
0 1 2 3 4 5km
© Hema Maps Pty Ltd
N
INDIAN
OCEAN
Joondalup
Lake Joondalup
Lakeside Shopping Centre
Edith Cowan Univ.
Wanneroo
Lake Jandabup
Jandabup
The Vines
Ocean Reef
Edgewater
Mullaloo
Beldon
Gnangara
Lake Gnangara
Ellenbrook
Mullaloo Beach
Kallaroo
Craigie
Woodvale
Wangara
Mullaloo Point
Hillarys
Padbury
Kingsley
Landsdale
Henley Brook
Hillarys Beach
Hillarys Boat Harbour
Sorrento
Cullacabardee
Alexander Heights
Marangaroo
Whiteman Park
Whiteman
Herne Hill
Duncraig
Greenwood
Sorrento Beach
Marmion Marine Park
Marmion Beach
Marmion
Warwick
Girrawheen
Koondoola
Ballajura
West Swan
Waterman
Watermans Beach
Carine
North Beach
Hamersley
Balga
Malaga
Beechboro
Middle Swan
Karrinyup
Balcatta
Westminster
Mirrabooka
Noranda
Caversham
Trigg Island
Trigg
Stirling
Nollamara
Dianella
Morley
Lockridge
Midland
South Trigg Beach
Scarborough Beach
Scarborough
Innaloo
Tuart Hill
Eden Hill
Osborne Park
Yokine
Woodlands
Joondanna
Bedford
Bayswater
Bassendean
Guildford
Bellevue
Brighton Beach
Coolbinia
Inglewood
South Guildford
Hazelmere
Wembley Downs
Herdsman Lake
Ashfield
Floreat Beach
Mt Hawthorn
Maylands
PERTH AIRPORT
Domestic Terminal
International Terminal
City Beach
Mt Lawley
Ascot
Wembley
North Perth
City Beach
Floreat
Highgate
Redcliffe
North Swanbourne Beach
Jolimont
Northbridge
Bold Park
Subiaco
West Perth
Belmont
Shenton Park
East Perth
Mt Claremont
PERTH
Burswood
High Wycombe
Maida Vale
Kings Park
Rivervale
Cloverdale
Newburn
Swan
Swanbourne
Karrakatta
Swanbourne Beach
Claremont
Victoria Park
Carlisle
Kewdale
Nedlands
Crawley
South Perth
East Victoria Park
Forrestfield
Cottesloe
Kensington
Welshpool
Cottesloe Beach
Peppermint Grove
Dalkeith
River
Como
Swan
Mosman Park
Applecross
Bentley
Cannington
Wattle Grove
Manning
Waterford
Leighton Beach
North Fremantle
Bicton
Attadale
Mt Pleasant
Salter Point
Beckenham
Orange Grove
East Fremantle
Melville
Shelley
Riverton
Ferndale
Alfred Cove
Rossmoyne
Port Beach
Palmyra
Booragoon
Langford
Kenwick
Rous Head
Fremantle
Arthur Head
Winthrop
Willetton
Parkwood
Maddington
White Gum Valley
O'Connor
Bull Creek
Kardinya
Thornlie
Hilton
Samson
Murdoch
Leeming
Canning Vale
South Fremantle
South Beach
Murdoch University
Huntingdale
Gosnells
Hamilton Hill
Catherine Point
Bibra Lake
Jandakot Airport
Jandakot
Spearwood
South Lake
Southern River
Westfield
KWINANA FWY
MITCHELL FWY
WA

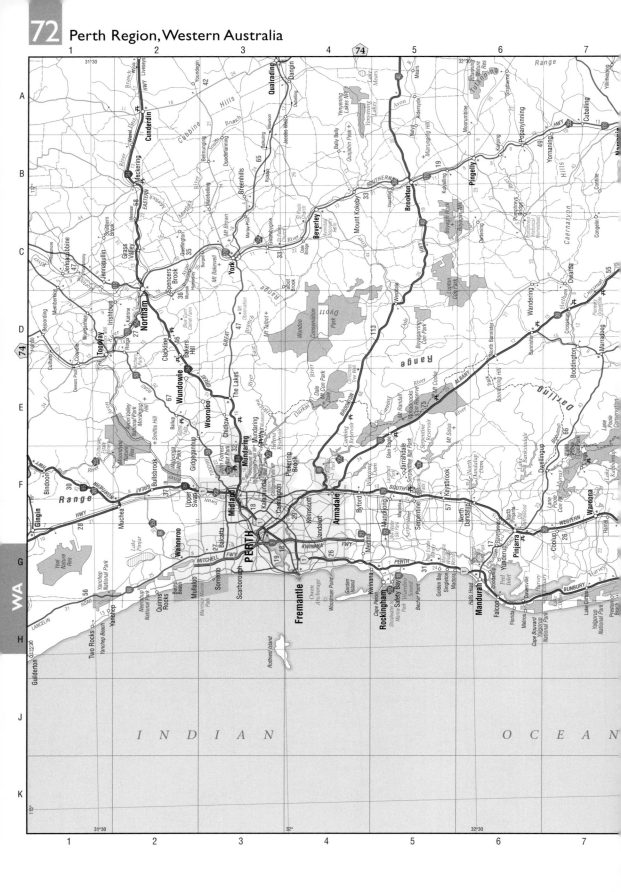

WA

INDIAN OCEAN

**PERTH**
**Fremantle**

Nambung Nat Park
Pinnacles
'Cooljarloo' Cataby
'Mimegarra'
Wanagarren Nature Res
Wedge Is
Dide Bay
Lancelin
Ledge Pt
Breton Bay
Sea Bird
Guilderton
Two Rocks
Yanchep
Neerabup Nat Park
Quinns Rocks
Marmion Marine Pk
Wanneroo
Mullaloo
Scarborough

**Moora**
Dandaragan
Walebing
Lake Hinds
New Norcia
Calingiri
Bolgart
Toodyay
Grass Valley
Mogumber
Wannamal
Bindoon
Moondyne
Gingin
Muchea
Lake Pinjar
Upper Swan
Wundowie
Woolooloo
Clackline
The Lakes **York**
Greenhills
Midland
Kalamunda
Mundaring
Glen Forrest
Armadale
Byford
Jarrahdale
Kelmscott
Dale
Canning Dam
Beverley
Con Park
Dangin
**Quairading**

**Wongan Hills** 108
Cowcowing Lakes
Cadoux
Koorda
Lake Wallambin
Bencubbin
Mukinbudin
Chiddarcooping
Lake Campion NR
Lake Brown
Lake Campion
Weston
Walgoolan
Burracopp
**Merredin**
Trayning
Nungarin
Dowerin
Wyalkatchem
180
**Goomalling**
Tammin 162 EASTERN
Doodlakine
Korbel
Meckering
**Cunderdin**
**Kellerberrin**
Muntadgin
**Northam**
**Bruce Rock**
Erikin
Shackleton
117
Narembeen
Sth Kumminin
Nth Karlgarin
125
135
Yenyening Lakes
Bulyee
Brookton
79 92
**Corrigin**
Kondinin 60
48 40
Jilakin Lake
Pingaring
Kulin
161
Yealering
Wandering
Popanyinning
**Pingelly**
Tutanning
Boyagin NR
Cuballing
Yomaning
Narrogin
94
Dwarda
Marradong
Wickepin
Harrismith
Jitarning
Dudinin
Taarblin Lake
Williams
Highbury
120
Tarin Rock NR
Kukerin
Lake Grace
Chinocup NR
Lake Pingrup
Piesseville
Dumbleyung
Lake NR
**Wagin**
Dumbleyung
119
**Mandurah**
Falcon
Peel Inlet
Cape Bouvard
182
Lake Clifton
Yalgorup Nat Park
Preston Beach
**Pinjarra**
Coolup
Dwellingup
Boddington
Bannister
128
Quindanning
Williams
Lupton Con Park
**Waroona**
Yarloop
Lane Poole Con Res
Stirling Dam
**Harvey**
Wokalup
Binningup
**Brunswick Junction**
Darkan
Arthur River
Lake Preston
98
Myalup
Harris Dam
**Bunbury**
Picton
Dardanup
Stratham
**Collie** 175
107
Bowelling
Duranillin
Woodanilling
Beaufort
Badgebup
Nyabing
Pingr
Eagle Bay
Geographe Bay
Cape Naturaliste
Dunsborough
**Busselton**
Yallingup
Capel
Tuart Forest NP
Argyle
Boyanup
Lowden
Mumballup
Mia Opencut
**Katanning** 200
Cape Clairault
Ludlow
Kirup
Grimwade
Noggerup
Broomehill
Moses Rock
143
Caves
130
Balingup
Dinninup
**Kojonup**
**Gnowangerup** 243
Leeuwin-Naturaliste
Cowaramup Bay
Gracetown
Cowaramup
Jarrahwood
Greenbushes
**Boyup Brook**
Mayanup
Onger
179
**Margaret River**
Prevelly Park
**Nannup**
**Bridgetown**
Tambellup
Borden
Witchcliffe
Lake Cave
Blackwood
Corack
Cape Freycinet
National Park
Hamelin Bay
Karridale
Kudardup
Jewel Cave
Gingilup Swamps NR
Deanmill
**Manjimup**
Cranbrook
Camel Lake NR
Amelup
STIRLING RANGE NAT PARK
Chillin
Augusta
Flinders Bay
Cape Leeuwin
Scott NP
Warren
Unicup NR
Quindinup
Frankland
Rocky Gully
Kendenup
Wellstead
Pemberton
Gloucester Tree
Warren NP
SHANNON NATIONAL PARK
162
Lake Muir
102
Kent
Porongurup Nat Park
Porongurup
Hassell NP
Warri
**Mt Barker**
Narrikup
Hass Beach
D'Entrecasteaux National Park
Northcliffe
Redmond
Manypeaks
Cheyne Beach
Waychinic
Looko
Windy Harbour
Point D'Entrecasteaux
239
**Walpole**
Valley of the Giants
**Denmark**
Nanarup
Two Peoples Bay
Cape Vancouver
King George Sou
Broke Inlet
Cliffy Head
Walpole-Nornalup National Park
Nornalup
Nornalup Inlet
Pt Nuyts
Pt Irwin
Pt Hillier
William Bay
West Cape Howe Nat Park
**ALBANY**
Torndirrup Nat Park
Bald Head
Torbay Bay
Cave Pt

For more detail on this area, see Hema's South West WA map

Rottnest Island
Garden Is
**Rockingham**
Kwinana
Safety Bay
Becher Pt
Shoalwater Is Marine Pk

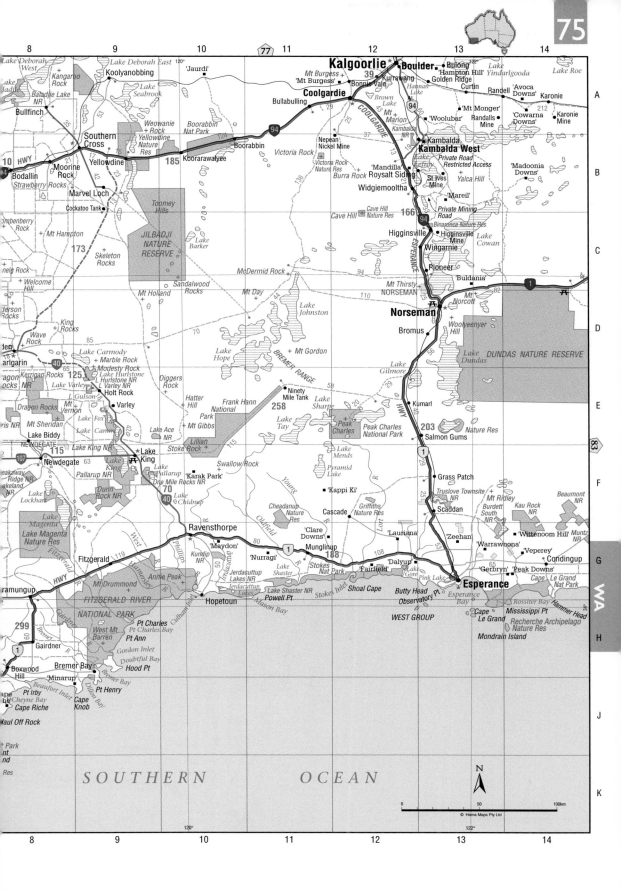

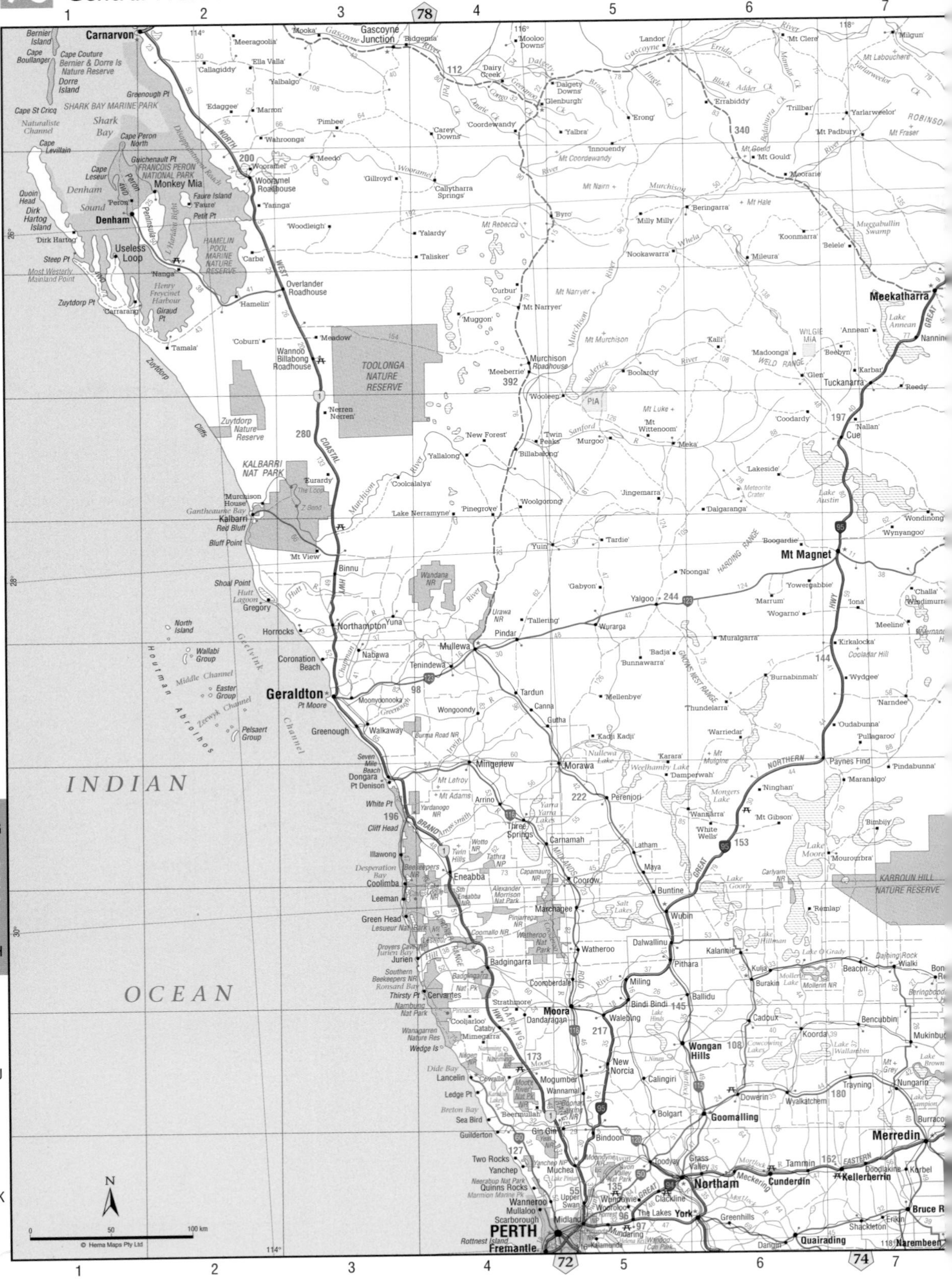

INDIAN

OCEAN

**WA**

Carnarvon

Denham
Monkey Mia

Meekatharra

Kalbarri

Mt Magnet

Geraldton

Yalgoo

Northampton

Mullewa
Morawa

Perenjori

Moora

Wongan Hills

Goomalling

New Norcia

Merredin

Northam
York

**PERTH**
Fremantle

Rottnest Island

Wanneroo

© Hema Maps Pty Ltd

0    50    100 km

N

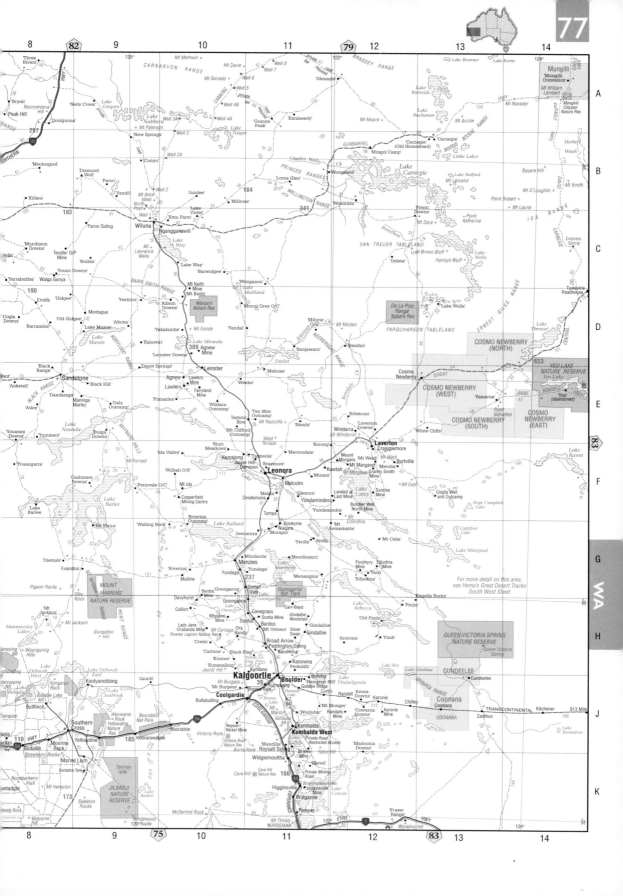

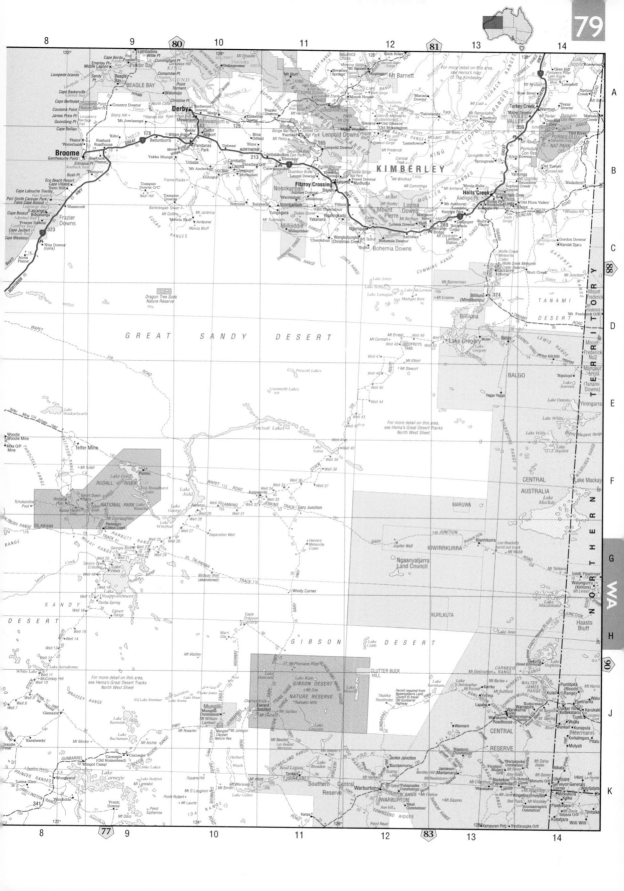

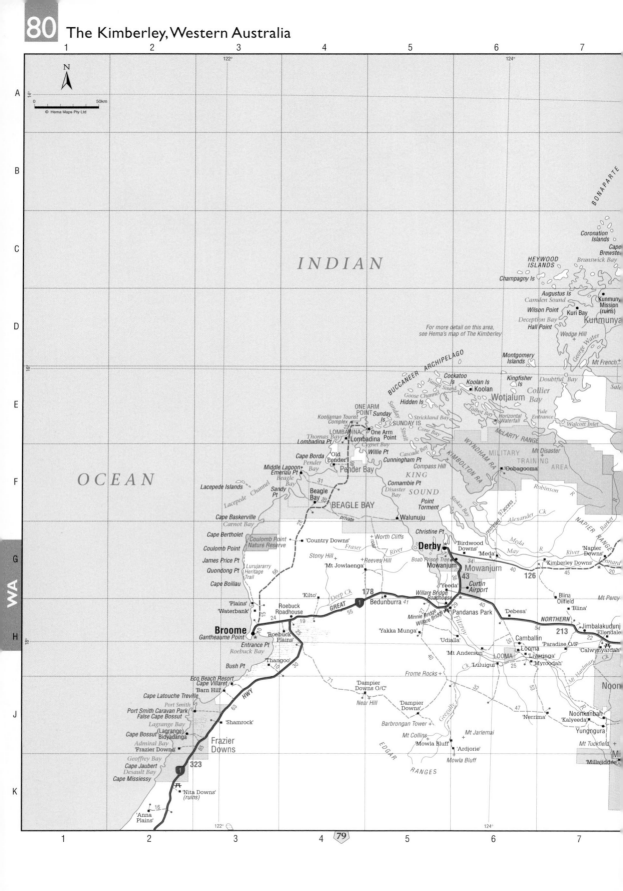

N

0    50km
© Hema Maps Pty Ltd

INDIAN

OCEAN

BONAPARTE

Coronation
Islands
Cape
Brewster
HEYWOOD
ISLANDS
Brunswick Bay
Champagny Is
Augustus Is
Camden Sound
Wilson Point
Kunmun
Mission
(ruins)
Deception Bay
Kuri Bay
Hall Point
Kunmunya
Wedge Hill
George Water
Mt French

For more detail on this area,
see Hema's map of The Kimberley

Montgomery
Islands

BUCCANEER ARCHIPELAGO

Cockatoo
Is
Koolan Is
Kingfisher
Is
Doubtful Bay
Koolan
Sal
Hidden Is
Yampi Sound
Collier
Bay
Wotjalum
Goose Channel
ONE ARM
POINT
Sunday
SUNDAY IS
Kooljaman Tourist
Complex
Strickland Bay
Yule
Entrance
Horizontal
Waterfall
Walcott Inlet
Thomas Bay
LOMBADINA
One Arm
Point
Cone Bay
McLARTY RANGE
Lombadina
Lombadina Pt
Cygnet Bay
Cascade Bay
WYNDHAM RA
Willie Pt
Cape Borda
Pender
Bay
'Old
Pender'
Cunningham Pt
Compass Hill
Mt Disaster
KIMBOLTON RA
MILITARY
Middle Lagoon
Emeriau Pt
Pender Bay
KING
'Oobagooma
TRAINING
Comambie Pt
Disaster
Bay
Lacepede Islands
Sandy
Pt
Beagle
Bay
SOUND
AREA
Beagle
Bay
Point
Torment
Robinson
R
Cape Baskerville
BEAGLE BAY
Walunuju
Stokes Bay
Alexander Ck
NAPIER
Carnot Bay
Private
Christine Pt
Cape Bertholet
Coulomb Point
Nature Reserve
'Country Downs'
Worth Cliffs
Fraser
Birdwood
Downs
Derby
Meda
R
Napier
Downs
RANGE
Coulomb Point
Stony Hill
River
Reeves Hill
May
R
'Kimberley Downs'
Chinnard
James Price Pt
Lurujararry
Heritage
Trail
'Mt Jowlaenga'
Boab Prison Tree
Mowanjum
Mowanjum
40
126
20
Quondong Pt
34
36
43
Cape Boiliau
'Yeeda'
Curtin
Airport
Blina
Oilfield
Mt Percy
'Kilto'
Deep Ck
178
Willare Bridge
Roadhouse
'Blina'
'Plains'
'Waterbank'
Roebuck
Roadhouse
GREAT
1
Bedunburra
41
Minnie Bridge
Pandanas Park
'Debesa'
'Yakka Munga'
54
'Paradise O/S'
Broome
Gantheaume Point
Roebuck
Plains'
55
Willare Bridge
NORTHERN
213
Jimbalakudunj
'Ellendale
Entrance Pt
Roebuck Bay
24
19
'Udialla'
Camballin
22
Bush Pt
Thangoo
'Mt Anderson'
LOOMA
'Livaringa'
'Calwynyardah
Eco Beach Resort
Frome Rocks
Ck 'Luluigui'
25
'Myroodah'
Cape Villaret
71
'Dampier
Downs O/C'
32
Cape Latouche Treville
Port Smith
'Barn Hill'
HWY
Near Hill
'Dampier
Downs'
47
'Nerrima'
Noonkanbah
Port Smith Caravan Park
False Cape Bossut
63
'Kalyeeda'
Lagrange Bay
'Shamrock'
Barbrongan Tower
Yungngura
Cape Bossut
(Lagrange)
Bidyadanga
Frazier
Downs
Mt Collins
Mt Jarlemai
Mt Tuckfield
Admiral Bay
'Frazier Downs'
'Mowla Bluff'
'Ardjorie'
'Millajiddee
Geoffrey Bay
Cape Jaubert
Desault Bay
Cape Missiessy
1
323
Mowla Bluff
EDGAR
RANGES
'Nita Downs'
(ruins)
16
'Anna
Plains'

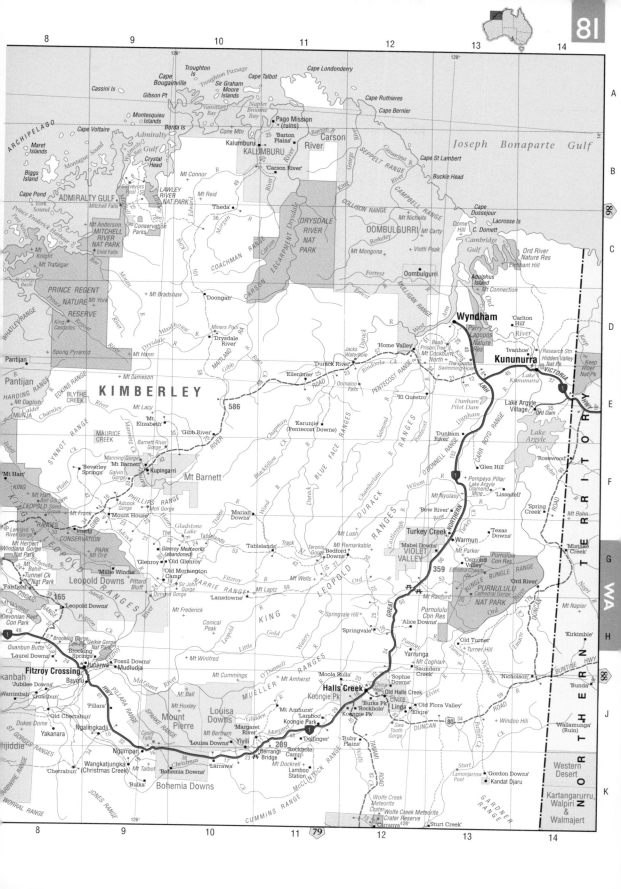

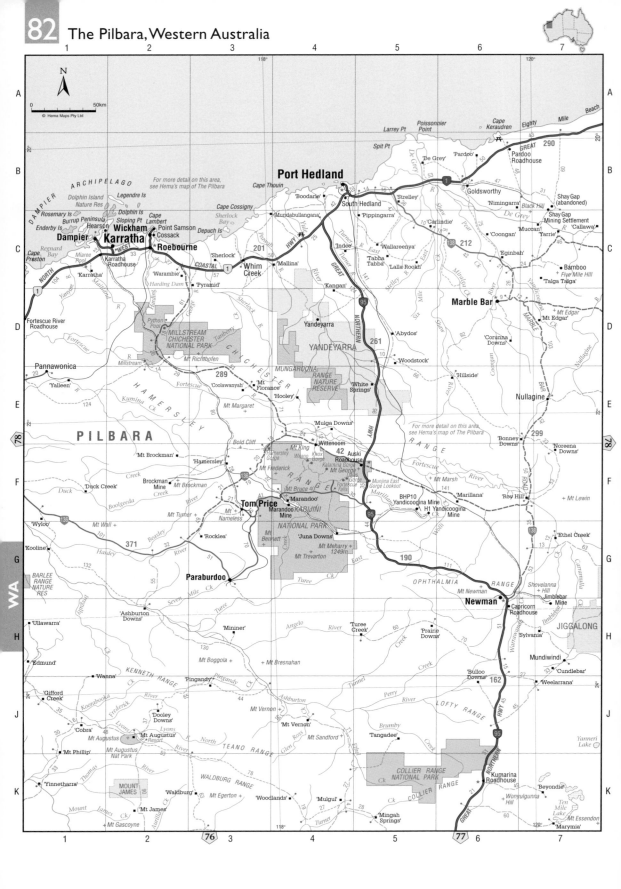

**N**

0          50km
© Hema Maps Pty Ltd

**Port Hedland**

**Karratha**
**Dampier**
**Wickham**
**Roebourne**

**PILBARA**

**Marble Bar**

**Nullagine**

**Tom Price**

**Paraburdoo**

**Newman**

**JIGGALONG**

MILLSTREAM
CHICHESTER
NATIONAL PARK

KARIJINI
NATIONAL PARK

YANDEYARRA

COLLIER RANGE
NATIONAL PARK

MOUNT
JAMES

**WA**

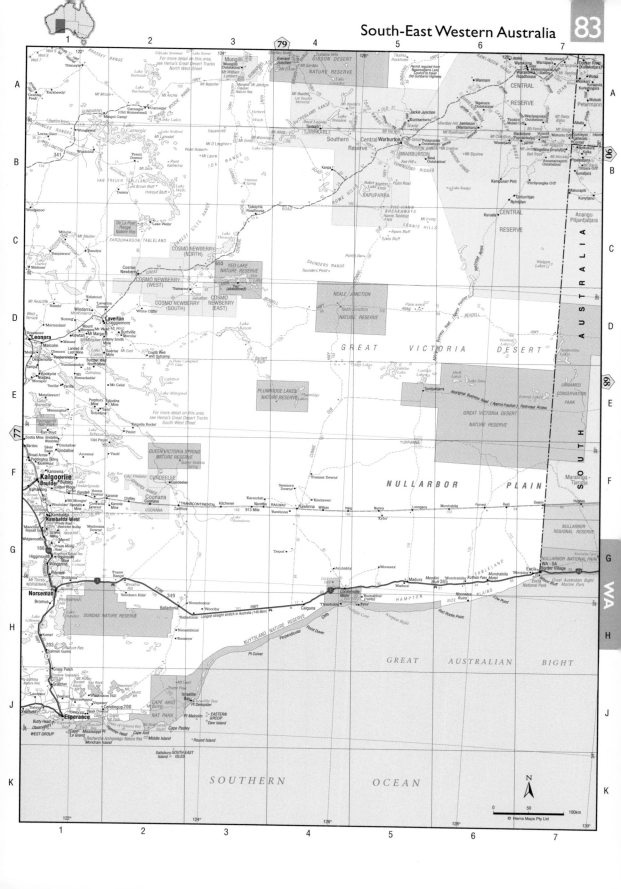

# Northern Territory

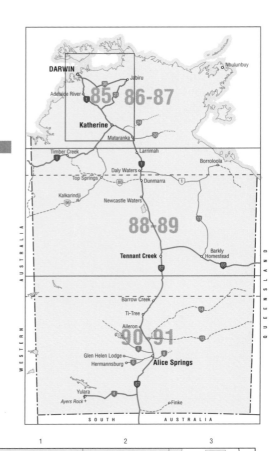

## Distance Chart

| | | | | | | | | | | | | | |
|---|---|---|---|---|---|---|---|---|---|---|---|---|---|
| **Alice Springs** | | | | | | | | | | | | | |
| **Ayers Rock** | 448 | | | | | | | | | | | | |
| **Barrow Creek** | 735 | 287 | | | | | | | | | | | |
| **Borroloola** | 924 | 1659 | 1211 | | | | | | | | | | |
| **Camooweal** | 755 | 699 | 1434 | 986 | | | | | | | | | |
| **Darwin** | 1439 | 986 | 1234 | 1969 | 1521 | | | | | | | | |
| **Jabiru** | 254 | 1415 | 962 | 1210 | 1945 | 1497 | | | | | | | |
| **Katherine** | 300 | 324 | 1115 | 662 | 910 | 1645 | 1197 | | | | | | |
| **Kulgera** | 1472 | 1772 | 1796 | 1261 | 1486 | 562 | 321 | 275 | | | | | |
| **Kununurra** | 1809 | 507 | 807 | 831 | 1452 | 1071 | 1247 | 1982 | 1534 | | | | |
| **Mataranka** | 612 | 1367 | 105 | 405 | 429 | 1010 | 557 | 805 | 1540 | 1092 | | | |
| **Nhulunbuy** | 708 | 1212 | 2074 | 705 | 1005 | 1029 | 1718 | 1265 | 1513 | 2247 | 1799 | | |
| **Tennant Creek** | 1290 | 582 | 1024 | 785 | 687 | 987 | 1011 | 476 | 701 | 223 | 958 | 510 | |

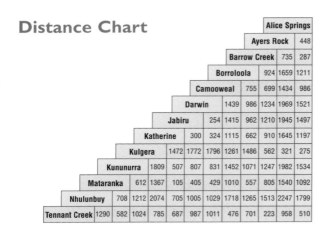

Darwin CBD

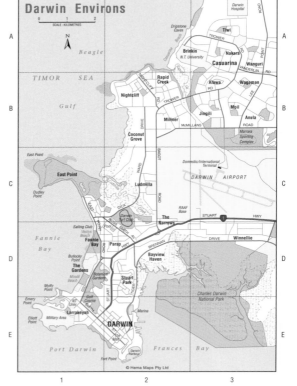

Darwin Environs

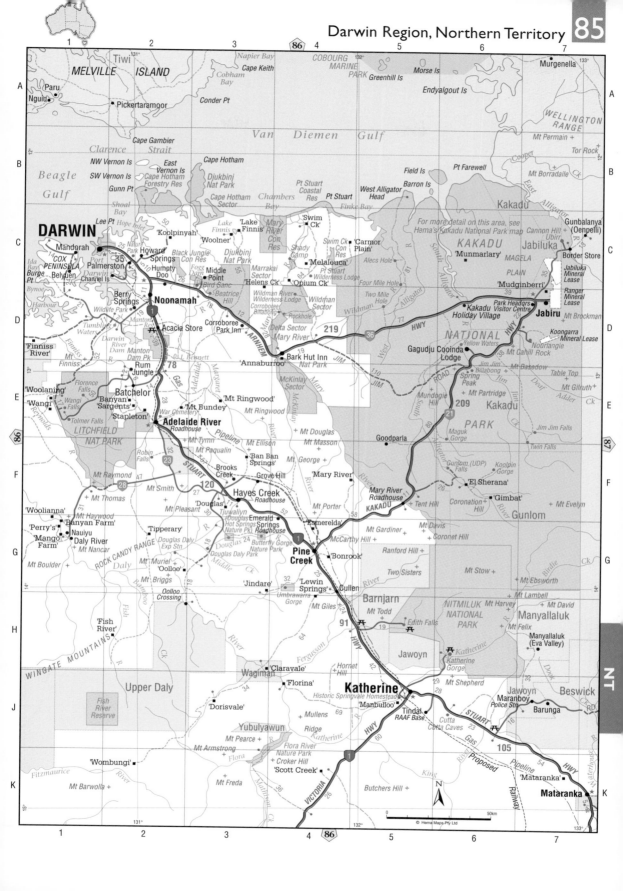

## Map labels

**DARWIN**

MELVILLE ISLAND

Tiwi

Paru
Nguiu
Pickertaramoor
Conder Pt
Napier Bay
Cape Keith
Cobham Bay

COBOURG MARINE PARK
Greenhill Is
Morse Is
Endyalgout Is
Murgenella

WELLINGTON RANGE
Mt Permain +
Tor Rock

Van Diemen Gulf

Clarence Strait
NW Vernon Is
SW Vernon Is
East Vernon Is
Cape Hotham
Cape Gambier
Field Is
Pt Farewell
Mt Borradaile
Cooper

Beagle Gulf
Gunn Pt
Cape Hotham Forestry Res
Djukbinj Nat Park
Cape Hotham Sector
Chambers Bay
Pt Stuart Coastal Res
Pt Stuart
Barron Is
West Alligator Head
Finke Bay

Shoal Bay
Lee Pt
Hope Inlet
'Lake Finniss'
Lake Finniss
Mary River Con Res
'Swim Ck'
Swim Ck Con Res
'Carmor Plain'
Kakadu

KAKADU
MAGELA PLAIN
Gunbalanya (Oenpelli)
Cannon Hill +
Ubirr
Border Store
Jabiluka
Jabiluka Mineral Lease

Ida Bay
Burge Pt
Bynoe
Harbour
Mandorah
COX PENINSULA
Belyuen
Channel Is
Palmerston
Howard Springs
Koolpinyah
'Woolner'
Black Jungle Con Res
Djukbinj Nat Park
Shady Camp
'Melaleuca'
Pt Stuart Wilderness Lodge
'Opium Ck'
Alecs Hole
'Munmarlany'
'Mudginberri'
Ranger Mineral Lease

Berry Springs
Humpty Doo
Marrakai Sector
'Helens Ck'
Beatrice Hill
Bird Sanc
Wildman River Wilderness Lodge
Corroboree Billabong
Wildman Sector
Rockhole
Four Mile Hole
Two Mile Hole
Kakadu Holiday Village
Park Headqrs Visitor Centre
Jabiru
Mt Brockman

Noonamah
Acacia Store
Corroboree Park Inn
Delta Sector Mary River
**219**
Gagudju Cooinda Lodge
Yellow Waters
Koongarra Mineral Lease
Nourlangie
Mt Cahill Rock

Tumbling Waters
Finniss River
Mt Finniss
Manton Res
Darwin River Dam
Manton Dam Pk
J.J.Bennett
'Annaburroo'
Bark Hut Inn Nat Park
McKinlay Sector
NATIONAL
Jim Jim
Mt Basedow
Table Top
Mt Gilruth
Deaf Adder Ck

'Woolaning'
'Wangi'
Florence Falls
Wangi Falls
Batchelor
Rum Jungle
'Banyan Sargents'
'Stapleton'
**78**
Gas
Mt Ringwood'
McKinlay Sector
Spring Peak
Mundogie Hill
Mt Partridge
**209**
Maguk Gorge
Kakadu
Jim Jim Falls
Twin Falls

LITCHFIELD NAT PARK
Tolmer Falls
'Mt Bundey'
War Cemetery
Adelaide River Roadhouse
'Mt Ringwood'
Mt Ringwood
Mt Ellison
Mt Masson
Mt Douglas
Goodparla
PARK
Gunlom (UDP) Falls
Koolpin Gorge
Jim Jim Falls

Mt Raymond
Robin Falls
**23**
'Mt Tymn
'Mt Paqualin
Brooks Creek
'Ban Ban Springs'
Grove Hill
Mt George
'Mary River'
'El Sherana'
'Gimbat'
Mt Evelyn

**28**
Mt Smith
STUART
**120**
Hayes Creek Roadhouse
Mt Porter
Mary River Roadhouse
KAKADU
Tent Hill
Coronation Hill
Mt Davis
Coronet Hill
Gunlom

Mt Thomas
'Douglas'
Tjuwaliyn
Douglas Hot Springs Nature Park
Emerald Springs Roadhouse
'Esmerelda'
McCarthy Hill
Mt Gardiner
'Woolianna'
'Perry's'
'Banyan Farm'
Mt Haywood
Nauiyu
Daly River
Mt Nancar
Mt Pleasant
'Mango Farm'
Tipperary
Douglas Daly Exp Stn
Butterfly Gorge Nature Park
Douglas Daly Park
Pine Creek
'Bonrook'
Ranford Hill
Two Sisters
Mt Stow +
Mt Ebsworth

Mt Boulder
ROCK CANDY RANGE
Mt Muriel
'Ooloo'
Mt Briggs
'Jindare'
'Lewin Springs'
Cullen
Barnjarn
NITMILUK NATIONAL PARK
Mt Harvey
Mt David
Manyallaluk
Ooloo Crossing
Umbrawarra Gorge
Mt Giles
Mt Todd
Edith Falls
Mt Lambell
Mt Felix
Manyallaluk (Eva Valley)

'Fish River'
Mt Harvey
**91**
Jawoyn
Katherine Gorge
Mt Shepherd

WINGATE MOUNTAINS
Upper Daly
Wagiman
Claravale'
'Florina'
Historic Springvale Homestead
Katherine
Jawoyn
Maranboy Police Stn
Barunga
Beswick

Fish River Reserve
'Dorisvale'
Mullens Ridge
'Manbulloo'
Tindal RAAF Base
Cutta Cutta Caves
STUART
Gas
**105**

'Wombungi'
Yubulyawun
Mt Pearce
Mt Armstrong
Flora River Nature Park
Croker Hill
'Scott Creek'
'Matarnka'
Proposed Pipeline

Fitzmaurice
Mt Barwolla
Mt Freda
VICTORIA HWY
Butchers Hill
King River
Railway
**Mataranka**

For more detail on this area, see Hema's Kakadu National Park map

© Hema Maps Pty Ltd

50km

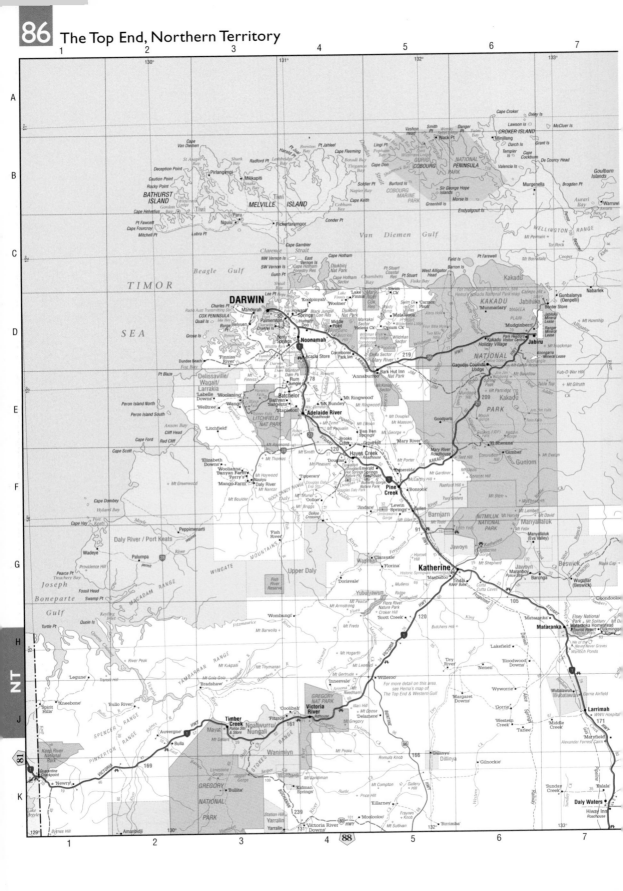

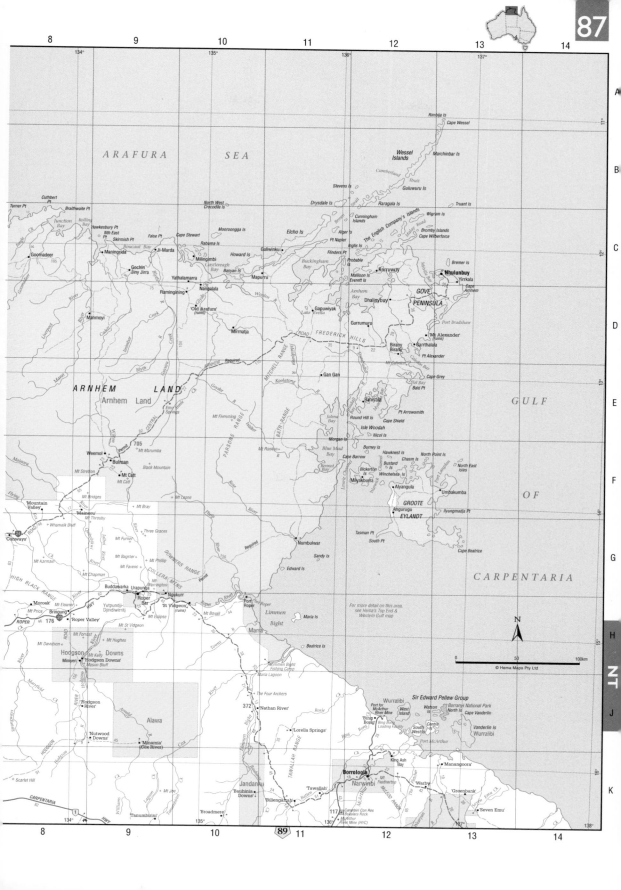

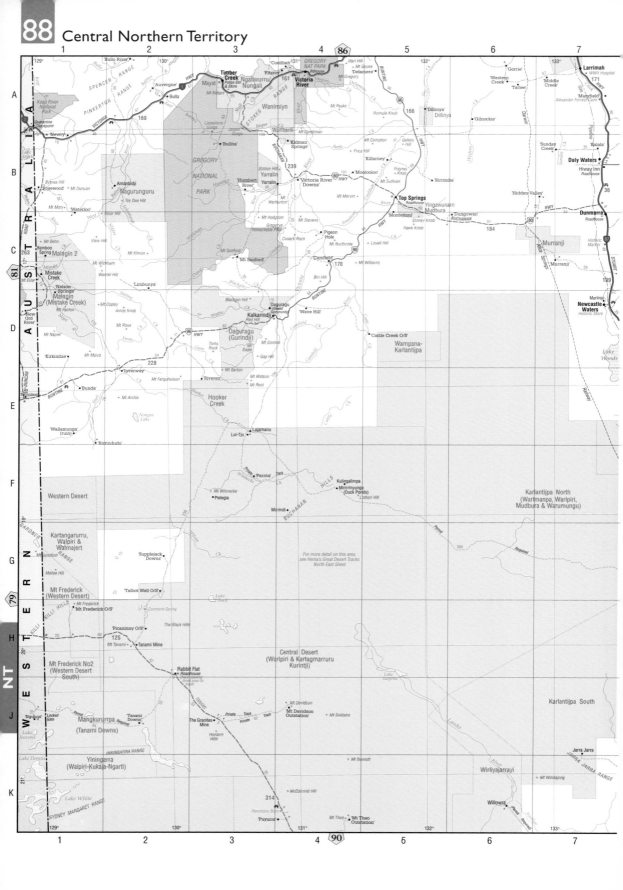

Central Desert
(Warlpiri & Kartagmarruru
Kurintji)

Karlantijpa North
(Warimanpa, Warlpiri,
Mudbura & Warumungu)

Karlantijpa South

Western Desert

Kartangarurru,
Walpiri &
Walmajert

Mt Frederick
(Western Desert)

Mt Frederick No2
(Western Desert
South)

Mangkururrpa
(Tanami Downs)

Yiningarra
(Walpiri-Kukaja-Ngarti)

Wirliyajarrayi

Nagurunguru

Malngin 2

Malngin
(Mistake Creek)

GREGORY
NATIONAL
PARK

Wampana-
Karlantijpa

Murranji

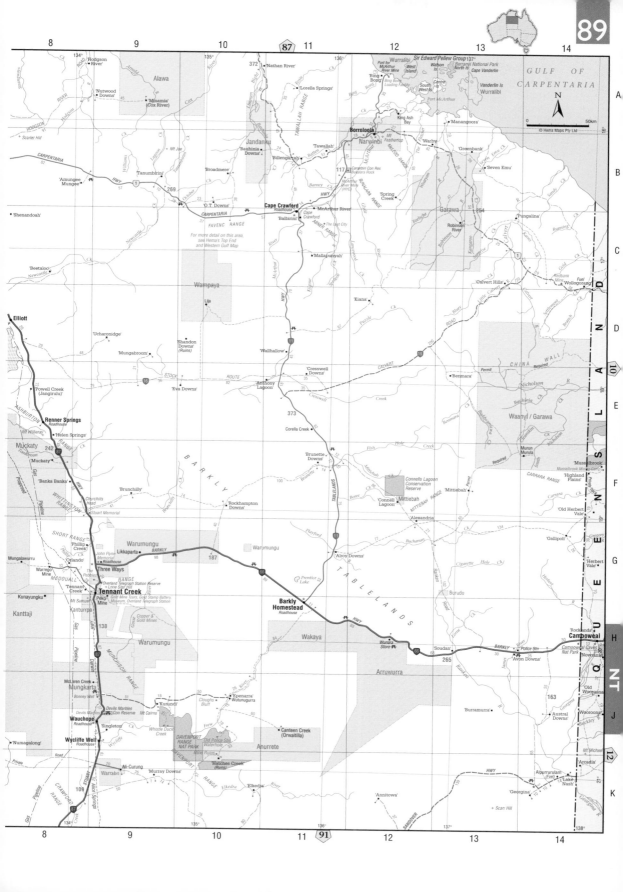

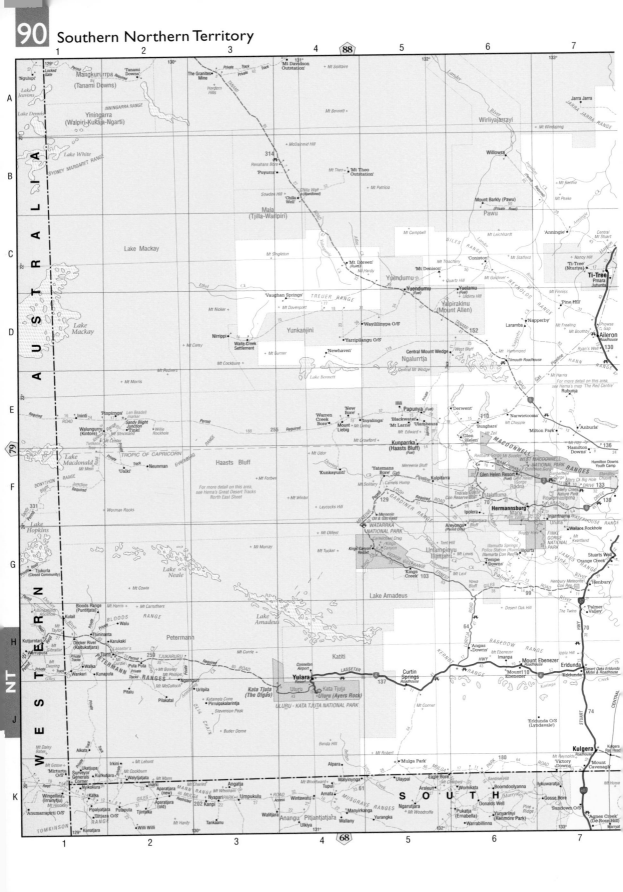

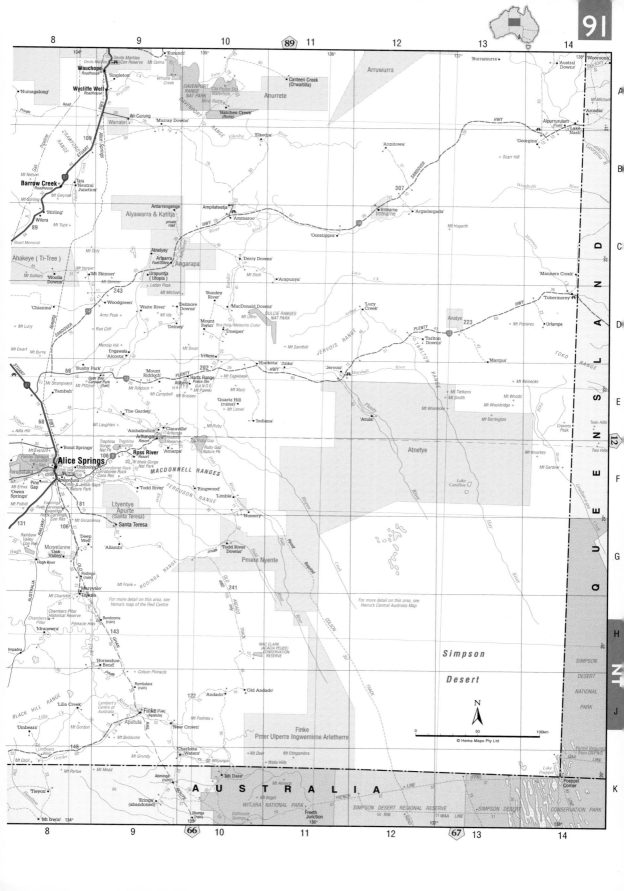

92 913 Mile – Beachmere

# A


913 Mile WA 77 J14 83 F3
A1 Mine Settlement VIC 42 H6 44 A7 46 C1
Abbeyard VIC 43 F8
Abbot Bay QLD 8 B6
Abbotsbury NSW 21 E9
Abbotsford NSW 19 E4
Abbotsham TAS 54 E6
Abercorn QLD 7 B9
Abercrombie NSW 22 H5
Abercrombie River Nat Park NSW 22 J6 31 A10
Aberdeen NSW 23 C8
Aberfeldy VIC 42 J7 44 B7 46 D1
Aberfoyle Park SA 60 J2 61 C6
Abergowie QLD 11 F13
Abminga SA 66 A4 91 K9
Acacia Ridge QLD 3 H4 5 E9
Acacia Store NT 85 D2 86 D4
Acheron VIC 42 G4
Acland QLD 7 F10
Acraman Creek Con Park SA 64 D3
Actaeon Island TAS 53 K9
Acton ACT 32 A1
Adamsfield TAS 52 F7
Adavale QLD 13 K11 15 C11
Addington VIC 39 D10
Adelaide SA 59 G4 60 G2 61 A6 62 F7 65 J10
Adelaide CBD SA 58
Adelaide River NT 85 E2 86 E4
Adelong NSW 29 H14 30 D7
Adjungbilly NSW 30 D7
Adminaby NSW 31 F8
Advancetown QLD 5 C13
Adventure Bay TAS 53 J10
Afterlee NSW 25 B12
Agery SA 62 H5 65 G8
Agnes Banks NSW 20 G7
Agnes Waters QLD 9 J12
Agnew WA 77 E10
Agnew Mine WA 77 D10
Aileron NT 90 D7
Ailsa VIC 40 K6
Aireys Inlet VIC 36 K1 39 J11
Airlie VIC 45 D11 46 E4
Airlie Beach QLD 9 B8
Akuna Bay NSW 19 A6
Alawa NT 84 B3
Alawoona SA 62 B6 65 J13
Albacutya VIC 28 K3 40 H4
Albany WA 74 K6
Albany Creek QLD 3 B2 4 F7
Albany Island QLD 16 B2
Albatross Bay QLD 16 F1
Alberrie Creek SA 67 H8
Albert NSW 22 C1 27 K13 29 A13
Albert Park VIC 36 D7
Alberton QLD 5 C10
Alberton SA 59 E2 60 F1
Alberton TAS 55 E12
Alberton VIC 45 G9 46 H2
Albion QLD 3 D4
Albion VIC 36 C6 39 F13 42 K1 44 B1
Albury NSW 29 K12 30 F4 43 B9
Alcomie TAS 54 C3
Alderley QLD 3 D3
Aldersyde WA 72 A5
Aldgate SA 59 J7 60 H4 61 B7
Aldinga SA 61 E5 62 F7 65 K10
Aldinga Bay SA 61 F4
Aldinga Beach SA 61 E4 62 F7 65 K9
Aldinga Scrub Con Park SA 61 E4
Alectown NSW 22 E2
Alexander Heights WA 71 C4
Alexander Morrison Nat Park WA 76 H4
Alexandra VIC 30 K1 42 G4
Alexandra Bridge WA 73 J13
Alexandra Headland QLD 4 E1 7 E13
Alexandra Hills QLD 5 D8
Alford SA 62 G4 65 G9
Alfords Point NSW 19 H3
Alfred Cove WA 71 H3
Alfred Nat Park VIC 47 C12
Alfred Town NSW 29 H13 30 D5
Algebuckina Bridge SA 66 E6
Alger Island NT 87 C11
Algester QLD 3 J4
Alice NSW 7 K12 25 C12
Alice QLD 8 H3 13 F13
Alice Springs NT 91 F8
Ali-Curung NT 89 K9 91 A9
Alkata NT 68 A1 79 K14 83 A7 90 J1
Allambie NSW 19 D6
Allans Flat VIC 43 C9
Allansford VIC 38 H7
Allanson WA 73 F9
Alleena NSW 29 E13 30 A4
Allen Island QLD 10 D3
Allenby Gardens SA 59 F3
Allendale East SA 38 G1 63 B14
Allestree VIC 38 H4
Allies Creek QLD 7 D9
Allora QLD 7 H11
Allworth NSW 23 D11
Alma SA 62 F5 65 H10
Almaden QLD 11 E11
Almonds VIC 42 C6
Almoola QLD 8 C6
Almurta VIC 37 K12 44 F4
Alonnah TAS 53 J10
Aloomba QLD 11 D13
Alpara NT 68 A4 90 K4
Alpha QLD 8 H4 13 F14
Alpine Nat Park VIC 30 K4 43 F10 46 B3
Alpurrurulam NT 12 A1 89 K14 91 A14
Alstonville NSW 7 K13 25 C14
Althorpe Islands SA 63 J8
Alton QLD 6 H6
Alton Nat Park QLD 6 H6
Altona VIC 35 E1 36 D6 39 F13 42 K1 44 C1
Altona Bay VIC 36 D6
Altona Meadows VIC 35 E1
Alum Cliffs State Res TAS 54 F7
Alva Beach QLD 8 A6
Alvie VIC 39 H9
Alyangula NT 87 F12
Amamoor QLD 7 D12
Amanbidji NT 86 K2 88 B2
Amata SA 68 A4 90 K4
Ambarvale NSW 21 E11
Amberley QLD 5 H9
Ambleside SA 60 H4
Amboola QLD 6 D3
Amboyne VIC 43 G14 47 A9
Ambrose QLD 9 H11
Amby QLD 6 D4
Amelup WA 74 H7
Amen Corner SA 63 J8 65 K8
American River SA 63 H9
Amherst VIC 39 C10
Amity QLD 4 B7 7 G13
Amoonguna NT 91 F8
Amosfield NSW 25 B10
Amphitheatre VIC 39 C9
Ampilatwatja NT 91 C10
Anakie QLD 8 H6
Anakie VIC 36 E2 39 F12
Anakie East VIC 36 E2
Anakie Junction VIC 36 D2 39 F12
Ancona VIC 42 F5
Andamooka SA 67 K8
Anderson VIC 44 G3
Anderson Bay TAS 55 D11
Anderson Inlet VIC 44 G5
Anderson Island TAS 55 C9
Ando NSW 31 H9
Andover TAS 53 D11
Andrews QLD 5 B14
Andrews SA 62 F4 65 F10
Anembo NSW 31 F10
Angahook Lorne State Park VIC 39 J11
Angaston SA 60 A7 62 E6 65 H10
Angatja SA 68 A2 90 K3
Angellala QLD 6 D1 13 K14
Angip VIC 40 J5
Angle Vale SA 60 C3
Anglers Rest VIC 30 J5 43 F11 46 A5
Anglesea VIC 36 K2 39 H11
Angorichina Village SA 65 B10
Angourie NSW 25 E13
Angurugu NT 87 F12
Anna Bay NSW 23 E11
Annerley QLD 3 F4 5 E8
Anne's Corner SA 68 E5
Annuello VIC 28 G5 40 D7
Anser Group VIC 44 K7 46 K1
Ansons Bay TAS 55 D14
Antarrengenge NT 91 C9
Antill Plains QLD 8 A5 11 H14
Antill Ponds TAS 53 C11 55 K11
Antwerp VIC 40 K5
Anula NT 84 B3
Anxious Bay SA 64 F4
Aparatjara (new) SA 68 A2 90 K2
Aparatjara (old) SA 68 A2 90 K2
Apollo Bay VIC 39 K10
Appila SA 62 F2 65 E10
Appin NSW 21 E12 23 J8 31 A13
Appin VIC 41 H10
Appin South VIC 41 H10
Apple Tree Flat NSW 22 D6
Applecross WA 71 H3
Apslawn TAS 53 B13 55 J13
Apsley TAS 53 D10
Apsley VIC 38 C2
Aquila Island QLD 9 E9
Arabella QLD 13 K14 15 D14
Arakoon NSW 25 J12
Araleun SA 68 A4 90 K5
Araluen NSW 31 E11
Aramac QLD 8 G2 13 E12
Aramara QLD 7 C11
Arana Hills QLD 3 C2
Ararat VIC 39 D8
Aratula QLD 5 J12 7 H12
Arawata VIC 37 J14
Arcadia NSW 19 A3 20 D6
Arcadia VIC 42 D3
Archdale VIC 39 B9
Archer River Roadhouse QLD 16 G3
Archerfield QLD 3 G3 5 E9
Archies Creek VIC 44 G4
Ardeer VIC 35 D1
Ardglen NSW 23 B8
Ardlethan NSW 29 F12 30 A4
Ardno VIC 38 F2
Ardrossan SA 62 G5 65 H9
Areyonga NT 90 G6
Argents Hill NSW 25 H12
Argyle WA 73 G10 74 G3
Ariah Park NSW 29 F13 30 A5
Aringa VIC 38 H5
Arkaroola SA 67 J11
Arkona VIC 40 K5
Arlparra NT 91 C9
Arltunga NT 91 F9
Arltunga Historic Res NT 91 F9
Armadale VIC 35 E4
Armadale WA 72 F4 74 D3
Armatree NSW 22 A3 24 K1
Armidale NSW 25 G9
Armstrong VIC 38 D7
Armuna QLD 8 B6
Armytage VIC 39 H10
Arncliffe NSW 19 G4
Arno Bay SA 62 K4 64 G7
Arnold VIC 39 A10
Arrino WA 76 G4
Artarmon NSW 21 C8
Arthur East WA 73 B10
Arthur Pieman Con Area TAS 54 F2
Arthur Point QLD 9 F9
Arthur River TAS 54 D1
Arthur River WA 73 B9 74 F5
Arthurs Creek VIC 37 A9
Arthurs Lake TAS 53 B9 55 J9
Arthurs Seat State Park VIC 36 J7 39 H14 44 F1
Arthurton SA 62 H5 65 H8
Arthurville NSW 22 D3
Arundel QLD 5 B12
Asbestos Range Nat Park TAS 55 D8 56 C1
Ascot QLD 3 D4 4 E7
Ascot VIC 39 D10
Ascot WA 71 F5
Ashbourne SA 63 F8 65 K10
Ashbury NSW 21 C9
Ashfield NSW 21 C9
Ashfield WA 71 E5
Ashford NSW 25 D8
Ashgrove QLD 3 D3
Ashley NSW 24 D5
Ashmore QLD 5 B12
Ashton SA 59 G7 60 G4 61 A7
Ashville SA 63 D8 65 K11
Aspen Island ACT 32 C4
Aspendale VIC 37 F8
Aspley QLD 3 B4 4 E7
Aspley VIC 63 A12
Asquith NSW 20 D7
Astrelba Downs Nat Park QLD 12 G5
Athelstone SA 59 E7 60 F3
Atherton QLD 11 D12
Athlone VIC 37 H13 44 E6
Athol Park SA 59 E3
Atitjere NT 91 E10
Atnelyey NT 91 C9
Attadale WA 71 H2
Attunga NSW 24 H7
Aubigny QLD 7 G10
Aubrey VIC 40 K5
Auburn NSW 19 F3 21 D9
Auburn SA 62 F5 65 G10
Auburn River Nat Park QLD 7 C9
Audley NSW 21 C10
Augathella QLD 6 C1 13 J14 15 C14
Augusta WA 73 J14 74 J2
Augustus Island WA 80 D7
Auldana SA 59 G6
Aurukun Community QLD 16 G1
Auski Roadhouse WA 78 F5 82 F5
Austinmer NSW 21 C13
Austinville QLD 5 C14
Austral NSW 21 F10
Australia Plains SA 62 E5 65 G11
Australind WA 73 G9
Avalon NSW 20 B6
Avalon Beach VIC 36 F3
Avenel VIC 42 F3
Avenue SA 63 C12
Avisford Nat Res NSW 22 D5
Avoca TAS 53 A12 55 H12
Avoca VIC 39 C9
Avoca Beach NSW 20 B4
Avon SA 62 F5 65 H9
Avon Plains VIC 38 A7
Avon Reservoir NSW 21 E14
Avon Valley Nat Park WA 72 E2 74 C3 76 K5
Avon Wilderness Park VIC 43 J8 45 A9 46 C3
Avondale QLD 7 A11 9 K12
Avonsleigh VIC 37 E11
Axedale VIC 39 B12
Ayr QLD 8 A6
Ayrford VIC 38 J7
Ayton QLD 11 B12


# B


Baan Baa NSW 24 G5
Babel Island TAS 55 B10
Babinda QLD 11 E13
Bacchus Marsh VIC 36 B3 39 E12
Backstairs Passage SA 61 K1 63 G8
Backwater NSW 25 F10
Baddaginnie VIC 42 D5
Baden TAS 53 D11
Badgebup WA 74 G6
Badger Island TAS 55 C8
Badgerys Creek NSW 21 F9
Badgingarra WA 76 H4
Badgingarra Nat Park WA 76 H4
Badja NSW 31 F10
Badu Island QLD 16 A1
Baerami NSW 23 D8
Baerami Creek NSW 22 D7
Bagdad TAS 53 E10
Bagot Well SA 62 E5 65 H10
Bailieston VIC 39 A14 42 E2
Bailup WA 72 E2
Baird Bay SA 64 E3
Bairnsdale VIC 43 K11 45 C13 46 D6
Bajool QLD 9 H10
Bakara SA 62 C6 65 J12
Baker VIC 40 J3
Baker Gully SA 60 J2 61 C6
Bakers Creek QLD 9 D8
Bakers Hill WA 72 D2
Bakers Swamp NSW 22 E4
Baking Board QLD 7 E8
Baladjie Lake Nat Res WA 75 A8 77 J8
Balaklava SA 62 F5 65 G9
Balbarrup WA 73 E13
Balcatta WA 71 D3 72 G3
Balcombe Bay VIC 36 H7
Bald Hills QLD 3 A3
Bald Island WA 74 K7
Bald Knob NSW 25 E10
Bald Knob QLD 4 F2
Bald Rock VIC 28 K7 41 J11
Bald Rock Nat Park NSW 7 K11 25 C10
Baldry NSW 22 E3
Balfe's Creek QLD 8 B3 11 J13
Balfour TAS 54 E2
Balga WA 71 D3
Balgo WA 79 D13
Balgowan SA 62 H5 65 H8
Balgowlah NSW 19 D6 21 B8
Balgownie NSW 21 D14
Balhannah SA 60 G5 62 E7 65 J10
Balingup WA 73 F11 74 G3
Balkuling WA 72 B3
Balladonia WA 83 H2
Balladoran NSW 22 B3
Ballajura WA 71 C5
Ballalaba NSW 31 E10
Ballan VIC 36 B2 39 E11
Ballan North VIC 36 A2
Ballandean QLD 25 B10
Ballangeich VIC 38 H7
Ballarat VIC 39 E10
Ballark VIC 36 C1
Ballbank NSW 28 J7 41 F11
Balldale NSW 29 K11 30 F3 42 A7
Ballendella VIC 41 K13 42 C1
Balliang VIC 36 D3 39 F12
Balliang East VIC 36 D3 39 F12
Ballidu WA 76 H5
Ballimore NSW 22 C4
Ballina NSW 7 K14 25 C14
Bally Bally WA 72 B4
Balmain NSW 19 F5 21 C8
Balmattum VIC 42 E4
Balmoral NSW 19 E6 21 B8 21 G14
Balmoral QLD 3 E5
Balmoral VIC 38 D4
Balnarring VIC 37 J8 39 H14 44 F2
Balnarring Beach VIC 37 J8
Balook VIC 45 F8 46 G2
Balranald NSW 28 G6 41 C9
Balwyn VIC 35 D5 37 D8
Bamaga QLD 16 B2
Bamawm VIC 41 K13 42 C1
Bamawm Extension VIC 41 J13 42 B1
Bambaroo QLD 11 G13
Bambill VIC 28 G2 40 B3
Bamboo WA 78 E7 82 C7
Bamboo Spring NT 88 C1
Bambra VIC 39 H11
Bambrough Island QLD 9 E10
Ban Ban Springs QLD 7 C11
Banana QLD 9 J9
Bancroft QLD 7 A9 9 K11
Bandiana VIC 43 B9
Bandon NSW 22 G2
Bandon Grove NSW 23 C10
Banealla SA 63 B9
Bangalow NSW 7 K13 25 B14
Bangerang VIC 40 J6
Bangham SA 38 A1
Bangham Con Park SA 38 A1 63 A11
Bangholme VIC 35 H6
Bangor NSW 21 C10 55 E10
Bangor TAS 56 D5
Baniyala NT 87 E12
Banks Strait TAS 55 B13
Banksia Beach QLD 4 D4
Banksia Park SA 59 D1
Banksmeadow NSW 19 H6
Bankstown NSW 19 G2 21 D9
Bannaby NSW 22 K6 31 B11
Bannerton VIC 28 G5 40 C7
Bannister NSW 22 K5 31 B10
Bannister WA 72 D6 74 E4
Bannockburn VIC 36 F1 39 G11
Banora Point NSW 5 A14
Banyan VIC 40 G7
Banyan Island NT 87 C10
Banyena VIC 38 A7
Banyenong VIC 41 K8
Banyo QLD 3 C5
Barabon QLD 13 A9
Baradine NSW 24 H3
Barakula QLD 7 D8
Baralaba QLD 9 J9
Baranduda VIC 43 B9
Barcaldine QLD 8 H2 13 F12
Bardoc WA 77 H11 83 F1
Bardoc Mine WA 77 G10
Bardon QLD 3 E3
Barduthulla QLD 13 K14 15 C14
Barellan NSW 29 F11 30 A3
Barfold VIC 39 C12
Bargara QLD 7 A12 9 K13
Bargo NSW 21 F13 22 J7 31 A12
Bargo State Rec Park NSW 21 G14
Barham NSW 28 J7 41 G11
Baring VIC 40 F5
Baringhup VIC 39 C11
Barjarg VIC 30 J2 42 F5
Bark Hut Inn NT 85 D4 86 E5
Barkly Homestead NT 89 H11
Barkstead VIC 39 E11
Barlee WA 73 G13
Barlee Range Nat Res WA 78 G3 82 G1
Barmah VIC 41 H14 42 B2
Barmah State Park VIC 41 H14 42 A2
Barmedman NSW 29 F13 30 A5
Barmera SA 62 B5 65 H13
Barmundu QLD 9 J11
Barnawartha VIC 43 B8
Barnes NSW 41 J13 42 B1
Barnes Bay TAS 50 H6 53 H10
Barongarook VIC 39 J10
Barooga NSW 29 K10 30 F1 42 A4
Baroota SA 62 G2 65 E9
Barossa Reservoir SA 60 C5
Barpinba VIC 39 G10
Barraba NSW 24 G7
Barrabool VIC 36 G2 39 G11
Barradale WA 78 G2
Barramunga VIC 39 J10
Barranyi Nat Park NT 87 J13 89 A13
Barraport VIC 41 H10
Barratta QLD 8 A5
Barrington NSW 23 B11
Barrington TAS 54 F7
Barrington Tops Nat Park NSW 23 C10
Barringun NSW 15 K13 27 B10
Barrogan NSW 22 F3
Barron Gorge Nat Park QLD 11 D12
Barron Island NT 85 B5 86 C6
Barrow Creek NT 91 B8
Barrow Island WA 78 E2
Barrow Island Nat Res WA 78 E3
Barry NSW 22 G5 23 A10 25 K8
Barrys Beach VIC 44 H7 46 H1
Barrys Reef VIC 39 E12
Barton ACT 32 D3
Barton SA 66 K1 68 H6
Barton VIC 38 D7
Barton Nat Res NSW 22 F4
Barunga NT 85 J7 86 G7
Barunga Gap SA 62 G4 65 G9
Barwell Con Park SA 64 F5
Barwon Downs VIC 39 J10
Barwon Heads VIC 36 H4 39 H12
Baryulgil NSW 25 D12
Bascombe Well Con Park SA 64 F5
Basket Range SA 60 G4
Bass VIC 37 K11 44 F3
Bass Hill NSW 21 D9
Bass Landing VIC 37 K11
Bass Strait 39 K12 44 K5 54 B3 56 A3
Bassendean WA 71 E6
Batchelor NT 85 E2 86 E4
Batchica VIC 40 J6
Bate Bay NSW 19 K5 21 B10
Bateau Bay NSW 20 B3
Batehaven NSW 31 F11
Batemans Bay NSW 31 E11
Batesford VIC 39 G12
Bathumi VIC 42 B6
Bathurst NSW 22 F5
Bathurst Bay QLD 16 H5
Bathurst Island NT 86 B2
Batlow NSW 29 J14 30 E7
Battery Point TAS 49 C2
Bauhinia QLD 9 K8
Baulkham Hills NSW 21 E8
Bauple QLD 7 C12
Baw Baw Nat Park VIC 42 K6 44 B7 46 D1
Bawley Point NSW 31 E12
Baxter VIC 37 G9
Bay of Fires Con Res TAS 55 E14
Bay of Islands Coastal Park VIC 38 J7
Bayles VIC 37 G12 44 E4
Bayley Island QLD 10 D3
Baynton VIC 39 C13 42 G1
Bayswater VIC 35 E7 37 D9
Bayswater WA 71 E5
Bayulu WA 79 B11 81 J9
Bayview NSW 19 B7 20 B6
Bayview Haven NT 84 D2
Beachamp VIC 41 G9
Beachmere QLD 4 E5

Beachport – Brahma Lodge 93


Beachport SA 63 C13
Beachport Con Park SA 63 C13
Beacon WA 76 H7
Beaconsfield NSW 19 G5
Beaconsfield TAS 55 E8 56 D2
Beaconsfield VIC 37 F10 44 D3
Beaconsfield Upper VIC 37 F11
Beagle Bay WA 79 A9 80 F4
Beagle Gulf NT 85 B1 86 C3
Bealiba VIC 39 B9
Bearbung NSW 22 A4 24 K2
Beardmore VIC 42 K7 45 C8 46 D2
Beargamil NSW 22 E2
Bearii VIC 42 A3
Bears Lagoon VIC 41 K11
Beatrice Island NT 87 H11
Beaudesert QLD 5 E12 7 H13
Beaufort VIC 39 D9
Beaufort WA 73 B10
Beaumaris TAS 55 F14
Beaumont SA 59 H5
Beaumont Nat Res WA 75 F14 83 J2
Beauty Point TAS 55 E9 56 D2
Beazleys Bridge VIC 39 A8
Bebeah NSW 20 D1
Beckenham WA 71 H6
Beckom NSW 29 F12 30 A4
Bedarra Island QLD 11 F13
Bedford WA 71 E4
Bedford Park SA 59 K3
Bedgerabong NSW 22 F1 29 D14
Bedourie QLD 12 G4
Bedunburra WA 80 H5
Beeac VIC 39 H10
Beech Forest VIC 39 J10
Beechboro WA 71 D5
Beechford TAS 55 D9 56 B3
Beechmont QLD 5 D14
Beechwood NSW 23 A13 25 K11
Beechworth VIC 30 G3 43 C8
Beechworth Historic Park VIC 30 G3 43 C8
Beecroft NSW 20 D7
Beedelup Nat Park WA 73 F14 74 J3
Beekeepers Nat Res WA 76 G3
Beela WA 73 F9
Beenak VIC 37 D12
Beenleigh QLD 5 D10 7 G13
Beerburrum QLD 4 F3 7 F13
Beerwah QLD 4 F2 7 E13
Bega NSW 31 H11
Beggan Beggan NSW 22 K2 30 B7
Beilpajah NSW 28 C6
Bejoording WA 72 D1
Belair SA 59 J4 60 H2 61 B6
Belair Nat Park SA 59 J5 60 H3 61 B7
Belalie North SA 62 E2 65 E10
Belaringar NSW 22 B1 27 J13
Belbora NSW 23 C12
Belconnen ACT 31 D9
Beldon WA 71 A1
Belgrave VIC 37 E10 42 K3 44 C3
Bell NSW 22 G7
Bell QLD 7 E10
Bell Bay TAS 55 D9 56 C3
Bellambi NSW 21 C13
Bellara QLD 4 D4
Bellarine VIC 36 G5 39 G13
Bellarine Peninsula VIC 36 G5 39 H13
Bellarwi NSW 29 F13 30 A5
Bellata NSW 24 E5
Bellbird NSW 23 E9
Bellbird Creek VIC 47 D10
Bellbird Park QLD 5 F9
Bellbrae VIC 36 J2 39 H12
Bellbridge VIC 43 B9
Bellbrook NSW 25 H11
Bellenden Ker QLD 11 D13
Bellerive TAS 50 C6 53 F11
Bellevue WA 71 E7
Bellevue Heights SA 59 K4 60 H2 61 B6
Bellingen NSW 25 G12
Bellinger River Nat Park NSW 25 G12
Bellingham TAS 55 D10 56 B5
Bellmere QLD 4 F4
Bellmount Forest NSW 31 C9
Belltrees NSW 23 B9
Belmont NSW 23 F10
Belmont QLD 3 F6
Belmont VIC 36 G2
Belmont WA 71 F5
Belmore NSW 19 G4 21 C9
Belmunging WA 72 B3
Beloka NSW 31 H8
Belowra NSW 31 G10
Belrose NSW 20 B7
Belsar Island VIC 40 C7
Beltana SA 65 A10 67 K10
Beltana Roadhouse SA 65 A10 67 K10
Belton SA 65 D10
Belyando Crossing QLD 8 E5 13 B14
Belyuen NT 85 C1 86 D3
Bemboka NSW 31 H10
Bemm River VIC 47 D10
Ben Boyd Nat Park NSW 31 K11 47 A14
Ben Bullen NSW 22 F6
Ben Halls Gap Nat Park NSW 23 A9
Ben Lomond NSW 25 F9
Ben Lomond Nat Park TAS 55 G12
Bena NSW 29 D13
Bena VIC 37 K13 44 F5
Benalla VIC 30 H2 42 D5
Benambra VIC 30 J6 43 F11
Benandarah NSW 31 E12
Benaraby QLD 9 J11
Benayoo VIC 38 C2
Bencubbin WA 74 A6 76 J7
Bendalong NSW 31 D12
Bendemeer NSW 25 H8
Bendick Murrel NSW 22 J3 31 A8
Bendidee Nat Park QLD 7 H8 24 A7
Bendigo VIC 39 B12
Bendoc VIC 31 K8 47 A10
Bendoc North VIC 47 A11
Bendolba NSW 23 D10
Beneree NSW 22 G4
Benetook VIC 28 F3 40 B4
Benger WA 73 G9
Bengerang NSW 6 K6 24 C4
Bengworden VIC 45 C12 46 E5
Beni NSW 22 C3
Benjeroop VIC 41 F10
Benjinup WA 73 E11
Benlidi QLD 8 K2 13 G11
Bennison Island VIC 44 H7 46 J1
Benowa QLD 5 B13
Bensville NSW 20 B4
Bentinck Island QLD 10 D3
Bentley NSW 25 B13
Bentley WA 71 H5
Bentleys Plain VIC 43 G12 46 B7
Benwerrin VIC 39 J11
Berajondo QLD 9 K12
Berala NSW 21 D9
Berambing NSW 20 K7 22 G7
Berdunburra WA 79 B9
Beremboke VIC 36 C2
Beresfield NSW 23 E10
Beresford SA 66 G7
Bergalia NSW 31 F11
Berkeley Vale NSW 20 B3
Berkshire Park NSW 20 F7
Bermagui NSW 31 H11
Bermagui South NSW 31 H11
Bernacchi TAS 53 A8 55 H8
Bernier and Dorre Island Nat Res WA 76 A1 78 J1
Bernier Island WA 76 A1 78 J1
Berowra NSW 19 A4 20 C6
Berowra Heights NSW 19 A5
Berowra Valley Bushland Park NSW 19 A4 20 D7
Berowra Waters NSW 20 D6
Berri SA 28 F1 62 B5 65 H13
Berridale NSW 31 G8
Berriedale TAS 50 B5
Berrigan NSW 29 J10 30 E2
Berrilee NSW 20 D6
Berrima NSW 22 K7 31 B12
Berringa VIC 39 F10
Berringama VIC 43 C11
Berriwillock VIC 28 J5 41 G8
Berrook VIC 28 H1 40 D1 62 A7 65 J13
Berry NSW 31 C13
Berry Springs NT 85 D2 86 D4
Berrybank VIC 39 G9
Berwick VIC 37 F10 44 D3
Bessiebelle VIC 38 H5
Bet Bet VIC 39 B10
Beta QLD 8 H4 13 F13
Bete Bolong VIC 43 K14 47 D8
Bethanga VIC 43 B9
Bethania QLD 3 K6
Bethany SA 60 B6
Bethungra NSW 22 K1 29 G14 30 C6
Betoota QLD 12 J5 14 C3 67 A14
Betsey Island TAS 51 G8 53 G11
Beulah TAS 54 F7
Beulah VIC 28 K4 40 H6
Beulah East VIC 40 H6
Beulah Park SA 59 G5
Beulah West VIC 40 H5
Bevendale NSW 22 K4 31 B9
Beverford VIC 28 H6 41 E9
Beveridge VIC 42 H2
Beveridge Station (site) VIC 43 F9
Beverley WA 72 C4 74 D4
Beverly Hills NSW 19 G4 21 C9
Bews SA 63 B8 65 K12
Bexhill NSW 25 B13
Bexley NSW 21 C9
Beyal VIC 40 J7
BHP10 Yandicoogina Mine WA 78 F6 82 F5
Biala NSW 22 K4 31 B9
Biamanga Nat Park NSW 31 H11
Bibbenluke NSW 31 J9
Biboohra QLD 11 D12
Bibra Lake WA 71 K3
Bicheno TAS 53 A14 55 H14
Bickerton Island NT 87 F12
Bicton WA 71 H2
Biddaddaba QLD 5 D12
Biddon NSW 22 A4 24 K2
Bidgeemia NSW 29 J11 30 E3
Bidyadanga (Lagrange) WA 79 C8 80 J2
Big Desert Wilderness Park VIC 28 J1 40 G2 63 A9 65 K14
Big Green Island TAS 55 C9
Big Heath Con Park SA 63 B12
Big Pats Creek VIC 37 C13
Bigga NSW 22 H4 31 A9
Biggara VIC 43 C13
Biggenden QLD 7 B11
Biggs Flat SA 60 H4
Biggs Island WA 81 B8
Bilambil NSW 5 B14 25 A14
Bilbaringa SA 60 C4
Bilgola NSW 20 B6
Billiatt Con Park SA 28 H1 62 B7 65 J13
Billiluna (Mindibungu) WA 79 D13
Billimari NSW 22 G3
Billinga QLD 5 A14
Billinooka Mine WA 78 G7
Billinudgell NSW 25 B14
Billys Creek NSW 25 F11
Biloela QLD 9 J10
Bilpin NSW 20 J6 23 G8
Bilyana QLD 11 F13
Bimbi NSW 22 H2 29 E14
Binalong NSW 22 K3 31 B8
Binalong Bay TAS 55 E14
Binaronca Nat Res WA 75 C13 83 G1
Binbee QLD 8 B6
Binda NSW 22 J5 31 A10
Bindango QLD 6 E4
Bindi VIC 43 G12 46 A7
Bindi Bindi WA 76 H5
Bindoon WA 72 F1 74 B3 76 K5
Bingara NSW 24 E7
Bingil Bay QLD 11 E13
Binginwarri VIC 45 G8 46 H2
Biniguy NSW 24 D6
Binjour QLD 7 B10
Binna Burra QLD 5 D14 7 H13 25 A13
Binnaway NSW 22 A5 24 K4
Binningup WA 73 G9 74 F2
Binnu WA 76 E3
Binnum SA 38 B1 63 A11
Binya NSW 29 F11 30 A3
Birany Birany NT 87 D12
Birchip VIC 28 K5 40 H7
Birchs Bay TAS 50 J4 53 H10
Bird Island TAS 54 B1
Birdsville QLD 12 K3 14 C1 67 A12
Birdwood NSW 23 A12 25 K11
Birdwood SA 60 E6 62 E6 65 J10
Birdwoodton VIC 28 F3 40 A4
Birkdale QLD 3 F7 5 D8
Birkenhead SA 59 D1
Birnam Range QLD 5 E12
Birralee QLD 8 C6
Birralee TAS 55 F8 56 G2
Birrego NSW 29 H12 30 C3
Birregurra VIC 39 H10
Birri Lodge QLD 10 C3
Birriwa NSW 22 C5
Birrong NSW 19 F2
Birru QLD 5 J9
Bishopsbourne TAS 55 G9 56 J4
Bittern VIC 37 J9
Black Forest SA 59 H3
Black Hill SA 62 D6 65 J11
Black Hill Con Park SA 59 E7 60 F3
Black Hills TAS 50 A2 53 F9
Black Jungle Con Res NT 85 C2 86 D4
Black Mountain NSW 25 G9
Black Mountain Nat Park QLD 11 B12 16 K7
Black Point NT 86 B5
Black Range State Park VIC 38 C5
Black River TAS 54 C3
Black Rock SA 62 E2 65 E10
Black Rock VIC 35 G4 36 E7
Black Springs NSW 22 H6
Black Springs SA 62 E4 65 G10
Black Swamp NSW 25 C11
Blackall QLD 8 J3 13 G12
Blackbull QLD 10 F7
Blackburn VIC 35 D6
Blackbutt QLD 7 E11
Blackdown Tableland Nat Park QLD 9 H8
Blackfellows Caves SA 63 B14
Blackheath NSW 21 K8 22 G7
Blackmans Bay TAS 50 F6 53 G10
Blacksmith Island QLD 9 C8
Blackstone (Papulankutja) WA 79 K13 83 B7
Blacktown NSW 19 D1 21 E8
Blackville NSW 22 A7
Blackwater QLD 9 H8
Blackwater Mine QLD 9 H8
Blackwood SA 59 K4 60 H3 61 B6 62 F7 65 J10
Blackwood VIC 39 E12
Blackwood Creek TAS 53 A9 55 H9
Blackwood Forest VIC 37 K12
Blackwood Nat Park QLD 8 D5 13 B14
Bladensburg Nat Park QLD 13 D9
Blair Athol QLD 8 F6
Blair Athol SA 59 E4
Blairgowrie VIC 36 J6
Blakehurst NSW 19 H4 21 C10
Blakeview SA 60 C3
Blakeville VIC 36 A2 39 E11
Blakney Creek NSW 22 K4 31 B9
Blanchetown SA 62 D5 65 H11
Bland NSW 22 H1 29 E13
Blandford NSW 23 B9
Blanket Flat NSW 22 J4 31 A9
Blaxland NSW 21 H8 23 H8
Blaxlands Ridge NSW 20 G6
Blayney NSW 22 G5
Blessington TAS 55 G11
Blewitt Springs SA 60 K2 61 D6
Bligh Park NSW 20 F7
Blighty NSW 29 J9
Blina Oilfield WA 79 B10 80 G7
Blinman SA 65 B10
Bloods Range (Puntitjata) NT 79 J14 90 H1
Bloomfield QLD 11 B12
Bloomsbury QLD 8 C7
Blow Clear NSW 22 E1 29 C14 29 E13
Blue Bay NSW 20 A3
Blue Lake Nat Park QLD 5 A8 7 G13
Blue Mountains Nat Park NSW 21 J8 22 H7 31 A11
Blue Rocks TAS 55 B9
Bluewater QLD 8 A4 11 H14
Bluewater Springs Roadhouse QLD 8 A3 11 H13
Bluff QLD 9 H8
Blyth SA 62 F4 65 G10
Blythdale QLD 6 E5
Boambee NSW 25 G13
Boat Harbour TAS 54 D4
Boat Harbour Beach TAS 54 C4
Boatswain Point SA 63 D12
Bobadah NSW 27 K12 29 A12
Bobbin Head NSW 19 A5 20 C6
Bobin NSW 23 B12
Bodalla NSW 31 G11
Bodallin WA 75 B8 77 J8
Bodangora NSW 22 D4
Boddington WA 72 D7 74 E4
Bogan Gate NSW 22 E1 29 C14
Bogantungan QLD 8 H5
Bogee NSW 22 E7
Boggabilla NSW 24 B6
Boggabri NSW 24 H5
Bogolong Creek NSW 22 H2 29 E14
Bogong VIC 30 J5 43 E10
Boho VIC 42 E5
Boho South VIC 42 E5
Boigbeat VIC 40 G7
Boinka VIC 28 H2 40 E3
Boisdale VIC 43 K9 45 C10 46 E4
Bokal WA 73 C10
Bokarina QLD 4 D1
Bolgart WA 74 B4 76 J5
Bolinda VIC 39 D13 42 H1
Bolivar SA 59 B4 60 D2
Bolivia NSW 25 D10
Bollon QLD 6 H2
Bolton VIC 28 H5 40 D7
Boltons Beach Con Area TAS 53 D13
Bolwarra VIC 38 H4
Bolwarrah VIC 36 A1 39 E11
Bomaderry NSW 31 C12
Bombala NSW 31 J9
Bombo NSW 23 K8 31 B13
Bomera NSW 22 A6 24 K5
Bonalbo NSW 7 K12 25 B12
Bonang VIC 31 K8 47 A10
Bonbeach VIC 37 F8
Bondi NSW 19 F7 21 B8
Bondi Junction NSW 19 F6
Bonegilla VIC 29 K12 30 G4 43 B9
Boneo VIC 36 K7
Bongaree QLD 4 D4 7 F13
Bongil Bongil Nat Park NSW 25 G13
Bonnells Bay NSW 20 B1
Bonnet Bay NSW 19 J3
Bonnie Doon VIC 42 F5
Bonnie Rock WA 76 H7
Bonnie Vale WA 75 A12 77 J11
Bonny Hills NSW 23 A13
Bonnyrigg NSW 21 E9
Bonogin QLD 5 C14
Bonshaw NSW 7 K9 25 C8
Bonville NSW 25 G12
Booborowie SA 62 F3 65 F10
Boobyalla TAS 55 C12
Booderee Nat Park ACT 31 D13
Boodie Island WA 78 E2
Bookabie SA 64 C1 68 K6
Bookaloo SA 65 C8
Bookar VIC 39 G8
Booker Bay NSW 20 B5
Bookham NSW 31 C8
Bookin QLD 10 K6 12 A6
Bool Lagoon SA 63 B12
Boolading WA 73 D9
Boolarra VIC 44 F7 46 G1
Boolba QLD 6 H3
Boolburra QLD 9 H9
Boolcunda SA 65 D9
Booleroo Centre SA 62 F2 65 E9
Booligal NSW 29 E8
Boolite VIC 40 K7
Boomi NSW 6 J6 24 B4
Boonah QLD 5 H12 7 H12
Boonanarring Nat Res WA 74 B3 76 J5
Boonarga QLD 7 E8
Boondall QLD 3 B5 4 E7
Boondooma QLD 7 D9
Boonmoo QLD 11 D12
Boonoo Boonoo NSW 25 C10
Boonoo Boonoo Nat Park NSW 7 K11 25 B11
Boonooroo QLD 7 C13
Boorabbin WA 75 B10 77 J10
Boorabbin Nat Park WA 75 A10 77 J9
Booragoon WA 71 J3
Booral NSW 23 D11
Boorcan VIC 39 H8
Boorhaman VIC 42 C6
Boorindal NSW 27 E11
Boorndoolyanna SA 90 K6
Boorongie North VIC 28 H4 40 E6
Booroopki VIC 38 B2
Booroorban NSW 29 G8 41 D13
Boorowa NSW 22 J3 31 B8
Boorrdoolyanna SA 68 A5
Boort VIC 28 K6 41 J10
Boosey VIC 42 B5
Booti Booti Nat Park NSW 23 D12
Boowillia SA 65 G9
Booyal QLD 7 B11
Bopeechee SA 67 H8
Boppy Mount NSW 27 H11
Borallon QLD 5 H8
Borambil NSW 22 B6
Borambola NSW 29 H14 30 D6
Boraning WA 73 C8
Borda Island WA 81 B9
Borden WA 74 H7
Border Island QLD 9 B8
Border Ranges Nat Park NSW 7 J12 25 A12
Border Store NT 85 C7 86 D7
Borderdale WA 73 A12
Bordertown SA 40 K1 63 B10
Boree NSW 22 F4
Boree QLD 8 C1 13 A10
Boree Creek NSW 29 H12 30 D3
Boreen Point QLD 7 D13
Boro NSW 31 D10
Boronia VIC 37 D9
Boronia Heights QLD 3 K4
Boroobin QLD 4 G2
Bororen QLD 9 J11
Borrika SA 62 C7 65 J12
Borroloola NT 87 K12 89 B12
Borung VIC 41 K10
Boscabel WA 73 B11
Bossley Park NSW 21 E9
Bostobrick NSW 25 G12
Boston Island SA 64 H6
Botany NSW 19 H6 21 B9
Botany Bay NSW 19 H5 21 B9
Botany Bay Nat Park NSW 19 J6 21 B10 23 H9 31 A14
Bothwell TAS 53 D9
Bouddi Nat Park NSW 20 B5 23 G10
Boulder WA 75 A12 77 J11 83 F1
Bouldercombe QLD 9 H10
Boulia QLD 12 E4
Boundain WA 73 A8
Boundary Bend VIC 28 G5 41 C8
Bountiful Island QLD 10 D4
Bourke NSW 27 E10
Bournda Nat Park NSW 31 J11
Bow NSW 22 C7
Bowden SA 58 A1
Bowelling WA 73 D10 74 F4
Bowen QLD 8 B7
Bowen Mountain NSW 20 H7
Bowen Park NSW 22 F4
Bowenvale VIC 39 C10
Bowenville QLD 7 F10
Bower SA 62 D5 65 G11
Boweya VIC 42 C6
Bowhill SA 62 D7 65 J11
Bowillia SA 62 F4
Bowling Alley Point NSW 23 A9 25 K8
Bowling Green Bay QLD 8 A5
Bowling Green Bay Nat Park QLD 8 A6
Bowma NSW 43 A9
Bowman QLD 9 F9
Bowmans SA 62 F5 65 H9
Bowna NSW 29 K13 30 F4
Bowning NSW 22 K4
Bowral NSW 22 K7 31 B12
Bowraville NSW 25 H12
Box Hill NSW 20 F7
Box Hill VIC 35 D6 37 D9 39 F14 42 K2 44 B2
Boxwood Hill WA 75 H8
Boyacup WA 73 A13
Boyagarring Con Park WA 72 D5
Boyagin Nat Res WA 72 C6 74 D4
Boyanup WA 73 G10 74 G3
Boydtown NSW 31 K11 47 A14
Boyeo VIC 40 K3
Boyer TAS 50 A3 53 F9
Boyland QLD 5 D12
Boyne Island QLD 9 J11
Boynedale QLD 9 J11
Boyup Brook WA 73 E11 74 G4
Bracalba QLD 4 G4
Brachina SA 65 B10
Bracken Ridge QLD 3 A4 4 E6
Brackendale NSW 25 J9
Bracknell TAS 55 G9 56 K3
Bradbury NSW 21 E11
Bradbury SA 60 H4 61 B7
Braddon ACT 32 A3
Bradvale VIC 39 F9
Braefield NSW 23 A8 24 K7
Braeside VIC 35 H5 37 F8
Brahma Lodge SA 59 B5

Braidwood NSW 31 E10
Bramble Bay QLD 3 A5
Bramfield SA 64 F4
Brampton Island QLD 9 C8
Brampton Islands Nat Park QLD 9 C8
Bramston Beach QLD 11 E13
Brandon QLD 8 A5
Brandy Creek VIC 37 G14
Branxholm TAS 55 E12
Branxholme VIC 38 F4
Branxton NSW 23 D10
Brawlin NSW 22 K2 29 G14 30 B7
Bray Junction SA 63 C12
Braybrook VIC 35 C1
Brayfield SA 64 G6
Brayton NSW 22 K6 31 B11
Brazendale Island TAS 53 B9 55 J9
Breadalbane NSW 31 C10
Breadalbane TAS 55 G10 56 H5
Break O'Day VIC 37 G14
Breakaway Ridge Nat Res WA 75 F8
Breakfast Creek NSW 22 D6 22 J3
31 A8
Breaksea Island TAS 52 J5
Bream Creek TAS 51 B12 53 F12
Breamlea VIC 36 H3
Bredbo NSW 31 F9
Breelong NSW 22 B4
Breeza NSW 24 J6
Bremer Bay WA 75 H9
Bremer Island NT 87 C13
Brendale QLD 3 A3
Brentwood SA 62 H6 65 J8
Brentwood VIC 40 H5
Breona TAS 53 A8 55 H8
Bretti NSW 23 B11
Brewarrina NSW 27 D12
Brewster VIC 39 E9
Briaba QLD 8 C6
Briagolong VIC 43 K9 45 C11 46 D4
Bribbaree NSW 22 J1 29 F14 30 A6
Bribie Island QLD 4 D3 7 F13
Bribie Island Nat Park QLD 4 E3 7 F13
Bridge Creek VIC 42 F6
Bridgeman Downs QLD 3 B3
Bridgenorth TAS 55 F9 56 F4
Bridgetown WA 73 F12 74 H3
Bridgewater QLD 60 H4
Bridgewater TAS 50 A4 53 F10
Bridgewater VIC 39 A11
Bridport TAS 55 D11 56 B7
Brigalow QLD 7 E9
Bright VIC 30 H4 43 E9
Brighton QLD 3 A4 4 E6
Brighton SA 59 K2 61 B5 62 F7
65 J10
Brighton TAS 53 F10
Brighton VIC 35 F3 36 E7
Brighton Beach WA 71 E1
Brighton-Le-Sands NSW 19 H5 21 C9
Brightview QLD 5 K8
Brightwaters NSW 20 B1
Brim VIC 40 J6
Brimbago SA 63 B10
Brimboal VIC 38 D3
Brimpaen VIC 38 C5
Brindabella NSW 31 D8
Brindabella Nat Park NSW 31 D8
Brinerville NSW 25 G11
Bringalbert VIC 38 B2
Bringelly NSW 21 F10
Bringung NT 87 H8
Brinkin NT 84 A2
Brinkley SA 62 E7 65 K11
Brinkworth SA 62 E4 65 G10
Brisbane QLD 3 E4 5 E8 7 G13
Brisbane CBD QLD 2
Brisbane Forest Park QLD 3 D1 4 G7
Brisbane Ranges Nat Park VIC 36 D2
39 F12
Brisbane Water Nat Park NSW 20 C5
23 G9
Brit Brit VIC 38 E4
Britannia Creek VIC 37 C12
Brittons Swamp TAS 54 C2
Brixton QLD 8 H2 13 F11
Broad Arrow WA 77 H11 83 F1
Broad Sound QLD 8 C6
Broadbeach QLD 5 B13 7 H13
Broadford VIC 39 C14 42 G2
Broadmarsh TAS 53 F10
Broadmeadows SA 60 D3
Broadmeadows VIC 35 B3 36 B7
Broadmont QLD 9 H10
Broadwater NSW 7 K13 25 C14
Broadwater VIC 38 F6
Broadwater Nat Park NSW 7 K13
25 C14
Brocklehurst NSW 22 C3
Brocklesby NSW 29 K12 30 F3 43 A8
Brockman WA 73 F14
Brockman Mine WA 82 F2
Brockman Nat Park WA 74 J3
Brodribb River VIC 43 K14 47 D9
Brogo NSW 31 H10
Broke NSW 23 E9
Broken Bay NSW 20 B5 23 G9
Broken Hill NSW 26 J2 28 A2 65 C14
Bromby Islands NT 87 C12

Bromelton QLD 5 F12
Brompton SA 59 F3
Bromus WA 75 D13 83 H1
Bronte NSW 21 B9
Bronte Park TAS 52 C7 54 K7
Bronzewing VIC 28 H4 40 E6
Brookdale NSW 29 H12 30 D4
Brooker SA 64 G6
Brookfield NSW 23 D11
Brookfield QLD 3 E1 5 G8
Brookfield Con Park SA 62 D5 65 H11
Brookhampton WA 73 F11
Brooking Gorge Con Park WA 79 B11
81 H8
Brooklands QLD 5 F11
Brooklyn NSW 20 C5
Brooklyn VIC 35 D1
Brooklyn Park SA 59 G3
Brooks Creek NT 85 F3 86 E4
Brooksby VIC 38 C4
Brookstead QLD 7 G10
Brookton WA 72 B5 74 D5
Brookvale NSW 19 D6 20 F7
Brooloo QLD 7 E12
Brooman NSW 31 E11
Broome WA 79 B8 80 H3
Broomehill WA 74 G6
Brooms Head NSW 25 E13
Brooweena QLD 7 C11
Broughton VIC 40 J2
Broughton Island NSW 23 D12
Broula NSW 22 H3
Broulee NSW 31 F11
Brovinia QLD 7 C9
Browning NSW 31 C8
Brownlow SA 62 D5 65 H11
Browns Creek NSW 22 G4
Browns Plains QLD 3 K4 5 E10
Bruarong VIC 30 G4 43 C8
Bruce SA 62 F1 65 D9
Bruce Rock WA 74 C7 76 K7
Brucknell VIC 39 J8
Bruinbun NSW 22 F5
Brukunga SA 60 H6
Brungle NSW 30 D7
Brunswick VIC 35 C3 36 C7
Brunswick Heads NSW 7 J13 25 B14
Brunswick Junction WA 73 G9 74 F3
Bruthen VIC 43 K12 45 B14 46 D7
Bryden QLD 4 J6
Buangor VIC 39 D8
Bucasia QLD 9 D8
Buccarumbi NSW 25 E11
Buccleuch SA 63 C8 65 K12
Buchan VIC 43 J13 47 C8
Buchan South VIC 43 J13 46 C7
47 C8
Bucheen Creek VIC 43 D11
Buchfelde SA 60 B3
Buckaroo NSW 22 D6
Buckenderra NSW 31 G8
Bucketty NSW 20 E1 23 F9
Buckingham QLD 8 G3
Buckingham WA 73 E10
Buckland TAS 53 E12
Buckland VIC 43 E8
Buckland Junction VIC 43 F8
Buckleboo SA 64 E3
Buckley VIC 36 H1 39 H11
Buckley Swamp VIC 38 F5
Buckrabanyule VIC 41 K9
Budawang Nat Park NSW 31 D11
Budbabadah NSW 27 J13
Buddawarka NT 87 G9
Budderoo Nat Park NSW 23 K8 31 B13
Buddigower NSW 29 E12
Buddina QLD 4 D1
Buderim QLD 4 E1 7 E13
Budgee Budgee NSW 22 D6
Budgeree VIC 44 F7 46 G1
Budgerum VIC 41 H9
Budgewoi NSW 20 A2 23 F10
Budgewoi Lake NSW 20 A2
Buenba Flat (site) VIC 43 E12
Buff Point NSW 20 A2
Buffalo VIC 44 G6
Buffalo River VIC 30 H3 43 E8
Bugaldie NSW 24 J3
Bugilbone NSW 24 F2
Builyan QLD 9 K11
Bukalong NSW 31 J9
Bukkulla NSW 25 D8
Bulahdelah NSW 23 D12
Bulart VIC 38 E4
Bulbararing Bay NSW 20 B4
Buldah VIC 47 B11
Bulga NSW 23 D9
Bulgandry NSW 29 J12 30 E3
Bulimba QLD 3 D4 5 E8
Bulkham Hills NSW 19 D2
Bull Creek WA 71 J4
Bull Swamp VIC 37 H14
Bulla NT 86 J2 88 A2
Bulla VIC 35 A1 36 B6 39 E13 42 J1
44 A1
Bullabulling WA 75 A11 77 J10

Bullaburra NSW 21 J9
Bullagreen NSW 22 A2 24 K1 27 H14
Bullarah NSW 24 D3
Bullarook VIC 39 E11
Bullarto VIC 39 D11
Bulleen VIC 35 C4
Bullenbung NSW 29 H12 30 D4
Bullengarook VIC 36 A4
Bulleringa Nat Park QLD 11 E10
Bullfinch WA 75 A8 77 J8
Bullhead Creek VIC 43 C10
Bulli NSW 21 C13 23 J8 31 B13
Bullioh VIC 29 K13 43 B10
Bullock Creek QLD 11 E11
Bullyard QLD 7 A11 9 K12
Bulman NT 87 F9
Buln Buln VIC 37 F14 44 D6
Bulong WA 75 A13 77 J11 83 F1
Bulumwaal VIC 43 J11 45 B12 46 D5
Bulwer QLD 4 B4
Bulwer Island QLD 3 C6
Bulyee WA 74 D6
Bumbaldry NSW 22 H3
Bumberry VIC 22 F3
Bumbunga SA 62 G4 65 G9
Bunbartha VIC 42 B3
Bunbury WA 73 G9 74 F2
Bundaberg QLD 7 A12 9 K13
Bundaburrah NSW 22 G1
Bundalaguah VIC 45 D10 46 E4
Bundall QLD 5 B12
Bundalong VIC 42 B6
Bundanoon NSW 22 K7 31 B12
Bundarra NSW 25 F8
Bundeela NSW 22 K7 31 C12
Bundeena NSW 19 K5 21 B10 23 J9
31 A14
Bundella NSW 22 A6 24 K5
Bunding VIC 36 A1
Bundjalung Nat Park NSW 25 D13
Bundook NSW 23 B11
Bundooma NT 91 H9
Bundoora VIC 35 B5 37 B8
Bundure NSW 29 H10 30 D2
Bung Bong VIC 39 C9
Bunga NSW 31 H11
Bungador VIC 39 H9
Bungal VIC 36 C1 39 F11
Bungallen VIC 12 B4
Bungarby NSW 31 H9
Bungaree VIC 39 E11
Bungeet VIC 42 C6
Bungendore NSW 31 D10
Bungil VIC 43 B10
Bungonia NSW 31 C11
Bungowannah NSW 29 K12 30 F4
43 A8
Bungulla NSW 25 C10
Bunguluke VIC 41 J9
Bungunya QLD 6 J6 24 A4
Bungwahl NSW 23 D12
Buninyong VIC 39 E10
Bunjurgen QLD 5 H13
Bunnaloo NSW 29 K8 41 H13
Bunnan NSW 23 C8
Buntine WA 76 H5
Bunya NSW 23 C12
Bunya QLD 3 C2
Bunya Mountains Nat Park QLD 7 E10
Bunyan NSW 31 G1
Bunyaville State Forest Park QLD 3 C2
Bunyip VIC 37 F13 44 D5
Bunyip State Park VIC 37 E13 44 C4
Buraja NSW 29 K11 30 F3 42 A7
Burakin WA 76 H6
Burbank QLD 3 G6 5 D8
Burcher NSW 29 D13
Burdett South Nat Res WA 75 F13
83 J1
Burekup WA 73 G9
Burford Island NT 86 B5
Burges WA 72 C3
Burgooney NSW 29 D12
Burke and Wills Roadhouse QLD 10 H5
Burketown QLD 10 E3
Burleigh VIC 37 D11
Burleigh Head Nat Park QLD 5 B13
Burleigh Heads QLD 5 B13 7 H13
Burma Road Nat Res WA 76 F4
Burnbank VIC 39 D10
Burndale VIC 37 K12
Burnett Heads QLD 7 A12
Burney Island NT 87 F12
Burnie TAS 54 D5
Burning Mountain Nat Res NSW 23 B9
Burns Creek TAS 55 F11
Burnside NSW 59 G6 60 G3 61 A6
Burnt Bridge NSW 25 J12
Buronga NSW 28 F3 40 A5
Burpengary QLD 4 F5
Burra NSW 31 E9
Burra QLD 8 C2 11 K12 13 A12
Burra SA 62 E4 65 G10
Burraboi NSW 28 J7 41 F12
Burracoppin WA 74 B7 76 J7
Burraga NSW 22 H5
Burragate NSW 31 J10 47 A13
Burragorang State Rec Park NSW
21 H11
Burramine North VIC 42 A5
Burramine South VIC 42 B5

Burrandana NSW 29 J13 30 E5
Burraneer NSW 19 K4
Burrapine NSW 25 H11
Burrell Creek NSW 23 B12
Burren Junction NSW 24 F3
Burrendong Dam NSW 22 D5
Burrill Lake NSW 31 E12
Burringbar NSW 25 A14
Burrinjuck NSW 31 C8
Burroin VIC 40 G3
Burrowa - Pine Mountain Nat Park VIC
29 K14 30 F6 43 B12
Burrowye VIC 29 K13 30 F5 43 B11
Burrum VIC 38 A7
Burrum Coast Nat Park QLD 7 A12
Burrum Heads QLD 7 B12
Burrumbeet VIC 39 D9
Burrumboot VIC 39 A13 42 D1
Burrumbuttock NSW 29 K12 30 F4
43 A8
Burswood WA 71 F4
Burton SA 59 A4 60 D2
Burtville WA 77 F12 83 D2
Burwood VIC 35 E5 37 D8 39 F14
42 K2 44 C2
Burwood East VIC 35 E6
Busbys Flat NSW 25 C12
Bushfield VIC 38 H6
Bushy Park TAS 53 F9
Bushy Park VIC 43 K9 45 C10 46 E4
Busselton WA 73 J11 74 G2
Bustard Bay QLD 9 J12
Bustard Island NT 87 F12
Butcher Well North Mine WA 77 F12
83 E1
Butchers Ridge VIC 43 H13 47 B8
Bute SA 62 G4 65 F9
Butler Tanks SA 64 G6
Butru QLD 12 B4
Butterfly Gorge Nature Park NT 85 G3
86 F5
Buxton NSW 21 G13
Buxton VIC 30 K1 42 H4
Buxtonville QLD 7 B12
Byabarra NSW 23 A13 25 K11
Byaduk VIC 38 G5
Byaduk North VIC 38 F5
Byawatha VIC 42 C7
Byee QLD 7 C11
Byfield QLD 9 G11
Byfield Nat Park QLD 9 G11
Byford WA 72 F4 74 D3
Bylong NSW 22 C7
Byrneside VIC 41 K14 42 C3
Byrnestown QLD 7 B10
Byrock NSW 27 F11
Byron Bay NSW 7 K14 25 B14
Bywong NSW 31 D10

## C

Cabanandra NSW 47 A10
Cabanda QLD 5 J9
Cabawin QLD 7 F8
Cabbage Tree Creek VIC 47 D10
Caboolture QLD 4 F4 7 F12
Caboonbah QLD 4 K5
Cabramatta NSW 19 F1 21 E9
Cabramurra NSW 30 F7 43 A14
Caddens Flat VIC 38 C8
Cadell SA 62 C5 65 G12
Cadney Homestead SA 66 E3
Cadney Park SA 66 E3
Cadoux WA 74 A5 76 J6
Caiguna WA 83 H3
Cairns QLD 11 D13
Cairns Bay TAS 50 J1 53 H9
Cairns Bay VIC 36 K7
Cal Lal NSW 28 F1 40 A1 62 A5
65 G14
Calamvale VIC 3 J4 5 E9
Calca SA 64 E3
Calcifer QLD 11 D11
Calcium QLD 8 A5 11 H14
Calder VIC 54 D4
Calder Island QLD 9 C9
Caldermeade VIC 37 H12
Caldwell NSW 29 J8 41 G12
Calen QLD 9 C8
Calga NSW 20 C4
Calingiri WA 74 A4 76 J5
Calivil VIC 41 K11
Callanna SA 67 H9
Callaroy NSW 22 C7
Callawadda VIC 38 B7
Calleen NSW 29 E12
Callide QLD 9 J10
Callide Coalfields QLD 9 J10
Callington SA 60 J7 62 E7 65 J10
Callion WA 77 H10
Calliope QLD 9 J11
Caloona NSW 6 K6 24 B3
Caloundra QLD 4 D2 7 E13
Calpatanna Con Park SA 64 E3
Caltowie SA 62 F3 65 F9
Calulu VIC 43 K11 45 B12 46 D5
Calvert QLD 5 J10
Calvert VIC 38 E7
Camballin WA 79 B10 80 H6
Cambarville VIC 37 A14 42 J5 44 A5
Camberwell NSW 23 D9
Camberwell VIC 35 D5 37 D8

Camboon QLD 7 A8 9 K10
Cambooya QLD 7 G10
Cambrai SA 62 D6 65 H11
Cambray WA 73 G12
Cambrian Hill VIC 39 E10
Cambridge NSW 21 G8
Cambridge TAS 50 C7 53 F11
Cambridge Gulf WA 81 C13
Cambridge Ruins QLD 11 K9
Camburinga NT 87 D12
Camden NSW 21 F11 23 H8 31 A13
Camden South NSW 21 F11
Camena TAS 54 E6
Cameron Corner SA QLD NSW 14 K4
26 C1 67 G14
Camira QLD 3 J1 5 F9
Camira Creek NSW 25 D12
Camooweal QLD 10 J1 89 H14
Camooweal Caves Nat Park QLD 10 J1
89 H14
Camp Hill QLD 3 F5 5 E8
Camp Mountain QLD 3 C1 4 G7
Campania TAS 53 E11
Campbell Town TAS 53 B11 55 J11
Campbellfield VIC 36 B7
Campbells Bridge VIC 38 B7
Campbells Creek VIC 39 C11
Campbells Forest VIC 39 A11
Campbelltown NSW 21 E11 23 J8
31 A13
Campbelltown SA 59 F6 60 F3
Campbelltown VIC 39 C11
Campbellville QLD 4 E2
Campellfield VIC 35 B3
Camperdown NSW 19 F5 21 C9
Camperdown VIC 39 H8
Campup WA 73 A13
Campwin Beach QLD 9 D8
Camurra NSW 24 D5
Canaga QLD 7 E9
Canbelego NSW 27 H11
Canberra ACT 31 D9
Canberra CBD ACT 32
Candelo NSW 31 J10
Canegrass WA 77 H11
Cangai NSW 25 D11
Cania Gorge Nat Park QLD 7 A9 9 K11
Caniambo VIC 42 D4
Cann River VIC 47 C11
Canna WA 76 F4
Cannawigara SA 63 B10
Cannie VIC 41 G9
Canning Vale WA 71 J5
Cannington NSW 71 H5 72 F3
Cannington Mine QLD 12 C5
Cannon Creek QLD 5 H13
Cannon Hill QLD 3 E5 5 E8
Cannon Vale QLD 8 B7
Cannons Creek VIC 37 H10
Cannum VIC 40 K5
Canoble NSW 29 C8
Canonba NSW 27 H13
Canowie SA 63 E5 65 F10
Canowindra NSW 22 G3
Canteen Creek (Orwaitilla) NT 89 J11
91 A11
Canterbury NSW 19 G4 21 C9
Canunda Nat Park SA 63 C13
Canungra QLD 5 D13 7 H13
Canyonleigh NSW 22 K6 31 B11
Cap Island Con Park SA 64 G4
Capalaba QLD 3 G7 5 D8 7 G13
Capalaba West QLD 3 F7
Capamauro Nat Res WA 76 G4
Caparra NSW 23 B12
Cape Arid Nat Park WA 83 J2
Cape Barren Island TAS 55 A13
55 A14
Cape Bridgewater VIC 38 J3
Cape Clear VIC 39 F10
Cape Conran Coastal Park VIC 47 D10
Cape Crawford NT 89 C11
Cape Cuvier WA 78 H1
Cape Gantheaume Con Park SA 63 H9
Cape Hart Con Park SA 63 G9
Cape Hillsborough Nat Park QLD 9 C8
Cape Hotham Forestry Res NT 85 B2
86 C4
Cape Howe VIC 47 C14
Cape Jervis SA 61 K1 63 G8 65 K9
Cape Le Grand Nat Park WA 75 G14
83 J1
Cape Melville Nat Park QLD 16 H5
Cape Nelson State Park VIC 38 J3
Cape Palmerston Nat Park QLD 9 E9
Cape Paterson VIC 44 G4
Cape Range Nat Park WA 78 F1
Cape River QLD 8 C3 11 K12
Cape Schanck VIC 36 K7 39 J14
44 F1
Cape Torrens Con Park SA 63 K8
Cape Upstart Nat Park QLD 8 A6
Cape York Peninsula QLD 16 F2
Capel WA 73 H10 74 G2
Capel Sound VIC 36 J6
Capella QLD 8 G6
Capels Crossing VIC 41 G11
Capercup WA 73 C10
Capertee NSW 22 E7
Capital Hill ACT 32 D2
Capricorn Coast QLD 9 G11
Capricorn Coast Nat Park QLD 9 G11
Capricorn Roadhouse WA 78 G6
82 H6

Capricornia Cays Nat Park QLD 9 H13
Captain Billy Landing QLD 16 D3
Captains Flat NSW 31 E10
Carabost NSW 29 J14 30 E6
Caragabal NSW 22 H1 29 E14
Caralue SA 64 F6
Caramut VIC 38 G6
Caranbiri Con Res NT 87 K11 89 B12
Carapooee VIC 39 B9
Carapook VIC 38 E3
Caravan Head NSW 19 J4
Carawa SA 64 D3
Carboor VIC 42 E7
Carbrook QLD 5 C9
Carbunup River QLD 73 J11
Carcoar NSW 22 G4
Carcuma Con Park SA 63 C8 65 K12
Cardinia VIC 37 E11
Cardinia Reservoir VIC 37 E11 44 C3
Cardross VIC 28 F4 40 B5
Cardwell QLD 11 F13
Carey Gully SA 60 G4
Cargerie VIC 39 F11
Cargo NSW 22 F4
Carina SA 3 F5
Carina VIC 28 H2 40 F2
Carina Heights QLD 3 F5
Carinda NSW 27 F14
Carindale QLD 5 E8
Carine WA 71 D2
Caringbah NSW 19 J4 21 B10
Carisbrook VIC 39 C10
Carlecatup WA 73 F11
Carlingford NSW 19 D3 21 D8
Carlisle NSW 24 J4
Carlisle Island Nat Park QLD 9 C8
Carlisle River VIC 39 J9
Carlisle State Park VIC 39 J9
Carlotta WA 73 G13
Carlsruhe VIC 39 D12
Carlton TAS 51 C10 53 F11
Carlton VIC 34 A3 35 D3
Carlyam Nat Res WA 76 G6
Carmila QLD 9 E9
Carmila Beach QLD 9 E9
Carnamah WA 76 G4
Carnarvon WA 76 A2 78 J1
Carnarvon Nat Park QLD 6 A4 8 K6
  13 H14
Carne SA 66 J4
Carnes Hill NSW 21 E10
Carngham VIC 39 E10
Caroda NSW 24 F6
Caroona NSW 22 A7 24 K6
Carpa SA 62 K4 64 G7
Carpendeit VIC 39 H9
Carpenter Rocks SA 63 C14
Carrajung VIC 45 F9 46 G3
Carramar NSW 21 D9
Carranballac VIC 39 F8
Carrara QLD 5 B13
Carrathool NSW 29 F9 30 B1
Carr-Boyd WA 77 H11 83 E1
Carrick TAS 55 G9 56 H4
Carrickalinga SA 61 G3 63 G8 65 K9
Carrieton SA 62 F1 65 D10
Carroll NSW 24 J6
Carroll Gap NSW 24 H6
Carrolup WA 73 A11
Carrow Brook NSW 23 C9
Carrowidgin NSW 31 J8
Carrum VIC 35 J5 37 F8 39 G14
  44 D2
Carrum Downs VIC 35 J6 37 F9
Carseldine QLD 3 B4 4 E7
Cartwright NSW 21 E9
Carwarp VIC 28 G3 40 B5
Cascade WA 75 F12
Cashmere QLD 3 A1 4 F4
Cashmore VIC 38 H3
Casino NSW 7 K13 25 C13
Cassilis NSW 22 D7
Cassilis VIC 43 G11 46 B6
Cassini Island WA 81 A9
Castambul SA 60 F4
Castella VIC 37 A11
Casterton VIC 38 E3 63 A13
Castle Forbes Bay TAS 50 H1 53 H9
Castle Hill NSW 19 C2 21 D8
Castle Rock NSW 23 C8
Castle Tower Nat Park QLD 9 J11
Castleburn VIC 43 J10 45 A11 46 C4
Castlecrag NSW 19 D6
Castlemaine VIC 39 C11
Castlereagh NSW 21 G8
Castleton QLD 11 G10
Casuarina NT 84 A3
Casula NSW 21 E9
Cataby WA 76 J4
Catamaran TAS 53 K9
Catani VIC 37 G12 44 E4
Cataract Reservoir NSW 21 D13
Cathcart NSW 31 J10
Cathcart VIC 38 D7
Cathedral Beach QLD 7 B13
Cathedral Range State Park VIC 30 K2
  42 H5
Cathedral Rock Nat Park NSW 25 G10
Catherine Field NSW 21 F9
Catherine Hill Bay NSW 20 A1
Cathkin VIC 30 K1 42 G4
Cathundral NSW 22 B1 27 J14
Cattai NSW 20 F6
Cattai Nat Park NSW 20 F6 23 G8

Catumnal VIC 41 J10
Caulfield VIC 35 E5 37 D8
Cavan SA 60 E2
Cave Hill Nat Res WA 75 B12 77 K11
Caveat VIC 42 F4
Cavendish VIC 38 E5
Caversham WA 71 D6
Caveside TAS 54 G7
Cawarral QLD 9 G10
Cecil Park NSW 21 E9
Cecil Plains QLD 7 G9
Cedar Bay Nat Park QLD 11 B12
Cedar Brush NSW 20 D2
Cedar Creek QLD 4 G6 5 D11
Cedar Grove QLD 5 E11
Cedar Point NSW 25 B13
Cedarton QLD 4 G2
Ceduna SA 64 C2 68 K7
Cement Creek VIC 37 C13
Central Castra TAS 54 E6
Central Mangrove NSW 20 D3
Central McDonald NSW 20 F4
Central Mount Wedge NT 90 D5
Central Plateau Con Area TAS 52 A7
  54 H7
Central Tilba NSW 31 G11
Centre Bore SA 68 B5
Centre Island NT 87 J13 89 A13
Ceratodus QLD 7 B9
Ceres NSW 22 C2
Ceres VIC 36 G2 39 G12
Cervantes WA 76 H4
Cessnock NSW 23 E10
Chadinga Con Res SA 64 C1 68 K6
Chadstone VIC 35 E5
Chaelundi Nat Park NSW 25 F11
Chain of Lagoons TAS 55 G14
Chain of Ponds SA 60 E5
Chain Valley Bay NSW 20 A1
Chakola NSW 31 G9
Chalky Island TAS 55 B8
Chambers Flat QLD 5 E10
Chambers Pillar Historical Res NT
  91 H8
Champagny Island WA 80 C6
Chandada SA 64 E4
Chandler QLD 3 F7 5 D8
Chandler SA 66 C2 68 B7
Chandlers Creek VIC 31 K9 47 B11
Channel Island NT 85 C2
Chapel Hill QLD 3 F2 5 F8
Chappell Islands TAS 55 C8
Chapple Vale VIC 39 J9
Charam VIC 38 C3
Charbon NSW 22 E6
Charles Darwin Nat Park NT 84 D3
Charleston SA 60 G5
Charleston Con Park SA 60 G6
Charleville QLD 13 K13 15 D14
Charleyong NSW 31 E9
Charleys Creek VIC 39 J9
Charlotte Pass NSW 30 H7 43 D14
Charlton VIC 41 K9
Charlwood QLD 5 J13
Charmhaven NSW 20 B2
Charra SA 64 C2 68 K7
Charters Towers QLD 8 B4 11 J13
Chasm Island NT 87 F12
Chatsbury NSW 22 K6 31 B11
Chatswood NSW 19 D5 21 C8
Chatswood West NSW 19 D5
Chatsworth NSW 25 D13
Chatsworth VIC 38 F7
Cheadanup Nat Res WA 75 F11
Cheepie QLD 15 E11
Chelmer QLD 3 F3
Chelsea VIC 35 H5 37 F8
Cheltenham NSW 19 C3 21 D8
Cheltenham SA 59 E2
Cheltenham VIC 35 G4 37 E8
Cherbourg QLD 7 D11
Chermside QLD 3 C4 4 E7
Chermside West QLD 3 C3
Cherry Gardens SA 60 H3 61 C7
Cherry Tree Hill NSW 25 D8
Cherry Tree Pool WA 73 A11
Cherrybrook NSW 19 C3 20 D7
Cherrypool VIC 38 C5
Cherryville SA 60 F4
Cheshunt VIC 42 E7
Chester Hill NSW 21 D9
Chesterton Range Nat Park QLD 6 D2
Chetwynd VIC 38 D3
Cheviot VIC 42 G4
Cheviot Island QLD 9 E10
Chewton VIC 39 C12
Cheyne Beach WA 74 J7
Cheynes Bridge VIC 43 K8 45 B9
  46 D3
Chichester NSW 23 C10
Chiddarcooping Nat Res WA 74 A7
  77 J8
Chidlow WA 72 E3
Chifley NSW 21 B9
Chifley WA 77 J12 83 F2
Childers QLD 7 B11
Childers VIC 44 E6 46 F1
Chillagoe QLD 11 D11
Chillagoe-Mungana Caves Nat Park
  QLD 11 D11
Chilli Beach QLD 16 E4

Chillingham NSW 25 A13
Chillingollah VIC 28 H5 41 E8
Chilowlah NSW 31 C8
Chiltern VIC 29 K12 43 B8
Chiltern Box-Ironbark Nat Park VIC
  29 J12 30 G3 43 B8
Chinaman Creek QLD 62 G1 65 E9
Chinaman Island VIC 37 H10
Chinamans Wells SA 63 D10
Chinbi QLD 13 B10
Chinchilla QLD 7 E8
Chinderah NSW 25 A14
Chinkapook VIC 28 H5 40 E7
Chinocup Nat Res WA 74 F7
Chipping Norton NSW 21 D9
Chitern VIC 30 G3
Chorregon QLD 13 D9
Chowerup WA 73 C13
Chowilla Reg Res SA 28 E1 62 A4
  65 G13
Christies Beach SA 60 J1 61 C5
Christmas Creek QLD 5 F14
Christmas Hills TAS 54 C2
Christmas Hills VIC 37 B10
Christmas Island TAS 54 A6
Chudleigh TAS 54 G7
Chum Creek VIC 37 B11
Church Point NSW 19 A7 20 B6
Churchill VIC 45 E8 46 G2
Churchill Island VIC 37 H10
Churchill Nat Park VIC 37 E9 44 C3
Chute VIC 39 D9
City ACT 32 A3
City Beach WA 71 F2
Clackline WA 72 D2 74 C4 76 K5
Clairview QLD 9 F9
Clandulla NSW 22 E6
Clapham SA 59 J4
Clare QLD 8 B5
Clare SA 62 F4 65 G10
Claremont NSW 23 B8
Claremont WA 71 G2
Claremont Isles Nat Park QLD 16 G4
Clarence Gardens SA 59 H3
Clarence Point TAS 56 C2
Clarence Town NSW 23 D11
Clarendon NSW 20 G7
Clarendon SA 60 J2 61 C6 62 F7
  65 J10
Clarendon TAS 55 G10 56 K6
Clarendon VIC 39 F11
Clareville NSW 20 B6
Clarina QLD 10 E6
Clarke Island TAS 55 B13
Clarkefield VIC 39 E13 42 H1
Claude Road TAS 54 F7
Claverton QLD 15 F13
Clayfield QLD 3 D4
Claymore NSW 21 F9
Clayton SA 63 E8 65 K10
Clayton VIC 35 F5 37 E8
Clear Island Waters QLD 5 B13
Clear Lake VIC 38 C4
Clear Mountain QLD 3 A1
Clear Ridge NSW 29 E13
Clearview SA 59 E4
Cleland Con Park SA 59 H6 60 G3
  61 A7
Clematis VIC 37 E11
Clermont QLD 8 G6
Cleve SA 62 K4 64 G7
Cleveland QLD 5 C8
Cleveland TAS 53 A11 55 H11
Clifton NSW 21 C12
Clifton QLD 7 H11
Clifton Beach QLD 11 D13
Clifton Beach TAS 51 E8 53 G11
Clifton Creek VIC 43 K11 45 B13
  46 D6
Clifton Gardens NSW 19 E6
Clifton Springs VIC 36 G4 39 G13
Clinton SA 62 G5 65 H9
Clinton Centre SA 62 G5 65 H9
Clinton Con Park SA 62 G5 65 H9
Cloncurry QLD 10 K5 12 A5
Clonmel Island VIC 45 H9 46 H3
Clontarf NSW 19 E6 21 B8
Clouds Creek NSW 25 F12
Clovelly NSW 21 B9
Clovelly Park SA 59 J3
Cloverdale WA 71 G6
Cluan TAS 55 G9 56 J2
Club Terrace VIC 47 C10
Clunes NSW 25 B14
Clunes VIC 39 D10
Clybucca NSW 25 J12
Clyde VIC 37 G10 44 D3
Clydebank VIC 45 D11 46 E4
Coal Creek VIC 37 K14
Coalcliff NSW 21 C12
Coaldale NSW 25 D12
Coalstoun Lakes QLD 7 C11
Cobains VIC 45 D11 46 E4
Cobaki NSW 5 A14
Cobar NSW 27 H10
Cobargo NSW 31 H11
Cobark NSW 23 B10
Cobaw VIC 39 D13 42 G1
Cobbadah NSW 24 F7
Cobba-da-mana QLD 7 J9 25 A8
Cobbannah VIC 43 J10 45 A11 46 C4
Cobbity NSW 21 F11
Cobbora NSW 22 B5

Cobby Cobby Island QLD 5 B10
Cobden VIC 39 H8
Cobdogla SA 62 B5 65 H13
Cobera SA 62 B6 65 J12
Coboco NSW 22 B4
Cobourg Marine Park NT 85 A4 86 B5
Cobourg Peninsula NT 86 B5
Cobram VIC 29 K10 30 F1 42 A4
Cobrico VIC 39 H8
Cobungra VIC 30 J5 43 G10 46 A5
Coburg VIC 35 C3 36 C7 39 F14
  42 K2 44 B1
Cocamba VIC 40 E7
Cocata Con Park SA 64 F5
Cochranes Creek VIC 39 B10
Cockaleechie SA 64 H6
Cockatoo VIC 37 E11 42 K4 44 C4
Cockatoo Island WA 80 E5
Cockatoo Tank WA 75 B9 77 K9
Cockatoo Valley SA 60 C5
Cockburn SA 26 K1 28 A1 65 D14
Cockermouth Island QLD 9 C9
Cockle Creek TAS 53 K9
Cocklebiddy Motel WA 83 G4
Coconut Grove NT 84 B2
Cocoparra Nat Park NSW 29 F11
  30 A2
Cocoparra Nat Res NSW 29 E11
Codrington VIC 38 H5
Coen QLD 16 H3
Coffin Bay SA 64 H5
Coffin Bay Nat Park SA 64 H5
Coffs Harbour NSW 25 G13
Coghills Creek VIC 39 D10
Cohuna VIC 28 K7 41 H11
Coila Creek NSW 31 F11
Cokum VIC 41 G9
Colac VIC 39 H10
Colbinabbin VIC 39 A13 42 D1
Coldstream VIC 37 C10 42 J3 44 B3
Coleambally NSW 29 G10 30 C2
Colebee NSW 21 F8
Colebrook TAS 53 F9
Coledale NSW 21 C13 23 J8 31 A13
Coleraine VIC 38 E4
Coles Bay TAS 53 C14 55 K14
Coleyville QLD 5 J11
Colignan VIC 28 G4 40 B5
Colinroobie NSW 29 F12 30 B3
Colinton NSW 31 F9
Collarenebri NSW 24 D2
Collaroy NSW 19 C7 20 B7
Collector NSW 31 C10
Colley SA 64 E4
Collie NSW 22 A2
Collie WA 73 B9 74 F3
Collie Cardiff WA 73 E10
Collier Range Nat Park WA 78 H6
  82 K5
Collingullie NSW 29 H13 30 D4
Collingwood VIC 35 D4 37 D7
Collins TAS 73 F14
Collins Cap TAS 50 C3 53 F10
Collins Island QLD 9 F10
Collinsvale TAS 50 C4 53 F10
Collinsville QLD 8 C6
Colly Blue NSW 22 A7 24 K5
Colo NSW 20 G5
Colo Heights NSW 20 H5 23 F8
Colton SA 64 F4
Colton QLD 7 B10
Columboola QLD 7 E8
Colyton NSW 21 F8
Comara NSW 25 H11
Comaum SA 63 A12
Combaning NSW 22 J1 29 F14 30 B6
Combara NSW 24 J1
Combienbar VIC 47 C11
Combo Waterhole Con Park QLD 12 B7
Comboyne NSW 23 A12
Come-By-Chance NSW 24 G1
Comet QLD 8 H7
Comet Vale WA 77 G11
Comleroy Road NSW 20 H6
Commodore Heights NSW 20 B5
Como NSW 19 J3 21 C10
Como WA 71 H4
Conara TAS 53 A11 55 H11
Conargo NSW 29 H9 41 F14
Concord NSW 19 E4 21 C8
Concordia SA 60 B4
Condah VIC 38 G4
Condamine QLD 6 E7
Condell Park NSW 21 D9
Condingup WA 75 G14 83 J2
Condobolin NSW 29 C13
Condong NSW 25 A14
Condoulpe NSW 41 C9
Condowie SA 62 F4 65 G9
Congelin NSW 27 F8
Congo NSW 31 F11
Congupna VIC 42 C3
Conimbla NSW 22 G3
Conimbla Nat Park NSW 22 H3
Coningham TAS 50 G5
Coniston NSW 21 C14
Conjola NSW 31 D12
Conjola Nat Park NSW 31 D12
Conmurra SA 63 C12

Connells Lagoon Con Res NT 89 F12
Connells Point NSW 19 H4
Connemarra NSW 22 A6 24 K4
Connewarre VIC 36 H3
Connewirrecoo VIC 38 D3
Conondale QLD 4 H1 7 E12
Conondale Nat Park QLD 4 J1 7 E12
Contine WA 72 B7
Conway Beach QLD 9 C8
Conway Nat Park QLD 9 C8
Coober Pedy SA 66 G4
Coobowie SA 62 H7 65 J8
Coochiemudlo Island QLD 5 C9
Coochin Creek QLD 4 E3
Coodanup WA 72 G6
Cooee TAS 54 C5
Coogee NSW 19 G6 21 B9
Coojar VIC 38 D4
Cook SA 68 H3
Cookamidgera NSW 22 F2
Cookardinia NSW 29 J13 30 E5
Cooke Plains SA 63 D8 65 K11
Cookernup WA 73 G8
Cooks Gap NSW 22 C7
Cooktown QLD 11 A12 16 K7
Coolabah NSW 27 F7
Coolac NSW 29 G14 30 C7
Cooladdi QLD 15 E12
Coolah NSW 22 B6
Coolah Tops Nat Park NSW 22 B7
Coolamon NSW 29 G13 30 C5
Coolana QLD 5 J8
Coolangatta QLD 5 A14 7 H13 25 A14
Coolaroo VIC 35 A2 36 B7
Coolatai NSW 24 D7
Coolbinia WA 71 E4
Coolgardie WA 75 A12 77 J10
Coolimba WA 76 G3
Coolmunda Dam QLD 7 J9
Coolongolook NSW 23 C12
Cooltong SA 28 F1 65 H13
Coolum Beach QLD 7 E13
Coolup WA 72 H7 73 H8
Cooma NSW 31 G9
Cooma VIC 41 K14 42 C2
Coomallo Nat Res WA 76 H4
Coomandook SA 63 D8 65 K11
Coombabah QLD 5 A11
Coombah NSW 28 C2
Coombogolong NSW 24 G1
Coomera QLD 5 C11 7 H13
Coomera Island QLD 5 B11
Cominya QLD 4 K7 7 G12
Coonabarabran NSW 24 J3
Coonalpyn SA 63 C9
Coonamble NSW 24 H1
Coonana WA 77 J13 83 F2
Coonawarra SA 38 D1 63 B12
Coondle WA 72 D1
Coongoola QLD 15 G13
Coonooer Bridge NSW 39 A9 41 K9
Coopernook NSW 23 B13
Coopers Creek VIC 45 C8 46 E2
Coopers Plains QLD 3 G4
Cooplacurripa NSW 23 A11
Coopracambra Nat Park VIC 31 K9
  47 B12
Coorabie SA 68 K5
Cooran QLD 7 D12
Cooranbong NSW 20 C1 23 F10
Cooranga North QLD 7 E10
Cooranup WA 73 C13
Cooriemungle VIC 39 H9
Coorong Nat Park SA 63 D9
Coorow WA 76 G5
Cooroy QLD 7 D13
Coorparoo QLD 3 E4
Cootamundra NSW 22 K2 29 G14
  30 B7
Coothalla QLD 15 E13
Cooyal NSW 22 D6
Cooyar QLD 7 F12
Copacabana NSW 20 B4
Cope Cope VIC 41 K8
Copeville SA 62 C6 65 J12
Copley SA 65 A10 67 K10
Copmanhurst NSW 25 E12
Coppabella QLD 8 E7
Copperfield QLD 8 G6
Copperfield Mining Centre WA 77 F10
Copperhannia Nat Res NSW 22 H4
Copping TAS 51 B12 53 F12
Cora Lynn VIC 37 G12 44 D4
Corack VIC 41 J8
Corack East VIC 41 J8
Corackerup Nat Park WA 74 H7
Coragulac VIC 39 H9
Coraki NSW 7 K13 25 C13
Coral Bay WA 78 G1
Coral Coast QLD 7 A12 9 K13
Coral Sea QLD 11 A14
Coramba NSW 25 G12
Cordalba QLD 7 B11
Cordeaux Reservoir NSW 21 E14
Cordering WA 73 C10
Coree NSW 29 J10 30 D1
Coreen NSW 29 J11 30 E3
Corella Creek NT 89 E11

96 Corfield – Dunedoo


Corfield QLD 13 C9
Coridhap VIC 39 F10
Corinda QLD 3 G3
Corindi Beach NSW 25 F13
Corinella VIC 37 K11 44 F3
Corinna TAS 54 G2
Corio VIC 36 F3
Corio Bay QLD 9 G11
Corio Bay VIC 36 G3
Cornella VIC 39 A13 42 E1
Corner Inlet VIC 44 H7
Cornucopia VIC 37 F12
Cornwall TAS 55 G13
Cornwallis NSW 20 G7
Corny Point SA 62 J7 62 J7 64 J7
Corobimilla NSW 29 G11 30 C3
Coromandel East SA 59 K5
Coromandel Valley SA 59 K4 60 H3 61 B6
Coromby VIC 38 A6
Coronation Beach WA 76 F3
Coronation Islands WA 80 C7
Coronet Bay VIC 37 K11
Corop VIC 41 K13 42 D1
Cororooke VIC 39 H9
Corowa NSW 29 K11 30 F3 42 A7
Corridgery NSW 22 F1 29 D14
Corrigin WA 74 D6
Corrimal NSW 21 C14 23 J8 31 B13
Corroboree Park Inn NT 85 D3 86 D4
Corroboree Rock Con Res NT 91 F9
Corrowong NSW 31 J8
Corryong VIC 29 K14 30 G6 43 C12
Cosgrove VIC 42 C4
Cosmo Newberry WA 77 E13 83 C2
Cossack WA 78 E4 82 C2
Costerfield VIC 39 B13 42 F1
Cotabena SA 65 C9
Cottage Point NSW 20 C6
Cottesloe WA 71 G1
Cottles Bridge VIC 37 B9
Cougal NSW 25 A13
Coulomb Point Nat Res WA 79 A8 80 G3
Coulson QLD 5 H12
Coulston Park QLD 9 E8
Coulta SA 64 H5
Countegany NSW 31 G10
Couta Rocks TAS 54 E1
Coutts Crossing NSW 25 E12
Cowabbie West NSW 29 F12 30 B4
Cowan NSW 20 D6
Cowan Cowan QLD 4 B5
Cowangie VIC 28 H2 40 E2 65 K14
Cowaramup WA 73 J12 74 G2
Coward Springs SA 66 H7
Cowell SA 62 J4 64 G7
Cowes VIC 37 K9 44 F3
Cowley QLD 11 E13
Cowper NSW 25 E13
Cowra NSW 22 H3
Cowwarr VIC 45 D9 46 E3
Cox Peninsula NT 85 C1 86 D3
Cox Scrub Con Park SA 61 F7
Crab Island QLD 16 C1
Crabtree TAS 50 E3 53 G9
Cracow QLD 7 B8
Cradle Mountain - Lake St Clair Nat Park TAS 52 A5 54 H5
Cradle Valley TAS 54 G5
Cradoc TAS 50 H2 53 H9
Cradock SA 65 C10
Crafers SA 59 J6 60 G3
Crafers West SA 59 J6
Craiggiemore WA 77 F12 83 D2
Craigie NSW 31 J9 47 A11
Craigie WA 71 B2
Craigieburn VIC 36 B7 39 E14 42 J2 44 A1
Craiglie QLD 11 C12
Cramenton VIC 28 G4 40 D6
Cramps TAS 53 A9 55 H9
Cramsie QLD 8 H1 13 E10
Cranbourne VIC 35 K7 37 G9 44 D3
Cranbrook TAS 53 B13 55 J13
Cranbrook WA 74 H6
Cranebrook NSW 21 G8
Craneford SA 60 C7
Craven NSW 23 C11
Cravensville VIC 43 C11
Crawley WA 71 G3
Crayfish Creek TAS 54 C4
Creek Junction VIC 42 E5
Creek View VIC 39 A13 42 D1
Cremorne NSW 19 E6 21 B8
Cremorne TAS 51 E8 53 G11
Crescent Head NSW 25 J12
Cressy TAS 55 G9 56 K5
Cressy VIC 39 G10
Crestmead QLD 3 K5 5 E10
Creswick VIC 39 D10
Crib Point VIC 37 J9
Croajingolong Nat Park VIC 47 D12
Croftby QLD 5 J14
Croker Island NT 86 B6
Cromer Con Park SA 60 E6
Cronulla NSW 19 K5 21 B10
Crooble NSW 24 C6
Crooked River VIC 43 H9 46 B4
Crookwell NSW 22 K5 31 B10
Croppa Creek NSW 24 C6
Cross SA 60 F2
Crossdale QLD 4 J5
Crossman WA 72 D7
Crow Mountain NSW 24 G7
Crowdy Bay Nat Park NSW 23 B13
Crowes VIC 39 K9
Crowlands VIC 39 C8
Crows Nest NSW 19 E5
Crows Nest QLD 7 F11
Crows Nest Nat Park QLD 7 F11
Croxton East VIC 38 F5
Croydon QLD 10 F7
Croydon SA 59 F3 60 F2
Croydon VIC 37 C10 42 K3 44 B3
Crusoe Island QLD 5 B10
Crymelon VIC 40 J5
Cryon NSW 24 F2
Crystal Brook SA 62 G3 65 F9
CSA Mine NSW 27 H10
Cuballing WA 72 A7 74 E5
Cubbaroo NSW 24 F3
Cuckoo TAS 55 E11
Cudal NSW 22 F3
Cudgee VIC 38 H7
Cudgegong NSW 22 E6
Cudgen NSW 25 A14
Cudgera Creek NSW 25 A14
Cudgewa VIC 29 K14 30 G6 43 C12
Cudgewa North VIC 43 B12
Cudlee Creek SA 60 F5
Cudlee Creek Con Park SA 60 F5
Cudmirrah NSW 31 D12
Cudmirrah Nat Park NSW 31 D12
Cudmore Nat Park QLD 8 G4 13 D13
Cue WA 76 D7
Culbin WA 73 C9
Culburra NSW 31 C13
Culburra SA 63 C9
Culcairn NSW 29 J12 30 E4
Culgoa VIC 28 J5 41 G8
Culgoa Floodplain Nat Park QLD 6 K1 27 B12
Culgoa Nat Park NSW 6 K1 27 C12
Culgoora NSW 24 F4
Culham WA 72 D1
Cullacabardee WA 71 C4
Cullen NT 85 G4 86 F5
Cullen Bullen NSW 22 F6
Cullendulla NSW 31 E11
Cullerin NSW 31 C10
Cullulleraine VIC 28 F2 40 B3 65 H14
Cumborah NSW 27 D14
Cummins SA 64 H5
Cumnock NSW 22 E3
Cundare VIC 39 G10
Cundeelee WA 77 J13 83 F2
Cunderdin WA 72 A2 74 C5 76 K6
Cundinup WA 73 G12
Cungena SA 64 D4
Cunliffe SA 62 H5 65 G8
Cunnamulla QLD 15 H13
Cunningham SA 62 H5 65 H9
Cunningham Islands NT 87 C12
Cunninyeuk NSW 28 H7 41 E10
Cuprona TAS 54 D6
Curacoa Island QLD 11 G14
Curban NSW 22 A3 24 K2
Curdie Vale VIC 38 J7
Curdimurka SA 67 H8
Curl Curl NSW 19 D7 20 B7
Curlew Island QLD 9 E9
Curlewis NSW 24 J6
Curlewis VIC 36 G4
Curlwaa NSW 28 F3 40 A4
Currabubula NSW 24 J6
Curramulka SA 62 H6 65 J8
Currarong NSW 31 D13
Currawang NSW 31 C10
Currawarna NSW 29 H12 30 C4
Currawinya Nat Park QLD 15 J11 26 B7
Currency Creek SA 63 F8 65 K10
Currie TAS 54 B6
Curries VIC 38 H3
Currimundi QLD 4 D2
Currumbin QLD 5 A14
Currumbin Valley QLD 5 B14
Currumbin Waters QLD 5 B14
Curtin WA 75 A13 77 J11 83 F1
Curtin Airport WA 80 G6
Curtin Springs NT 90 J5
Curtis Island QLD 9 H11
Curtis Island Nat Park QLD 9 H11
Curyo VIC 28 K5 40 H7
Cuttabri NSW 24 G3
Cygnet TAS 50 H3 53 H9
Cygnet River SA 63 H8 65 K8
Cynthia QLD 7 B9

## D

Daandine QLD 7 F9
Dadswells Bridge VIC 38 B6
D'Aguilar QLD 4 G3
D'Aguilar Nat Park QLD 4 G7 7 F12
Daguragu NT 88 D3
Dahlen VIC 38 A5
Daintree QLD 11 C12
Daintree Nat Park QLD 11 C12
Daisy Dell TAS 54 G6
Daisy Hill QLD 3 J7 5 D9
Daisy Hill State Forest QLD 3 J7
Dajarra QLD 12 C3
Dakabin QLD 4 F5
Dalbeg QLD 8 B5
Dalby QLD 7 F9
Dale Bridge WA 72 C4
Dale Con Park WA 72 E4 74 D4
Dales Creek VIC 36 A2
Dalgety NSW 31 H8
Dalkeith WA 71 H2
Dallarnil QLD 7 B11
Dalma QLD 9 H10
Dalmeny NSW 31 G11
Dalmore VIC 37 G11
Dalmorton NSW 25 F11
Dalrymple Nat Park QLD 8 B4 11 J13
Dalton NSW 22 K4 31 C9
Dalwallinu WA 76 H5
Daly River NT 85 G1 86 F3
Daly Waters NT 86 K7 88 B7
Dalyston VIC 44 G4
Dampier WA 78 E4 82 C1
Dandaloo NSW 22 C1 27 K13 29 A13
Dandaragan WA 74 A2 76 J4
Dandenong VIC 35 G7 37 E9 44 C2
Dandenong North VIC 35 G7
Dandenong Ranges Nat Park VIC 37 D10 42 K3 44 C3
Dandenong South VIC 35 H7
Dandongadale VIC 30 J3 43 E8
Dangarfield NSW 23 C9
Dangarsleigh NSW 25 H9
Danggali Con Park SA 28 D1 62 A3 65 F13
Dangin WA 72 A4 74 C5 76 K6
Danyo VIC 28 H2 40 F2
Dapper Nat Res NSW 22 C5
Dapto NSW 23 K8 31 B13
Daradgee QLD 11 E13
Darbalara NSW 30 C7
Darbys Falls NSW 22 H4
Darch Island NT 86 B6
Dardadine WA 73 C9
Dardanup WA 73 G10 74 F3
Dareton NSW 28 F3 40 A4
Dargo VIC 43 H10 46 C4
Dark Corner NSW 22 F6
Darkan WA 73 C9 74 F4
Darke Peak SA 64 F6
Darkes Forest NSW 21 D12
Darkwood NSW 25 G12
Darley VIC 36 B3
Darling Harbour NSW 18 C1
Darling Point NSW 19 F6
Darlinghurst NSW 18 D3 19 F6
Darlington QLD 5 E14
Darlington SA 59 K3
Darlington TAS 53 E13
Darlington VIC 39 G8
Darlington Point NSW 29 G10 30 B2
Darnick NSW 28 C6
Darnum VIC 44 E6
Daroobalgie NSW 22 F2 29 D14
Darr QLD 8 G1 13 E10
Darra QLD 3 G2
Darradup WA 73 H13
Darraweit Guim VIC 39 D14 42 H1
Darriman VIC 45 F10 46 G3
Dartmoor VIC 38 G3 63 A14
Dartmouth QLD 8 H2 13 E11
Dartmouth VIC 43 D11
Darwin NT 84 E2 85 C1 86 D3
Darwin CBD NT 84
Dattening WA 72 C6
Davenport Range Nat Park NT 89 J10 91 A10
Daveyston SA 60 A5
Davidson NSW 19 C5 20 C7
Davies Creek Nat Park QLD 11 D12
Davies Plain VIC 43 E13
Davis Creek NSW 23 C9
Davistown NSW 20 B4
Davyhurst WA 77 H10
Daw Island WA 83 J3
Dawes Point NSW 18 A2
Dawesley SA 60 H6
Dawesville WA 72 G6
Dawson SA 62 E2 65 E10
Dawsons Hill NSW 23 C9
Dayboro QLD 4 G5 7 F12
Daydream Island QLD 9 B8
Daylesford VIC 39 D11
Daymar QLD 6 J5 24 B3
Daysdale NSW 29 J11 30 E3
Daytrap VIC 28 H5 40 E7
Daytrap Corner VIC 28 H4 40 F7
De La Poer Range Nat Res WA 77 D12 83 C2
De Witt Island TAS 52 K7
Dead Horse Gap NSW 30 H7 43 D13
Deagon QLD 3 A5
Deakin WA 68 H1 83 F7
Dean VIC 39 E11
Dean Park NSW 21 F8
Deanmill WA 73 F13 74 H3
Deans Marsh VIC 39 H11
Deception Bay QLD 4 E5 7 F13
Deddington TAS 55 G11
Dederang VIC 30 H4 43 D9
Dee Why NSW 19 C7 20 B7
Deeford QLD 9 J10
Deep Creek Con Park SA 61 K2 63 G8 65 K9
Deep Lead VIC 38 C7
Deepwater NSW 25 D10
Deepwater Nat Park QLD 9 J12
Deer Park VIC 36 C6 39 F13 42 K1
Deer Vale NSW 25 G11
Deeragun QLD 8 A4 11 H14
Deeral QLD 11 D13
Delamere SA 61 J2 63 G8 65 K9
Delaneys Creek QLD 4 G4
Delatite VIC 42 G6 46 A1
Delegate NSW 31 J8 47 A10
Delegate River VIC 31 J8 47 A10
Delfin Island SA 59 E1
Dellicknora VIC 47 A10
Dellyanine WA 73 B10
Deloraine TAS 55 F8 56 H1
Delta Gas Field SA 14 H3 67 E13
Delungra NSW 24 E7
Denham WA 76 B1 78 K1
Denham Group Nat Park QLD 16 C3
Denham Island QLD 10 D3
Denham Sound WA 76 B2
Denial Bay SA 64 C2 68 K7
Denicull Creek VIC 38 D7
Deniliquin NSW 29 J9 41 G14
Denman NSW 23 D8
Denman SA 68 H2
Denmark WA 74 K5
Dennes Point TAS 50 G6 53 G10
Dennington VIC 38 H6
D'Entrecasteaux Nat Park WA 73 G14 74 J3
Deptford VIC 43 J11 45 A13 46 C6
Depuch Island WA 82 C3
Derby TAS 55 E12
Derby VIC 39 A11
Derby WA 79 A10 80 G5
Dereel VIC 39 F10
Dergholm VIC 38 D2 63 A13
Dergholm State Park VIC 38 D2 63 A12
Dering VIC 40 F5
Deringulla NSW 22 A5 24 K3
Dernancourt SA 59 E6
Deroora QLD 8 H2 13 F11
Derrinallum VIC 39 G8
Derriwong NSW 29 C13
Derwent Bridge TAS 52 C6 54 K6
Desdemona WA 77 F11 83 E1
Detpa VIC 40 J4
Deua Nat Park NSW 31 F10
Devenish VIC 42 C5
Devils Marbles Con Res NT 89 J9 91 A9
Devoit TAS 55 E9 56 E3
Devon VIC 45 G9 46 G2
Devon Meadows VIC 37 G10
Devoncourt QLD 12 B4
Devonian Reef Con Park WA 79 B11 81 H8
Devonport TAS 54 E7
Dewars Pool WA 72 E1
Dhalinybuy NT 87 D12
Dharug Nat Park NSW 20 E4 23 G9
Diamantina Gates Nat Park QLD 12 F6
Diamond Creek VIC 35 A6 37 B9 39 E14 42 J2 44 B2
Dianella WA 71 D4
Diapur VIC 40 K3
Dicky Beach QLD 4 D2
Didleum Plains TAS 55 F11
Digby VIC 38 F3
Digby Island QLD 9 D9
Diggers Rest VIC 36 B5 39 E13 42 J1
Dillalah Ridge QLD 15 E13
Dillcar QLD 13 D9
Dilpurra NSW 28 H6 41 E10
Dilston TAS 55 F9 56 F4
Dimboola VIC 38 A5 40 K5
Dimbulah QLD 11 D12
Dingee VIC 41 K11
Dingley Village VIC 35 G5 37 E8
Dingo QLD 9 H8
Dingup WA 73 E13
Dingwall VIC 28 K6 41 H10
Dinmore QLD 5 G9
Dinner Plain VIC 30 J5 43 F10 46 A5
Dinninup WA 73 D11 74 G4
Dinoga NSW 24 F7
Dinyarrak VIC 40 K2
Dipperu (Scientific) Nat Park QLD 8 E7
Direk SA 59 A4 60 D2
Dirk Hartog Island WA 76 B1 78 K1
Dirnaseer NSW 22 K1 29 G14 30 B6
Dirranbandi QLD 6 J4 24 A1
Discovery Bay VIC 38 H2
Discovery Bay Coastal Park VIC 38 H2 63 A14
Dixie VIC 39 H8
Dixons Creek VIC 37 B11 42 J3 44 A3
Djukbinj Nat Park NT 85 C3 86 D4
Dobbyn QLD 10 J4
Docker VIC 30 H3 42 D7
Docker River (Kaltukatjara) NT 79 J14 83 A7 90 H1
Doctors Flat VIC 30 K6 43 H12 46 B6
Dodges Ferry TAS 51 C9 53 F11
Dolphin Island WA 78 D4 82 C2
Dolphin Island Nat Res WA 78 D3 82 B1
Don TAS 54 E7
Don Valley VIC 37 C12
Donald VIC 41 K8
Donalds Well SA 68 A5 90 K6
Doncaster VIC 35 C6 37 C9
Dongara WA 76 G3
Donnelly River WA 73 F13
Donnybrook QLD 4 E4
Donnybrook VIC 36 A7
Donnybrook WA 73 G10 74 G3
Doo Town TAS 51 F13
Dooboobetic VIC 41 K8
Doodenanning WA 72 B3
Doodlakine WA 74 C6 76 K7
Dooen VIC 38 A5
Dookie VIC 30 G1 42 C4
Doolandella QLD 3 J3
Doomadgee QLD 10 F2
Doomben QLD 3 D5 4 E7
Doonside NSW 21 E8
Dooragan Nat Park NSW 23 B13
Dooralong NSW 20 C2
Doreen NSW 24 F4
Doreen VIC 37 B9 39 E14 42 J2 44 A2
Dorodong VIC 38 D2
Dorre Island WA 76 A1 78 J1
Dorrigo NSW 25 G12
Dorrigo Nat Park NSW 25 G12
Dorset Vale SA 60 J3 61 C7
Double Bay NSW 21 B8
Double Bridges (site) VIC 43 J12 45 A14 46 C7
Double Sandy Point Con Area TAS 55 D10 56 A7
Doughboy NSW 31 D10
Douglas VIC 38 C4
Douglas Apsley Nat Park TAS 53 A13 55 H13
Douglas Park NSW 21 E12
Douglas River TAS 53 A14 55 H14
Dover TAS 53 J9
Dover Heights NSW 19 F7 21 B8
Doveton VIC 35 G7
Dowerin WA 74 B5 76 J6
Downside NSW 29 H13 30 C5
Doyalson NSW 20 B1 23 F10
Dragon Rocks Nat Res WA 75 E8
Dragon Tree Soak Nat Res WA 79 D9
Drake NSW 25 C11
Dreeite VIC 39 H9
Drewvale QLD 3 J4
Driffield VIC 44 E7 46 F1
Drik Drik VIC 38 G3
Drillham QLD 6 E7
Dripstone NSW 22 D4
Dromana VIC 36 J7 39 H14 44 E1
Dromedary TAS 50 A4 53 F10
Dronfield QLD 12 B4
Drouin VIC 37 G14 44 D5
Drouin South VIC 37 G13 44 D5
Drouin West VIC 37 F14
Drovers Cave Nat Park WA 76 H3
Drumborg VIC 38 G3
Drummond QLD 8 H5
Drummoyne NSW 19 E5 21 C8
Drung Drung VIC 38 B6
Dry Creek SA 59 D4
Dry Creek VIC 42 F5
Dryander Nat Park QLD 8 B7
Drysdale VIC 36 G4 39 G13
Drysdale Island NT 87 B11
Drysdale River Nat Park WA 81 C11
Duaringa QLD 9 H9
Dubbo NSW 22 C3
Dubelling WA 72 A4
Dublin SA 62 F5 65 H9
Duchess QLD 12 B4
Duck Island VIC 36 H5
Duddo VIC 28 H2 40 E2
Dudinin WA 74 E6
Dudley VIC 44 G4
Dudley Con Park SA 63 G9
Dudley Park SA 59 E4
Duffys Forest NSW 19 B5 20 C6
Duke Islands QLD 9 E10
Dulacca QLD 6 E7
Dularcha Nat Park QLD 4 F2
Dulbolla QLD 5 F14
Dulbydilla QLD 6 D2
Dulcie Ranges Nat Park NT 91 D11
Dullingari Oil & Gas Field SA 14 H4 67 E14
Dululu QLD 9 H10
Dulwich SA 59 G5
Dumaresq NSW 25 G9
Dumbalk VIC 44 G6 46 H1
Dumbalk North VIC 44 F7 46 G1
Dumberning WA 73 B8
Dumbleyung WA 74 F6
Dumbleyung Lake Nat Res WA 74 F
Dumosa VIC 28 K5 41 H8
Dunalley TAS 51 D12 53 F12
Duncraig WA 71 C2
Dundas NSW 21 D8
Dundas QLD 4 J6
Dundas TAS 52 A4 54 H4
Dundas Nat Res WA 75 D14 83 H1
Dundas Valley NSW 19 D3
Dundee NSW 25 E10
Dundee Beach NT 86 D3
Dundonnell VIC 39 F8
Dundurrabin NSW 25 G11
Dunedoo NSW 22 B5

Dunggir Nat Park NSW 25 H12
Dungog NSW 23 D11
Dungowan NSW 25 J8
Dunk Island QLD 11 F13
Dunkeld NSW 22 F5
Dunkeld QLD 6 E3
Dunkeld VIC 38 E6
Dunluce QLD 13 A10
Dunmarra NT 88 C7
Dunmore NSW 22 D2 29 B14
Dunnstown VIC 39 E11
Dunorlan TAS 54 F7
Dunrobbin Bridge TAS 53 E8
Dunrobin VIC 38 E3
Dunsborough WA 73 K11 74 G2
Dunwich QLD 5 B8 7 G13
Durack QLD 3 H3
Dural NSW 19 B3 20 D7
Duramana NSW 22 F5
Duranillin WA 73 C10 74 G4
Durdidwarrah VIC 36 D1 39 F11
Durham QLD 11 F9
Durham Lead VIC 39 F10
Durham Ox VIC 28 K7 41 J11
Duri NSW 24 J7
Durong South QLD 7 D9
Durras NSW 31 E12
Durundur QLD 4 G3
Dutton SA 62 E5 65 H11
Dutton Park QLD 3 F4
Duverney VIC 39 G10
Dwarda WA 72 C7 74 E4
Dwellingup WA 72 F7 74 E3
Dwyers NSW 27 F11
Dykehead QLD 7 B9
Dynnyrne TAS 49 D1
Dysart QLD 8 F7
Dysart SA 53 E10

# E

Eagle Bay WA 73 K10 74 G1
Eagle Bore SA 68 A5 90 K5
Eagle Farm QLD 3 D5
Eagle Heights QLD 5 D12
Eagle on the Hill SA 59 H6
Eagle Point VIC 43 K11 45 C13 46 E6
Eagle Vale NSW 21 E11
Eagleby QLD 5 D10
Eaglehawk VIC 39 B12
Eaglehawk Neck TAS 51 F13 53 G12
Eaglevale VIC 43 H9 46 B4
Earlston VIC 42 D4
Earlwood NSW 21 C9
East Brisbane QLD 3 E4
East Fremantle WA 71 H2
East Gosford NSW 20 B4
East Guyong NSW 22 F5
East Haydon QLD 10 F6
East Hills NSW 19 H2 21 D10
East Kangaroo Island TAS 55 C8
East Killara NSW 19 D5
East Kurrajong NSW 20 G6
East Lynne NSW 31 E12
East Melbourne VIC 34 C4
East Palmerston QLD 11 E13
East Perth WA 70 B4 71 F4
East Point NT 84 C1
East Ryde NSW 19 E4
East Sassafras TAS 55 E8
East Strait Island QLD 16 B2
East Vernon Island NT 85 B2 86 C4
East Victoria Park WA 71 G5
Eastbrook WA 73 F14
Easter Group WA 76 F2
Eastern Creek NSW 21 E8
Eastern View VIC 39 J11
Eastwood NSW 19 D3 21 D8
Eastwood SA 58 D3
Eaton WA 73 G9
Eatons Hills QLD 3 B2
Eba Island SA 64 E3
Ebenezer NSW 20 F6
Ebor NSW 25 F11
Eccleston NSW 23 C10
Echo Hill SA 66 B1 68 B6
Echuca VIC 29 K8 41 J13 42 B1
Echunga SA 60 J4 62 E7 65 J10
Ecklin South VIC 39 H8
Eco Beach Resort WA 79 B8 80 J3
Eddington QLD 10 K7 12 A6
Eddington VIC 39 B10
Eden NSW 31 J11 47 A14
Eden Hills SA 59 K4 60 H2 61 B6
Eden Island QLD 5 D3
Eden Valley SA 60 C7 62 E6 65 H11
Edenhope VIC 38 C2 63 A12
Edensor Park NSW 21 E9
Edgecliff NSW 21 B8
Edgeroi NSW 24 F5
Edgewater WA 71 A2
Edi VIC 30 H3 42 E7
Edillilie SA 64 H5
Edith NSW 23 H6
Edith Creek TAS 55 B8
Edithburgh SA 62 H7 65 J8
Edithvale VIC 35 H5 37 F8 39 G14 44 D2
Edjudina Mine WA 77 G12 83 E2

Edmondson Park NSW 21 E10
Edmonton QLD 11 D13
Edmund Kennedy Nat Park QLD 11 F13
Edrom NSW 31 K11 47 A14
Edungalba QLD 9 H9
Edward Island NT 87 G11
Edward River SA 64 C1
Edwards Creek SA 66 F6
Edwardstown SA 59 J3
Egg Island TAS 50 G2
Egg Lagoon TAS 54 A6
Eidsvold QLD 7 B9
Eight Mile Plains QLD 3 H5 5 E9
Eildon VIC 30 K2 42 G5
Einasleigh QLD 11 H2
El Alamein SA 62 H1 65 D8
El Arish QLD 11 E13
Elaine VIC 39 F11
Elalie QLD 13 E9
Elands NSW 23 B12
Elanora Heights NSW 19 B7 20 B7
Elbow Hill SA 62 A4 64 G7
Elcho Island NT 87 C11
Elcombe NSW 24 E6
Elderslie TAS 53 E9
Eldon TAS 53 E11
Eldorado VIC 42 C7
Electrona TAS 50 G5 53 G10
Elgin WA 73 H10
Elgin Vale QLD 7 D11
Elimbah QLD 4 F4
Elizabeth SA 59 A5 60 D3 62 F6 65 J10
Elizabeth Bay NSW 23 C12
Elizabeth East SA 59 A6
Elizabeth Grove SA 59 A6
Elizabeth Heights SA 59 A6
Elizabeth Island VIC 37 K10
Elizabeth Town TAS 55 F8
Ella Bay Nat Park QLD 11 E13
Ellam VIC 40 J5
Ellenborough NSW 23 A12 25 K11
Ellenbrook WA 71 B6
Ellendale TAS 53 E8
Ellerslie VIC 38 G7
Ellerston NSW 23 B10
Ellery Creek Nature Park NT 90 F7
Elliminyt VIC 39 H10
Ellinbank VIC 37 H14 44 E6
Elliott NT 89 D8
Elliott QLD 7 A12 9 K13
Elliott TAS 54 D5
Elliott Heads QLD 7 A12 9 K13
Elliston SA 64 F4
Elmhurst VIC 39 C9
Elmore VIC 39 A13 41 K13 42 D1
Elong Elong NSW 22 C4
Elphin TAS 56 G5
Elphinstone QLD 8 D7
Elphinstone VIC 39 C12
Elsey Nat Park NT 86 H7
Elsmore NSW 25 E8
Eltham NSW 25 B14
Eltham VIC 35 B6 37 C9 39 F14 42 J2 44 B2
Elura Mine NSW 27 G10
Elwood VIC 35 E3
Emerald QLD 8 H7
Emerald VIC 37 E11 42 K3 44 C3
Emerald Hill NSW 24 H5
Emerald Springs NT 85 G4 86 F5
Emeriau Point WA 80 F4
Emily and Jessie Gaps Nature Park NT 91 F8
Emita TAS 55 B8
Emmaville NSW 25 D9
Emmdale NSW 26 J7
Emmet QLD 8 K1 13 G11
Empire Bay NSW 20 B5
Empire Vale NSW 25 C14
Emu VIC 39 B9
Emu Bay SA 63 H8 65 K8
Emu Downs SA 62 E4 65 G10
Emu Flat VIC 39 C13 42 G1
Emu Junction SA 68 E5
Emu Park QLD 9 G11
Emu Plains NSW 21 G8
Emuford QLD 11 E12
Encounter Bay SA 61 J7 63 F8
Endeavour Mine QLD 10 J3
Endeavour River Nat Park QLD 11 A12 16 K7
Enderby Island WA 78 E3
Endyalgout Island NT 85 A6 86 C6
Eneabba WA 76 G4
Enfield NSW 21 C9
Enfield SA 59 E4 60 F2
Enfield VIC 39 F11
Enfield State Park VIC 39 F10
Engadine NSW 19 K2 21 C10
Engawala NT 91 D9
Englefield VIC 38 D4
English Town TAS 55 G11
Enmore NSW 21 C9 25 H9
Enngonia NSW 27 C10
Enoggera QLD 3 C3
Ensay VIC 30 K6 43 H12 46 B7
Ensay North VIC 43 H12 46 B7
Ensay South VIC 43 H12 46 B7
Eppalock VIC 39 B12
Epping NSW 19 D3 21 D8
Epping VIC 35 A4 37 B8 39 E14 42 J2 44 A2
Epping Forest TAS 53 A10 55 H10

Epping Forest (Scientific) Nat Park QLD 8 F4 13 D14
Epsom QLD 9 D8
Epsom VIC 39 A12
Ercildoun VIC 39 D10
Eribung NSW 22 D1 29 B14
Eric Bonython Con Park SA 61 K3
Erica VIC 44 C7 46 E1
Erigolia NSW 29 E11
Erikin WA 74 C6 76 K7
Erina NSW 20 B4
Erindale SA 59 G6
Erldunda NT 90 H7
Ermington NSW 19 E3 21 D8
Ernest QLD 5 B12
Ernest Henry Mine QLD 10 K5
Eromanga QLD 15 E8
Erriba TAS 54 F6
Erringibba Nat Park QLD 6 F7
Errinundra VIC 47 B10
Errinundra Nat Park VIC 31 K8 47 B10
Errolls WA 77 D8
Erskine Island QLD 9 H12
Erskine Park NSW 21 F9
Erskineville NSW 21 B9
Esk QLD 4 K6 7 F12
Eskdale VIC 30 H5 43 D10
Esmond VIC 29 K11 30 F2 42 B6
Esperance WA 75 G13 83 J1
Essendon VIC 35 C2 36 C7
Estcourt VIC 37 G2
Eton QLD 9 D8
Ettalong Beach NSW 20 B5
Ettrick NSW 7 J12 25 B12
Etty Bay QLD 11 E13
Euabalong NSW 29 C11
Euabalong West NSW 29 C11
Eubanangee Swamp Nat Park QLD 11 E13
Euchareena NSW 22 E4
Eucla WA 68 K1 83 G7
Eucla Nat Park WA 68 K1 83 G7
Eucumbene Cove NSW 31 G8
Eudlo QLD 4 F1
Eudlo Creek Nat Park QLD 4 F1
Eudunda SA 62 E5 65 H11
Euegnana TAS 54 F7
Eugowra NSW 22 F3
Eulo QLD 15 H11
Eumundi QLD 7 E13
Eumungerie NSW 22 B3
Eungai NSW 25 H12
Eungella QLD 8 D7
Eungella Nat Park QLD 8 C7
Eurack VIC 39 G10
Eurambeen VIC 39 D9
Euramo QLD 11 F13
Eurelia SA 62 F1 65 D10
Eurilla Con Park SA 60 G3 61 A7
Eurimbula Nat Park QLD 9 J12
Euroa VIC 30 H1 42 E4
Eurobin VIC 43 E8
Eurobodalla NSW 31 G11
Eurobodalla Nat Park NSW 31 F11
Eurong QLD 7 B13
Eurongilly NSW 29 G14 30 C6
Euston NSW 28 G4 40 C7
Evandale TAS 55 G10 56 J6
Evans Head NSW 7 K13 25 C14
Evans Island SA 64 D2
Evanston SA 60 C4
Evanston WA 77 G9
Everard Junction WA 79 J11 83 A4
Everett Island NT 87 C12
Eversley VIC 39 C9
Everton VIC 30 G3 42 C7
Everton Hills QLD 3 C2
Everton Park QLD 3 C3 4 E7
Ewaninga Rock Carvings Con Res NT 91 F8
Ewens Ponds SA 38 G1
Exeter NSW 22 K7 31 B12
Exeter TAS 55 E9 56 E3
Exford VIC 36 C4
Exmouth WA 78 F1
Exmouth Gulf WA 78 F2
Expedition Nat Park QLD 6 B5 9 K8
Exton QLD 55 G8 56 H1
Eyre Island SA 64 D2
Eyre Peninsula SA 62 K3 64 E5

# F

Failford NSW 23 C12
Fairbank VIC 37 K14
Fairfax Islands QLD 9 J13
Fairfield NSW 19 F1 21 D9
Fairfield West NSW 19 F1
Fairhaven VIC 36 K1 37 J10 39 J11 47 C13
Fairholme NSW 29 D13
Fairleigh QLD 9 D8
Fairley VIC 41 G10
Fairneyview QLD 5 H8
Fairview Con Park SA 63 B11
Fairview Park SA 59 C7
Fairy Hill NSW 25 B13
Fairy Meadow NSW 21 C14
Fairy Mine WA 77 E10
Falcon WA 72 H6 74 E2
Falls Creek NSW 31 C12
Falls Creek Alpine Village VIC 30 J5 43 F10

Falmouth TAS 55 G14
Family Islands Nat Park QLD 11 F13
Fannie Bay NT 84 D1
Farina SA 67 J10
Farnham NSW 22 E4
Farrar WA 73 B12
Farrell Flat SA 62 E4 65 G10
Fassifern QLD 5 J12
Faulconbridge NSW 21 H8
Faulkland NSW 23 C11
Faure Island WA 76 B2
Fawcett VIC 42 G4
Fawkner VIC 35 B3
Federal NSW 25 B14
Feilton TAS 50 B1
Felixstow SA 59 F5
Feluga QLD 11 E13
Fentonbury TAS 53 E8
Fentons Creek VIC 39 A9
Ferguson SA 64 A4 66 K4
Ferguson VIC 39 J9
Fern Tree TAS 50 D5 53 G10
Fernances NSW 20 F3
Fernbank VIC 43 K10 45 C12 46 E5
Fernbrook WA 73 F9
Ferndale NSW 29 J12 30 E3
Ferndale VIC 37 J14
Ferndale WA 71 H5
Ferndene TAS 54 E6
Fernihurst VIC 41 J10
Fernlees QLD 8 H7
Fernleigh NSW 25 B14
Fernshaw VIC 37 B12
Ferntree Gully VIC 37 D10
Fernvale QLD 5 H8
Ferny Glen QLD 5 D13
Ferny Grove QLD 3 C1 4 F7
Ferny Hills QLD 3 C2
Ferryden Park SA 59 E3
Fiddletown NSW 20 D6
Field Island NT 85 B5 86 C6
Fiery Flat VIC 41 K10
Fifield NSW 29 B13
Fig Tree NSW 21 D14
Fig Tree Pocket QLD 3 F2
Finch Hatton QLD 8 D7
Finders SA 59 F3
Findon SA 59 F2 60 F1
Fine Flower NSW 25 E12
Fingal NSW 5 A14 25 A14
Fingal TAS 55 G13
Finger Post NSW 22 D4
Finke (Apatula) NT 91 J9
Finke Gorge Nat Park NT 90 G7
Finley NSW 29 J10 30 E1
Finniss SA 63 E8 65 K10
Finniss Con Park SA 61 F7
Fish Creek VIC 44 H6
Fish Point VIC 41 F10
Fish River Res NT 85 J2 86 G3
Fisher SA 68 H4
Fisherman Islands QLD 3 C7 4 D7
Fishermens Bend VIC 35 D2
Fiskville VIC 36 B2
Fitzgerald TAS 53 F8
Fitzgerald WA 75 H9
Fitzgerald River Nat Park WA 75 H9
Fitzgibbon QLD 3 B4
Fitzroy SA 58 A2 59 F4
Fitzroy VIC 34 A4 35 D3
Fitzroy Crossing WA 79 B11 81 J8
Fitzroy Falls NSW 22 K7 31 B12
Fitzroy Island NSW 11 C13
Fitzroy Island Nat Park QLD 11 D13
Five Day Creek NSW 25 H11
Five Ways NSW 27 J2 29 A12
Fiveways VIC 37 G10
Flaggy Rock QLD 9 E9
Flagstaff Hill SA 59 K4 60 H2 61 B6
Flat Rocks WA 73 A12
Flat Witch Island TAS 52 K7
Flaxley SA 60 J5
Flaxton QLD 4 F1
Fleurieu Peninsula SA 61 J3 63 F8
Flinders SA 5 H11
Flinders VIC 37 K8 39 J14 44 F2
Flinders Bay WA 73 J14 74 J2
Flinders Chase Nat Park SA 63 H5
Flinders Group Nat Park QLD 16 H5
Flinders Island QLD 16 H5
Flinders Island SA 64 G3
Flinders Island TAS 55 B9
Flinders Ranges Nat Park SA 65 B10
Flintstone TAS 53 B9 55 J9
Flora River Nature Park NT 85 J4 86 H5
Floreat WA 71 F2
Florida NSW 27 H11
Florida WA 72 H6
Florieton SA 62 D4 65 G11
Flowerdale TAS 54 D5
Flowerdale VIC 42 H3
Flowerpot SA 50 J3 53 H10
Flowery Gully TAS 55 E9 56 E2
Fluorspar QLD 11 D12
Foleyvale QLD 9 H9
Footscray VIC 35 D2 36 C6
Forbes NSW 22 F2 29 D14
Forcett TAS 51 B10 53 F11
Fords Bridge NSW 27 D9

Forest TAS 54 C3
Forest Den Nat Park QLD 8 E2 13 C12
Forest Glen NSW 20 E6
Forest Lake SA 3 J2 5 F9
Forest Range SA 60 G4
Forest Reefs NSW 22 G4
Forestdale QLD 3 K3 5 E9
Forester TAS 55 D12
Foresters Beach NSW 20 B4
Forestier Peninsula TAS 51 D13 53 G13
Foreston SA 60 D3
Forestville NSW 19 D6 20 C7
Forge Creek VIC 43 K11 45 C13 46 E6
Formby Bay SA 62 J7
Forrest ACT 32 D2
Forrest NSW 39 J10
Forrest WA 83 F6
Forrest Beach QLD 11 G13
Forrestfield WA 71 G7
Forsayth QLD 11 G9
Forster NSW 23 C12
Forsyth Island QLD 10 D3
Forsyth Island TAS 55 A14
Forsyth Islands QLD 10 D3
Fort Glanville Con Park SA 60 F1
Fort Lytton Nat Park QLD 3 D6 4 D7
Fortescue River Roadhouse WA 78 E3 82 D1
Forth TAS 54 E7
Fortis Creek Nat Park NSW 25 D12
Fortitude Valley QLD 2 A3 3 E4
Forty Mile Scrub Nat Park QLD 11 F11
Foster VIC 44 G7 46 H1
Fosterton NSW 23 C11
Fosterville VIC 39 A12
Four Mile Creek TAS 55 G14
Fowlers Bay SA 68 K6
Fowlers Gap NSW 26 G2
Foxdale QLD 8 C7
Foxhow VIC 39 G9
Framlingham VIC 38 H7
Frampton NSW 22 K1 29 G14 30 B6
Frances SA 38 B1 63 A11
Francois Peron Nat Park WA 76 B2 78 K1
Frank Hann Nat Park WA 75 E10
Frankford TAS 55 F8 56 F2
Frankland WA 73 B14 74 H5
Franklin - Gordon Wild Rivers Nat Park TAS 52 D5 54 K5
Franklin TAS 50 G2 53 H9
Franklin Harbour Con Park SA 62 J4 64 G7
Franklin Island SA 64 D2
Franklin Vale QLD 5 K10
Franklinford VIC 39 D11
Frankston VIC 35 K5 37 G8 39 G14 44 D2
Frankton SA 62 E5 65 H11
Fraser Island QLD 7 B13
Frederick Henry Bay TAS 51 D9
Freeling SA 62 E5 65 H10
Freemans Reach NSW 20 F6
Freemans Waterhole NSW 23 E10
Freeth Junction SA 86 B6 91 K11
Fregon (Kaltjiti) SA 68 B5
Fremantle WA 71 J1 72 G4 74 D2 76 K4
French Island VIC 37 J10 44 E3
French Island Nat Park VIC 37 J10 44 E3
French Park NSW 29 H12 30 D4
Frenchmans VIC 39 C8
Frenchs Forest NSW 19 C6 20 B7
Freshwater Creek VIC 36 H2 39 H12
Freshwater Nat Park QLD 4 E7 5 D11
Frewhurst QLD 11 F11
Freycinet Nat Park TAS 53 C14 55 K14
Freycinet Peninsula TAS 53 C14
Friday Island QLD 16 B2
Frogmore NSW 22 J4 31 A8
Fulham SA 59 G2 60 F1
Fulham Gardens SA 59 F2
Fulham Island TAS 51 D11
Fulham Vale QLD 4 K4
Fullarton SA 59 H5 60 G2 61 A6
Fullerton NSW 22 J5 31 A10
Fumina VIC 42 K6 44 C6 46 E1
Furner SA 63 C13
Furracabad NSW 25 E9
Fyans Creek VIC 38 C6
Fyansford VIC 36 G2

# G

Gabba Island QLD 16 A2
Gabo Island VIC 47 C14
Gaffneys Creek VIC 42 H6 46 C1
Gagebrook TAS 50 A5 53 F10
Gagudju Cooinda Lodge NT 85 D6 86 D6
Gailes QLD 3 J1 5 F9
Gairdner WA 75 H8
Galah VIC 28 H4 40 E5
Galaquil VIC 40 J6
Galaquil East VIC 40 J6
Galga SA 62 C6 65 J12

Galiwinku NT 87 C11
Galong NSW 22 K3 31 B8
Galore NSW 29 H12 30 C4
Galston NSW 19 A3 20 D7
Gama VIC 40 G6
Gammon Ranges Nat Park SA 65 A11 67 K11
Gan Gan NT 87 E11
Ganmain NSW 29 G12 30 C4
Gannawarra VIC 28 J7 41 G11
Gapsted VIC 43 D8
Gapuwiyak NT 87 D11
Garah NSW 24 G4
Garden Island SA 59 C2 60 E1
Garden Island TAS 50 K3
Garden Island WA 72 G4 74 D2
Garden Island Creek TAS 50 K3 53 H10
Gardens Of Stone Nat Park NSW 22 F6
Gardners Bay TAS 50 J3 53 H10
Garema NSW 22 G2 29 D14
Garfield VIC 37 F13 44 D4
Garfield North VIC 37 F12
Gargett QLD 9 D8
Garie NSW 21 C11
Garigal Nat Park NSW 19 C5 23 H9
Garland NSW 22 G4
Garnpung Lake NSW 28 D5
Garra NSW 22 F3
Garrawilla VIC 24 J4
Garrthalala NT 87 D12
Garvoc VIC 38 H7
Gary Junction WA 79 F11
Gascoyne Junction WA 76 A3 78 J2
Gatton QLD 7 G11
Gatum VIC 38 D4
Gaven QLD 5 C12
Gawler SA 60 B4 62 E6 65 H10
Gawler TAS 54 E6
Gayndah QLD 7 C10
Gaythorne QLD 3 D3
Gazette VIC 38 G5
Geebung QLD 3 C4
Geehi NSW 30 G7 43 C13
Geelong VIC 36 G3 39 G12
Geeralying WA 73 B8
Geeveston TAS 53 H9
Geikie Gorge Nat Park WA 79 B12 81 H9
Gelantipy VIC 43 G13 47 A8
Gellibrand VIC 39 J9
Gembrook VIC 37 E12 44 C4
Gemoka QLD 11 K9 13 A8
Genoa VIC 47 C13
Geographe Bay WA 73 J10 74 G2
George Town TAS 55 D9 56 C2
Georges Hall NSW 19 F9
Georges Creek Nat Res NSW 25 H10
Georges Junction NSW 25 H10
Georges Plains NSW 22 G5
Georges River Nat Park NSW 19 H2
Georgetown QLD 11 F9
Georgetown SA 62 F3 65 F10
Georgica NSW 25 B13
Gepps SA 60 F2
Gepps Cross SA 59 D4
Geraldton WA 76 F3
Gerang Gerung VIC 40 K4
Geranium SA 63 C8 65 K12
Gerard SA 62 B5 65 H13
German Creek Mine QLD 8 G7
Gerogery NSW 29 K12 30 F4 43 A9
Gerra QLD 8 H3 13 F12
Gerringhap VIC 36 F2
Gerringong NSW 23 K8 31 C13
Gerroa NSW 31 C13
Getullai Island QLD 16 A2
Geurie NSW 22 C4
Gherang VIC 36 J1
Gibinbell QLD 7 J8 24 B7
Gibraltar Range Nat Park NSW 25 E11
Gibson Desert Nat Res WA 79 J11 83 A4
Gibson Island QLD 3 D6
Gidgegannup WA 72 E2
Gidginbung NSW 29 F13 30 A5
Giffard VIC 45 F10 46 G4
Gilbert River QLD 11 F8
Gilberton SA 58 A3
Gilderoy VIC 37 D13
Gilead NSW 21 E11
Giles Meteorological Station WA 79 J13
Gilgai NSW 25 E8
Gilgandra NSW 22 A3
Gilgooma NSW 24 H2
Gilgunnia NSW 27 K10 29 B10
Gilles Plains SA 59 E5 60 F3
Gilliat QLD 10 K6 12 A6
Gillingall VIC 43 H13 47 B8
Gilston QLD 5 C13
Gin Gin NSW 22 B2 27 J14
Gin Gin QLD 7 A11 9 K12
Gina SA 66 J4
Gindalbie WA 77 H11 83 F1
Gindie QLD 8 H7
Gingilup Swamps Nat Res WA 73 H14 74 H2
Gingin WA 72 G1 74 B3 76 J5

Gippsland Lakes Coastal Park VIC 45 D12 46 F6
Gipsy Point VIC 47 C13
Girgarre VIC 41 K14 42 C2
Girilambone NSW 27 G12
Girral NSW 29 E12
Girraween NSW 21 E8
Girraween Nat Park QLD 7 K11 25 C10
Girrawheen WA 71 C3
Giru QLD 8 A5
Girvan NSW 23 D11
Gisborne VIC 39 E13
Gladesville NSW 19 E4
Gladfield VIC 41 J11
Gladstone NSW 25 J12
Gladstone QLD 9 H11
Gladstone SA 62 F3 65 F9
Gladstone TAS 55 D13
Gladysdale VIC 37 D12 42 K4 44 B4
Glamis NSW 23 A11
Glamorgan Vale QLD 5 J8
Glance Creek TAS 54 D5
Glandore SA 59 H3
Glass House Mountains QLD 4 F3
Glass House Mountains Nat Park QLD 4 F3 7 F12
Glastonbury QLD 7 D12
Glaziers Bay TAS 50 H2 53 H9
Glebe NSW 19 F5 21 C8
Glebe TAS 49 B2
Glen Alice NSW 22 E7
Glen Alvie VIC 37 K12 44 F4
Glen Davis NSW 22 F7
Glen Eagle WA 72 E5
Glen Elgin NSW 25 E10
Glen Forbes VIC 37 K12
Glen Fyne VIC 39 H8
Glen Gallic NSW 23 D8
Glen Helen Resort NT 90 F6
Glen Huon TAS 50 F1 53 G9
Glen Innes NSW 25 E9
Glen Morrison NSW 25 J9
Glen Nayook VIC 37 E14
Glen Osmond SA 59 H5 60 G3 61 A7
Glen Patrick VIC 39 C7
Glen Roy Con Park SA 38 D1 63 B12
Glen Valley VIC 30 J5 43 F11
Glen Waverley VIC 35 E6 37 D9
Glenaire VIC 39 K9
Glenaladale VIC 43 K10 45 B11 46 D5
Glenalbyn VIC 39 A10
Glenalta SA 59 J5
Glenariff NSW 27 F11
Glenaroua VIC 39 C14 42 G2
Glenbawn Dam NSW 23 C9
Glenbrae VIC 39 D9
Glenbrook NSW 21 G9
Glenburn VIC 30 K1 42 H3
Glenburnie SA 38 F1 63 B14
Glencairn VIC 42 J7 45 A8 46 C2
Glencoe NSW 25 F9
Glencoe SA 63 B13
Glencoe West SA 63 B13
Glendambo SA 64 A5
Glenden QLD 8 D7
Glendevie TAS 50 K1 53 H9
Glendon Brook NSW 23 D10
Gleneagle QLD 5 F12
Glenelg SA 59 J2 60 G1 61 A5 62 F7 65 J10
Glenelg North SA 59 H2
Glenfern QLD 4 J3
Glenfern TAS 50 B1 53 F9
Glenfield NSW 21 E10
Glenfyne VIC 39 H8
Glengarrie NSW 5 B14
Glengarry NSW 27 D14
Glengarry TAS 55 F9 56 F2
Glengarry VIC 45 D8 46 F2
Glengower VIC 39 D10
Glenhaven SA 59 J2
Glenhaven NSW 20 E7
Glenhope VIC 39 C13 42 G1
Glenisla VIC 38 D3
Glenlee VIC 40 K4
Glenlofty VIC 39 C8
Glenlusk TAS 50 B4 53 F10
Glenlyon VIC 39 D12
Glenlyon Dam QLD 7 K10
Glenmaggie VIC 43 K8 45 C9 46 E3
Glenmore NSW 21 G11
Glenmore VIC 36 C2
Glenmore Park NSW 21 G9
Glenmorgan QLD 6 F6
Glennie Group VIC 44 K7 46 K1
Glenora TAS 53 E9
Glenoran WA 73 F13
Glenorchy TAS 50 C5 53 F10
Glenorchy VIC 38 B7
Glenore QLD 10 E6
Glenore TAS 55 G9 56 J3
Glenorie NSW 20 E6
Glenormiston North VIC 39 G8
Glenormiston South VIC 39 H8
Glenreagh NSW 25 F12
Glenrowan VIC 30 H2 42 D6
Glenside SA 59 G5

Glenstuart QLD 8 J2 13 G12
Glenthompson VIC 38 E6
Glentulloch WA 73 E12
Glenunga SA 59 H5
Glenusk QLD 8 J3 13 G12
Glenwarrin NSW 23 A12
Glenwood NSW 21 E8
Glenwood QLD 7 C12
Glossodia NSW 20 G6
Glossop SA 62 B5 65 H13
Gloucester NSW 23 D11
Gloucester Island Nat Park QLD 8 B7
Gloucester Nat Park WA 73 F14 74 J3
Gnangara WA 71 B4
Gnarpurt VIC 39 G9
Gnarwarree VIC 36 G1
Gnotuk VIC 39 H8
Gnowangerup WA 74 G6
Goangra NSW 24 F1
Goat Island SA 64 D2
Gobarralong NSW 30 C7
Gobur VIC 42 F4
Gochin Jiny Jirra NT 87 C9
Gocup NSW 29 H14 30 D7
Godfreys Creek NSW 22 J3 31 A8
Godwin Beach QLD 4 E4
Gogango QLD 9 H9
Gogeldrie NSW 29 G11 30 B3
Gol Gol NSW 28 F3 40 A5
Golconda TAS 55 E10 56 D7
Gold Coast QLD 5 A12 7 H14
Golden Bay WA 72 G5
Golden Beach QLD 4 E2
Golden Beach VIC 45 E12 46 F5
Golden Grove SA 59 C7 60 E3
Golden Ridge WA 75 A13 77 J11 83 F1
Golden Valley TAS 55 G8 56 K1
Goldsborough VIC 39 B10
Goldsmith TAS 53 B10 55 J10
Goldsmith Island QLD 9 C8
Goldsworthy WA 78 D6 82 B6
Gollan NSW 22 C4
Golspie NSW 22 J5 31 A10
Gomersal SA 60 B5
Goneaway Nat Park QLD 13 F8
Gongolgon NSW 27 E12
Goobang Nat Park NSW 22 E3
Good Hope NSW 31 C8
Goodedulla Nat Park QLD 9 G9
Goodger QLD 7 E10
Goodna QLD 3 J1 5 F9
Goodnight NSW 41 D9
Goodnight Scrub Nat Park QLD 7 B11
Goodooga NSW 6 K2 27 B13
Goodparla NT 85 F5 86 E5
Goods Island QLD 16 B2
Goodwood QLD 7 B12
Goodwood SA 59 H4
Goohi NSW 24 J5
Goold Island QLD 11 F13
Goold Island Nat Park QLD 11 F13
Goolgowi NSW 29 E10
Goolma NSW 22 C5
Goolmangar NSW 25 B13
Gooloogong NSW 22 G3
Goolwa SA 61 B5 65 K10
Goomadeer NT 87 C8
Goomalibee VIC 42 D5
Goomalling WA 74 B4 76 J6
Goombi QLD 7 E8
Goombungee QLD 7 F10
Goomeri QLD 7 D11
Goon Nure VIC 45 C12 46 E5
Goonawarra Nat Res NSW 29 E8
Goondah NSW 22 K3 31 B8
Goondiwindi QLD 7 8J 24 A6
Goongarrie NSW 4 F11
Goongarrie Nat Park WA 77 G11 83 E1
Goongee VIC 28 H2 40 A2
Goongerah VIC 31 K8 47 B10
Goonumbla NSW 22 E2 29 C14
Goonyella Mine QLD 8 E6
Goorabin NSW 29 J11 30 C2
Gooram VIC 42 F4
Goorambat VIC 42 C5
Goorawin NSW 29 E10
Goornong VIC 39 A12
Gooroc VIC 39 A8 41 K8
Goose Island QLD 16 A2
Gooseberry Hill Nat Park WA 72 F3
Goovigen QLD 9 J10
Goowarra QLD 9 H9
Gorae VIC 38 H3
Gorae West VIC 38 H3
Goranba QLD 7 F8
Gordon NSW 19 D5 20 C7
Gordon TAS 50 K4 53 H10
Gordon VIC 36 A1 39 E11
Gordon Park QLD 3 D4
Gordon Ruins SA 65 D9
Gordonvale QLD 11 D13
Gormandale VIC 45 E9 46 F3
Gormanston TAS 52 B4 54 J4
Gorokan NSW 20 B2
Goroke VIC 38 B3
Goschen VIC 28 J6 41 F9
Gosford NSW 20 B4 23 G9
Goshen SA 55 E13
Gosnells WA 71 K6
Gosse Bore SA 66 A1 68 A6 90 K7
Gostwyck NSW 25 H9
Goughs Bay VIC 42 G6
Goulburn NSW 22 K6 31 C10

Goulburn Islands NT 86 B7
Goulburn River Nat Park NSW 22 C7
Goulburn Weir VIC 39 A14 42 E2
Goulds Country TAS 55 E13
Gove Peninsula NT 87 D13
Gowanford VIC 41 F8
Gowar East VIC 39 A9
Gowrie Park TAS 54 F6
Goyura VIC 40 H6
Grabben Gullen NSW 22 K5 31 B10
Gracefield WA 73 A13
Gracemere QLD 9 H10
Gracetown WA 73 K12 74 H1
Graceville QLD 3 F3
Gradule QLD 6 J5 24 A3
Grafton NSW 25 E12
Graham NSW 22 J4 31 A9
Grahamstown NSW 30 D7
Grahamvale VIC 42 C3
Graman NSW 24 D7
Grampians Nat Park VIC 38 C6
Grandchester QLD 5 K9
Grange QLD 3 D3
Grange SA 59 F2 60 F1
Granite Flat VIC 43 D10
Granite Island SA 61 J6
Granite Island VIC 44 H7 46 J2
Granite Point Con Area SA 55 D11 56 A7
Granite Tor Con Area TAS 52 A5 54 H5
Granny Smith Mine WA 77 F12 83 D1
Grant (site) VIC 43 H9 46 B4
Granton TAS 50 A4 53 F10
Granton VIC 37 A13
Grantville VIC 37 K11 44 F4
Granville NSW 19 E2 21 D8
Granville Harbour TAS 52 A2 54 H2
Granya VIC 43 B10
Granya State Park VIC 30 G5
Grass Flat VIC 38 A4
Grass Hut NSW 27 D10
Grass Patch WA 75 F13 83 J1
Grass Valley WA 72 C2 74 C4 76 K6
Grassdale VIC 38 F4
Grassmere VIC 38 H6
Grassy TAS 52 C5
Grattai NSW 22 D5
Gravelly Beach TAS 55 E9 56 E4
Gravesend NSW 24 D6
Grawin NSW 27 D14
Gray TAS 55 G14
Grays Point NSW 19 K3
Graytown VIC 39 B14 42 E2
Great Australian Bight 68 K2 83 H5
Great Australian Bight Marine SA 68 K4 83 G7
Great Barrier Reef QLD 9 C11 11 C13 16 F5
Great Basalt Wall Nat Park QLD 8 B2 11 J12
Great Dog Island TAS 55 C9
Great Keppel Island QLD 9 G11
Great Lake TAS 53 A8 55 H8
Great Oyster Bay TAS 53 C13 55 K13
Great Palm Island QLD 11 G14
Great Sandy Island Nat Res WA 78 E3
Great Sandy Nat Park QLD 7 B11 7 D13 9 K14
Great Victoria Desert Nat Res WA 68 F1 83 B6
Great Western VIC 38 C7
Great Western Tiers Con Park TAS 53 B10 55 J10
Gredgwin VIC 41 H10
Green Fields SA 59 C4
Green Head WA 76 H3
Green Island QLD 4 C7 11 D13
Green Island TAS 50 J5
Green Island Nat Park QLD 11 D13
Green Lake VIC 38 B5
Green Pigeon NSW 25 B13
Green Point NSW 20 B4
Green Valley NSW 21 E9
Greenacre NSW 19 G3 21 C9
Greenacres SA 59 E5
Greenbank SA 5 F10
Greenbushes WA 73 F12 74 G3
Greendale NSW 21 G10
Greendale VIC 36 A2 39 E12
Greenethorpe NSW 22 H3
Greengrove NSW 20 D4
Greenhill QLD 9 E9
Greenhill SA 60 G5
Greenhill Island NT 85 A5 86 B5
Greenhills WA 72 B3 74 C5 76 K6
Greenmount QLD 7 G11
Greenmount VIC 45 E9 46 H3
Greenock SA 60 A6 62 E5 65 H10
Greenough WA 76 F3
Greenpatch SA 64 H5
Greens Beach TAS 55 D8 56 C1
Greens Creek VIC 39 C8
Greensborough VIC 35 B5 37 C8
Greenslopes QLD 3 F4
Greenvale NSW 29 H11 30 C3
Greenvale QLD 11 G11
Greenvale VIC 35 A2 36 B6
Greenvale Reservoir VIC 36 B7
Greenwald VIC 38 G3
Greenways SA 62 D6 63 C12 65 J11
Greenwell Point NSW 31 C13

Greenwich NSW 21 C8
Greenwich Park NSW 22 K6 31 B11
Greenwith SA 59 B7
Greenwood WA 71 C2
Gregors Creek QLD 4 K3
Gregory WA 76 E2
Gregory Downs QLD 10 G3
Gregory Mine QLD 8 G7
Gregory Nat Park NT 86 J4 88 B3
Greigs Flat NSW 47 A14
Grenfell NSW 22 H2 29 E14
Grenville VIC 39 F10
Gresford NSW 23 D10
Greta VIC 42 D6
Greta West VIC 42 D6
Gretna TAS 53 E9
Grevillia NSW 25 A12
Grey Peaks Nat Park QLD 11 D13
Greystanes NSW 19 E1 21 E8
Griffin QLD 4 E6
Griffith NSW 29 F11 30 A2
Griffiths Island VIC 38 H6
Griffiths Nat Res WA 75 F12 83 J1
Grimwade WA 73 F11 74 G3
Gringegalgona VIC 38 E4
Grogan NSW 22 J1 29 F14 30 A6
Groganville QLD 11 C11
Grong Grong NSW 29 G12 30 B4
Gronos Point NSW 20 F6
Groote Eylandt NT 87 F12
Groper Creek QLD 8 A6
Grose Island NT 86 D3
Grose Vale NSW 20 H7
Grose Wold NSW 20 G7
Grove TAS 50 E3 53 G9
Grove Hill NT 85 F3 86 F4
Grovedale VIC 36 H2
Grovely QLD 3 C2
Gruyere VIC 37 C11
Guanaba QLD 5 C12
Gubbata NSW 29 D11
Gubbata Nat Res NSW 29 D12
Guilderton WA 72 H1 74 B2 76 K4
Guildford NSW 19 F2 21 D9
Guildford TAS 54 F5
Guildford VIC 39 C11
Guildford WA 71 E6
Gular NSW 24 J1
Gulargambone NSW 24 K1
Gulera QLD 7 F9
Gulf of Carpentaria 10 B3 87 E14
Gulf St Vincent SA 59 G1 60 H1 61 62 66 65 J9
Gulgong NSW 22 C5
Gull Creek NSW 24 F7
Gulnare SA 62 F3 65 F10
Gulpa NSW 41 G13
Guluguba QLD 7 E9
Guluwuru Island NT 87 B12
Gum Creek NSW 26 G9 30 B1
Gum Flat VIC 30 J3
Gum Lagoon Con Park SA 63 C10
Gum Lake NSW 28 B5
Gumble NSW 22 E3
Gumdale QLD 3 F6
Gumeracha SA 60 E5 62 E6 65 J10
Gumlu QLD 8 B6
Gunalda QLD 7 D12
Gunbalanya (Oenpelli) NT 85 C7 86
Gunbar NSW 29 E9
Gunbower VIC 29 K8 41 H12
Gundabooka Nat Park NSW 27 F10
Gundagai NSW 29 H14 30 C7
Gundaroo NSW 31 C9
Gunderman NSW 20 E5
Gundowring VIC 43 D9
Gundy NSW 23 B9
Gunebang NSW 29 C12
Gungal NSW 23 C8
Gunnary NSW 22 J4 31 A8
Gunnedah NSW 24 J6
Gunner VIC 28 H3 40 E4
Gunnewin QLD 6 C4
Gunning NSW 31 C9
Gunning Grach NSW 31 H9
Gunningband NSW 22 F1 29 C14
Gunns Plains TAS 54 E6
Gunpowder QLD 10 J3
Gununa QLD 10 D3
Gunyarra QLD 8 C7
Gurig Nat Park NT 86 B5
Gurley NSW 24 E5
Gurrai SA 28 H1 62 B7 65 K13
Gurrumuru NT 87 D12
Gurulmundi QLD 6 D7
Gutha WA 76 F4
Guthalungra QLD 8 B6
Guthega NSW 30 G7 43 C14
Guy Fawkes River Nat Park NSW 25 F11
Guy Fawkes River Nat Res NSW 25 G11
Guyra NSW 25 F9
Guys Forest VIC 43 B11
Gwabegar NSW 24 G3
Gwambygine WA 72 C3
Gwandalan NSW 20 A1
Gwandalan TAS 51 F10 53 G12
Gwindinup WA 73 G10
Gymbowen VIC 38 B3
Gymea NSW 21 C10
Gympie QLD 7 D12
Gypsum VIC 28 H4 40 F6

H1 Yandicoogina Mine – Junortoun 99

## H


**H1 Yandicoogina Mine WA** 78 G6 82 F5
**Hackham SA** 60 K1 61 D5
**Hackney SA** 58 B3 59 F5
**Haddon VIC** 39 E10
**Haddon Corner QLD SA** 12 K6 14 C4 67 A14
**Haden QLD** 7 F11
**Hadleigh NSW** 24 D6
**Hadspen TAS** 55 F9 56 H4
**Hagley TAS** 55 F9 56 H3
**Hahndorf SA** 60 H4 62 E7 65 J10
**Haig WA** 83 F4
**Haigslea QLD** 5 J9
**Haines Junction VIC** 39 J10
**Halbury SA** 62 F5 65 G10
**Hale Con Park SA** 60 C5
**Halekulani NSW** 20 A2
**Halfway Creek NSW** 25 F13
**Halidon SA** 62 C7 65 J12
**Halifax QLD** 11 G13
**Halifax Bay Wetlands Nat Park QLD** 11 G14
**Hall ACT** 31 D9
**Hall NSW** 19 G2
**Hallett SA** 62 E3 65 F10
**Hallett Cove SA** 60 J1 61 C5
**Hallett Cove Con Park SA** 60 H1 61 C5
**Hallidays Point NSW** 23 C12
**Hallora VIC** 37 H14
**Halls Creek WA** 79 B13 81 J12
**Halls Gap VIC** 38 C6
**Hallston VIC** 44 F6
**Halton NSW** 23 C10
**Hambidge Con Park SA** 64 F6
**Hamel WA** 72 F7
**Hamelin Bay WA** 73 K13 74 H1
**Hamelin Pool Marine Nat Res WA** 76 B2 78 K2
**Hamersley WA** 71 D3 72 C2
**Hamilton QLD** 3 D4 12 D5
**Hamilton SA** 62 E5 65 H10
**Hamilton TAS** 53 E9
**Hamilton VIC** 38 F5
**Hamilton Hill WA** 71 K2
**Hamilton Island QLD** 9 C8
**Hamley Bridge SA** 62 F5 65 H10
**Hammond SA** 62 F1 65 D9
**Hammond Island QLD** 16 B2
**Hampshire TAS** 54 E5
**Hampton NSW** 22 G6
**Hampton QLD** 7 F11
**Hanging Rock NSW** 23 A9 25 K8
**Hann River Roadhouse QLD** 11 A10 16 K4
**Hann Tableland Nat Park QLD** 11 D12
**Hannahs Bridge NSW** 22 B6
**Hannan NSW** 29 D11
**Hannaville QLD** 9 D8
**Hansborough SA** 62 E5 65 H10
**Hanson SA** 62 E4 65 G10
**Hansonville VIC** 42 D6
**Hanwood NSW** 29 F11 30 A2
**Happy Valley QLD** 7 B13
**Happy Valley SA** 60 J2 61 C6
**Happy Valley VIC** 28 G4 40 C7 43 D8 43 H9 46 B4
**Happy Valley Reservoir SA** 60 J2 61 C6
**Harcourt VIC** 39 C12
**Harden NSW** 22 K3 30 B7
**Hardwicke Bay SA** 62 H6 65 J8
**Harefield NSW** 29 H13 30 C5
**Harford TAS** 55 E8
**Hargraves NSW** 22 E5
**Harlin QLD** 7 F11
**Harrietville VIC** 30 J4 43 F9
**Harrington NSW** 23 B13
**Harris Nat Res WA** 75 E8
**Harrismith WA** 74 E6
**Harrisville QLD** 5 H11
**Harrogate SA** 60 G7 62 E7 65 J10
**Harrow VIC** 38 D3
**Hart SA** 62 F4 65 G10
**Hartley NSW** 22 G7
**Hartley SA** 60 K7
**Harts Range NT** 91 E10
**Hartz Mountains Nat Park TAS** 53 H8
**Harvey WA** 73 G8 74 F3
**Harwood NSW** 25 D13
**Haslam SA** 64 D3
**Hassell Nat Park WA** 74 J7
**Hastings TAS** 53 J9
**Hastings VIC** 37 J9 39 H14 44 E2
**Hastings Point NSW** 25 A14
**Hat Head Nat Park NSW** 25 J12
**Hatfield NSW** 28 E6
**Hatherleigh SA** 63 C13
**Hattah VIC** 28 G4 40 C5
**Hattah-Kulkyne Nat Park VIC** 28 G4 40 C5
**Hatton Vale QLD** 5 K9
**Havanna Island QLD** 11 G14
**Havelock VIC** 39 C10
**Haven VIC** 38 B5
**Hawker SA** 65 C10
**Hawkesbury Island QLD** 16 B2
**Hawkesdale VIC** 38 G6
**Hawkesdale West VIC** 38 G5
**Hawknest Island NT** 87 F12
**Hawks Nest NSW** 23 E11
**Hawley Beach TAS** 55 E8
**Hawthorn VIC** 35 D4
**Hawthorndene SA** 59 K5
**Hawthorne QLD** 3 E4
**Hay NSW** 29 F8 41 B13
**Hay Point QLD** 9 D8
**Haydens Bog VIC** 47 A10
**Hayes TAS** 50 A2 53 F9
**Hayes Creek NT** 85 F3 86 F4
**Hayman Island QLD** 9 B8
**Haysdale VIC** 28 G5 41 D8
**Hazelbrook NSW** 21 J9
**Hazeldean QLD** 4 J4
**Hazelmere WA** 71 E7
**Hazelwood VIC** 44 E7 46 F1
**Hazelwood Island QLD** 9 B8
**Hazelwood Park SA** 59 G5
**Healesville VIC** 37 B11 42 J4 44 A4
**Hearson WA** 82 C1
**Heartlea WA** 73 D13
**Heath Hill VIC** 37 H13
**Heathcote NSW** 21 C11
**Heathcote VIC** 39 B13 42 F1
**Heathcote Nat Park NSW** 19 K2 21 D11 23 J8 31 A13
**Heathfield SA** 59 K7 60 H4 61 B7
**Heathlands QLD** 16 D2
**Heathmere VIC** 38 H4
**Heathwood QLD** 3 J3
**Hebden NSW** 23 D9
**Hebel QLD** 6 K3 27 B14
**Hectorville SA** 59 F6
**Heidelberg VIC** 35 C4 37 C8
**Heirisson Island WA** 70 C4
**Heka TAS** 54 E6
**Helena Reservoir WA** 72 E3
**Helensburgh NSW** 21 C12 23 J9 31 A13
**Helensvale QLD** 5 C12
**Helenvale QLD** 11 B12 16 K7
**Helidon QLD** 7 G11
**Hell Hole Gorge Nat Park QLD** 13 J10 15 B10
**Hells Gate Roadhouse QLD** 10 E2
**Hellyer TAS** 54 C4
**Hellyer Gorge State Res TAS** 54 E4
**Hemmant QLD** 3 E6
**Henbury Meteorite Con Res NT** 90 G7
**Hendon QLD** 7 H11
**Henley Beach SA** 59 F2 60 F1 61 A5
**Henley Brook WA** 71 B6
**Henrietta TAS** 54 E4
**Henry Freycinet Harbour WA** 76 C2
**Hensley Park VIC** 38 E5
**Henty NSW** 29 J12 30 E4
**Henty VIC** 38 F3
**Hepburn Springs VIC** 39 D11
**Herberton QLD** 11 E12
**Heritage Park QLD** 3 K5
**Hermannsburg NT** 90 F6
**Hermidale NSW** 27 H12
**Hernani NSW** 25 G11
**Herne Hill WA** 71 C7
**Heron Island QLD** 9 H12
**Herons Creek NSW** 23 A13
**Herrick TAS** 55 D12
**Hervey Bay QLD** 7 A12 7 B13
**Hesso SA** 65 D8
**Hester WA** 73 E12
**Hewetsons Mill NSW** 25 A11
**Hewitt NSW** 21 F9
**Hexham VIC** 38 G7
**Hexham Island QLD** 9 E10
**Heybridge TAS** 54 D6
**Heyfield VIC** 45 C9 46 E3
**Heywood VIC** 38 H4
**Heywood Islands WA** 80 C7
**Hicks Island QLD** 16 D3
**Hidden Island WA** 80 E5
**Hidden Vale QLD** 5 K10
**Hidden Valley QLD** 11 G13
**Hidden Valley Nat Park WA** 81 D14
**Higginsville WA** 75 C13 77 K11 83 G1
**Higginsville Mine WA** 75 C13 77 K11 83 G1
**High Island QLD** 11 D13
**High Peak Island QLD** 9 E10
**High Range NSW** 22 J7 31 B12
**High Wycombe WA** 71 F7
**Highbury SA** 59 E6 60 F3
**Highbury WA** 73 A8 74 F5
**Highclere TAS** 54 E5
**Highcroft TAS** 51 H11 53 H12
**Higher McDonald NSW** 20 F3
**Highgate WA** 71 F4
**Highlands VIC** 42 G3
**Highton VIC** 36 G2
**Hilgay VIC** 38 E3
**Hill End NSW** 22 E5
**Hill End VIC** 44 D6 46 E1
**Hillarys WA** 71 B1
**Hillbank SA** 59 B6
**Hillcrest QLD** 3 K4
**Hillcrest SA** 59 E5
**Hillgrove NSW** 25 H10
**Hillier SA** 60 C3
**Hillman WA** 73 C9
**Hillside VIC** 43 K11 45 C12 46 D5
**Hillston NSW** 29 D10
**Hilltop NSW** 21 G14
**Hilltown SA** 62 F4 65 G10
**Hillview NSW** 27 J10
**Hillview QLD** 5 E14
**Hillwood TAS** 55 E9 56 E4
**Hilton QLD** 10 K3 12 A3
**Hilton WA** 71 J2
**Hinchinbrook Island QLD** 11 F13
**Hinchinbrook Island Nat Park QLD** 11 F13
**Hincks Con Park SA** 64 G6
**Hindmarsh SA** 59 F3 60 F2
**Hindmarsh Island SA** 63 E8
**Hindmarsh Valley SA** 61 H6
**Hinnomunjie VIC** 30 J6 43 F11 46 A6
**Hivesville QLD** 7 D10
**Hiway Inn NT** 86 K7 88 B7
**HMAS Cerberus VIC** 37 J9
**Hobart TAS** 49 C2 50 C6 53 F10
**Hobart CBD TAS** 49
**Hobbys Yards NSW** 22 G5
**Hobson Bay VIC** 36 D7
**Hoddles Creek VIC** 37 D12
**Hodgson QLD** 6 E4
**Hoffman WA** 73 F8
**Holbrook NSW** 29 J13 30 E5
**Holden Hill SA** 59 E6
**Holdfast Bay SA** 59 H2 60 G1 61 A5
**Holey Plains State Park VIC** 45 E10 46 F3
**Holgate NSW** 20 B4
**Holland Landing VIC** 45 D12 46 E5
**Holland Park QLD** 3 F4
**Hollow Tree TAS** 53 E9
**Holmwood NSW** 22 H3
**Holsworthy NSW** 19 H1 21 D10
**Holt Rock WA** 75 E9
**Holts Flat NSW** 31 H9
**Holwell TAS** 55 E8 56 E2
**Home Hill QLD** 8 A6
**Home Rule NSW** 22 D6
**Homebush NSW** 21 D9
**Homebush QLD** 9 D8
**Homebush Bay NSW** 19 E3
**Homecroft VIC** 40 K6
**Homerton VIC** 38 G4
**Homestead QLD** 8 B3 11 K13
**Homevale Nat Park QLD** 8 D7
**Homewood VIC** 42 G3
**Hook Island QLD** 9 B8
**Hookina SA** 65 C9
**Hope Vale QLD** 11 A12 16 K6
**Hope Valley SA** 59 D6 60 E3
**Hopefield NSW** 29 K11 30 F3 47 A7
**Hopetoun VIC** 28 J4 40 G6
**Hopetoun WA** 75 G10
**Hopetoun West VIC** 40 G5
**Hopevale VIC** 28 K4 40 H5
**Hoppers Crossing VIC** 36 D5
**Horfield VIC** 41 H11
**Horn Island QLD** 16 B2
**Hornsby NSW** 19 B3 20 D7 23 H9
**Hornsby Heights NSW** 19 B4
**Horrocks WA** 76 E3
**Horsham VIC** 38 B5
**Horsley Park NSW** 21 E9
**Horsnell Gully Con Park SA** 59 G7 60 G3 61 A7
**Hoskinstown NSW** 31 E10
**Hoskyn Islands QLD** 9 H13
**Hotspur VIC** 38 G3
**Hotspur Island QLD** 9 D10
**Houtman Abrolhos WA** 76 F2
**Howard QLD** 7 B12
**Howard Island NT** 87 C10
**Howard Springs NT** 85 C2 86 D4
**Howden TAS** 50 F5 53 G10
**Howes Valley NSW** 23 E8
**Howick Group Nat Park QLD** 16 H6
**Howick Island QLD** 16 H6
**Howlong NSW** 29 K12 30 F3 43 A8
**Howqua VIC** 30 K2 42 G6 46 B1
**Howqua Hills VIC** 42 G7 46 A1
**Howth TAS** 54 D6
**Hoxton Park NSW** 21 E9
**Hoyleton SA** 62 F4 65 G10
**Hugh River NT** 91 G8
**Hughenden QLD** 8 C1 11 K10 13 A10
**Hughes SA** 68 H2 83 F7
**Hull Heads QLD** 11 F13
**Humbug Point Con Area TAS** 55 E14
**Hume Weir NSW** 29 K12 30 F4 43 B9
**Humevale VIC** 37 A9 39 E14 42 H3 44 A2
**Humpty Doo NT** 85 C2 86 D4
**Humula NSW** 29 J14 30 E6
**Hungerford QLD** 15 K10 26 B7
**Hunter VIC** 41 K12
**Hunter Island TAS** 54 A1
**Hunters Hill NSW** 19 E5 21 C8
**Huntingdale WA** 71 K6
**Huntly VIC** 39 A12
**Huonville TAS** 50 F2 53 G9
**Hurstbridge VIC** 35 A6 37 B9 39 E14 42 J3 44 A2
**Hurstville NSW** 19 H4 21 C9
**Huskisson NSW** 31 D13
**Hyden WA** 75 D8
**Hynam SA** 38 C1 63 B12


## I


**Iandra NSW** 22 H3 30 A7
**Ida Bay TAS** 53 J9
**Idalia Nat Park QLD** 8 K2 13 H11 15 A11
**Iguana Creek VIC** 43 K10 45 B12 46 D5
**Ilbilbie QLD** 9 E8
**Ilbunga SA** 66 B4 91 E3 91 K10
**Ilford NSW** 22 E6
**Ilfracombe QLD** 8 H1 13 F11
**Ilfraville TAS** 55 E9 56 D2
**Illabarook VIC** 39 F10
**Illabo NSW** 29 G14 30 C6
**Illalong Creek NSW** 22 K3 31 B8
**Illamurta Con Res NT** 90 G6
**Illawarra Coast NSW** 31 D13
**Illawong WA** 76 G3
**Illili NT** 90 E5
**Illilliwa NSW** 29 F9 41 B14
**Illowa VIC** 38 H6
**Illpurta NT** 90 G6
**Iltur SA** 68 C3
**Iluka NSW** 25 D13
**Ilykuwaratja SA** 66 A1 68 A6 90 K7
**Imanpa NT** 90 H6
**Imbil QLD** 7 E12
**Imintji WA** 79 A11 81 G8
**Immarna SA** 68 H5
**Impadna NT** 91 H8
**Inala QLD** 3 H2 5 F9
**Inarki SA** 68 A2 90 K2
**Indented Head VIC** 36 G5 39 G13
**Indooroopilly QLD** 3 F3
**Indulkana (Iwantja) SA** 66 C1 68 B7
**Ingebyra NSW** 31 H8 43 E14
**Ingham QLD** 11 G13
**Ingle Farm SA** 59 D5 60 E3
**Ingleburn NSW** 21 E10
**Inglegar NSW** 27 H14
**Ingleside NSW** 19 B6 20 B6
**Inglewood QLD** 7 J9 25 A8
**Inglewood SA** 60 E4
**Inglewood VIC** 39 A10
**Inglewood WA** 71 E4
**Inglis Island NT** 87 C12
**Ingliston VIC** 36 B2
**Ininti NT** 79 G14 90 E1
**Injarrtnama NT** 90 F7
**Injinoo QLD** 16 B2
**Injune QLD** 6 C4
**Inkerman QLD** 8 A6
**Inkerman SA** 62 G5 65 H9
**Inman Valley SA** 61 H5 63 F8 65 K9
**Innaloo WA** 71 E2
**Innamincka SA** 14 G3 67 E14
**Innamincka Reg Res SA** 14 G3 67 D13
**Inner Sister Island TAS** 55 A8
**Innes Nat Park SA** 62 J7 64 K7
**Innisfail QLD** 11 E13
**Innisplain QLD** 5 F14
**Innot Hot Springs QLD** 11 E12
**Interlaken TAS** 53 C10 55 K10
**Inveralochy NSW** 31 C10
**Inverell NSW** 25 E8
**Invergordon VIC** 42 B4
**Inverleigh VIC** 36 G1 39 G11
**Inverloch VIC** 44 G5
**Investigator Group Con Park SA** 64 G3
**Investigator Strait SA** 63 J8
**Iona VIC** 37 G13 44 D4
**Ipolera NT** 90 F6
**Ipswich QLD** 5 G9 7 G12
**Irishtown TAS** 54 C3
**Irishtown WA** 72 D1
**Irkini NT** 68 A1 79 K14 83 B7 90 K2
**Iron Baron SA** 62 J2 65 E8
**Iron Knob SA** 62 J1 65 E8
**Iron Range QLD** 16 F3
**Iron Range Nat Park QLD** 16 E3
**Ironbank SA** 59 K6 60 H3 61 B7
**Ironwood Bore SA** 68 B5
**Irrapatana SA** 66 G7
**Irrewarra VIC** 39 H10
**Irrewillipe VIC** 39 H9
**Irrmarne NT** 91 C12
**Irvinebank QLD** 11 E12
**Irymple VIC** 28 F3 40 A5
**Isabella NSW** 22 H5
**Isis TAS** 53 A10 55 H10
**Isis Junction QLD** 7 B12
**Isisford QLD** 8 J1 13 G11
**Isla Gorge Nat Park QLD** 6 B7
**Island Bend NSW** 31 G8 43 C14
**Island Lagoon SA** 64 B7
**Isle of the Dead TAS** 51 H13
**Isle Woodah NT** 87 E12
**Israelite Bay WA** 83 J3
**Ivanhoe NSW** 28 C7
**Iveragh QLD** 9 J11


## J


**Jabiru NT** 85 D7 86 D6
**Jabuk SA** 63 C8 65 K12
**Jack River VIC** 45 G8 46 H2
**Jack Smith Lake VIC** 46 G4
**Jackadgery NSW** 25 E11
**Jackeys Marsh TAS** 55 G8 56 K1
**Jackie Junction WA** 79 K12
**Jackson QLD** 6 E6
**Jackson Oil Field QLD** 14 G6
**Jacobs Well QLD** 5 B11
**Jacobs Well WA** 72 A4
**Jalbarragup WA** 73 H12
**Jallukar VIC** 38 D7
**Jallumba VIC** 38 C4
**Jam Jerrup VIC** 37 J11
**Jamberoo NSW** 23 K8 31 B13
**Jambin QLD** 9 J10
**Jamboree Heights QLD** 3 G2
**Jamestown SA** 62 F3 65 F10
**Jamieson VIC** 30 K2 42 H6 46 B1
**Jamieson (Mantamaru) WA** 79 K13 83 A6
**Jamisontown NSW** 21 G8
**Jan Juc VIC** 36 J2 39 H12
**Jancourt VIC** 39 H8
**Jancourt East VIC** 39 H8
**Jandabup WA** 71 A4
**Jandakot WA** 71 K4 72 G4
**Jandowae QLD** 7 E9
**Jannali NSW** 19 J3
**Japoonvale QLD** 11 E13
**Jaraga QLD** 8 B6
**Jardee WA** 73 E14
**Jardin Valley QLD** 8 C1 13 A10
**Jardine River Nat Park QLD** 16 C2
**Jarklin VIC** 41 K11
**Jarra Jarra NT** 88 J7 90 A7
**Jarrahdale WA** 72 F5 74 D3
**Jarrahwood WA** 73 G11 74 G3
**Jasper Hill/Dominion WA** 77 F11
**Jaspers Brush NSW** 31 C13
**Jeetho VIC** 37 J13
**Jeffcott North VIC** 41 K8
**Jennacubbine WA** 72 C1
**Jennapullin WA** 72 C1
**Jenolan Caves NSW** 22 H6
**Jeogla NSW** 25 H10
**Jeparit VIC** 40 J4
**Jerangle NSW** 31 F10
**Jerdacuttup Lakes Nat Res WA** 75 G10
**Jericho QLD** 8 H4 13 F13
**Jericho TAS** 53 D10
**Jericho VIC** 42 J6 44 A7 46 C1
**Jerilderie NSW** 29 H10 30 D1
**Jerramungup WA** 75 G8
**Jerrawa NSW** 31 C9
**Jerrys Plains NSW** 23 D9
**Jerseyville NSW** 25 J12
**Jervis Bay NSW** 31 D13
**Jervois SA** 62 D7 65 K11
**Jetsonville TAS** 55 D11
**Jiggalong WA** 78 G7
**Jil Jil VIC** 28 K5 41 H8
**Jilbadji Nat Res WA** 75 C9 77 K9
**Jilliby NSW** 20 C2
**Ji-Marda NT** 87 C9
**Jimaringle NSW** 28 H7 41 F11
**Jimbalakudunj WA** 79 B11 80 H7
**Jimblebar Mine WA** 78 G7 82 H7
**Jimboomba QLD** 5 E11 7 H13
**Jimbour QLD** 7 F9
**Jimenbuen NSW** 31 H8
**Jimna QLD** 4 K1 7 E12
**Jindabyne NSW** 31 H8
**Jindalee QLD** 3 G2 5 F8
**Jindera NSW** 29 K12 30 F4 43 A9
**Jindivick VIC** 37 F14 44 D5
**Jindivick North VIC** 37 F14
**Jindivick West VIC** 37 F14
**Jindong WA** 73 J11
**Jingalup WA** 73 B12
**Jingellic NSW** 29 K14 30 F6 43 A11
**Jingera NSW** 31 F10
**Jingili NT** 84 B3
**Jinglemoney NSW** 31 E10
**Jip Jip Con Park SA** 63 C10
**Jitarning WA** 74 E6
**Joadja NSW** 22 K7 31 B12
**Joanna SA** 38 C1 63 B12
**Joel VIC** 39 C8
**Johanna VIC** 39 K9
**John Forrest Nat Park WA** 72 F3 74 C3 76 K5
**Johnburgh SA** 62 E1 65 D10
**Johns River NSW** 23 B13
**Jolimont WA** 71 F3
**Jondaryan QLD** 7 F10
**Joondalup WA** 71 A2
**Joondanna WA** 71 E3
**Josbury WA** 73 C8
**Joseph Banks (Round Hill Head) Con Park QLD** 9 J12
**Joseph Bonaparte Gulf NT WA** 81 B14 86 G1
**Josephville QLD** 5 F13
**Joycedale QLD** 8 H4 13 F13
**Joyces Creek VIC** 39 C11
**Judbury TAS** 50 E1 53 G9
**Jueburra QLD** 12 B4
**Jugiong NSW** 30 C7
**Julatten QLD** 11 C12
**Julia SA** 62 E5 65 G10
**Julia Creek QLD** 10 K7 12 A7
**Julius River Forest Res TAS** 54 E2
**Jumbunna VIC** 37 K13 44 F5
**Jundah QLD** 13 H9 15 A8
**Junee NSW** 29 G13 30 C6
**Junee Reefs NSW** 22 K1 29 G13 30 B6
**Jung VIC** 38 A6
**Junjuwa WA** 79 B11 81 H9
**Junortoun VIC** 39 B12

Jurema QLD 8 G6
Jurien WA 76 H3

## K

Kaarimba VIC 42 B3
Kaban QLD 11 E12
Kabelbara QLD 8 G6
Kabra QLD 9 H10
Kadina SA 62 H4 65 G8
Kadnook VIC 38 C3
Kadungle NSW 22 D1 29 B13
Kagara QLD 5 F11
Kaimkillenbun QLD 7 F10
Kainton SA 62 G5 65 G9
Kainton Corner SA 62 G5 65 G9
Kairi QLD 11 D12
Kaiserstuhl Con Park SA 60 B7
Kajabbi QLD 10 J4
Kajuligah Nat Res NSW 29 B8
Kakadu Holiday Village NT 85 D6 86 D6
Kakadu Nat Park NT 85 C6 86 D6
Kalamunda WA 72 F3 74 C3 76 K5
Kalamunda Nat Park WA 72 F3 74 C3 76 K5
Kalang NSW 25 G12
Kalangadoo SA 38 E1 63 B13
Kalannie WA 76 H6
Kalarka QLD 9 F9
Kalaru NSW 31 H11
Kalbar QLD 5 J12 7 H12
Kalbarri WA 76 D2
Kalgoorlie WA 75 A12 77 J11 83 F1
Kalimna West VIC 43 K12 45 C14 46 E7
Kalka SA 68 A1 79 K14 83 B7 90 K1
Kalkadoon Mine QLD 10 J4
Kalkallo VIC 36 A7 39 E14 42 J2 44 A1
Kalkaringji NT 88 D3
Kalkee VIC 38 A5
Kallangur QLD 4 E6
Kallaroo WA 71 B1
Kallista VIC 37 D10
Kalorama VIC 37 D10
Kalpi SA 68 C5
Kalpowar QLD 7 A10 9 K11
Kalumburu WA 81 B10
Kalyan SA 62 C7 65 J12
Kamarah NSW 29 F12 30 A4
Kamarooka VIC 39 A12 41 K12
Kamarooka State Park VIC 39 A12
Kambalda WA 75 B13 77 J11 83 G1
Kambalda Nat Res WA 75 B12 77 J11 83 G1
Kambalda West WA 75 B13 77 J11 83 F1
Kamber NSW 22 A3 24 K2
Kamona TAS 55 E12
Kampurarr Pirti WA 79 K13 83 B6
Kanaguik VIC 38 C4
Kanangra-Boyd Nat Park NSW 22 H6 31 A11
Kandanga QLD 7 D12
Kandat Djaru WA 79 C14 81 K13
Kandos NSW 22 E6
Kangarilla SA 60 K3 61 D7 62 F7 65 J10
Kangaroo Creek Res SA 60 F4
Kangaroo Flat SA 60 B3
Kangaroo Flat VIC 39 B12
Kangaroo Ground VIC 35 B7 37 B9
Kangaroo Island SA 5 B10
Kangaroo Island SA 63 J9
Kangaroo Island TAS 54 B1
Kangaroo Point QLD 2 C4
Kangaroo Valley NSW 22 K7 31 C12
Kangarooby NSW 22 G3
Kangawall VIC 38 B3
Kangy Angy NSW 20 C3
Kaniva SA 63 A10
Kaniva VIC 40 K2
Kanmantoo SA 60 H7
Kanowna WA 77 H11 83 F1
Kanpa WA 79 H11 83 B4
Kanpi SA 68 A2 90 K3
Kanumbra VIC 42 F4
Kanunnah Bridge TAS 54 D2
Kanwal NSW 20 B2
Kanya VIC 38 A8
Kanyaka Ruins SA 65 C9
Kaoota TAS 50 F4 53 G10
Kapinnie SA 64 G5
Kapunda SA 62 G5 65 H10
Kara Kara State Park VIC 39 B9
Karabeal VIC 38 E5
Karadoc VIC 28 F4 40 B5
Karana Downs QLD 5 G8
Karanja TAS 53 E9
Karara QLD 7 H10 25 A9
Karatta SA 63 J9
Karawatha QLD 3 J5
Karawinna VIC 28 F3 40 B3
Kardella VIC 37 K14
Kardella South VIC 37 K14
Kardinya WA 71 J3

Kareela NSW 19 J3 21 C10
Kariah VIC 39 H8
Karijini Nat Park WA 78 G5 82 F4
Kariong NSW 20 C4
Karkoo SA 64 G5
Karlgarin WA 75 D8
Karonie WA 75 A14 77 J12 83 F2
Karonie Mine WA 75 A14 77 J12 83 F2
Karook VIC 39 A14 42 D2
Karoola TAS 55 E10 56 E5
Karoon QLD 8 C2 13 A11
Karoonda SA 62 C7 65 J12
Karping VIC 72 B6
Karragarra Island QLD 5 B9
Karrakatta WA 71 G2
Karramomus North VIC 42 D4
Karratha WA 78 E4 82 C2
Karratha Roadhouse WA 78 E4 82 C1
Karridale WA 73 J13 74 H2
Karrinyup WA 71 D2
Karrku WA 79 J13
Karroun Hill Nat Res WA 76 G7
Kars Springs NSW 23 B8
Karte SA 28 H1 62 B7 65 J13
Karte Con Park SA 28 H1 62 B7 65 K13
Karuah NSW 23 D11
Karukaki NT 79 J14 90 H2
Karween VIC 28 F2 40 B2
Katamatite VIC 29 K10 30 F1 42 B4
Katandra VIC 42 C4
Katanning WA 74 G6
Katoomba NSW 21 K9
Katrine WA 72 D2
Kattyoong VIC 28 H3 40 E4
Katunga VIC 29 K10 30 F1 42 A4
Katyil VIC 40 K5
Kau Rock Nat Res WA 75 F14 83 J1
Kawana Waters QLD 4 D1
Kawarren VIC 39 J10
Kayena TAS 55 E9 56 D3
Kedron QLD 3 C4 4 E7
Keep River Nat Park NT 81 E14 86 J1 88 A1
Keera NSW 24 F7
Keilor VIC 35 B1 36 C6 39 F13 42 J1 44 B1
Keilor North VIC 35 B1
Keith SA 63 B10
Kellalac VIC 40 K6
Kellatier SA 54 D4
Kellerberrin WA 74 C6 76 K7
Kellevie TAS 51 B12 53 F12
Kellidie Bay Con Park SA 64 H5
Kelly Hill Caves Con Park SA 63 J9
Kellys Creek NSW 22 H3
Kellyville NSW 19 B1 20 E7
Kelmscott WA 72 F4 74 D3
Kelso TAS 55 D8 56 C2
Kelvin NSW 24 H6
Kelvin Grove QLD 2 A2 3 E3
Kembla Heights NSW 21 D14
Kemps Creek NSW 21 F9
Kempsey NSW 25 J12
Kempton TAS 53 E10
Kendall NSW 23 B13
Kendenup WA 74 J6
Kenebri NSW 24 H3
Kenilworth QLD 7 E12
Kenley VIC 41 D9
Kenmare VIC 40 H5
Kenmore QLD 3 F2 5 F8
Kenmore Hills QLD 3 F2
Kenmore Park SA 68 A2
Kennedy QLD 11 F13
Kennedy Range Nat Park WA 78 H2
Kennedys Creek VIC 39 J9
Kenneth Stirling Con Park SA 60 G4
Kennett River VIC 39 K10
Kennys Creek NSW 22 J4 31 B9
Kensington NSW 21 B9
Kensington SA 59 G5 60 G3 61 A7
Kensington VIC 35 D3
Kensington WA 71 G4
Kensington Gardens SA 59 G6
Kent Town SA 58 C3
Kentbruck VIC 38 H1
Kenthurst NSW 19 B2
Kentlyn Ruse NSW 21 E11
Kenton Valley SA 60 F5
Kentucky NSW 25 H9
Kentville SA 5 K8
Kenwick WA 71 J6
Keperra QLD 3 D2 4 F7
Keppel Bay QLD 9 H11
Keppel Bay Islands Nat Park QLD 9 G11
Keppel Sands QLD 9 H10
Keppoch SA 63 B11
Kerang VIC 28 J7 41 G10
Kerang East VIC 41 H11
Kerang South VIC 41 H11
Kerein Hills NSW 29 B12
Kergunyah VIC 30 G4 43 C9
Kernot VIC 37 K12 44 F14
Kerrabee NSW 22 D7

Kerrisdale VIC 42 G3
Kerriwah NSW 27 K13 29 B13
Kerrs Creek NSW 22 E4
Kerry QLD 5 E13
Kersbrook SA 60 E5 62 E6 65 J10
Keswick SA 58 D1
Kettering TAS 50 H5 53 H10
Kevin QLD 64 C1 68 K6
Kevington VIC 30 K2 42 H6 46 B1
Kew NSW 23 B13
Kew VIC 35 D4
Kewdale WA 71 G6
Kewell VIC 38 A6
Keyneton SA 62 E6 65 H11
Keysborough VIC 35 H6 37 F9
Keysbrook WA 72 F5
Khancoban NSW 29 K14 30 G7 43 C13
Kholo QLD 5 H8
Ki Ki SA 63 D8 65 K11
Kia Ora VIC 38 E7
Kiacatoo NSW 29 C12
Kiah NSW 31 K11 47 B14
Kialla NSW 22 K5 31 B10
Kialla VIC 42 D3
Kiama NSW 23 K8 31 B13
Kiamal VIC 28 H4 40 D5
Kiandra NSW 31 F8 43 A14
Kianga NSW 31 G11
Kianga QLD 9 K9
Kiata VIC 40 K4
Kidman Park SA 59 F2
Kidston QLD 11 G10
Kielpa SA 64 F6
Kiewa VIC 30 G4 43 C9
Kikoira NSW 29 D12
Kilburn SA 59 E4 60 F2
Kilcunda VIC 44 G4
Kilcunda Road VIC 37 K13
Kilkenny SA 59 F3
Kilkivan QLD 7 D11
Killabakh NSW 23 B12
Killara NSW 19 D5 20 C7
Killara VIC 37 C11
Killarney QLD 7 J11 25 A11
Killarney VIC 38 H6
Killarney Heights NSW 19 D6 20 C7
Killarney Vale NSW 20 B3
Killcare NSW 20 B5 23 G9
Killi Killi WA 79 D14
Killiecrankie TAS 55 A8
Kilmany VIC 45 D10 46 F3
Kilmore VIC 39 D14 42 G2
Kimba SA 62 K2 64 E6
Kimberley TAS 54 F7
Kimbriki NSW 23 B12
Kimburra QLD 8 C3 11 K12
Kin Kin QLD 7 D12
Kinalung NSW 26 K3 28 A3
Kinchega Nat Park NSW 26 K3 28 B3
Kinchela Creek NSW 25 J12
Kincumber NSW 20 B4
Kindee NSW 23 A12 25 K11
Kindred TAS 54 E7
King Ash Bay NT 87 K12 89 A12
King George Island TAS 51 E12
King Island VIC 16 H5
King Leopold Ranges Con Park WA 81 G9
King Sound WA 79 A10 80 F5
King Valley VIC 30 H3 42 E7
Kingaroy QLD 7 E10
Kingfisher Bay QLD 7 B13
Kingfisher Island WA 80 E6
Kinglake VIC 37 A10 42 J3 44 A3
Kinglake Central VIC 37 A10 42 H3 44 A3
Kinglake East VIC 37 A10
Kinglake Nat Park VIC 37 A10 39 D14 42 H3 44 A3
Kinglake West VIC 42 H3
Kingoonya SA 64 A5
Kingower VIC 39 A10
Kings Cross NSW 18 C3 21 B8
Kings Langley NSW 19 C1
Kings Plains Nat Park NSW 25 E9
Kingsborough QLD 11 D12
Kingscliff NSW 7 J13 25 A14
Kingscote SA 63 H8 65 K8
Kingsdale NSW 22 K6 31 B10
Kingsford NSW 19 G6 21 B9
Kingsholme QLD 5 C11
Kingsley WA 71 B2
Kingston ACT 32 D4
Kingston QLD 3 K5 5 E9
Kingston SA 50 E5 53 G10
Kingston VIC 39 D11
Kingston OM SA 62 B5 65 H12
Kingston SE SA 63 D11
Kingstown NSW 25 G8
Kingsvale NSW 22 J2 31 A9
Kingswood NSW 21 H9
Kingswood SA 59 H4
Kinimakatka VIC 40 K3
Kinnabulla VIC 40 H7
Kioloa NSW 31 E12
Kirkstall VIC 38 H6
Kirrawee NSW 19 J3
Kirup WA 73 H3 74 G3
Kitchener NSW 77 J14 83 F3
Kithbrook VIC 42 E5

Kiwirrkurra WA 79 G13
Klemzig SA 59 E5
Knight Island QLD 9 D9
Knorrit Flat NSW 23 B11
Knowsley VIC 39 B13
Knoxfield VIC 37 D9
Kobyboyn VIC 42 F3
Koetong VIC 29 K13 30 G5 43 B11
Kogan QLD 7 F8
Kogarah NSW 19 H4
Koimbo VIC 28 H5 40 D7
Kojonup WA 73 A11 74 G5
Kokotungo QLD 9 J9
Koloona NSW 24 E7
Koloro VIC 38 G7
Komungla NSW 31 C10
Kondalilla Nat Park QLD 4 G1
Kondinin WA 74 D7
Kongal SA 63 B10
Kongorong SA 63 B14
Kongwak VIC 44 F5
Konongwootong VIC 38 E4
Kononup SA 8 K1 13 H10 15 A10
Kookaburra NSW 25 J11
Kookynie WA 77 G11 83 E1
Koolamarra QLD 10 J4
Koolan SA 80 E6
Koolan Island WA 80 E6
Koolewong NSW 20 C4
Koolgera Con Res SA 64 D4
Kooloonong VIC 28 G5 41 D8
Kooltandra QLD 9 H9
Koolunga SA 62 F3 65 F9
Koolyanobbing WA 75 A9 77 J9
Koombooloomba QLD 11 E12
Koonda VIC 28 H2 40 E3 42 D4
Koondoola WA 71 C4
Koondrook VIC 28 J7 41 G11
Koongawa SA 64 F6
Koongie Park WA 79 C13 81 J11
Koonibba SA 64 D3 68 J6
Koonibba Community SA 64 C2 68 K7
Koonoomoo VIC 42 A4
Koonunga SA 62 E5 65 H10
Koonwarra VIC 44 G6
Koonya TAS 51 G12 53 G12
Kooralbyn QLD 5 G13
Koorarawalyee WA 75 B10
Koorawatha NSW 22 H3
Koorboora QLD 11 E11
Koorda WA 74 A5 76 J6
Kooreh VIC 39 A9
Kooringal QLD 4 B7
Koorkab VIC 28 G5 41 D8
Koorlong VIC 28 F3 40 A5
Kooroocheang VIC 39 C11
Kootingal NSW 25 J8
Koo-wee-rup VIC 37 H11 44 E4
Koo-wee-rup North VIC 37 G11
Kooyoora State Park VIC 39 A10
Kopi SA 64 F5
Koppio SA 64 H6
Korbel WA 74 C7 76 K7
Koriella VIC 30 K1 42 G4
Korobeit VIC 36 A3
Koroit VIC 38 H6
Korong Vale VIC 41 K10
Koroop VIC 41 G11
Korora NSW 25 G9
Korrak Korrak VIC 41 G10
Korumburra VIC 37 K13 44 F5
Korumburra South VIC 37 K14
Korunye SA 60 A1
Kosciuszko Nat Park NSW 30 G7 43 C14
Kotta VIC 41 J12
Kotupna VIC 41 J14 42 B2
Koumala QLD 9 E8
Koumala South QLD 9 E8
Kowanyama QLD 10 A7 16 K1
Kowguran QLD 6 D7
Kowtah WA 77 F11 83 D1
Kowulka SA 64 C1 68 K6
Koyuga VIC 41 J14 42 B2
Krambach NSW 23 C12
Kroombit Tops Nat Park QLD 9 J11
Krowera VIC 37 K12 44 F4
Kudardup WA 73 J13 74 H2
Kudla SA 60 C3
Kukerin WA 74 E7
Kulai NT 79 J14 90 H1
Kulde SA 62 D7 65 K11
Kulgera NT 66 A1 68 A6 90 J7
Kulgera Rail Head NT 66 A2 68 A7 90 J7
Kulikup WA 73 C11
Kulin WA 74 E7
Kulingalimpa NT 88 F4
Kulitjara SA 68 B5
Kulja WA 76 H6
Kulkami SA 62 B7 65 K12
Kulliparu Con Park SA 64 E4
Kulnine VIC 28 F2 40 A3
Kulnine East VIC 40 A3
Kulnura NSW 20 D2 23 F9
Kulpara SA 62 G5 65 G9
Kulpi QLD 7 F10
Kulpitarra NT 90 F5
Kultanaby SA 64 A5
Kulwin VIC 28 H4 40 E6
Kulyalling WA 72 G7
Kumarina Roadhouse WA 78 J6 82 K6
Kumarl WA 75 E12 83 H1

Kumbarilla QLD 7 F9
Kumbia QLD 7 E10
Kunamata SA 68 B3
Kunapula NT 79 J14 83 A7 90 H1
Kunat VIC 41 G9
Kunatjara SA 68 B1 79 K14 83 B7 90 K1
Kunawarara QLD 9 G10
Kunawarritji WA 79 F11
Kunayangku NT 89 H8
Kundana WA 77 H11
Kundip Nat Res WA 75 G10
Kundora QLD 12 B4
Kungala NSW 25 F12
Kunghur NSW 7 J13 25 B13
Kunlara SA 62 C6 65 J12
Kunmunya Mission WA 80 D7
Kunparrka (Haasts Bluff) NT 90 F5
Kununurra WA 81 E14
Kunytjanu SA 68 B1 83 B7
Kupingarri WA 79 A12 81 F9
Kuraby QLD 3 J5 5 E9
Kuranda QLD 11 D12
Kurbayia QLD 12 B4
Kuri Bay WA 80 D7
Kuridala QLD 12 B5
Ku-ring-gai Chase Nat Park NSW 19 A6 20 C6 23 G9
Kurkatingara NT 79 J14 83 A7
Kurkutjara NT 68 A1 90 K1
Kurmond NSW 20 G6
Kurnbrunin VIC 40 H4
Kurnell NSW 19 J6 21 B10
Kurnwill VIC 28 G2 40 B2
Kurraca VIC 39 A10
Kurraca West VIC 39 A9
Kurrajong NSW 20 H7 23 G8
Kurrajong WA 77 F10
Kurrajong Heights NSW 20 H6
Kurralta Park SA 59 H3
Kurrawang WA 75 A12 77 J11 83 F1
Kurri Kurri NSW 23 E10
Kurrimine QLD 11 E13
Kurrimine Beach Nat Park QLD 11 E1
Kuruala WA 83 C6
Kurumbul QLD 7 J8 24 B7
Kurwongbah QLD 4 G6
Kutjurntari WA 90 H1
Kuttabul QLD 9 D8
Kwinana WA 72 G5 74 D3
Ky Valley VIC 41 K14 42 C2
Kyabram VIC 41 K14 42 C2
Kyalite VIC 28 H6 41 D9
Kyancutta SA 64 E5
Kybeyan NSW 31 G10
Kybunga SA 62 F4 65 G10
Kybybolite SA 38 B1 63 A11
Kydra NSW 31 H10
Kyeamba NSW 29 J13 30 E6
Kyeema Con Park SA 61 E7
Kylie WA 73 B10
Kyndalyn VIC 40 C7
Kyneton VIC 39 D12
Kynuna QLD 12 B7
Kyogle NSW 7 J12 25 B13
Kywong NSW 29 H12 30 C4

## L

La Perouse NSW 19 H6 21 B9
Laanecoorie VIC 39 B10
Laang VIC 38 H7
Labertouche VIC 37 F13 44 D5
Labrador QLD 5 B12
Lacepede Islands WA 79 A8 80 F3
Lachlan TAS 50 C2 53 F9
Lackrana TAS 55 B9
Lacmalac NSW 30 D7
Lacrosse Island WA 81 C13
Lady Annie Mine QLD 10 J3
Lady Barron TAS 55 C9
Lady Bay SA 61 H3
Lady Elliott Island QLD 9 J13
Lady Jane - Orabanda Mine WA 77 H10
Lady Julia Percy Island VIC 38 J5
Lady Loretta Mine QLD 10 J3
Lady Musgrave Island QLD 9 J13
Ladys Pass VIC 39 B13 42 E1
Laen VIC 40 K7
LaFevre Peninsula SA 59 B2
Laggan NSW 22 J5 31 B10
Lagoon Island QLD 5 C10
Laguna Quays QLD 9 C8
Lah VIC 40 J6
Lah-Arum VIC 38 C6
Laheys Creek NSW 22 C5
Laidley QLD 5 K9 7 G11
Lajamanu NT 88 E3
Lake Ace Nat Res WA 75 E9
Lake Albacutya Park VIC 28 J3 40 G4
Lake Albert SA 63 E8
Lake Alexandrina SA 63 E8 65 K10
Lake Amadeus NT 90 H3
Lake Argyle WA 79 A14 81 E14
Lake Argyle Village WA 81 E14
Lake Auld WA 79 F10
Lake Austin WA 76 D7
Lake Barambah QLD 7 D11
Lake Barlee WA 77 F9
Lake Barrington TAS 54 F6
Lake Bathurst NSW 31 C10
Lake Biddy WA 75 E8

Lake Bindegolly Nat Park QLD 15 H10
Lake Blanche SA 67 G12
Lake Blanche WA 79 H4
Lake Boga VIC 28 J6 41 F10
Lake Bolac VIC 38 F7
Lake Boondoona QLD 7 D10
Lake Borumba QLD 7 E12
Lake Buchanan QLD 8 E3 13 B13
Lake Buloke VIC 40 K7
Lake Burbury TAS 52 B4 54 J4
Lake Burnside WA 79 J9
Lake Burley Griffin ACT 32 B1
Lake Burragorang NSW 21 H11 22 H7
Lake Callabonna SA 67 K11
Lake Campion Nat Res WA 74 A7
Lake Cania QLD 9 K11
Lake Carey WA 77 F12 83 D1
Lake Cargelligo NSW 29 D11
Lake Carnegie WA 77 B12 79 K9 83 B2
Lake Cathie NSW 23 A13
Lake Cawndilla NSW 28 B3
Lake Cethana TAS 54 G6
Lake Charm VIC 28 J6 41 G10
Lake Chisolm Forest Res TAS 54 D2
Lake Clifton WA 72 G7 72 G7
Lake Conjola SA 31 D12
Lake Connewarre VIC 36 H3
Lake Cootharaba QLD 7 D13
Lake Cowal NSW 29 D13 29 E13
Lake Cowan WA 75 C13 77 K12
Lake Dalrymple QLD 8 C5 13 A14
Lake Dartmouth QLD 15 C12
Lake Dartmouth VIC 30 H6 43 D11
Lake Dennis WA 79 E14
Lake Disappointment WA 79 G9
Lake Dora WA 79 F9
Lake Dundas WA 83 H1
Lake Echo TAS 53 C8 55 K8
Lake Eildon VIC 30 K2 42 G5 46 A1
Lake Eildon Nat Park VIC 30 K2 42 G5
Lake Eucumbene NSW 31 G8
Lake Everade SA 64 B4
Lake Eyre Nat Park SA 67 E8
Lake Eyre North SA 67 F8
Lake Eyre South SA 67 G8
Lake Frome SA 65 A12
Lake Frome Reg Res SA 65 A12 67 K12
Lake Gairdner SA 64 C6
Lake Gairdner Nat Park SA 64 B6
Lake Galilee QLD 8 F3 13 D13
Lake George NSW 31 D10
Lake Gilles SA 62 K2
Lake Gilles Con Park SA 62 K2 64 E7
Lake Gleeson SA 8 A5
Lake Goldsmith VIC 39 E9
Lake Gordon TAS 52 F6
Lake Grace WA 74 F7
Lake Gregory WA 79 D13
Lake Harris SA 64 G5
Lake Hindmarsh VIC 40 J4
Lake Hope WA 75 D10
Lake Hume NSW 29 K13 30 F4 43 B9
Lake Hurlstone Nat Res WA 75 E9
Lake Illawara NSW 23 K8
Lake Innes Nat Res NSW 23 A13 25 K12
Lake Jasper WA 74 J3
Lake Jindabyne NSW 31 G8
Lake Johnston WA 75 D11
Lake Joondalup WA 71 A2
Lake Julius QLD 10 J4
Lake Kajarabie QLD 6 G4
Lake Keepit NSW 24 H6
Lake King VIC 45 C13 46 E6
Lake King WA 75 F9
Lake King Nat Res WA 75 F9
Lake King William TAS 52 C7 54 K7
Lake Koombooloomba QLD 11 E12
Lake Leagur NSW 28 D5
Lake Leake TAS 53 B12 55 J12
Lake Lefroy WA 75 B13
Lake Logue Nat Res WA 76 H4
Lake Macdonald WA 79 H14
Lake Machattie SA 12 H4 14 J1
Lake Mackay WA 79 F14 90 D1
Lake Mackintosh TAS 54 G5
Lake MacLeod WA 78 H1
Lake Macquarie NSW 23 F10
Lake Magenta Nat Res WA 75 G8
Lake Marabon QLD 8 H6
Lake Marmal VIC 41 J9
Lake Maroon QLD 7 H12
Lake Maurice SA 68 F4
Lake McFarlane SA 64 F7
Lake Meering WA 28 K6 41 H10
Lake Menindee NSW 28 B3
Lake Minigwal WA 83 E2
Lake Mokoan VIC 30 G2 42 D6
Lake Moogerah QLD 7 H12
Lake Moondarra QLD 10 K4
Lake Moore WA 76 G6
Lake Muir Nat Res WA 73 C14 74 J4
Lake Mundi VIC 38 J7
Lake Munmorah NSW 20 A1
Lake Muir WA 78 J7
Lake Neale NT 90 J2
Lake Noondie WA 77 E8
Lake Nuga Nuga QLD 6 A5 8 K7
Lake Paloona TAS 54 E7
Lake Pamamaroo NSW 28 A4
Lake Pedder TAS 52 G6

Lake Philipi QLD 12 G3
Lake Pieman TAS 52 A3 54 H3
Lake Raeside WA 77 G11
Lake Rason WA 77 F14 83 D3
Lake Rebecca WA 77 H12 83 E1
Lake Rowallan TAS 54 H6
Lake Rowan VIC 30 G2 42 C5
Lake Samsonvale QLD 4 F6 7 F12
Lake Shaster Nat Res VIC 75 G11
Lake Somerset QLD 4 F4 7 F12
Lake Sorell TAS 53 B10 55 J10
Lake St Clair TAS 52 B6 54 J6
Lake Thomson VIC 44 B7
Lake Throssel WA 77 D14 83 C3
Lake Tinaroo QLD 11 D12
Lake Torrens SA 65 A9
Lake Torrens Nat Park SA 65 A9 67 K9
Lake Trevallyn TAS 56 G4
Lake Tyers VIC 43 K13 46 H2
Lake Tyers State Park VIC 43 K12 46 D7
Lake Tyrrell VIC 28 J5 40 F7
Lake Urana NSW 28 F2
Lake Varley Nat Res WA 75 E9
Lake Victoria NSW 28 F2
Lake Victoria VIC 45 D13 46 E6
Lake View SA 62 G4 65 F9
Lake Waulkarlcarly WA 79 E8
Lake Wells WA 77 C13 83 B2
Lake White WA 79 E14
Lake Wills WA 79 E14
Lake Wivenhoe QLD 4 J6 7 F12
Lake Woods NT 88 D7
Lake Wyangan NSW 29 F11 30 A2
Lake Wyara QLD 15 J10
Lake Yamma Yamma QLD 12 K7 14 D5
Lake Yindarlgooda WA 83 F1
Lakefield Nat Park QLD 11 A10 16 J5
Lakeland QLD 11 B11
Lakeland Nat Res WA 75 F8
Lakes Entrance VIC 43 K12 45 C14 46 E7
Lakeside VIC 37 E11
Lal Lal VIC 39 E11
Lalbert VIC 28 J6 41 G9
Lalbert Road VIC 41 G9
Lalla TAS 55 E10 56 E5
Lalor Park NSW 21 E8
Lamb Island QLD 5 B9
Lamboo Station WA 79 C13 81 K11
Lameroo SA 63 B8 65 K13
Lamington Nat Park QLD 5 D14 7 J13 25 A13
Lamplough VIC 39 C9
Lana QLD 13 C9
Lancaster VIC 41 K14 42 C2
Lancefield VIC 39 D13 42 G1
Lancelin WA 42 76 J4
Lancevale QLD 8 H3 13 F13
Landed at Last Mine WA 77 F12 83 D1
Landsborough QLD 4 F2 7 E13
Landsborough VIC 39 C8
Landsdale WA 71 B4
Landsdowne NSW 23 B12
Lane Cove NSW 19 E5 21 C8
Lane Cove Nat Park NSW 19 D4 21 C8
Lane Poole Con Park WA 72 F7 73 E8 74 E3
Lane Poole Con Res WA 73 E8 74 F4
Lang Lang VIC 37 H12 44 E4
Langford WA 71 J5
Langhorne Creek SA 63 E8 65 K10
Langi-Ghiran State Park VIC 39 D8
Langkoop VIC 38 C2 63 A12
Langlo Crossing QLD 13 K12 15 C13
Langtree NSW 29 D10
Langwarrin VIC 37 G9
Lankeys Creek NSW 29 K13 30 F6 43 A11
Lannercost QLD 11 G13
Lansdowne NSW 19 F2
Lansvale NSW 21 C9
Lapaku WA 79 J13 83 A6
Lapoinya TAS 54 D4
Lappa QLD 11 E11
Lapstone NSW 21 G9
Lara VIC 36 F3 39 G12
Lara Lake VIC 39 G12
Laramba NT 90 D6
Laravale QLD 5 F13
Lardner VIC 37 H14
Largs Bay SA 59 C1 59 D1 60 E1
Lark Quarry Env Park QLD 13 E8
Larpent VIC 39 H9
Larrakeyah NT 84 E1
Larras Lee NSW 22 E4
Larrimah NT 86 J7 88 A7
Lascelles VIC 28 J4 40 G6
Latham WA 76 J2
Lathami Con Park SA 63 J8 65 K9
Latrobe TAS 54 E7
Lauderdale TAS 51 D8 53 G11
Launceston TAS 55 F10 56 G5
Launching Place VIC 37 C12 42 K4 44 B4
Laura QLD 11 B11 16 K4
Laura SA 62 F2 65 F9
Laura Bay SA 64 D2 68 K7
Laurieton NSW 23 B13
Lauriston VIC 39 D12
Lavers Hill VIC 39 K9

Laverton VIC 36 D6 39 F13 42 K1
Laverton WA 77 F12 83 D1
Lavington NSW 29 K12 30 F4 43 B9
Lavinia Nat Res TAS 54 A6
Lawler VIC 40 K7
Lawlers WA 77 E10
Lawlers Mine WA 77 E10
Lawley River Nat Park WA 81 B9
Lawloit VIC 40 K3
Lawn Hill Nat Park QLD 10 G2
Lawnton QLD 4 F6
Lawrence NSW 25 E13
Lawrence QLD 21 J9 22 G7
Lawrenny TAS 53 E8
Lawson NSW 21 G9 22 H7
Lawson Island NT 86 A6
Leadville NSW 22 B5
Leaghur VIC 28 K6 41 H10
Leaghur State Park VIC 28 K6 41 H10
Learmonth VIC 39 D11
Learmonth WA 78 F1
Lebrina TAS 55 E10 56 D6
Ledge Point WA 74 B2 76 J4
Ledknapper Crossing NSW 27 C11
Leeka TAS 55 B8
Leeman WA 76 H3
Leeming WA 71 J4
Leeor VIC 40 K2
Leeton NSW 29 E11 30 B3
Leeuwin-Naturaliste Nat Park WA 73 K13 74 G1
Lefroy TAS 55 D9 56 C4
Legana TAS 55 F9 56 F4
Legendre Island WA 78 D4 82 B2
Legerwood TAS 55 E12
Legume NSW 25 A11
Legunia TAS 55 E12
Leicester Island QLD 9 F10
Leichhardt NSW 19 F5 21 C9
Leigh Creek SA 65 A10 67 K10
Leighton SA 62 E4 65 G10
Leinster WA 77 E10
Leitchville VIC 28 K7 41 H12
Leith TAS 54 E7
Leitinna TAS 55 E12
Leitpar VIC 28 H4 40 E6
Lemana TAS 55 G8
Lemon Tree Passage NSW 23 E11
Lemont TAS 53 D11 55 K11
Leneva VIC 29 K12 30 G4 43 C9
Lennox Head NSW 7 K14 25 C14
Lenswood SA 60 G5
Leonards Hill VIC 39 D11
Leonay NSW 21 G9
Leongatha VIC 37 K14 44 F6
Leongatha South VIC 44 G5
Leonora WA 77 F11 83 D1
Leopold VIC 36 G4 39 H12
Leopold Ranges Con Park WA 79 A11
Leppington NSW 21 E10
Leprena TAS 53 K9
Lerderderg State Park VIC 36 A3 39 E12
Leslie Dam QLD 7 H10
Leslie Manor VIC 39 G9
Leslie Vale TAS 50 E5 53 G10
Lesmurdie Falls Nat Park WA 71 G7 72 F3
Lesueur Nat Park WA 76 H3
Lethbridge VIC 36 E1 39 G11
Leumeah NSW 21 E11
Levendale TAS 53 E11
Lewana WA 73 F12
Lewisham TAS 51 C9 53 F11
Lewiston SA 60 B2
Lexton VIC 39 D9
Leyburn QLD 7 H10
Liamana QLD 22 B5
Liawenee TAS 53 A8 55 H8
Licola VIC 43 J8 45 A9 46 C2
Lidcombe NSW 19 F3 21 D9
Liddell NSW 23 D9
Liena TAS 54 G8
Liffey TAS 55 G9 56 K2
Light Pass SA 60 A7
Lightning Ridge NSW 27 C14
Liguanea Island SA 64 J5
Lija NT 89 D10
Likkaparta NT 89 G9
Lileah TAS 54 D3
Lilli Pilli NSW 21 C10
Lillimur VIC 40 K2
Lillimur South VIC 38 A2 40 K2
Lilydale TAS 55 E10 56 D6
Lilydale VIC 37 C10 42 K3 44 B3
Lilyvale NSW 21 C12
Lima VIC 42 E5
Lima South VIC 30 J2 42 E5
Limbri NSW 25 J8
Lime Bay Nat Res TAS 51 E11 53 G12
Lime Lake WA 73 A10
Limeburners Creek Nat Res NSW 23 A14 25 K12
Limekilns NSW 22 F6
Limerick QLD 22 H5 31 A10
Limestone VIC 42 G4
Limevale QLD 7 J9 25 B8
Lincoln Gap SA 62 H1 65 E8
Lincoln Nat Park SA 64 J6
Lind Nat Park VIC 47 C10
Linda TAS 52 B4 54 J4
Lindeman Island QLD 9 C8
Lindeman Islands Nat Park QLD 9 C8
Linden NSW 21 H8

Lindenow VIC 43 K10 45 B12 46 D5
Lindfield NSW 19 D5 20 C7
Lindisfarne TAS 51 C5 53 F10
Lindsay Island VIC 40 A2
Linga VIC 28 H3 40 E3
Linga WA 79 B13 81 J12
Lingnoonganee Island QLD 10 C4
Linne Islands QLD 9 C8
Linton VIC 39 F9
Linville QLD 7 E11
Lipson SA 64 H6
Liptrap VIC 44 H5
Lisarow NSW 20 B4
Lisle TAS 55 E10 56 E7
Lismore NSW 7 K13 25 C13
Lismore VIC 39 G9
Liston NSW 25 B10
Litchfield WA 41 H10
Litchfield Nat Park NT 85 E1 86 E3
Lithgow NSW 22 G7
Littabella Nat Park QLD 9 K12
Little Adolphus Island QLD 16 B2
Little Billabong NSW 29 J13 30 E5
Little Desert Nat Park VIC 38 A3 63 A11
Little Dip Con Park SA 63 D12
Little Dog Island TAS 55 C9
Little Forest NSW 22 F5
Little Green Island TAS 55 C9
Little Mulgrave QLD 11 D13
Little Para Reservoir SA 60 D4
Little Plain NSW 24 E7
Little River VIC 36 E4 39 G12
Little Snake Island VIC 45 H8 46 H2
Little Swanport TAS 53 D13
Littlehampton SA 60 H5
Littlemore QLD 9 K11
Liverpool NSW 19 G1 21 D8
Liveseys WA 72 A2
Lizard Island Nat Park QLD 16 J7
Llandaff TAS 53 B14 55 J13
Llandilo NSW 21 G9
Llangothlin NSW 25 F9
Loamside QLD 5 H10
Lobethal SA 60 F5 62 E7 65 J10
Loch VIC 37 J13 44 F5
Loch Sport VIC 45 D13 46 E6
Lochaber SA 63 B11
Lochern Nat Park QLD 13 F9
Lochiel NSW 31 J10 47 A13
Lochiel SA 62 G4 65 G9
Lochinvar NSW 23 E10
Lochnagar QLD 8 H3 13 F12
Lock SA 64 F5
Lockhart NSW 29 H12 30 D4
Lockhart River QLD 16 F4
Lockington VIC 41 K12
Lockleys SA 59 G2 60 G1 61 A5
Lockridge WA 71 D6
Lockrose QLD 5 K8
Locksley VIC 42 E3
Lockwood VIC 39 B11
Lockwood South VIC 39 B11
Loddon QLD 15 E12
Loddon Vale VIC 28 K7 41 H11
Loftus NSW 19 K3 21 C10
Logan QLD 7 G13
Logan VIC 39 A9
Logan Central QLD 3 J5
Logan Village QLD 5 D10
Loganholme QLD 3 K7 5 D10
Loganlea QLD 3 K6 5 D10
Lombadina WA 79 A9 80 E4
Londonderry NSW 21 G8
Long Flat NSW 23 A12 25 K11
Long Gully VIC 37 B11
Long Island QLD 4 E3 5 B10 9 C8 9 F9
Long Island TAS 55 A13
Long Island WA 78 F2
Long Plains SA 62 F5 65 H9
Long Plains VIC 40 F7
Long Pocket QLD 3 F3
Longerenong VIC 38 B6
Longford TAS 55 G10 56 J5
Longford VIC 45 E11 46 F4
Longlea VIC 39 B12
Longley TAS 50 E4 53 G10
Longreach QLD 8 H3 13 F10
Longwarry VIC 37 G13 44 D5
Longwarry North VIC 37 F13
Longwood VIC 59 K7 60 H3 61 B7
Longwood VIC 42 E3
Lonnavale VIC 53 G9
Lonsdale SA 60 J1 61 C5
Looma WA 79 B10 80 H6
Loongana TAS 54 F6
Loongana WA 83 F5
Loorana TAS 54 B6
Lorinna TAS 54 G6
Lorne NSW 23 B13
Lorne SA 62 G5 65 H9
Lorne VIC 39 J11
Lorquon VIC 40 J4
Lostock NSW 23 C10
Lota QLD 3 E7
Lottah TAS 55 E13
Loughnan Nat Res NSW 29 D10
Louisville TAS 53 E12

Louth NSW 27 F9
Louth Bay SA 64 H6
Louth Island SA 64 H6
Loveday SA 62 B5 65 H13
Lovett Bay NSW 19 A7
Low Head TAS 55 D8 56 B2
Low Hill SA 64 D7
Lowden WA 73 F10 74 G3
Lowdina TAS 53 E11
Lower Barrington TAS 54 E7
Lower Beechmont QLD 5 C13
Lower Beulah TAS 54 F7
Lower Bucca NSW 25 F13
Lower Creek NSW 25 H11
Lower Cresswell QLD 4 K4
Lower Frankland WA 73 F7
Lower Gellibrand VIC 39 K9
Lower Glenelg Nat Park VIC 38 G3 63 A14
Lower Hawkesbury NSW 20 E5
Lower Hermitage SA 60 E4
Lower Heytesbury VIC 39 J8
Lower Light SA 62 E5 65 H9
Lower Longley TAS 50 E3
Lower Mangrove NSW 20 C4
Lower Marshes TAS 53 D10
Lower Mookerawa NSW 22 E4
Lower Mount Hicks TAS 54 D5
Lower Mount Walker QLD 5 J10
Lower Norton VIC 38 B5
Lower Portland NSW 20 F5
Lower Turners Marsh TAS 55 E10 56 D5
Lower Wilmot TAS 54 E6
Lowesdale NSW 29 K11 30 F3 42 A7
Lowlands NSW 20 G7 29 C9
Lowmead QLD 9 K12
Lowood QLD 5 J8 7 G12
Loxton SA 62 B6 65 H13
Loxton North SA 28 G1 62 B6 65 H13
Loy Yang VIC 45 E8 46 F2
Loyetea TAS 54 F5
Lubeck VIC 38 B6
Lucas Heights NSW 19 J2 21 D10
Lucaston TAS 50 E2 53 G9
Lucinda QLD 11 G14
Lucindale SA 63 B12
Lucknow NSW 22 F4
Lucknow VIC 43 K11 45 C13 46 D6
Lucky Bay SA 62 J4 64 G7
Lucky Flat NSW 24 G4
Lucyvale VIC 43 C11
Luddenham NSW 21 F10
Ludlow WA 73 H11 74 G2
Ludmilla NT 84 C2
Lue NSW 22 C10
Lugarno NSW 21 C10
Luina TAS 54 F3
Lul-Tju NT 88 E3
Lulworth TAS 55 D9 56 B4
Lumeah WA 73 A12
Lumholtz Nat Park QLD 11 F13
Lunawanna TAS 53 J10
Lune River TAS 53 J9
Lupton Con Park WA 72 C5 74 D4
Lurg VIC 42 D6
Lurnea NSW 21 E10
Luscombe QLD 5 D11
Lutwyche QLD 3 D4
Lymington TAS 50 J2 53 H9
Lymwood TAS 54 C6
Lynchford TAS 52 C4 54 K4
Lyndbrook QLD 11 E11
Lyndenham NSW 22 G4
Lyndhurst SA 67 J10
Lyndhurst VIC 35 H7 37 F9 44 D2
Lyndoch SA 60 A5 60 B5 62 E6 65 H10
Lyons SA 64 A3 66 K3 68 H7
Lyons VIC 38 G3
Lyonville VIC 39 D12
Lyrup SA 28 F1 62 B5 65 H13
Lysterfield Lake Park VIC 37 E10
Lysterfield State Park VIC 44 C3
Lytton QLD 3 D6 4 D7

## M

Maaroom QLD 7 C13
Maatsuyker Island TAS 52 K7
Mabuiag Island QLD 16 A2
Mac Clark (Acacia Peuce) Con Res NT 91 H10
Macalister QLD 7 F9
Macarthur VIC 38 G5
Macclesfield SA 60 K5 62 E7 65 J10
Macclesfield VIC 37 D11
Macedon VIC 39 D13
MacGregor QLD 3 G5 5 E9
Mackay QLD 9 D8
MacKenzie QLD 3 G6
Macksville NSW 25 H13
Maclean NSW 25 D13
Macleay Island QLD 5 C9
Macleod VIC 35 B5 37 C8
Macorna VIC 41 H11
Macquarie Fields NSW 21 E10
Macquarie Marshes Nat Res NSW 27 F13 27 G13

102 Macquarie Pass Nat Park – Monash

**Macquarie Pass Nat Park NSW** 23 K8 31 B13
**Macquarie Plains TAS** 53 F9
**Macrossan QLD** 8 B4 11 J14
**Macumba Well SA** 66 B7
**Maddington WA** 71 J7
**Madora WA** 72 G5
**Madura WA** 83 G5
**Mafeking VIC** 38 D6
**Maffra NSW** 31 H9
**Maffra VIC** 45 C10 46 E4
**Maggea SA** 62 C6 65 H12
**Magill SA** 59 F6 60 F3
**Magnetic Island QLD** 11 G14
**Magnetic Island Nat Park QLD** 11 G14
**Magra TAS** 50 A2 53 F9
**Magrath Flat SA** 63 D9
**Maharatta NSW** 31 J9 47 A11
**Maianbar NSW** 21 B10
**Maida Vale WA** 71 F7
**Mailers Flat VIC** 38 H6
**Maimuru NSW** 22 J2 30 A7
**Main Beach QLD** 5 B12
**Main Creek NSW** 23 C11
**Main Range Nat Park QLD** 5 K13 7 H11 25 A11
**Maindample VIC** 30 J2 42 F5
**Maingon Bay TAS** 51 K13 53 H12
**Mairjimmy NSW** 29 J10 30 E1
**Maitland NSW** 23 E10
**Maitland SA** 62 H5 65 H8
**Maitland Bay NSW** 20 B5
**Major Plains VIC** 42 C5
**Majorca VIC** 39 C10
**Majors Creek NSW** 31 E10
**Makiri SA** 68 C4
**Makowata QLD** 9 J12
**Makurapiti SA** 68 B1 83 B7
**Malabar NSW** 19 H6
**Malaga WA** 71 D5
**Malanda QLD** 11 E12
**Malbina TAS** 50 B3 53 F10
**Malbon QLD** 12 B5
**Malbooma SA** 64 A3 66 K3
**Malcolm WA** 77 F11 83 D1
**Maldon NSW** 21 F12
**Maldon VIC** 39 C11
**Malebelling WA** 72 B3
**Malebo NSW** 29 H13 30 C5
**Maleny QLD** 4 G1 7 E12
**Malinong SA** 63 D8 65 K11
**Mallacoota VIC** 47 C13
**Mallala SA** 62 F5 65 H10
**Mallanganee NSW** 25 C12
**Mallee Cliffs Nat Park NSW** 28 F4 40 A6
**Mallison Island NT** 87 C12
**Malmsbury VIC** 39 C12
**Malua Bay NSW** 31 F11
**Malvern SA** 59 H4
**Malvernton QLD** 8 J2 13 G12
**Mamboo QLD** 8 H5 13 F14
**Mambray Creek SA** 62 G2 65 E9
**Mammoth Mines QLD** 10 J3
**Manangatang VIC** 28 H5 40 E7
**Mandagery NSW** 22 F3
**Mandalong NSW** 20 C1
**Mandalup WA** 73 E12
**Mandorah NT** 85 C1 86 D3
**Mandurah WA** 72 G6 74 E2
**Mandurama NSW** 22 G4
**Mangalo SA** 62 K 64 F7
**Mangalore QLD** 15 E13
**Mangalore TAS** 53 E10
**Mangalore VIC** 39 B14 42 F3
**Mangana TAS** 55 G12
**Mangkili Claypan Nat Res WA** 77 A14 79 J10 83 A3
**Mangoplah NSW** 29 H13 30 D5
**Mangrove Creek NSW** 20 D4
**Mangrove Creek Dam NSW** 20 E2
**Mangrove Mountain NSW** 20 D3 23 F9
**Manguri SA** 66 G3
**Manildra NSW** 22 F3
**Manilla NSW** 24 H7
**Maninga Marley WA** 77 E9
**Maningrida NT** 87 C9
**Manjimup WA** 73 E13 74 H3
**Manly NSW** 19 D7 20 B7 23 H9
**Manly QLD** 3 D7 5 D8
**Manly Vale NSW** 19 D6 20 B7
**Manly West QLD** 3 E7
**Manmoyi NT** 87 D8
**Mann River Nat Res NSW** 25 E10
**Mannahill SA** 62 C1 65 D12
**Mannanarie SA** 62 F2 65 E10
**Mannerim VIC** 36 H4
**Mannering Lake NSW** 20 B1
**Mannering Park NSW** 20 B1
**Manning WA** 71 H4
**Manns Beach VIC** 45 G9 46 H3
**Mannum SA** 62 D7 65 J11
**Mannus NSW** 29 J14 30 F6 43 A12
**Manobalai Nat Res NSW** 23 C8
**Manoora SA** 62 E4 65 G10
**Manor VIC** 36 E4 39 F13
**Manorina VIC** 47 D10
**Manowar Island QLD** 10 C3
**Mansfield QLD** 3 G5
**Mansfield VIC** 30 J2 42 F6 46 A1
**Manton Dam Park NT** 85 D2 86 E4
**Mantung SA** 62 C6 65 H12
**Manumbar QLD** 7 D11
**Many Peaks QLD** 9 K11
**Manyallaluk (Eva Valley) NT** 85 H7 86 G6
**Manyirkanga SA** 68 A4 90 K4
**Manypeaks WA** 74 J7
**Manyung QLD** 7 D11
**Mapleton QLD** 7 E12
**Mapoon QLD** 16 D1
**Mapurru NT** 87 C10
**Maralinga SA** 68 G4
**Marama SA** 62 C7 65 K12
**Marananga SA** 60 A6
**Maranboy NT** 85 J7 86 G6
**Marandoo Mine WA** 82 F4
**Marangaroo WA** 71 C3
**Marathon QLD** 13 A9
**Marathon South QLD** 13 A9
**Maraylya NSW** 20 F6
**Marayong NSW** 21 E8
**Marble Bar WA** 78 E6 82 D6
**Marble Hill SA** 60 F4
**Marble Island QLD** 9 E10
**Marburg QLD** 5 J9 7 G12
**Marchagee WA** 76 H5
**Marchinbar Island NT** 87 B12
**Marcus Hill VIC** 36 H4 39 H12
**Mardan VIC** 44 F6 46 G1
**Mardella WA** 72 F5
**Mareeba QLD** 11 D12
**Maret Islands WA** 81 B8
**Margaret River WA** 73 K12 74 H2
**Margate QLD** 4 E6
**Margate TAS** 50 F5 53 G10
**Margooya VIC** 28 G5 40 D7
**Maria Island NT** 87 H11
**Maria Island TAS** 53 F13
**Maria Island Nat Park TAS** 53 E13
**Mariala Nat Park QLD** 13 K12 15 C11
**Marian QLD** 9 D8
**Marimo QLD** 10 K5 12 A5
**Marino SA** 59 K2 60 H1 61 B5
**Marino Con Park SA** 60 H1 61 B5
**Marion SA** 59 J3 60 H2 61 B6
**Marion Bay SA** 62 J7 64 K7
**Marion Bay TAS** 51 B13 53 F12
**Mark Oliphant Con Park SA** 60 H3 61 B7
**Markdale NSW** 22 J5 31 A9
**Markwood VIC** 30 H3 42 D7
**Marla SA** 66 D2 68 C7
**Marlborough QLD** 9 G9
**Marlee NSW** 23 B12
**Marleston SA** 59 G3
**Marley Pool WA** 72 C3
**Marlinja NT** 88 D7
**Marlo VIC** 43 K14 47 D9
**Marma VIC** 38 B6
**Marmion WA** 71 C1
**Marmion Marine Park WA** 76 K4
**Marmor QLD** 9 H10
**Marnoo VIC** 38 A7
**Marnoo East VIC** 39 A8
**Marong VIC** 39 B11
**Maroochydore QLD** 4 E1 7 E13
**Maroon QLD** 5 H14
**Maroona VIC** 38 E7
**Maroota NSW** 20 E5
**Maroota South NSW** 20 E6
**Maroubra NSW** 19 G6 21 B9
**Maroubra Bay NSW** 21 B9
**Marp VIC** 38 F2
**Marraba QLD** 12 A5
**Marrabel SA** 62 E5 65 G10
**Marradong WA** 72 D7 74 E4
**Marramarra Nat Park NSW** 20 D5 23 G9
**Marrar NSW** 29 G13 30 C5
**Marrawah TAS** 54 C1
**Marraweeny VIC** 42 E4
**Marree SA** 67 H9
**Marrickville NSW** 21 C9
**Marryat SA** 66 B2 68 B7 90 K7
**Marsden NSW** 22 G1 29 E13
**Marsden QLD** 3 K5 5 E10
**Marsden Park NSW** 20 F7
**Marsfield NSW** 19 D4 21 C8
**Marshall VIC** 36 H3
**Marshdale NSW** 23 D11
**Martindale NSW** 23 D8
**Martins Washpool Con Park SA** 63 D10
**Marulan NSW** 22 K6 31 C11
**Marvel Loch WA** 75 B9 77 K9
**Mary Kathleen QLD** 10 K4 12 A4
**Mary River Con Res NT** 85 C4 86 D5
**Mary River Nat Park NT** 85 D4 86 D5
**Mary River Roadhouse NT** 85 F5 86 F5
**Maryborough QLD** 7 C12
**Maryborough VIC** 39 C10
**Maryfarms QLD** 11 C12
**Maryknoll VIC** 37 F12
**Marysville VIC** 37 A13 42 H4 44 A5
**Maryvale NSW** 22 D4
**Mascot NSW** 19 G5 21 B9
**Maslin Beach SA** 61 E5 62 F7 65 K10
**Massey VIC** 40 J7
**Masthead Island QLD** 9 H12
**Matakana NSW** 29 C10
**Mataranka NT** 85 K7 86 H7
**Mataranka Homestead NT** 86 H7
**Matcham NSW** 20 B4
**Matheson NSW** 25 E9
**Mathiesons VIC** 39 A14
**Mathinna TAS** 55 F12
**Mathoura NSW** 29 K9 41 H14 42 A1
**Matlock VIC** 42 J6 44 A7 46 C1
**Matong NSW** 29 G12 30 C4
**Matraville NSW** 19 H6 21 B9
**Maude NSW** 28 F7 41 B12
**Maude VIC** 36 E1 39 G11
**Maudsland QLD** 5 C12
**Mawbanna TAS** 54 D3
**Mawson WA** 72 A3
**Mawson Lakes SA** 59 C4
**Maxwelton QLD** 11 K8 13 A8
**Maya WA** 76 G5
**Mayanup WA** 73 D12 74 G4
**Mayberry TAS** 54 G7
**Maybole NSW** 25 F9
**Maydena TAS** 53 F8
**Mayfield Bay Con Area TAS** 53 C13 55 K13
**Maylands WA** 71 F5
**Maynard Bore SA** 68 C5
**Mayrung NSW** 29 J9
**Maytown QLD** 11 B10
**Mazeppa Nat Park QLD** 8 F5
**McAlinden WA** 73 E10
**McCluer Island NT** 86 A7
**McCoys Bridge VIC** 41 J14 42 B2
**McCullys Gap NSW** 23 C9
**McDowall QLD** 3 C3
**McGraths Hill NSW** 20 F7
**McKenzie Creek VIC** 38 B5
**McKillops Bridge VIC** 43 G14 47 A9
**McKinlay QLD** 12 B6
**McKinnon VIC** 35 F4
**McLaren Creek NT** 89 J9
**McLaren Flat SA** 60 K2 61 D6
**McLaren Vale SA** 60 K2 61 E5 62 F7 65 K10
**McIntyres VIC** 39 A10
**McMahons Creek VIC** 37 C14 42 J5 44 B5
**McMahons Reef NSW** 22 K3 30 B7
**McMasters Beach NSW** 20 B4
**McMillans VIC** 41 H11
**McPhail NSW** 22 D2
**Mead VIC** 41 H11
**Meadow Flat NSW** 22 G6
**Meadows SA** 60 K4 62 F7 65 K10
**Meandarra QLD** 6 F7
**Meander TAS** 55 G8
**Mears WA** 72 A5
**Meatian VIC** 41 G9
**Meckering WA** 72 B2 74 C5 76 K6
**Medina WA** 72 G4
**Medindie SA** 58 A3
**Medlow Bath NSW** 21 K9
**Meeandah QLD** 3 D5
**Meekatharra WA** 76 C7 78 K5
**Meelup WA** 73 K10
**Meenaar WA** 72 C2
**Meeniyan VIC** 44 G6
**Meerlieu VIC** 45 D12 46 E5
**Megan NSW** 25 G12
**Mekaree QLD** 8 K2 13 G11
**Melba Gully State Park VIC** 39 K9
**Melbourne VIC** 35 D3 36 C7 39 F14 42 K2 44 B1
**Melbourne CBD VIC** 34
**Meldale QLD** 4 E4
**Mella TAS** 54 C2
**Melros WA** 72 H6
**Melrose NSW** 29 B12
**Melrose SA** 62 F2 65 E9
**Melrose TAS** 54 E7
**Melrose Park SA** 59 J4
**Melton SA** 62 G5 65 G9
**Melton VIC** 36 B4 39 E13
**Melton Mowbray TAS** 53 D10
**Melton South VIC** 36 C4
**Melville WA** 71 J2
**Melville Forest VIC** 38 E4
**Melville Island NT** 85 A1 86 B3
**Melwood VIC** 43 K11 45 B12 46 D5
**Memana TAS** 55 B9
**Memerambi QLD** 7 D10
**Mena Park VIC** 39 E9
**Menai NSW** 19 J2 21 D10
**Menangle NSW** 21 E12
**Menangle Park NSW** 21 E11
**Mendooran NSW** 22 B4
**Mengha TAS** 54 C3
**Menindee NSW** 26 K4 28 B4
**Meningie SA** 63 D9 65 K11
**Mentone VIC** 35 G5 37 E8 39 G14 44 C2
**Menzies WA** 77 G10
**Menzies Creek VIC** 37 E11
**Mepunga East VIC** 38 J7
**Mepunga West VIC** 38 J7
**Merah North NSW** 24 F4
**Merbein VIC** 28 F3 40 A4
**Merbein South VIC** 28 F3 40 A4
**Merbein West VIC** 40 A4
**Mercunda SA** 62 C6 65 J12
**Merebene NSW** 24 H3
**Meredith VIC** 36 D1 39 F11
**Meribah SA** 28 G1 40 C1 62 A6 65 J13
**Merimbula NSW** 31 J11
**Merinda QLD** 8 B7
**Meringadan QLD** 7 G11
**Meringur VIC** 28 F2 40 B2 65 H14
**Meringur North VIC** 40 B2
**Merino VIC** 38 F3
**Mermaid Beach QLD** 5 B13
**Mernda VIC** 37 B8 39 E14 42 J2 44 A2
**Merredin WA** 74 B7 76 K7
**Merriang VIC** 43 D8
**Merricks VIC** 37 J8 39 H14 44 F2
**Merricks Beach VIC** 37 K8
**Merricks North VIC** 37 J8
**Merrigum VIC** 41 K14 42 C2
**Merrijig VIC** 30 K3 42 G6 46 A1
**Merrimac QLD** 5 B13
**Merrinee VIC** 28 F3 40 B4
**Merrinee North VIC** 28 F3 40 B4
**Merriton SA** 62 G3 65 F9
**Merriwa NSW** 22 C7
**Merriwagga NSW** 29 E10
**Merrygoen NSW** 22 B5
**Merrylands NSW** 19 E2 21 D8
**Merryvale QLD** 5 J11
**Merrywinebone NSW** 24 E2
**Mersey White Water Forest Res TAS** 54 G6
**Merseylea TAS** 54 F7
**Merton NSW** 29 K11 30 F2 42 A6
**Merton VIC** 30 J1 42 F4
**Metcalfe VIC** 39 C12
**Methul NSW** 29 G13 30 B5
**Metricup WA** 73 J11
**Metung VIC** 43 K12 45 C14 46 E7
**Meunna TAS** 54 D4
**Mia Mia VIC** 39 C13
**Miallo QLD** 11 C12
**Miami QLD** 5 B13
**Miandetta NSW** 27 H12
**Miara QLD** 7 A11 9 K12
**Michaelmas and Upolu Cays Nat Park QLD** 11 C13
**Michelago NSW** 31 E9
**Mickleham VIC** 36 A7
**Middingbank NSW** 31 G8
**Middle Beach SA** 62 F6 65 H9
**Middle Camp NSW** 20 A1
**Middle Dural NSW** 19 A2
**Middle Island QLD** 9 E10
**Middle Island WA** 83 J2
**Middle Lagoon WA** 79 A9
**Middle Park QLD** 5 F9
**Middle Point NT** 85 C3 86 D4
**Middle Swan WA** 71 D7
**Middlecamp Hills Con Park SA** 62 K4 64 F7
**Middlemount QLD** 8 G7
**Middleton QLD** 12 D6
**Middleton SA** 61 H7 63 F8 65 K10
**Middleton TAS** 50 K5 53 H10
**Midge Point QLD** 9 C8
**Midland WA** 71 D7 72 F3 76 K5
**Midway Point TAS** 51 B8 53 F11
**Miena TAS** 53 B8 55 J8
**Miepoll VIC** 30 H1 42 D4
**Miga Lake VIC** 38 C3
**Mike O/P Mine WA** 79 F8
**Mil Lel SA** 38 F1 63 B14
**Mila NSW** 31 J9 47 A11
**Milabena TAS** 54 D4
**Milang SA** 63 E8 65 K10
**Milawa VIC** 42 D7
**Milbrook Res SA** 60 E4
**Milbrulong NSW** 29 H12 30 D4
**Milchomi NSW** 24 G2
**Mildura VIC** 28 F3 40 A5
**Mile End SA** 58 C1 59 G3
**Miles QLD** 6 E7
**Milford QLD** 5 H13
**Milguy NSW** 24 D6
**Milikapiti NT** 86 B3
**Miling WA** 76 H5
**Milingimbi NT** 87 C10
**Milkshake Hills Forest Res TAS** 54 D3
**Mill Park VIC** 35 A4
**Millaa Millaa QLD** 11 E12
**Millaroo QLD** 8 B5
**Millbank NSW** 25 H11
**Millchester QLD** 8 B4 11 J14
**Miller NSW** 21 E10
**Millers Point NSW** 18 A1
**Millfield NSW** 23 E9
**Millgrove VIC** 37 C12 42 K4 44 B4
**Millicent SA** 63 C13
**Millie NSW** 24 E4
**Millmerran QLD** 7 H9
**Milloo VIC** 41 K12
**Millstream Chichester Nat Park WA** 78 E4 82 D2
**Millstream Falls Nat Park QLD** 11 E12
**Millswood SA** 59 H4
**Millthorpe NSW** 22 G4
**Milltown VIC** 38 G4
**Millwood NSW** 29 H13 30 C5
**Milner NT** 84 B2
**Milparinka NSW** 26 D2
**Milperra NSW** 19 G2 21 D9
**Milton NSW** 31 D12
**Milton QLD** 5 F8
**Milvale NSW** 22 J1 29 F14 30 A6
**Milyakburra NT** 87 F12
**Milyu Nat Res WA** 70 C1
**Mimili (Everard Park) SA** 68 B6
**Mimosa Rocks Nat Park NSW** 31 H11
**Mincha VIC** 41 H11
**Mindarie SA** 62 C6 65 J12
**Minden QLD** 5 J8
**Miners Rest VIC** 39 E10
**Minerva QLD** 8 J6
**Minerva Hills Nat Park QLD** 8 J6
**Mingary SA** 65 D13
**Mingay VIC** 39 F9
**Mingela QLD** 8 B4 11 J14
**Mingenew WA** 76 G4
**Mingoola QLD** 25 C9
**Minhamite VIC** 38 G6
**Minilya Roadhouse WA** 78 H1
**Minimay VIC** 38 B2
**Mininera VIC** 39 E8
**Miniyeri NT** 87 H8
**Minjan VIC** 38 G6
**Minjilang NT** 86 B6
**Minlaton SA** 62 H6 65 J8
**Minnamurra NSW** 23 K8 31 B13
**Minnie Water NSW** 25 E13
**Minnipa SA** 64 E4
**Minore NSW** 22 C3
**Mintabie SA** 66 D1 68 C7
**Mintaro SA** 62 F4 65 G10
**Minto NSW** 21 E10
**Minyip VIC** 38 A6 40 K6
**Miralie VIC** 28 H5 41 E9
**Miram VIC** 40 K2
**Miram South VIC** 38 A3 40 K3
**Miranda NSW** 19 J4 21 C10
**Mirani QLD** 9 D8
**Mirannie NSW** 23 D10
**Mirboo VIC** 44 F7 46 G1
**Mirboo North VIC** 44 F7 46 G1
**Miriam Vale QLD** 9 J12
**Mirikata SA** 66 J5
**Mirimbah VIC** 42 G7 46 A2
**Mirirrinyunga (Duck Ponds) NT** 88 F4
**Miriwinni QLD** 11 E13
**Mirrabooka QLD** 15 F13
**Mirrabooka WA** 71 D4
**Mirranatwa VIC** 38 D6
**Mirrindi NT** 88 F4
**Mirrnatja NT** 87 D10
**Mirrool NSW** 29 F12 30 A4
**Missabotti NSW** 25 H12
**Mission Beach QLD** 11 E13
**Missouri Mine WA** 77 H10
**Mistake Creek NT** 88 C1
**Mitakooki QLD** 12 A5
**Mitcham SA** 59 J4 60 G2 61 A6
**Mitcham VIC** 35 D7
**Mitchell - Alice Rivers Nat Park QLD** 10 A7 16 K2
**Mitchell QLD** 6 D3
**Mitchell River Nat Park VIC** 43 J10 45 A12 46 C5
**Mitchell River Nat Park WA** 81 C9
**Mitchells (site) VIC** 42 H7 46 B1
**Mitchellville SA** 62 J3 65 F8
**Mitchelton QLD** 3 D2
**Mitiamo VIC** 41 J11
**Mitre VIC** 38 B4
**Mitta Mitta VIC** 30 H5 43 D10
**Mittagong NSW** 22 K7 31 B12
**Mittyack VIC** 28 H4 40 E6
**Moa Island QLD** 16 A2
**Moama NSW** 29 K8 41 J13 42 B1
**Moana SA** 60 K1 61 D5
**Moana Sands Con Park SA** 60 K1 61 D5
**Mobrup WA** 73 B13
**Mockinya VIC** 38 C5
**Modbury SA** 59 D6 60 E3
**Modbury Heights SA** 59 C6
**Modbury North SA** 59 D6
**Modella VIC** 37 G13 44 E5
**Modewarre VIC** 36 H1
**Moe VIC** 44 D7 46 F1
**Moganemby VIC** 42 D4
**Moggill QLD** 3 H1 5 F9
**Mogo NSW** 31 F11
**Mogriguy NSW** 22 B3
**Mogumber WA** 74 A3 76 J5
**Moil NT** 84 B3
**Moina TAS** 54 F6
**Moira NSW** 42 A1
**Moira VIC** 41 H13
**Mokepilly VIC** 38 C7
**Mole Creek TAS** 54 G7
**Mole Creek Karst Nat Park TAS** 54 G
**Mole River NSW** 25 C9
**Molesworth TAS** 50 B3 53 F10
**Molesworth VIC** 42 G4
**Moliagul VIC** 39 B10
**Molka VIC** 42 E3
**Molle Islands Nat Park QLD** 9 B8
**Mollerin Nat Res WA** 76 H6
**Mollymook NSW** 31 D12
**Molong NSW** 22 F4
**Moltema TAS** 54 F7
**Molyullah VIC** 42 D6
**Mona Vale NSW** 19 B7 20 B6 23 G9
**Mona Vale TAS** 53 B11 55 J11
**Monadnocks Con Res WA** 72 E5 74 D3
**Monak NSW** 28 F4 40 A5
**Monarto Con Park SA** 60 K7
**Monash SA** 62 B5 65 H13

Monbulk VIC 37 D11 42 K3 44 C3
Mondarra State Park VIC 46 E1
Mondrain Island WA 75 H14
Monduran Dam QLD 7 A11 9 K12
Monea VIC 42 E3
Monegeetta VIC 39 D13 42 H1
Monga NSW 31 E11
Mongarlowe NSW 31 E11
Monkey Mia WA 76 B2 78 K1
Monogorilby QLD 7 B9
Monomeith VIC 37 H11
Monsildale 4 K1
Montacute SA 59 F7 60 F4
Montacute Con Park SA 60 F4
Montagu TAS 54 C2
Montagu Island TAS 54 C2
Montague WA 77 D9
Montague Bay TAS 49 B4
Montague Island NSW 31 G11
Montana TAS 55 G8
Monteagle NSW 22 J2 30 A7
Montebello Islands WA 78 D3
Montebello Islands Con Park WA 78 D3
Montefiores NSW 22 D4
Monterey NSW 19 H5 21 B9
Montesquieu Islands WA 81 A9
Montgomery Island WA 80 D6
Monto QLD 7 A9 9 K11
Montumana TAS 54 D4
Montville QLD 4 F1 7 E12
Mooball NSW 7 J14 25 A14
Moockra SA 61 F5 65 D10
Moodiarrup WA 73 C10
Moodlu QLD 4 F4
Moogara SA 53 F9
Moogerah QLD 5 J13
Moogerah Peaks Nat Park QLD 5 J13
Moojeeba QLD 16 H4
Moolap VIC 36 G3
Mooloolaba QLD 4 D1 7 E13
Mooloolah QLD 4 F2
Mooloolah River Nat Park QLD 4 E1
Moolort VIC 39 C11
Moolpa NSW 28 H6 41 D10
Moomba SA 14 H2 67 E13
Moombooldool NSW 29 F12 30 A3
Moombra QLD 4 K4
Moona Plains NSW 25 J10
Moonambel VIC 39 C9
Moonan Flat NSW 23 B9
Moonaran NSW 24 F7
Moonbah NSW 31 H8 43 D14
Moonbi NSW 25 J8
Moondarra VIC 44 D7 46 E1
Moondarra State Park VIC 44 D7
Moondyne Nat Res WA 74 C3 76 K5
Moonee Beach NSW 25 G13
Mooney Mooney NSW 20 C5
Moonford QLD 7 A9 9 K11
Moongobulla QLD 11 G14
Moonie QLD 7 G8
Moonlight Flat SA 64 E4
Moonta SA 62 H5 65 G8
Moonta Bay SA 62 H4 65 G8
Moonyoonooka WA 76 F3
Moora WA 74 B3 76 J5
Moorabbin VIC 35 F5 37 E8 39 F14 42 K2 44 J2
Moorabool VIC 36 F2
Mooralla VIC 38 D5
Moore QLD 7 F11
Moore Creek NSW 24 J7
Moore Park QLD 7 A12 9 K13
Moore River Nat Park WA 74 B2 76 J4
Moorebank NSW 19 G1 21 D9
Mooreville TAS 54 D5
Moorilim VIC 42 D3
Moorina TAS 55 E12
Moorine Rock WA 75 B8 77 J8
Moorland NSW 23 B13
Moorlands SA 63 D8 65 K11
Moorleah TAS 54 D4
Moormbool VIC 39 B14 42 E2
Moorook SA 62 B5 65 H12
Moorooka QLD 3 G4
Mooroongga Island NT 87 C10
Mooroopna VIC 42 C3
Moorowie SA 62 H7 65 J8
Moorrinya Nat Park QLD 8 D2 13 B11
Moorundie Wildlife Park SA 65 H11
Moppin NSW 24 C5
Morago NSW 29 H8 41 F13
Moranbah QLD 8 E6
Morangarell NSW 22 J2 29 F14 30 A6
Morans Crossing NSW 31 H10
Morawa WA 76 G5
Morayfield QLD 4 F5
Morchard SA 62 F1 65 E10
Mordalup WA 73 C14
Mordialloc VIC 35 H5 37 F8 39 G14 44 C2
Morea (Carlopac) VIC 38 B2
Moree NSW 24 D5
Moree VIC 38 D3
Morella QLD 13 E10
Moresby QLD 11 E13
Moreton Bay QLD 3 A6 4 C6 7 F13
Moreton Island QLD 4 B5 7 F13
Moreton Island Nat Park QLD 4 B5 7 F13
Moreton Telegraph Station QLD 16 E2

Morgan SA 62 D5 65 G11
Morgan Island NT 87 E11
Moriac VIC 36 H1 39 H11
Morialpa SA 65 D12
Morialta Con Park SA 59 F7 60 F3
Moriarty TAS 54 E7
Morisset NSW 20 B1 23 F10
Morisset Park NSW 20 B1
Morkalla VIC 28 F2 40 B2
Morley WA 71 D5
Morna Point NSW 23 E11
Morningside QLD 3 E4
Mornington VIC 36 H7 39 H14 44 E2
Mornington Island QLD 10 C3
Mornington Peninsula VIC 37 J8 39 H14 44 E2
Mornington Peninsula Nat Park VIC 36 K7 39 H13 44 F1
Morongla Creek NSW 22 H3
Morphett Vale SA 60 J1 61 C5 62 F7 65 J10
Morphettville SA 59 J3
Morri Morri VIC 38 B7
Morrisons VIC 36 C1 39 F11
Morse Island NT 85 A5 86 B6
Mortchup VIC 39 F10
Mortdale NSW 21 C9
Mortlake VIC 38 G7
Morton Nat Park NSW 31 C12
Morton Plains VIC 28 K5 40 J7
Morundah NSW 29 G11 30 C3
Moruya NSW 31 F11
Moruya Heads NSW 31 F11
Morven NSW 29 J13 30 E4
Morven QLD 6 D2
Morwell VIC 45 E8 46 F2
Morwell Nat Park VIC 45 F8 46 G2
Moselle QLD 11 K9 13 A9
Mosman NSW 19 E6 21 B8
Mosman Park WA 71 H1
Moss Vale NSW 22 K7 31 B12
Mossgiel NSW 29 D8
Mossiface VIC 43 K12 45 B14 46 D6
Mossman QLD 11 C12
Mossy Point NSW 31 F11
Moulamein NSW 28 H7 41 E11
Moule SA 64 C2
Mount Aberdeen Nat Park QLD 8 B6
Mount Adolphus Island QLD 16 B2
Mount Alford QLD 5 J13
Mount Annan NSW 21 E11
Mount Arapiles - Tooan State Park VIC 38 B4
Mount Archer Nat Park QLD 9 H10
Mount Augustus Nat Park WA 78 H4 82 J2
Mount Barker SA 60 H5 62 E7 65 J10
Mount Barker WA 74 J6
Mount Barker Junction SA 60 H5
Mount Barney Nat Park QLD 7 J12 25 A12
Mount Bauple (Scientific) Nat Park QLD 7 C12
Mount Baw Baw Alpine Village VIC 42 K6 44 B7 46 D1
Mount Beauty VIC 43 E10
Mount Benson SA 63 D12
Mount Beppo QLD 4 K5
Mount Bold Reservoir SA 60 J3 61 C7
Mount Boothby Con Park SA 63 D9
Mount Bryan SA 62 E3 65 F10
Mount Buangor State Park VIC 39 D8
Mount Buffalo Chalet VIC 30 H4 43 E8
Mount Buffalo Nat Park VIC 30 H4 43 E8
Mount Buller Alpine Village VIC 30 K3 42 G7 46 A2
Mount Burnett VIC 37 E11
Mount Burr SA 63 B13
Mount Bute VIC 39 F9
Mount Camel VIC 39 B13 42 E1
Mount Carbine QLD 11 C12
Mount Catt NT 87 F9
Mount Chapple Island TAS 55 C8
Mount Christie SA 66 K1
Mount Christie Siding SA 68 H7
Mount Claremont WA 71 F2
Mount Colah NSW 19 B4 20 C7
Mount Colosseum Nat Park QLD 9 J12
Mount Compass SA 61 F6 63 F8 65 K10
Mount Cook Nat Park QLD 11 A12 16 K6
Mount Coolon QLD 8 D5
Mount Coot-tha QLD 3 E2 5 F8
Mount Cotton QLD 5 D9
Mount Cottrell VIC 36 C5 39 F13
Mount Crosby QLD 5 G8
Mount Damper SA 64 B4
Mount Dandenong VIC 37 D10
Mount Dangar QLD 8 B7
Mount David NSW 22 H5
Mount Direction TAS 55 E9 56 E4
Mount Drummond SA 64 H5
Mount Duneed VIC 36 H3 39 H12
Mount Dutton SA 66 E5
Mount Ebenezer NT 90 H6
Mount Eccles VIC 44 F6
Mount Eccles Nat Park VIC 38 G4
Mount Eckersley VIC 38 G4
Mount Egerton VIC 36 B1 39 E11
Mount Eliza VIC 37 G8 39 H14 44 E2

Mount Emu VIC 39 E9
Mount Ernest Island QLD 16 A2
Mount Etna Caves Nat Park QLD 9 G10
Mount Field Nat Park TAS 53 E8
Mount Fitton SA 67 J11
Mount Frankland Nat Park WA 74 J5
Mount Gambier SA 38 F1 63 B14
Mount Garnet QLD 11 E12
Mount George NSW 23 B12
Mount Gipps NSW 26 J2 28 A2
Mount Glorious QLD 4 G6
Mount Gordon Mine QLD 10 H3
Mount Granya State Park VIC 29 K13 43 B10
Mount Gravatt QLD 3 G5 5 E8
Mount Grenfell Historic Park NSW 27 H9
Mount Hawthorn WA 71 E3
Mount Helen VIC 39 E10
Mount Hill SA 64 G6
Mount Hope NSW 29 C10
Mount Hope SA 64 G5
Mount Hotham Alpine Village VIC 30 J5 43 F9
Mount Hunter NSW 21 F11
Mount Hyland Nat Res NSW 25 F11
Mount Hypipamee Nat Park QLD 11 E12
Mount Ida NSW 77 F10
Mount Imlay Nat Park NSW 31 K10 47 A13
Mount Irvine NSW 20 K6
Mount Isa QLD 10 K3 12 A3
Mount Jerusalem Nat Park NSW 7 J13 25 B14
Mount Kaputar Nat Park NSW 24 F5
Mount Keith Mine WA 77 C10
Mount Kokeby WA 72 B4
Mount Kororoit VIC 36 B5
Mount Ku-ring-gai NSW 19 A5 20 D6
Mount Larcom QLD 9 H11
Mount Lawley WA 71 F4
Mount Lawson State Park VIC 29 K13 30 F5 43 B11
Mount Leyson Mine QLD 8 B4 11 J14
Mount Liebig NT 90 E4
Mount Lion NSW 25 A13
Mount Lloyd TAS 50 C1 53 F9
Mount Lonarch VIC 39 D9
Mount Macedon VIC 39 D13
Mount Magnet WA 76 E7
Mount Magnificent Con Park SA 61 F7
Mount Manning Nat Res WA 77 G9
Mount Margaret WA 77 F12 83 D1
Mount Martha VIC 39 H14 44 E1
Mount Mary SA 62 D5 65 G11
Mount Mee QLD 4 G4
Mount Mercer VIC 39 F10
Mount Molloy QLD 11 C12
Mount Morgan QLD 9 H10
Mount Morgans WA 77 F12 83 D1
Mount Moriac VIC 36 H1
Mount Mort QLD 5 K11
Mount Mulligan QLD 11 D11
Mount Napier State Park VIC 38 G5
Mount Nathan QLD 5 C12
Mount Nebo QLD 4 G7
Mount O'Connell Nat Park QLD 9 G9
Mount Olive NSW 23 D9
Mount Ommaney QLD 3 G2
Mount Ossa QLD 9 D8
Mount Oxide Mine QLD 10 H3
Mount Perry QLD 7 B10
Mount Pleasant QLD 4 G5
Mount Pleasant SA 60 E7 62 E6 65 J10
Mount Pleasant WA 71 H3
Mount Pritchard NSW 19 G1 21 E9
Mount Remarkable Nat Park SA 62 G2 65 E9
Mount Rescue Con Park SA 63 B9
Mount Richmond Nat Park VIC 38 H3
Mount Royal Nat Park NSW 23 C9
Mount Russell NSW 24 E7
Mount Samaria State Park VIC 30 J2 42 F6
Mount Samson QLD 4 G6
Mount Scott Con Park SA 63 C11
Mount Seaview NSW 23 A11 25 K10
Mount Selwyn NSW 30 F7 43 A14
Mount Seymour TAS 53 D11
Mount Shaugh Con Park SA 40 H1 63 A9
Mount Stirling Alpine Resort VIC 42 G7 46 A2
Mount Surprise QLD 11 F11
Mount Tamborine QLD 5 D12
Mount Tarampa QLD 5 K8
Mount Taylor VIC 43 K11 45 B13 46 D6
Mount Torrens SA 60 F6 62 E7 65 J10
Mount Vernon NSW 75 G14 83 J2
Mount Victoria NSW 22 G7
Mount Walker WA 75 C11
Mount Wallace VIC 36 C2 39 F11
Mount Walsh Nat Park QLD 7 C11
Mount Warning Nat Park NSW 7 J13 25 A13
Mount Waverley VIC 35 E6
Mount Webb Nat Park QLD 11 A12 16 J6
Mount Wedge SA 64 F4
Mount White NSW 20 D4
Mount William Nat Park TAS 55 D14

Mount Wilson NSW 20 K7 22 G7
Mount Worth State Park VIC 44 E6
Mountain Creek NSW 29 J13
Mountain Creek QLD 4 E1
Mountain River TAS 50 E3 53 G10
Mountain View VIC 37 H14
Moura QLD 9 K9
Mourilyan QLD 11 E13
Mourilyan Harbour QLD 11 E13
Moutajup VIC 38 E5
Mowanjum WA 79 A10 80 G6
Mowbray TAS 56 G5
Mowbray Park NSW 21 G12
Mowen WA 73 J12
Moyarra VIC 37 K13
Moyhu VIC 30 H3 42 D7
Moyston VIC 38 D7
Muchea WA 72 F2 74 C3 76 K5
Muckadilla QLD 6 E4
Muckatah VIC 30 F1 42 A4
Muckaton VIC 29 K10
Mud Island QLD 4 C7
Mud Island VIC 36 H6
Mudamuckla SA 64 D3
Mudgee NSW 22 D5
Mudgeeraba QLD 5 B13 7 H13
Mudgegonga VIC 30 H4 43 D8
Mudludja WA 79 B12 81 H9
Muggabullin Swamp WA 78 K5
Muiron Islands WA 78 F2
Mukinbudin WA 74 A7 76 J7
Mulan WA 79 D13
Mulbring NSW 23 D10
Mulca VIC 28 H2 40 E2
Mulga Bore SA 68 B5
Mulgildie QLD 7 A9 9 K11
Mulgoa NSW 21 G9
Mulgrave NSW 20 F7
Mulgrave VIC 37 E9
Mullaley NSW 24 J5
Mullaloo WA 71 A1 72 G2 74 C2 76 K4
Mullalyup WA 73 F11
Mullaway NSW 25 F13
Mulline WA 77 G10
Mullion Creek NSW 22 F4
Mullumbimby NSW 7 J13 25 B14
Mulpata SA 62 B7 65 K12
Mulwala NSW 29 K11 30 F2 42 A5
Mulyandry NSW 22 G2 29 D14
Mulyati NT 79 J14 83 A7
Mumballup WA 73 F10 74 G3
Mumbannar VIC 38 G2
Mumberkine WA 72 D1
Mumbil NSW 22 D4
Mummulgum NSW 7 K12 25 C12
Mumu QLD 13 A10
Mundaring WA 72 F3 74 C3 76 K5
Mundaring Weir WA 72 E3
Mundarlo NSW 29 H14 30 D6
Munderoo NSW 29 K14 30 F6 43 A12
Mundijong WA 72 F5 73 C6
Mundiwindi WA 78 H7 82 H7
Mundoona VIC 42 B3
Mundoora SA 62 G3 65 F9
Mundowey NSW 24 H7
Mundrabilla WA 83 F6
Mundrabilla Motel WA 83 G6
Mundubbera QLD 7 B10
Mundulla SA 63 B10
Mungalawurru NT 89 G8
Mungallala QLD 6 D3
Mungana QLD 11 D11
Mungar QLD 7 C12
Mungaroona Range Nat Res WA 78 F5
Mungerannie Roadhouse SA 67 E10
Mungeriba NSW 22 C9 29 A14
Mungeribar NSW 27 K14
Munghorn Gap Nat Res NSW 22 D6
Mungindi NSW 6 K5 24 C3
Mungkan Kandju Nat Park QLD 16 G3
Mungkarta QLD 89 D13
Mungonbar QLD 8 B7
Mungrave QLD 7 C12
Mungil NT 6 K5 24 C3
Munmorah State Rec Area NSW 20 A1 23 F10
Munno Para SA 60 C3
Munro VIC 43 K9 45 C11 46 E4
Muntadgin WA 74 C7 77 K8
Muntz Nat Res WA 75 G14 83 J2
Munyaroo Con Park SA 62 J3 65 F8
Muogamarra Nat Res NSW 20 D6
Muradup WA 73 B12
Muralag QLD 16 B2
Murarrie QLD 3 E6
Murbko SA 62 D5 65 H11
Murcheboluc VIC 36 G1
Murchison NSW 42 D3
Murchison East VIC 42 D3
Murchison Roadhouse WA 76 C4
Murdinga SA 64 G5
Murdoch WA 71 J3

Murdunna TAS 51 E13 53 G12
Muresk WA 72 C2
Murga NSW 22 F2
Murgenella NT 85 A7 86 B6
Murgon QLD 7 D11
Murninnie SA 62 H3 65 F8
Muronbung NSW 22 C4
Murphys Creek QLD 7 G11
Murra Warra VIC 40 K5
Murrabit VIC 28 J7 41 G11
Murradoc VIC 36 G5
Murramarang Nat Park NSW 31 E12
Murrami NSW 29 F11 30 B3
Murrawal NSW 22 A5 24 K3
Murray Bridge SA 62 D7 65 J11
Murray River Nat Park SA 28 F1 62 B6 65 H13
Murray Sunset Nat Park VIC 28 G2 40 D3 62 A6 65 J14
Murray Town SA 62 G2 65 E9
Murray-Kulkyne Park VIC 28 G4 40 C6
Murrayville VIC 28 J2 40 F2 63 A8 65 K14
Murrigal QLD 11 F13
Murrin Bridge NSW 29 C11
Murrindal VIC 43 H13 47 B8
Murrindindi VIC 42 H4
Murringo NSW 22 J3 31 A8
Murroon VIC 39 J10
Murrumbateman NSW 31 C9
Murrumburrah NSW 22 K3 30 B7
Murrungowar VIC 47 C10
Murrurundi NSW 23 B8
Murtoa VIC 38 A6
Murun Murula NT 89 F14
Murweh QLD 15 E13
Murwillumbah NSW 7 J13 25 A14
Musselboro TAS 55 F11
Musselroe Bay Con Res TAS 55 C13
Muswellbrook NSW 23 C9
Mutarnee QLD 11 G13
Mutawintji Nat Park NSW 26 H4
Mutawintji Nat Res NSW 26 G4
Mutchilba QLD 11 D12
Mutdapilly QLD 5 H10
Muttaburra QLD 8 F1 13 D11
Muttama NSW 29 G14 30 C7
Mutton Bird Island TAS 52 J5
Myall VIC 41 G11
Myall Lake NSW 23 D12
Myall Lakes Nat Park NSW 23 D12
Myalla TAS 54 D4
Myalup WA 73 G8 74 F2
Myamyn VIC 38 G4
Mylestom NSW 25 G12
Mylor SA 60 H4 62 F7 65 J10
Myola VIC 39 A13 42 D1
Mypolonga SA 62 D7 65 J11
Myponga SA 61 G5 63 F8 65 K10
Myponga Beach SA 61 F4 63 F8 65 K9
Myponga Con Park SA 61 G4
Myponga Reservoir SA 61 G4
Myrla SA 62 B6 65 H12
Myrniong VIC 36 B3 39 E12
Myrrhee VIC 42 E6
Myrtle Bank SA 59 H5
Myrtle Bank TAS 55 E10 56 E7
Myrtle Scrub NSW 23 A11 25 K10
Myrtleford VIC 30 H4 43 D8
Myrtletown QLD 3 C6
Myrtleville NSW 22 K6 31 B11
Mysia VIC 41 J10
Mystery Bay NSW 31 G11
Mystic Park VIC 41 G10
Myubee QLD 12 B4

# N

Nabageena TAS 54 D3
Nabarlek NT 86 D7
Nabawa WA 76 F3
Nabiac NSW 23 C12
Nabowla TAS 55 E10 56 D7
Naccowlah Oil Field QLD 14 G6
Nackara SA 62 F2 65 E11
Nadgee Nat Res NSW 31 K11 47 C14
Nagambie VIC 39 B14 42 E2
Nagoorin QLD 9 J11
Nailsworth SA 59 E4
Nairne SA 60 H6 62 E7 65 J10
Nakara NT 84 A3
Nala TAS 53 D11
Nalangil VIC 39 H9
Nalya WA 72 A5
Namadgi Nat Park ACT 31 E9
Nambour QLD 7 E13
Nambrok VIC 45 D10 46 E3
Nambucca Heads NSW 25 H12
Nambung Nat Park WA 74 A1 76 H4
Namming Nat Res WA 74 A2 76 J4
Nana Glen NSW 25 F12
Nanango QLD 7 E11
Nanarup WA 74 K6
Nandaly VIC 28 H4 40 F7
Nanga WA 72 F7
Nangalala NT 87 C10
Nangana VIC 37 D11

Nangar Nat Park **NSW** 22 F3
Nangiloc **VIC** 28 G4 40 B5
Nangkita **SA** 61 F7
Nangus **NSW** 29 H14 30 C6
Nangwarry **SA** 38 E1 63 B13
Nannine **WA** 76 C7
Nannup **WA** 73 G12 74 H3
Nantawarra **SA** 62 G4 65 G9
Napperby **SA** 62 G5 65 F9
Napranum **QLD** 16 E1
Nar Nar Goon **VIC** 37 F12 44 D4
Nar Nar Goon North **VIC** 37 F12
Naracoopa **TAS** 54 B7
Naracoorte **SA** 38 C1 63 B12
Naracoorte Caves Con Park **SA** 38 C1 63 B12
Naradhan **NSW** 29 D11
Narangba **QLD** 4 F5
Narara **NSW** 20 C4
Narbethong **VIC** 37 A12 42 J4 44 A4
Nardoo **SA** 15 G13
Nareen **VIC** 38 D3
Narellan **NSW** 21 F11
Narellan Vale **NSW** 21 F11
Narembeen **WA** 74 C7 76 K7
Naretha **WA** 83 F3
Nariel Creek **VIC** 30 G6 43 C12
Naringal **VIC** 38 H7
Narioka **VIC** 41 J14 42 B2
Narooma **NSW** 31 G11
Narrabarba **NSW** 31 K10 47 B13
Narrabeen **NSW** 19 C7 20 B7
Narrabeen Lakes **NSW** 20 B7
Narrabri **NSW** 24 G5
Narrabri West **NSW** 24 G5
Narraburra **NSW** 22 J1 29 F14 30 A6
Narran Lake **NSW** 27 D13
Narrandera **NSW** 29 G11 30 C3
Narraport **VIC** 28 K5 41 H8
Narrawa **NSW** 22 J4 31 B9
Narraweena **NSW** 19 C7 20 B7
Narrawong **VIC** 38 H4
Narre Warren **VIC** 37 F10
Narre Warren East **VIC** 37 E10
Narre Warren North **VIC** 37 E10
Narrewillock **VIC** 41 J9
Narridy **SA** 62 F3 65 F9
Narrien Range Nat Park **QLD** 8 G5 13 D14
Narrikup **WA** 74 J6
Narrogin **WA** 72 A7 74 E5
Narromine **NSW** 22 C2
Narrung **SA** 63 E8 65 K11
Narrung **VIC** 28 G5 41 C8
Narungar **SA** 64 B7
Nashdale **NSW** 22 F4
Nathalia **VIC** 29 K9 41 J14 42 B3
Nathan **QLD** 3 G4
Natimuk **VIC** 38 B4
National Park **TAS** 53 F8
Natone **TAS** 54 E5
Nattai **NSW** 21 H12 22 H7 31 A12
Nattai Nat Park **NSW** 21 H13 22 J7 31 A12
Natte Yallock **VIC** 39 B9
Natural Bridge **QLD** 5 C14
Naturi **SA** 62 D7 65 K11
Natya **VIC** 28 H5 41 D8
Nauiyu **NT** 86 F3
Navarre **VIC** 39 B8
Nayook **VIC** 37 E14 42 K5 44 C6
N'dhala Gorge Nature Park **NT** 91 F9
Nea **NSW** 24 J6
Neale Junction **WA** 83 D4
Neale Junction Nat Res **WA** 83 D4
Nearie Lake Nat Res **NSW** 28 D3
Nebo **QLD** 8 E7
Nectar Brook **SA** 62 G1 65 E9
Nedlands **WA** 71 G2
Neds Corner **VIC** 28 F2 40 A2
Needles **TAS** 55 G8
Neerabup Nat Park **WA** 72 G2 74 C2 76 K4
Neeralin Pool **WA** 73 A8
Neerim **VIC** 44 C6
Neerim South **VIC** 44 D6
Neeworra **NSW** 24 C3
Neilrex **NSW** 22 B5
Nelia **QLD** 10 K7 12 A7
Nelligen **NSW** 31 E11
Nelshaby **SA** 62 G2 65 E9
Nelson **NSW** 20 E7
Nelson **VIC** 38 G2 63 A14
Nelson Bay **NSW** 23 E11
Nemingha **NSW** 24 J7
Nene Valley Con Park **SA** 63 B14
Nepabunna **SA** 65 A11 67 K11
Nepean Nickel Mine **WA** 75 B12 77 J10
Nepean Reservoir **NSW** 21 F14
Neptune Island **SA** 64 K6
Nerang **QLD** 5 C12 7 H13
Neranwood **QLD** 5 C14
Nerriga **NSW** 31 D11
Nerrigundah **NSW** 31 G11
Nerrin Nerrin **VIC** 39 F8
Netherby **VIC** 40 J3
Nethercote **NSW** 31 J10 47 A14

Netherdale **QLD** 8 D7
Netherton **SA** 63 C8 65 K12
Netley **SA** 59 G3
Neuarpur **VIC** 38 B2
Neunman **NT** 90 F2
Neurea **NSW** 22 D4
Neurum **QLD** 4 H3
Neutral Bay **NSW** 19 E6
Nevertire **NSW** 20 D2 22 B1 27 J14
Neville **NSW** 22 G4
New Angledool **NSW** 6 K3 27 B14
New Beith **QLD** 5 F10
New England Nat Park **NSW** 25 G11
New Farm **QLD** 3 E4 5 E8
New Mollyann **NSW** 22 A5 24 K3
New Norcia **WA** 74 A3 76 J5
New Norfolk **TAS** 50 B2
New Residence **SA** 62 B5 65 H12
New Town **TAS** 49 A1
New Year Island **TAS** 54 A6
Newbridge **NSW** 22 G5
Newbridge **VIC** 39 B11
Newburn **WA** 71 G6
Newbury **VIC** 39 D12
Newcastle **NSW** 23 E11
Newcastle Bay **QLD** 16 B2
Newcastle Waters **NT** 88 D7
Newdegate **WA** 75 F8
Newell **QLD** 11 C12
Newfield **VIC** 39 J8
Newham **VIC** 39 D13
Newhaven **VIC** 44 F3
Newland Head Con Park **SA** 61 K5 63 F8 65 K10
Newlands **WA** 73 G11
Newlands Mine **QLD** 8 D6
Newlyn **VIC** 39 D11
Newman **WA** 78 G6 82 H6
Newmarket **QLD** 3 D3
Newmerella **VIC** 43 K14 47 D9
Newnes **NSW** 22 F7
Newport **NSW** 19 A7 20 B6
Newport **VIC** 35 E2 36 D6
Newry **WA** 43 K8 45 C10 46 E3
Newry Islands Nat Park **QLD** 9 C8
Newrybar **NSW** 25 B14
Newstead **SA** 3 E4
Newstead **VIC** 39 C11
Newton **SA** 59 F6
Newton Boyd **NSW** 25 E11
Newtown **NSW** 19 F5
Newtown **VIC** 36 G3
Ngalingkadji **WA** 79 C11 81 J9
Ngallo **VIC** 40 F1
Nganggawanili **WA** 77 C10 78 K7
Ngarkat Con Park **SA** 28 K1 40 H1 63 B9 65 K13
Ngarngurr **NT** 90 J2
Ngarutjara **SA** 68 A4 68 A4 90 K5
Nguiu **NT** 85 A1 86 C3
Ngukurr **NT** 87 H9
Ngumpan **WA** 79 C12 81 K9
Nhill **VIC** 40 K3
Nhulunbuy **NT** 87 C13
Niagara **WA** 77 G11 83 E1
Niagara Park **NSW** 20 C3
Niangala **NSW** 25 K8
Nicholls Rivulet **TAS** 50 J3 53 H10
Nicholson **VIC** 43 K11 45 C13 46 D6
Nicol Island **NT** 87 F2
Nicoll Scrub Nat Park **QLD** 5 B14
Niemur **NSW** 41 E11
Nierinna **TAS** 50 F4 53 G10
Nietta **TAS** 54 F6
Nifty Mine **WA** 78 F7
Night Island **QLD** 16 J4
Nightcap Nat Park **NSW** 7 J13 25 B13
Nightcliff **NT** 84 B2
Nildottie **SA** 62 D6 65 J11
Nile **TAS** 55 G10 56 K7
Nilgen Nat Res **WA** 74 A2 76 J4
Nillahcootie **VIC** 30 J2 42 F6
Nimaru **QLD** 15 D13
Nimbin **NSW** 7 J13 25 B13
Nimmitabel **NSW** 31 H9
Ninda **VIC** 40 F7
Nindigully **QLD** 6 H5 24 A2
Ninety Mile Tank **WA** 75 E11
Ningaloo Marine Park **WA** 78 F1
Ningi **QLD** 4 E4
Ninian Bay **QLD** 16 H6
Ninnes **SA** 62 G4 65 G9
Ninth Island **TAS** 55 C10
Nirranda **VIC** 38 J7
Nirranda East **VIC** 38 J7
Nirranda South **VIC** 38 J7
Nirrippi **NT** 90 D3
Nitmiluk Nat Park **NT** 85 H6 86 G6
Nixon Skinner Con Park **SA** 61 G4
Noarlunga Centre **SA** 60 J1 61 D5
Nobby **QLD** 7 H11
Noble Park **VIC** 35 G6 37 E9
Noccundra **QLD** 14 G7
Nocolche Nat Res **NSW** 26 D7
Noggerup **WA** 73 E10 74 G3
Noland Bay **TAS** 55 D10
Nollamara **WA** 71 D3
Nombinnie Nat Res **NSW** 29 C11
Nome **QLD** 8 A5 11 H14

Nonda **QLD** 11 K8 13 A8
Noogoora **QLD** 5 H8
Noojee **VIC** 44 C6
Nook **TAS** 54 F6
Noonaera Ruins **WA** 83 H6
Noonamah **NT** 85 D2 86 D4
Noondoo **QLD** 6 J4 24 B1
Noonkanbah **WA** 79 B11 80 J7
Noorat **VIC** 39 H8
Noorinbee **VIC** 47 C11
Noorinbee North **VIC** 47 C11
Noosa Heads **QLD** 7 D13
Noosa Nat Park **QLD** 7 D13
Nora Creina **SA** 63 D12
Noradjuha **VIC** 38 B4
Norah Head **NSW** 20 A2 23 F10
Noranda **WA** 71 D5
Noraville **NSW** 20 A1
Nords Wharf **NSW** 23 G10
Norfolk Bay **TAS** 51 F12 53 G12
Norlane **VIC** 36 F3
Normanhurst **NSW** 20 D7
Normanton **QLD** 10 H6
Normanville **SA** 61 G3 63 G8 65 K9
Nornalup **WA** 74 K4
Norseman **WA** 75 D13 83 H1
North Adelaide **SA** 58 A2 59 F4
North Bannister **WA** 72 D6
North Beach **WA** 71 D1
North Bondi **NSW** 21 B8
North Bourke **NSW** 27 E10
North Bruny Island **TAS** 50 H6 53 H10
North Dandalup **QLD** 72 F6
North East Island Nat Park **QLD** 9 E10
North East Isles **NT** 87 F13
North Fremantle **WA** 71 H1
North Goonyella **QLD** 8 E7
North Goonyella Mine **QLD** 8 E6
North Haven **SA** 23 B13
North Haven **NSW** 59 C2 60 E1
North Hobart **TAS** 49 B1
North Ipswich **QLD** 5 H9
North Isis **QLD** 7 B11
North Island **NT** 87 J13 89 A13
North Island **WA** 76 F7
North Karlgarin Nat Res **WA** 74 D7
North Keppel Island **QLD** 9 G11
North Lilydale **TAS** 55 E6
North Maclean **QLD** 5 G10
North Molle Island **QLD** 9 B8
North Motton **TAS** 54 E6
North Parkes Mine **NSW** 22 E2 29 C14
North Peak **SA** 66 E6
North Perth **WA** 71 F4
North Pinjarra **WA** 72 F6
North Point Island **NT** 87 F12
North Richmond **NSW** 20 G7
North Riverside **TAS** 55 F9 56 G5
North Ryde **NSW** 19 D4 21 C8
North Scottsdale **TAS** 55 D11
North Shields **SA** 64 H6
North Shore **VIC** 36 F3
North St Ives **NSW** 20 C7
North Star **NSW** 7 K8 24 C6
North Stradbroke Island **QLD** 5 B9 7 G13
North Sydney **NSW** 19 E6 21 B8
North Tamborine **QLD** 5 D12
North Turramurra **NSW** 19 B5
North West Cape **WA** 78 F1
North West Crocodile Island **NT** 87 B10
North West Island **QLD** 9 H12
North Willoughby **NSW** 19 D6
North Wollongong **NSW** 21 C8
Northam **WA** 72 D2 74 C4 76 K6
Northampton **WA** 76 E3
Northbridge **NSW** 19 E6
Northbridge **WA** 70 A2 71 F4
Northcliffe **WA** 74 J3
Northcote **VIC** 35 C4 37 C8
Northdown **TAS** 54 E7
Northfield **SA** 59 E5 60 F3
Northumberland Islands Nat Park **QLD** 9 D9
Norton Summit **SA** 59 G7 60 G4 61 A7
Norvill Park **QLD** 9 K12
Norwood **SA** 59 G5 60 G3 61 A6
Norwood **TAS** 56 G5
Notley Hills **TAS** 55 F9 56 F3
Notts Well **SA** 62 C6 65 H12
Novar Gardens **SA** 59 H2
Nowa Nowa **VIC** 43 K13 46 D7
Nowendoc **NSW** 23 A11 25 K9
Nowingi **VIC** 28 G3 40 C5
Nowley **NSW** 24 F3
Nowra **NSW** 31 C12
NSW Jervis Bay Nat Park **NSW** 31 D13
Nubeena **TAS** 51 H11 53 H12
Nudgee **QLD** 3 C5 4 E7
Nudgee Beach **QLD** 3 B5 4 E7
Nuga Nuga Nat Park **QLD** 6 A5 8 K7
Nugent **TAS** 51 A11 53 F12
Nullagine **WA** 78 F7 82 E7
Nullamanna **NSW** 25 D8
Nullawarre **VIC** 38 J7
Nullawil **VIC** 28 K5 41 H8
Number One **NSW** 23 B11
Numbla Vale **NSW** 31 H8
Numbugga **NSW** 31 H10

Numbulwar **NT** 87 G11
Numeralla **NSW** 31 G9
Numinbah Valley **QLD** 5 C14
Numurkah **VIC** 29 K9 30 G1 42 B3
Nunamara **TAS** 55 F10 56 G7
Nundah **QLD** 3 C4
Nundle **NSW** 23 A9 25 K8
Nundroo **SA** 68 K5
Nunga **VIC** 28 H4 40 E6
Nungarin **WA** 74 B6 76 J7
Nungatta **NSW** 31 K10 47 B12
Nunjikompita **SA** 64 D3
Nunniong Plains **VIC** 43 G12 46 A7
Nunnyah Con Res **SA** 64 C3
Nurina **WA** 83 F5
Nuriootpa **SA** 60 A6 62 E6 65 H10
Nurrabiel **VIC** 38 B5
Nutfield **VIC** 37 B9
Nuyts Archipelago Con Park **SA** 64 D2
Nuytsland Nat Res **WA** 83 H3
NW Vernon Island **NT** 85 B2 86 C3
Nyabing **WA** 74 G7
Nyah **VIC** 28 H6 41 E9
Nyah West **VIC** 28 H6 41 E9
Nyamup **WA** 73 E14
Nyapari **SA** 68 A2 90 K3
Nyarrin **VIC** 40 F7
Nyerimilang State Park **VIC** 43 K12 45 C14 46 E7
Nyikukura **SA** 68 A1 79 K14 83 B7 90 K1
Nyintjilan **WA** 83 B6
Nymagee **NSW** 27 J11 29 A11
Nymboi-Binderay Nat Park **NSW** 25 F12
Nymboida **NSW** 25 E11
Nymboida Nat Park **NSW** 25 E11
Nyngan **NSW** 27 H12
Nyora **NSW** 29 J10 30 E2
Nyora **VIC** 37 J12 44 E4
Nypo **VIC** 40 G5

## O

Oak Beach **QLD** 11 C12
Oak Valley **SA** 68 F3
Oakbank **SA** 60 G5
Oakey **QLD** 7 G10
Oakey Creek **NSW** 22 A6 24 K4
Oakhurst **NSW** 21 F8
Oaklands **NSW** 29 J11 30 E2
Oaklands Park **SA** 59 J3
Oakleigh **VIC** 35 F5 37 E8 39 F14 42 K2 44 C2
Oaks **TAS** 55 G9 56 J4
Oakvale **VIC** 41 H9
Oakville **NSW** 20 F7
Oakwood **NSW** 25 E8
Oakwood **TAS** 51 H12 53 H12
Oaky Creek Mine **QLD** 8 G7
Oasis Roadhouse **QLD** 11 G11
Oatlands **NSW** 21 D8
Oatlands **TAS** 53 D10 55 K10
Oatley **NSW** 21 C10
OB Flat **SA** 38 G1 63 B14
Oban **NSW** 25 F10
Oberne **NSW** 29 J14 30 D6
Oberon **NSW** 22 G6
Obley **NSW** 22 D3
Ocean Grove **VIC** 36 H4 39 H12
Ocean Reef **WA** 71 A1
Ocean Shores **NSW** 25 B14
Ocean View **QLD** 4 G5
O'Connell **NSW** 22 G6
O'Connor **WA** 71 J2
Offham **QLD** 15 A13
Officer **VIC** 37 F11
Officer Creek **SA** 68 B5
Ogmore **QLD** 9 F9
Olary **SA** 62 B5 65 D13
Old Adaminaby **NSW** 31 F8
Old Aparawilinitja **SA** 68 C5
Old Bar **NSW** 23 C13
Old Beach **TAS** 50 A5 53 F10
Old Bonalbo **NSW** 25 B12
Old Grevillia **NSW** 25 A12
Old Halls Creek **WA** 79 B13 81 J12
Old Junee **NSW** 29 G13 30 C5
Old Noarlunga **SA** 60 K1 61 D5 62 F7 65 J10
Old Onslow Historic Ruin **WA** 78 F2
Old Tyabb **VIC** 37 H9
Old Warburton **VIC** 37 C13
Old Warrah **NSW** 23 A8
Oldina **TAS** 54 D4
Olinda **NSW** 22 E7
Olinda **VIC** 37 D10 42 K3 44 C3
Olio **QLD** 13 C9
Olive Island Con Park **SA** 64 E3
Olympic Dam **SA** 66 K7
O'Malley **SA** 68 H4
Ombersley **VIC** 39 H10
Omeo **VIC** 30 J6 43 G11 46 A6
Ondit **VIC** 39 H10
One Arm Point **WA** 80 E5
One Mile Rocks Nat Res **WA** 75 F9
One Tree **NSW** 29 F8 41 A13
One Tree Hill **SA** 60 D4
One Tree Island **QLD** 9 H12
Ongerup **WA** 74 H7
Onkaparinga River Nat Park **SA** 60 K2 61 D6
Onslow **WA** 78 F2

Oodla Wirra **SA** 62 E2 65 E11
Oodnadatta **SA** 66 D5
Oolarinna Well **SA** 66 A7
Ooldea **SA** 68 H6
Ooma North **NSW** 22 G2 29 D14
Oombulgurri **WA** 81 C12
Oonah **TAS** 54 E4
Oondooroo **QLD** 13 C4
Oorindi **QLD** 10 K6 12 A6
Ootann **QLD** 11 E11
Ootha **NSW** 29 C13
Opalton **QLD** 13 E8
Ophir **NSW** 22 F4
Opossum Bay **TAS** 50 E7 53 G11
Ora Banda **WA** 77 H10
Oran Park **NSW** 21 F10
Orange **NSW** 22 F4
Orange Grove **WA** 71 H7
Orangeville **NSW** 21 G11
Oranmeir **NSW** 31 E10
Orbost **VIC** 43 K14 47 D9
Orchard Hills **NSW** 21 F8
Orchid Beach **QLD** 7 A13 9 K14
Orchid Valley **WA** 73 B12
Ord River Nat Res **WA** 81 C14
O'Reillys **QLD** 7 H13 25 A13
Orford **TAS** 53 E12
Orford **VIC** 38 H5
Organ Pipes Nat Park **VIC** 36 B6 39 E13 42 J1
Orielton **TAS** 51 A9 53 F11
Orkabie **QLD** 9 E9
Ormeau **QLD** 5 C11
Ormiston **QLD** 5 B9
Orpheus Island Nat Park **QLD** 11 G14
Orroroo **SA** 62 F1 65 E10
Orrvale **VIC** 42 C3
Osborne **NSW** 29 H12 30 D4
Osborne **SA** 59 C1
Osborne Park **WA** 71 E2
Osborne Well **NSW** 29 J10 30 E2
Osmington **WA** 73 J12
Osterley **TAS** 53 D8
O'Sullivan Beach **SA** 60 J1 61 C5
Otago **TAS** 50 B5 53 F10
Otford **NSW** 21 E10
Ottoway **SA** 59 D2
Otway Nat Park **VIC** 39 K10
Ourimbah **NSW** 20 B3 23 F10
Ournie **NSW** 29 K14 30 F6 43 A12
Ouse **TAS** 53 D8
Outer Harbor **SA** 59 B2 60 E1 62 F6 65 J10
Outer Sister Island **TAS** 55 A9
Ouyen **VIC** 28 H4 40 E5
Ovens **VIC** 43 D8
Overland Corner **SA** 62 B5 65 H12
Overland Telegraph Station Res **NT** 89 G9
Overlander Roadhouse **WA** 76 C3 78 K2
Owen **SA** 62 F5 65 H10
Owens Gap **NSW** 23 C8
Owingup Nat Res **WA** 74 K4
Oxenford **QLD** 5 C11
Oxford Bay **QLD** 16 C3
Oxford Falls **NSW** 19 C6 20 B7
Oxley **NSW** 41 A11
Oxley **QLD** 3 G2 5 F9
Oxley **VIC** 42 D7
Oxley Island **NT** 86 A6
Oxley Wild Rivers Nat Park **NSW** 25 J10
Oyster Bay **NSW** 21 C10
Oyster Cove **TAS** 50 H4 53 H10
Ozenkadnook **VIC** 38 B3

## P

Pacific Palms **NSW** 23 D12
Packsaddle **NSW** 26 F3
Padbury **WA** 71 B2
Paddington **NSW** 18 D3 21 B8
Paddington **QLD** 3 E3
Paddington Siding **WA** 77 H11 83 F1
Paddys Ranges State Park **VIC** 39 C10
Paddys River **NSW** 22 K7 31 B11
Padstow **NSW** 19 H3 21 D9
Padstow Heights **NSW** 19 H3
Padthaway **SA** 63 B11
Padthaway Con Park **SA** 63 B11
Pagewood **NSW** 21 B9
Pago Mission **WA** 81 A11
Paignie **VIC** 28 H3 40 E5
Pains Island **QLD** 10 D3
Pakenham **VIC** 37 F11 44 D4
Pakenham South **VIC** 37 G11
Pakenham Upper **VIC** 37 F11
Palana **TAS** 55 A8
Palgarup **WA** 73 E13
Pallamallawa **NSW** 24 D6
Pallamana **SA** 62 E7 65 J11
Pallara **QLD** 3 J3
Pallarang **VIC** 28 H2 40 E2
Pallarenda **QLD** 8 A5 11 H14
Pallarup Nat Res **WA** 75 F9
Palm Beach **NSW** 20 B6 23 G9
Palm Beach **QLD** 5 B14
Palm Cove **QLD** 11 D13
Palm Grove **NSW** 20 C3
Palmdale **NSW** 20 C3
Palmer **SA** 62 E7 65 J11
Palmer River Roadhouse **QLD** 11 C11

Palmers Oakey NSW 22 F6
Palmerston NT 85 C2 86 D3
Palmgrove (Scientific) Nat Park QLD 6 A6 9 K8
Palmview QLD 4 E1
Palmwoods QLD 4 F1
Palmyra WA 71 J2
Paloona TAS 54 E7
Paluma QLD 11 G13
Paluma Range Nat Park QLD 11 G13
Palumpa NT 86 G2
Pambula NSW 31 J11 47 A14
Pambula Beach NSW 31 J11 47 A14
Pandanas Park WA 79 B10 80 H6
Pandappa Con Park SA 62 E3 65 F11
Panitya VIC 28 H1 40 F1
Panmure VIC 38 H4
Pannawonica WA 78 F3 82 E1
Pannikin Island QLD 5 C9
Panorama SA 59 J4
Pantijan WA 81 E8
Panton Hill VIC 37 B9 42 J3 44 A3
Paper Beach TAS 55 E9 56 E3
Pappinbarra NSW 23 A12 25 K11
Papunya NT 90 E5
Para Hills SA 59 C6 60 E3
Para Vista SA 59 D6
Paraburdoo WA 78 G4 82 G3
Parachilna SA 65 B10
Paracombe SA 54 F7
Paradise SA 59 E6
Paradise TAS 54 F7
Paradise Beach VIC 45 E12 46 F5
Paradise Point QLD 5 B11
Parafield SA 59 C5 60 E2
Parafield Gardens SA 59 C4
Paralowie SA 59 B4
Parap NT 84 D2
Paraparap VIC 36 H2
Paratoo SA 62 D1
Parattah TAS 53 D11
Parawa SA 61 J4
Pardoo Roadhouse WA 78 D6 82 B6
Parenna TAS 54 B6
Parham SA 62 G5 65 H9
Parilla SA 63 B8 65 K13
Paringa SA 28 F1 62 A5 65 H13
Paris Creek SA 60 K4
Park Holme SA 59 J3 60 G2 61 A5
Park Orchards VIC 35 C7
Park Ridge QLD 5 E10
Parkes ACT 32 C3
Parkes NSW 22 F2 29 C14
Parkham TAS 55 F8
Parkhurst QLD 9 H10
Parkinson QLD 5 E7
Parkside SA 58 D3 59 G4 60 G2 61 A6
Parkville NSW 23 B9
Parkwood QLD 5 B12
Parkwood WA 71 J5
Parma NSW 31 C12
Parnabal QLD 9 H8
Parndana SA 63 J9
Parnngurr WA 79 G9
Paroo Siding WA 77 C9 78 K6
Parrakie SA 28 C8 65 K12
Parramatta NSW 19 E2 21 D8 23 H9
Parrawe TAS 54 E5
Parry Lagoons Nat Res WA 81 D13
Parsons Beach SA 62 H6 65 J8
Partridge Island TAS 55 J9
Paru NT 85 A1 86 C3
Paruna SA 28 G1 62 B6 65 J13
Parwan VIC 36 E3 39 F12
Pascoe Vale VIC 36 C7
Paskeville SA 62 G4 65 G9
Pasminco Century Mine WA 10 G2
Passage Island TAS 55 A14
Pastoria VIC 39 D13
Pata SA 62 B6 65 H13
Patchewollock VIC 28 J4 40 F5
Paterson NSW 23 D8
Patersonia TAS 55 F10 56 F7
Patho VIC 29 K8 41 H12
Patonga NSW 20 C5
Patterson Lakes VIC 37 F9
Paupong NSW 31 H8
Paw Paw SA 60 G9
Pawleena TAS 51 A9 53 F11
Pawtella TAS 53 C11 55 K11
Payne QLD 8 G1 13 E10
Payneham SA 59 F5 60 F3
Paynes Crossing NSW 23 E9
Paynes Find WA 76 G7
Paynesville VIC 45 C13 46 E6
Peachester QLD 4 F2
Peak Charles Nat Park WA 75 E12
Peak Crossing QLD 5 H11
Peak Downs Mine QLD 8 F7
Peak Hill NSW 22 D2 29 B14
Peak Hill WA 77 A8 78 J5
Peak Range Nat Park QLD 8 F6
Peak View NSW 31 F10
Peake SA 63 C8 65 K12
Peakhurst NSW 19 H3
Pearcedale VIC 37 G9 37 G9 44 E2
Pearl Beach NSW 20 B5
Pearshape TAS 54 C6
Pearson Isles SA 64 G3
Peats Ridge NSW 20 C3
Pebbly Beach NSW 31 E12
Pedirka SA 66 B5

Peebinga SA 28 H1 40 D1 62 A7 65 J13
Peebinga Con Park SA 28 H1 40 E1 62 A7 65 J13
Peechelba VIC 30 G2 42 B6
Peel NSW 22 F5
Peel Island QLD 5 B8
Peelwood NSW 22 J5 31 A10
Peen Inlet WA 72 G6
Peerabeelup WA 73 G14
Pegarah TAS 54 C6
Pekina SA 62 F2 65 E10
Peko Mine NT 89 H9
Pelham TAS 53 E9
Pelican Waters QLD 4 E2
Pella VIC 40 H4
Pelorus Island QLD 11 G14
Pelsaert Group WA 76 F2
Pelverata TAS 50 G3 53 G10
Pemberton WA 73 F14 74 J3
Pembroke NSW 23 A13 25 K12
Penarie NSW 28 F6 41 B9
Pencil Pine TAS 54 G5
Penfield SA 60 C2
Penguin TAS 54 D6
Penna TAS 51 B8 53 F11
Pennant Hills NSW 19 C3 20 D7
Penneshaw SA 63 J8
Penola SA 38 E1 63 B13
Penong SA 64 C1 68 K6
Penrice SA 60 A7
Penrith NSW 19 D2 23 H8
Penshurst VIC 38 F6
Pental Island VIC 41 F10
Pentland QLD 8 C3 11 K12 13 A12
Penwortham SA 62 F4 65 G10
Penzance TAS 55 H8
Peppermint Grove WA 71 G2
Peppers Plains VIC 40 J5
Peppimenarti NT 86 G2
Peranga QLD 7 F10
Percival Lakes WA 79 E10
Perekerten NSW 28 H6 41 D10
Perenjori WA 76 G5
Perenna VIC 40 J4
Perforated Island SA 64 H4
Pericoe NSW 31 K10 47 A13
Perisher NSW 30 G7 43 D14
Perkins Bay TAS 54 C3
Perkins Island TAS 54 C2
Peron Island North NT 86 E2
Peron Island South NT 86 E2
Peron Peninsula WA 76 B2
Perponda SA 62 C7 65 J12
Perth TAS 55 G10 56 J5
Perth WA 71 F4 72 G3 74 C3 76 K4
Perth CBD WA 70
Perth Water WA 70
Perthville NSW 22 G5
Petcheys Bay TAS 50 J2 53 H9
Peterborough SA 62 E2 65 E10
Peterborough VIC 38 J7
Peterhead SA 59 D2
Peters Island QLD 8 A6
Petersville SA 62 G5 65 H9
Petford QLD 11 E11
Petina SA 64 D3
Petrie QLD 4 F6 7 F13
Petrie Terrace QLD 2 B1
Pettavel VIC 36 H2
Pheasant Creek VIC 42 H3
Pheasants Nest NSW 23 J8 31 A13
Phegans Bay NSW 20 C5
Phillip Bay NSW 21 B9
Phillip Island VIC 37 K9 39 J14 44 F2
Phillott QLD 15 H13
Phils Creek NSW 22 J4 31 A9
Phosphate Hill Mine QLD 12 C4
Piallamore NSW 25 J8
Piallaway NSW 24 J6
Piambie VIC 28 G5 41 D8
Piangil VIC 28 H5 41 E9
Piangil West VIC 41 E8
Piccadilly SA 59 J7 60 G4
Piccaninnie Ponds Con Park SA 38 G1 63 B14
Pickanjinnie QLD 6 E5
Pickering Brook WA 72 F4
Pickertaramoor NT 85 A2 86 C3
Picnic Point NSW 29 K9 41 H14 42 A2
Picola VIC 41 H14 42 A1
Picton NSW 21 F2 23 J8 31 A12
Picton WA 73 G9 74 F3
Piedmont VIC 37 D14
Piednippie SA 64 E3
Pielegia NT 88 F3
Pieman River State Res TAS 54 G3
Pier Millan VIC 28 H4 40 E7
Piesseville WA 73 A14 74 F5
Pigeon Hole NT 88 C4
Pigeon Ponds VIC 38 D4
Piggabeen NSW 5 B14
Pikedale QLD 7 J10 25 B9
Pilakatal NT 90 J2
Pilgna SA 68 C3
Pilkinga SA 68 C4
Pillar Valley NSW 25 E13
Pilliga NSW 24 G2
Pilliga Nat Res NSW 24 H4
Pimba SA 64 B7
Pimpama QLD 5 C11
Pimpinio VIC 38 A5
Pinchgut Junction VIC 36 K1
Pindar WA 76 E4

Pine Clump NSW 24 K1 27 H14
Pine Corner SA 62 K4 64 G6
Pine Creek NT 85 G4 86 F5
Pine Gap NT 91 F8
Pine Hill QLD 8 H5 13 F14
Pine Lodge VIC 42 C4
Pine Peak Island QLD 9 E10
Pine Point SA 62 G6 65 H9
Pine Ridge NSW 23 A8 24 K6
Pinery SA 62 F5 65 H10
Piney Range NSW 22 H2 29 E14
Pingaring WA 74 E7
Pingelly WA 72 B6 74 E5
Pingrup WA 74 G6 74 E3
Pinjarra WA 72 G6 74 E3
Pinjarra Hills QLD 3 G1
Pink Lakes State Park VIC 65 J14
Pinkawillinie Con Park SA 64 E5
Pinkenba QLD 3 D6
Pinnacle QLD 8 D7
Pinnaroo SA 28 J1 40 F1 63 A8 65 K13
Pioneer TAS 55 D13
Pioneer WA 75 C13 77 K1 83 G1
Pioneer Bay VIC 37 J11
Pipalyatjara SA 68 A1 79 K14 83 B7 90 K7
Pipers Brook TAS 55 D6 56 C6
Pipers River TAS 55 D9 56 C4
Pipon Island QLD 16 H5
Piries VIC 30 K2 42 H6 46 A1
Pirlangimpi NT 86 B3
Pirlta VIC 28 F3 40 B4
Pirrinuan QLD 7 F9
Pirron Yallock VIC 39 H9
Pirrulpakalarintja NT 90 J3
Pitalu NT 78 J1 90 J2
Pitfield VIC 39 F10
Pithara WA 76 H5
Pitt Town NSW 20 F6
Pittong VIC 39 E9
Pittsworth QLD 7 G10
Pittwater TAS 51 B8
Plainland QLD 5 K9
Platts NSW 31 J9 47 A12
Pleasant Hills NSW 29 J12 30 E4
Plenty TAS 50 A1 53 F9
Plenty VIC 35 A5 37 B8 39 E14 42 J2 44 B2
Plumpton NSW 21 F8
Plumridge Lakes Nat Res WA 83 E4
Plympton SA 59 H3 60 G1 61 A5
Plympton Park SA 59 H3
Poatina TAS 53 A9 55 H9
Poeppel Corner NT QLD SA 12 K2 67 A9 91 K14
Point Bell Con Res SA 64 D1 68 K6
Point Clare NSW 20 C4
Point Cook VIC 36 E6 39 F13 42 K1
Point Davenport Con Park SA 62 H7 65 J8
Point Denison WA 76 G3
Point Leo VIC 37 K8 39 H14 44 F2
Point Lonsdale VIC 36 H5 39 H13
Point Lookout QLD 4 A7 7 G14
Point Pass SA 62 E5 65 G10
Point Quobba WA 78 H1
Point Samson WA 78 E4 82 C2
Point Souttar SA 62 H7 65 J8
Point Stuart Coastal Res NT 85 B4 86 C5
Point Turton SA 62 H7 65 J8
Pokataroo NSW 24 D2
Police Point TAS 50 K2 53 H9
Policemans Point SA 63 D9
Poltalloch SA 63 E8 65 K11
Pomborneit VIC 39 H9
Pomborneit North VIC 39 H9
Pomona QLD 7 D12
Pomonal VIC 38 D7
Pompapiel VIC 41 K11
Pontville TAS 53 E10
Poochera SA 64 E4
Pooginagoric SA 38 A1 40 K1
Pooginook Con Park SA 62 C5 65 G12
Poolaijelo VIC 38 D2
Poolawanna No. 1 Oil Well SA 67 B9
Poole TAS 55 C13
Poona QLD 7 C13
Poona Nat Park QLD 7 C12
Pooncarie NSW 28 D4
Poonindie SA 64 H6
Poopelloe Lake NSW 26 H6
Pooraka SA 59 D5 60 E3
Poothoura SA 66 F3
Pootilla VIC 39 E11
Poowong VIC 37 J13 44 E5
Poowong East VIC 37 J14 44 E5
Poowong North VIC 37 J13
Popanyinning VIC 72 B6 74 E5
Popran Nat Park NSW 20 D3 23 H9
Porcupine Gorge Nat Park QLD 8 C1 11 K11
Porepunkah VIC 30 H4 43 E9
Pormpuraaw QLD 10 A6 16 J1
Porongurup WA 74 J6
Porongurup Nat Park WA 74 J6
Porphyry Mine WA 77 G12 83 E1
Port Adelaide SA 59 E2 60 E1 62 F6 65 J10
Port Albert VIC 45 G9 46 H3
Port Alma QLD 9 H9
Port Arthur TAS 51 H12 53 H12
Port Augusta SA 62 H1 65 D9

Port Botany NSW 19 H6
Port Broughton SA 62 G3 65 F9
Port Campbell VIC 39 J8
Port Campbell Nat Park VIC 39 J8
Port Davis SA 62 G3 65 F9
Port Douglas QLD 11 C12
Port Elliot SA 61 J7 63 F8 65 K10
Port Fairy VIC 38 H5
Port Fairy - Warrnambool Coastal Park VIC 38 H6
Port Franklin VIC 44 H7 46 H1
Port Gawler SA 60 C1 62 F6 65 H10
Port Gawler Con Park SA 60 C1
Port Germein SA 62 G2 65 E9
Port Gibbon SA 62 K4 64 G7
Port Hacking NSW 19 K4
Port Hedland WA 78 D5 82 B4
Port Hughes SA 62 H5 65 G8
Port Huon TAS 50 H1 53 H9
Port Jackson NSW 19 E7
Port Julia SA 62 G6 65 J8
Port Kembla NSW 21 C14 23 K8 31 B13
Port Kenny SA 64 E4
Port Latta TAS 54 C3
Port Lincoln SA 64 J6
Port MacDonnell SA 38 G1 63 B14
Port Macquarie NSW 23 A13 25 K12
Port Melbourne VIC 35 D3
Port Minlacowie SA 62 H6 65 J8
Port Neill SA 64 G6
Port Noarlunga SA 60 K1 61 D5 62 F7 65 J10
Port of Bowen Bay QLD 8 B7
Port Phillip Bay VIC 36 F6 39 G13 44 D1
Port Pirie SA 62 G2 65 F9
Port Rickaby SA 62 H6 65 H8
Port Roper NT 87 H10
Port Smith Caravan Park WA 79 B8 80 J2
Port Sorell TAS 55 E8
Port Stewart QLD 16 H4
Port Victoria SA 62 H6 65 H8
Port Vincent SA 62 G6 65 J9
Port Wakefield SA 62 G5 65 H9
Port Welshpool VIC 45 H8 46 H2
Port Willunga SA 61 E5
Portarlington VIC 36 G5 39 G13
Porters Retreat NSW 22 H6
Portland NSW 22 F6
Portland VIC 38 H4
Portland Bay VIC 38 H4
Portland Roads QLD 16 E4
Portsea VIC 36 J5 39 H13
Possession Island Nat Park QLD 16 B2
Potato Point NSW 31 G11
Potts Point NSW 18 B4
Pottsville NSW 7 J14 25 A14
Pound Creek VIC 44 G5
Powelltown VIC 37 D13 42 K4 44 C5
Powers Creek VIC 38 D2
Powlathanga QLD 8 B4 11 J13
Powlett Plains VIC 41 K10
Poynter Island QLD 9 E9
Prahran VIC 35 E4 37 D8
Prairie QLD 8 C1 11 K11 13 A11
Prairie VIC 41 K11
Precipice Nat Park QLD 6 B7
Premaydena TAS 51 G3 53 G12
Premer NSW 22 A6 24 K5
Preolenna TAS 54 D4
Preservation Island TAS 55 A13
Preston TAS 54 E6
Preston VIC 35 B4 36 C7
Preston Beach WA 72 H7 74 E2
Pretty Beach NSW 20 B5
Pretty Gully NSW 25 B11
Pretty Pines NSW 29 J8 41 F13
Prevelly WA 73 K12
Prevelly Park WA 74 H1
Price SA 62 G5 65 H9
Priestdale QLD 3 H6
Prime Seal Island TAS 55 B8
Primrose Sands TAS 51 D10 53 G12
Prince of Wales Island QLD 16 B2
Prince Regent Nat Res WA 81 D8
Princess Charlotte Bay QLD 16 H4
Princetown VIC 39 K8
Princhester QLD 9 G9
Priors Pocket QLD 3 H1
Priory TAS 55 E14
Probable Island NT 87 C11
Propodollah VIC 40 K3
Proserpine QLD 8 C7
Prospect NSW 19 E1 21 E8
Prospect SA 59 F4 60 F2
Prospect TAS 56 H5
Proston QLD 7 D10
Prubi QLD 13 C9
Prudhoe Island QLD 9 D9
Pucawan NSW 29 F13 30 B5
Puckapunyal VIC 39 C14 42 F2
Pudman Creek NSW 22 K4 31 B9
Pukatja (Ernabella) SA 68 A5 90 K6
Pullabooka NSW 22 G1 29 E14
Pullen Island SA 61 J7
Pullen Island Con Park SA 61 J7
Pullenvale QLD 5 F8

Pulletop NSW 29 J13 30 E5
Pulletop Nat Res NSW 29 E10
Pullut VIC 40 J5
Pumphreys Bridge WA 72 C6
Punchbowl NSW 19 G3 21 C9
Punmu WA 79 F9
Punthari SA 62 D6 65 J11
Pura Pura VIC 39 F8
Pureba Con Park SA 64 C3
Pureba Con Res SA 68 K7
Purfleet NSW 23 B12
Purga QLD 5 H10
Purlewaugh NSW 24 K4
Purnim VIC 38 H7
Purnong SA 62 D6 65 J11
Purnululu Con Res WA 79 B14 81 H13
Purnululu Nat Park WA 79 B14 81 G13
Purrumbete South VIC 39 H8
Puta Puta NT 90 H2
Putaputa SA 68 A1 90 K2
Putty NSW 20 J1 23 E8
Pyalong VIC 39 C13 42 G1
Pyap SA 62 B6 65 H13
Pyengana TAS 55 E13
Pygery SA 64 E5
Pymble NSW 19 C5 20 C7
Pymurra QLD 10 K5 12 A5
Pyramid Hill VIC 28 K7 41 J11
Pyramul NSW 22 E5
Pyrete State Forest VIC 36 A4

## Q

Quaama NSW 31 H11
Quail Island NT 86 D3
Quail Island QLD 9 F9
Quail Island WA 37 H10 44 E3
Quairading WA 72 A3 74 C5 76 K6
Quakers Hill NSW 21 E8
Qualco SA 62 C5 65 G12
Qualeup WA 73 C11
Quambatook VIC 28 K6 41 H9
Quambone NSW 27 G14
Quamby QLD 10 K5
Quamby Brook TAS 55 G8 56 J1
Quanda Nat Res NSW 27 J12
Quandialla NSW 22 H1 29 E14
Quangallin WA 73 A14
Quantong VIC 38 B5
Quarram Nat Res WA 74 K4
Queanbeyan NSW 31 D9
Queen Lake NSW 23 B12
Queen Victoria Spring Nat Res WA 77 H13 83 F2
Queenscliff NSW 20 B7
Queenscliff VIC 36 H5 39 H13
Queensferry VIC 37 K11
Queenstown TAS 52 B4 54 J4
Quellington WA 72 C2
Quilberry QLD 15 F13
Quilpie QLD 15 E10
Quinalow QLD 7 F10
Quindalup WA 73 J11
Quindanning WA 73 D8 74 F4
Quindinup Nat Res WA 73 C14 74 H5
Quinninup WA 73 E14
Quinns Rocks WA 72 G2 74 C2 76 K4
Quipolly NSW 23 A8 24 K7
Quirindi NSW 23 A8 24 K7
Quobba WA 78 H1
Quoin Island NT 86 H1
Quondong NSW 26 K3 28 A3
Quorn SA 62 G1 65 D9

## R

Rabbit Flat Roadhouse NT 88 H2
Rabbit Island QLD 9 C8
Rabuma Island NT 87 C10
Raby NSW 21 E10
Raglan QLD 9 H10
Raglan VIC 39 D9
Railton TAS 54 F7
Rain Island QLD 16 D5
Rainbow VIC 28 K3 40 H4
Rainbow Beach QLD 7 C13
Rainbow Valley Con Res NT 91 G8
Raleigh NSW 25 G12
Raluana VIC 38 A7
Ramco SA 62 C5 65 G12
Raminea TAS 53 J9
Ramingining NT 87 D10
Ramsgate NSW 21 B9
Ranceby VIC 37 J14 44 E5
Rand NSW 29 J12 30 E3
Randalls Mine WA 75 A13 77 J12 83 F1
Randell WA 75 A14 77 J12 83 F1
Randwick NSW 19 G6 21 B9
Ranelagh TAS 50 F2 53 G9
Ranga TAS 55 C9
Rangal QLD 9 H8
Rangelands QLD 13 C9
Rankins Springs NSW 29 E11
Rannes QLD 9 J9
Rannock NSW 29 G13 30 B5
Ransome QLD 3 E7

Rapanyup South VIC 38 B7
Rapid Bay SA 61 J2 63 G8 65 K9
Rapid Creek NT 84 B2
Rappville NSW 25 C12
Raragala Island NT 87 B12
Rathdowney QLD 5 G14 7 H12 25 A12
Rathscar VIC 39 C9
Ravensdale NSW 20 D2
Ravenshoe QLD 11 E12
Ravensthorpe WA 75 G10
Ravenswood QLD 8 B5 11 J14
Ravenswood VIC 39 B11
Ravenswood WA 72 G6
Ravensworth NSW 23 D9
Rawbelle QLD 7 A9 9 K10
Rawdon Vale NSW 23 B10
Rawlinna WA 77 J14
Rawson VIC 45 C8 46 E2
Raymond Island VIC 46 E6
Raymond Terrace NSW 23 E10
Raywood VIC 39 A11
Razorback Nat Res NSW 22 H5 31 A9
Recherche Archipelago Nat Res WA 75 H14 83 J1
Red Banks SA 60 A2
Red Bluff Nat Res WA 28 K2 40 H1 63 A9
Red Cap Creek VIC 38 E2
Red Cliffs VIC 28 F3 40 B5
Red Hill QLD 2 A1 3 E3 5 E8
Red Hill VIC 37 J8
Red Hill South VIC 37 J8
Red Hills TAS 55 G8
Red Range NSW 25 E10
Red Rock NSW 25 F13
Redbank NSW 30 H4 39 B9 43 E9
Redbank Plains QLD 5 G9
Redbanks SA 62 E4 65 G11
Redcliffe QLD 4 D6 7 F13
Redcliffe WA 71 F5
Redesdale VIC 39 C12
Redfern NSW 19 F6 21 B9
Redhill SA 62 G3 65 F9
Redland Bay QLD 5 C9 7 G13
Redlynch QLD 11 D13
Redmond WA 74 K6
Redpa TAS 54 C1
Redwood Park SA 59 C7
Reedy Creek QLD 5 B13
Reedy Creek SA 63 C12
Reedy Creek VIC 39 D14 42 G2
Reedy Dam VIC 28 K4 40 H7
Reedy Flat VIC 43 H12 46 B3
Reedy Marsh TAS 55 F8 56 G1
Reefton NSW 29 F13 30 A5
Reefton VIC 37 B14 42 J5 44 B5
Reekara TAS 54 B6
Reeves Plains SA 60 A2
Reevesby Island SA 62 E11
Regatta Point TAS 52 C3 54 K3
Regency Park SA 59 E3
Regents Park NSW 19 F2 21 D9
Regents Park QLD 3 K4
Regentville NSW 21 G9
Reid ACT 32 A4
Reid WA 83 F6
Reid River QLD 8 A5 11 J14
Reids Creek VIC 43 C8
Reids Flat NSW 22 J4 31 A9
Relbia TAS 55 J10 56 H6
Remine TAS 52 B3 54 H3
Rendlesham SA 63 C13
Renison Bell TAS 52 A4 54 H4
Renmark SA 27 F1 62 A5 65 H13
Rennie NSW 29 K11 30 F2 42 A6
Renner Springs NT 89 E8
Repulse Bay QLD 9 C8
Research VIC 35 B6
Reservoir VIC 34 B4 36 C7
Retreat TAS 55 E10 56 D5
Retro QLD 8 G6
Revesby NSW 19 H3 21 D9
Reynella SA 60 J2 61 C5 62 F7 65 J10
Reynolds Island TAS 53 A8 55 H8
Reynolds Neck TAS 53 A8 55 H8
Rheban TAS 53 E12
Rheola VIC 39 A10
Rhodes NSW 21 C8
Rhyll VIC 37 K10 44 F3
Rhyndaston TAS 53 D11
Rhynie SA 62 F5 65 G10
Riana TAS 54 E6
Rich Avon VIC 38 A7 40 K7
Richlands NSW 22 J6 31 A11
Richlands QLD 3 H2
Richmond NSW 20 G7 23 G8
Richmond QLD 11 K9 13 A9
Richmond SA 59 E3
Richmond SA 59 G3 60 G2 61 A6
Richmond TAS 53 E9 53 F11
Richmond VIC 35 D4 37 D8
Richmond Range Nat Park NSW 7 J12 25 B12
Rickeys VIC 72 B3
Riddells Creek VIC 39 E13 42 H1
Ridgehaven SA 59 D7
Ridgelands QLD 9 G10
Ridgeway TAS 50 D5

Ridgley TAS 54 E5
Rifle Creek QLD 12 A3
Rimbanda QLD 13 D10
Rimbija Island NT 87 A13
Ringa WA 72 D2
Ringarooma TAS 55 E12
Ringarooma Bay TAS 55 C12
Ringarooma Coastal Res TAS 55 C13
Ringwood VIC 35 D7 37 D9 42 K3 44 B2
Ripley QLD 5 G10
Ripplebrook VIC 37 H13 44 E5
Risdon Vale TAS 50 B6 53 F10
Rita Island QLD 8 A6
River Heads QLD 7 B13
Riverhills QLD 3 G1
Riverside TAS 56 G5
Riverside Mine QLD 8 E6
Riverstone NSW 20 F7
Riverton SA 62 E5 65 H10
Riverton WA 71 H5
Rivervale WA 71 G5
Riverview QLD 5 G9
Riverwood NSW 19 H3 21 C9
Roadvale QLD 5 H12
Robbins Island TAS 54 B2
Roberts Point TAS 50 H5
Robertson NSW 23 K8 31 B12
Robertson QLD 3 G4
Robertstown SA 62 E4 65 G11
Robigana TAS 56 E3
Robin Hood VIC 37 F14
Robina QLD 5 B13
Robinson River NT 89 C13
Robinvale VIC 28 G5 40 C7
Rochedale QLD 3 G6 5 D9
Rochedale South QLD 3 H6
Rocherlea TAS 55 F10 56 F5
Rochester QLD 8 C7
Rochester VIC 41 K13 42 C1
Rochford VIC 39 D13 42 H1
Rock Flat NSW 31 D9
Rockbank VIC 36 C5 39 F13 42 K1
Rockdale NSW 19 H4 21 C9
Rockhampton QLD 9 H10
Rockingham WA 72 G5 74 D2
Rocklands Reservoir VIC 38 D5
Rocklea QLD 3 G3
Rockleigh SA 60 G7 62 E7 65 J10
Rockley NSW 22 G5
Rockley QLD 5 E8
Rocklyn VIC 39 D11
Rocksberg QLD 4 G4
Rockton NSW 31 K9 47 A12
Rockvale NSW 25 G10
Rocky Cape TAS 54 C4
Rocky Cape Nat Park TAS 54 C4
Rocky Creek NSW 24 F6
Rocky Glen NSW 24 J4
Rocky Gully WA 73 B14 74 J5
Rocky Hall NSW 31 J10
Rocky Island QLD 10 C3
Rocky River NSW 25 H9
Rocky River SA 63 K9
Rodds Bay QLD 9 J11 9 J12
Rodinga NT 91 G8
Roebourne WA 78 E4 82 C2
Roebuck Roadhouse WA 79 B9 80 H4
Roelands WA 73 G9
Roger Corner SA 62 H7 65 J8
Roger River TAS 54 D2
Roger River West TAS 54 D2
Rokeby TAS 50 D7 53 G11
Rokeby VIC 37 F14 44 D6
Rokewood VIC 39 F10
Rokewood Junction VIC 39 F10
Roland TAS 54 F7
Rollands Plains NSW 23 A13 25 K12
Rolleston QLD 8 J7
Rollingstone QLD 11 G14
Roma QLD 6 E5
Romsey VIC 39 D13 42 H1
Rookhurst NSW 23 B11
Rooty Hill NSW 21 F8
Roper Bar NT 87 H9
Rorruwuy NT 87 C12
Rosa Glen WA 73 J12
Rosanna VIC 37 C8
Rose Bay NSW 21 B8
Rose Bay TAS 49 A4
Rosebank NSW 25 C8
Rosebery VIC 28 K4 40 H6
Rosebery East VIC 40 H6
Rosebery TAS 52 A4 54 H4
Rosebrook VIC 38 H6
Rosebud VIC 36 J7 39 H13 44 F1
Rosedale QLD 9 K12
Rosedale SA 60 B5
Rosedale VIC 45 D10 46 F3
Rosegarland TAS 53 F9
Rosehill NSW 19 E3 21 D8
Rosemary Island WA 78 D3 82 B1
Rosemeadow NSW 21 E11
Roses Tier TAS 55 F12
Rosevale QLD 5 K11
Rosevale TAS 55 F9 56 F2
Rosevears TAS 55 F9 56 F4
Roseville NSW 19 D5 21 C8

Rosewater SA 59 E2
Rosewhite VIC 43 D9
Rosewood NSW 29 J14 30 E6
Rosewood QLD 5 J9 7 G12
Rosewood Island QLD 9 F9
Roseworthy SA 60 A4 62 F6 65 H10
Roseworthy College SA 60 A3
Roslyn NSW 22 K5 31 B10
Roslyn Bay QLD 9 G10
Roslynmead VIC 41 J12
Rosny TAS 49 B4
Rosny Park TAS 49 B4
Ross TAS 53 B11 55 J11
Ross River NT 91 F9
Rossarden TAS 55 G12
Rossbridge VIC 38 E7
Rossi NSW 31 E10
Rossmore NSW 21 F10
Rossmore WA 72 C1
Rossmoyne WA 71 H4
Rossville QLD 11 B12
Rostrevor SA 59 F6 60 F3
Rostron VIC 39 B8
Rothwell QLD 4 E3
Rothwell VIC 36 E3
Roto NSW 29 C9
Rottnest Island WA 72 H3 74 C2 76 K4
Rouchel Brook NSW 23 C9
Round Corner NSW 19 B2 20 D7
Round Hill Island NT 87 E12
Round Hill Nat Res NSW 29 C11
Round Island WA 83 J3
Rouse Hill NSW 20 E7
Rowella TAS 55 E9 56 D3
Rowena NSW 24 E3
Rowes NSW 31 J9 47 A11
Rowland Flat SA 60 B6
Rowles Lagoon Nat Res WA 77 H10
Rowsley VIC 36 C3 39 F12
Rowville VIC 37 E9
Roxby Downs SA 64 A7 66 K7
Roxby Island SA 62 E11
Royal George TAS 53 A12 55 H12
Royal Nat Park NSW 19 K3 21 C11 23 J9 31 A14
Royal Park SA 59 E2
Royalla NSW 31 E9
Roydon Island TAS 55 B8
Roysalt Siding WA 75 B13 77 J11 83 G1
Royston Park SA 59 F5
Rozelle NSW 21 C8
Rubunja NT 90 E7
Ruby VIC 37 K14
Ruby Gap Nature Park NT 91 F10
Rubyvale QLD 8 H6
Rudall SA 64 G2
Rudall River Nat Park WA 79 F9
Ruffy VIC 42 F4
Rufus River NSW 28 F2 40 A2 65 G14
Rugby NSW 22 J4 31 B9
Rules Beach QLD 9 K12
Rules Point NSW 31 E8
Rum Island TAS 55 A13
Rum Jungle NT 85 E2 86 E4
Rumbalara NT 91 J9
Rumula QLD 11 C12
Runaway Bay QLD 5 B12
Runcorn QLD 3 H5
Rundle Range Nat Park QLD 9 H11
Rungoo QLD 11 F13
Running Stream NSW 22 E6
Runnymede TAS 53 E11
Runnymede VIC 39 A13 42 D1
Rupanyup VIC 38 B7
Rupanyup North VIC 38 A7
Rushworth VIC 39 A14 42 D2
Rushy Lagoon TAS 55 C13
Russell Island QLD 5 B10
Russell River Nat Park QLD 11 D13
Russell Vale NSW 21 C13
Rutherglen VIC 29 K11 30 F3 42 B7
Ryan NSW 29 J12 30 E4
Ryans Creek VIC 42 E6
Rydalmere NSW 19 E3 21 D8
Ryde NSW 19 E4 21 C8
Rye VIC 36 J6 39 H13 44 F1
Rye Park NSW 22 K4 31 B9
Rylstone NSW 22 E6
Ryton VIC 44 G7 46 H1

## S

Sackville NSW 20 F6
Sackville North NSW 20 F5
Saddleworth SA 62 F5 65 G10
Safety Bay WA 72 G5 74 D2
Sale VIC 45 D10 46 F4
Salisbury NSW 23 C10
Salisbury QLD 3 G4
Salisbury SA 59 B5 60 D3 62 F6 65 J10
Salisbury VIC 40 K4
Salisbury Downs SA 59 B4
Salisbury East SA 59 C6
Salisbury Heights SA 59 B6
Salisbury Island WA 83 K2
Salisbury North SA 59 A5
Salisbury South SA 59 C5
Salisbury West VIC 39 A11
Sallys Flat NSW 22 E5
Salmon Gums WA 75 E13 83 H1

Salt Creek SA 63 D10
Salt Lake NSW 26 E3
Salter Point WA 71 H4
Saltern QLD 8 H2 13 F12
Saltwater River TAS 51 F11 53 G12
Samford QLD 7 G12
Samford State Forest QLD 3 C1
Samford Valley QLD 4 G7
Samford Village QLD 3 B1
Samson WA 71 J2
Samsonvale QLD 4 G6
San Remo VIC 44 G3
Sanctuary Cove QLD 5 B11
Sand Bay QLD 9 D8
Sandalwood SA 62 C7 65 J12
Sanderston SA 62 E6 65 J11
Sandfire Roadhouse WA 78 D7
Sandfly SA 50 E4 53 G10
Sandford QLD 8 C7
Sandford TAS 50 E6 53 G11
Sandford VIC 38 E3
Sandgate QLD 3 A4 4 E6
Sandigo NSW 29 G12 30 C3
Sandilands SA 62 H6 65 H9
Sandon NSW 25 E13
Sandringham NSW 19 J4
Sandringham VIC 35 G4 36 E7
Sandringham Bay QLD 9 D8
Sandsmere VIC 40 K2
Sandstone WA 77 E8
Sandstone Point QLD 4 D4
Sandy Bay TAS 49 D2
Sandy Blight Junction WA 90 E2
Sandy Creek SA 60 B5
Sandy Creek VIC 43 C9
Sandy Creek Con Park SA 60 B5
Sandy Hill NSW 25 C11
Sandy Hollow NSW 22 C8
Sandy Island NT 87 G11
Sandy Point NSW 19 H2
Sandy Point VIC 44 H6 46 J1
Sangar NSW 29 J11 30 E2
Sans Souci NSW 21 C10
Santa Teresa NT 91 G9
Sapphire NSW 25 E8
Sapphire QLD 8 H6
Sarah Island TAS 52 D3
Saraji Mine QLD 8 F7
Saratoga NSW 20 B4
Sarina QLD 9 D8
Sarsfield VIC 43 K11 45 B13 46 D6
Sassafras NSW 31 D12
Sassafras TAS 54 F7
Sassafras VIC 37 D10
Sassie Island QLD 16 A3
Saunders Beach QLD 11 H14
Savage River TAS 54 F3
Savage River Nat Park TAS 54 F3
Savernake NSW 29 J11 30 E2
Sawtell NSW 25 G13
Sawyers Lakes NSW 28 B5
Scaddan WA 75 F13 83 J1
Scamander TAS 55 F14
Scarborough NSW 21 C12 23 J9 31 A13
Scarborough QLD 4 D5
Scarborough WA 71 E2 72 G3 74 C2 76 K4
Scarsdale VIC 39 E10
Scawfell Island QLD 9 C9
Scheyville NSW 20 F7
Scheyville Nat Park NSW 20 F6 23 G8
Schofields NSW 20 E7
School Hill VIC 36 K7
Schouten Island TAS 53 D14
Scone NSW 23 C9
Scoresby VIC 35 E7 37 D9
Scorpion Springs Con Park SA 28 J1 40 G1 63 A8 65 K13
Scotia Mine WA 77 H11 83 F1
Scotland Island NSW 19 A7
Scotsburn VIC 39 E11
Scott Con Park SA 61 G7
Scott Creek SA 60 H3 61 B7
Scott Creek Con Park SA 60 J3 61 C7
Scott Nat Park WA 73 J13 74 H2
Scotts Creek VIC 39 J8
Scotts Head NSW 25 H12
Scottsdale TAS 55 E11
Scottville QLD 8 C6
Sea Bird WA 74 B2 76 J4
Sea Elephant TAS 54 B7
Sea Lake VIC 28 J5 40 F7
Sea View VIC 37 H14
Seabrook TAS 54 D5
Seacliff SA 59 K2 60 H1 61 B5
Seacliff Park SA 59 K2
Seacombe VIC 45 D12 46 F5
Seacombe Gardens SA 59 K3
Seaford SA 60 K1 61 D5
Seaforth NSW 21 B8
Seaforth QLD 9 C8
Seaham NSW 23 D10
Seal Island SA 61 J6 63 J8
Seal Rocks NSW 23 D12
Seal Rocks State Res TAS 54 C6
Seaspray VIC 45 F11 46 G4
Seaton SA 59 F2 60 F1
Seaton VIC 45 D9 46 E2
Seaview VIC 44 E6
Seaview Downs SA 59 K2
Sebastopol NSW 22 G1 29 G13 30 B5
Sebastopol VIC 39 E10
Second Valley SA 61 H2 63 G8 65 K9

Sedan SA 62 D6 65 H11
Sedan Dip QLD 11 J6
Sedgwick VIC 39 B12
Sefton NSW 21 D9
Seisia QLD 16 B2
Selbourne TAS 55 F9 56 G3
Sellheim QLD 8 B4 11 J14
Sellicks Beach SA 61 F4 63 F8 65 K9
Sellicks Hill SA 61 F5
Selwyn QLD 12 B5
Semaphore SA 59 D1 60 F1
Semaphore Park SA 59 E1
Seppeltsfield SA 60 A6
Serpentine VIC 41 K11
Serpentine WA 72 D1
Serpentine Lakes SA 83 D7
Serpentine Nat Park WA 72 F5 74 D3
Serviceton VIC 40 K1 63 A10
Seven Hills NSW 19 D1 21 E8
Seven Mile Beach TAS 51 C8 53 F11
Seven Mile Beach Nat Park NSW 31 C13
Sevenhill SA 62 F4 65 G10
Seventeen Seventy QLD 9 J12
Seville VIC 37 C11 42 K3 44 B3
Seymour TAS 53 A14 55 H14
Seymour VIC 39 C14 42 F2
Shackleton WA 74 C6 76 K7
Shadforth NSW 22 F4
Shailer Park QLD 3 J7 5 D9
Shallow Crossing NSW 31 E11
Shanes Park NSW 21 F8
Shannon TAS 53 B8 55 J8
Shannon Nat Park WA 74 J4
Shannon Vale NSW 25 E10
Shannons Flat NSW 31 F9
Shark Bay WA 76 A1
Shark Bay Marine Park WA 76 A1 78 J1
Shaw Island QLD 9 C8
Shay Gap WA 78 D7 82 B7
Shay Gap Mining Settlement WA 78 D7 82 C7
Sheans Creek VIC 42 E4
Shearwater TAS 54 E7
Sheep Hills VIC 40 K6
Sheffield TAS 54 F7
Shelbourne VIC 39 B11
Shelburne Bay QLD 16 D3
Sheldon QLD 3 H7
Shelford VIC 39 G11
Shelley VIC 29 K13 43 B11
Shelley WA 71 H4
Shelley Beach NSW 20 A3
Shellharbour NSW 23 K8 31 B13
Shelly VIC 30 G5
Shelly Beach QLD 4 D2
Shenton Park WA 71 F2
Sheoak Hill Con Park SA 62 K3 64 F7
Sheoak Log SA 60 A5
Sheoaks VIC 36 B1
Shepparton VIC 30 G1 42 C3
Sheringa SA 64 G5
Sherlock SA 63 D8 65 K12
Sherwood NSW 25 J12
Sherwood QLD 3 F3
Shinfield QLD 9 D8
Shoalhaven Heads NSW 31 C13
Shoalwater Bay QLD 9 F10
Shooters Hill NSW 22 H6
Shoreham VIC 37 K8
Shorncliffe QLD 3 B5 4 E6
Short Island QLD 5 B10
Shots WA 73 E10
Shute Harbour QLD 9 B8
Sidmouth TAS 55 E9 56 D3
Silkwood QLD 11 E13
Silky Oak QLD 11 F13
Silvan VIC 37 D11
Silvan Reservoir VIC 37 D11
Silver Sands SA 61 F4
Silver Spur QLD 7 K9 25 B8
Silver Swan WA 77 H11 83 F1
Silverdale NSW 21 G10
Silverdale QLD 5 J11
Silverton NSW 26 J1 28 A1 65 C14
Silverwater NSW 19 E3
Simmie VIC 41 K13 42 C1
Simpson VIC 39 J8
Simpson Desert Con Park SA 12 K1 6 B9 91 K13
Simpson Desert Nat Park QLD 12 J2 67 A10 91 J14
Simpson Desert Reg Res SA 67 C8 91 K12
Simpsons Bay TAS 53 J10
Sinclair Island Con Park SA 64 C1 68 K6
Singleton NSW 23 D9
Singleton WA 72 G5
Sinnamon Park QLD 3 G2
Sir Edward Pellew Group NT 87 J13
Sir George Hope Islands NT 86 B5
Sir Graham Moore Island WA 81 A10
Sir Joseph Banks Group Con Park SA 64 H6
Sisters Beach TAS 54 C4
Sisters Creek TAS 54 C4
Skenes Creek VIC 39 K10
Skipton VIC 39 F9
Skye SA 59 G6
Skye VIC 35 K7 37 G9
Slacks Creek QLD 3 J6
Slade Point QLD 9 D8

Slaty Creek – Terang 107


Slaty Creek VIC 39 A9
Sliding Rock Mine SA 65 A10 67 K10
Sloping Island TAS 51 E10 53 G11
Smeaton VIC 39 D11
Smeaton Grange NSW 21 F11
Smiggin Holes NSW 30 G7 43 D14
Smith Islands Nat Park QLD 9 C8
Smithfield NSW 19 E1 21 E9
Smithfield SA 60 C3 62 F6 65 J10
Smithton TAS 54 C2
Smithtown NSW 25 J12
Smokers Bank TAS 54 C3
Smoky Bay SA 64 D3
Smooth Island TAS 51 E11 53 G12
Smythesdale VIC 39 E10
Snake Island VIC 45 H8 46 J2
Snake Range Nat Park QLD 8 J6
Snake Valley VIC 39 E10
Snobs Creek VIC 42 G5
Snowtown SA 62 G4 65 G9
Snowy River Nat Park VIC 30 K7 43 G14 47 B9
Snug TAS 50 G5 53 G10
Snuggery SA 63 B13
Sofala NSW 22 F6
Somers VIC 37 J9 39 H14 44 F2
Somersby NSW 20 C3
Somerset TAS 54 D5
Somerset Dam QLD 4 J5 7 F12
Somerton NSW 24 H7
Somerton VIC 35 A3 36 B7
Somerton Park SA 59 J2 60 H1 61 B5
Somerville VIC 37 H9 39 H14 44 E2
Sommariva QLD 6 D1 13 K14 15 D14
Sorell TAS 51 B9 53 F11
Sorrento VIC 36 J6 39 H13
Sorrento WA 71 C1 72 G3
South Arm TAS 50 F7 53 G11
South Bank QLD 2 C2
South Blackwater Mine QLD 9 J8
South Brisbane QLD 2 D1
South Bruny Island TAS 53 J10
South Bruny Nat Park TAS 53 J10
South Coast NSW 31 J11
South Coogee NSW 19 G7
South Cumberland Island Nat Park QLD 9 C9
South East Forests Nat Park NSW 31 J10 47 A12
South Eneabba Nat Res WA 76 H4
South Forest TAS 54 C3
South Franklin TAS 50 H1 53 H9
South Fremantle WA 71 J1
South Glen QLD 7 F8
South Grafton NSW 25 E12
South Guildford WA 71 E6
South Hedland WA 78 D5 82 B4
South Hobart TAS 49 D1
South Island Nat Park QLD 9 E10
South Johnstone QLD 11 E13
South Kilkerran SA 62 H5 65 H8
South Kolan QLD 7 A11 9 K12
South Kumminin WA 74 D7
South Lake WA 71 K3
South Maclean QLD 5 E11
South Melbourne VIC 34 D2 35 D3
South Molle Island QLD 9 B8
South Morang VIC 37 B8 39 E14 42 J2 44 A2
South Mount Cameron TAS 55 D13
South Nietta TAS 54 F6
South Para Reservoir SA 60 D5
South Perth WA 70 D2 71 G4
South Preston TAS 54 E6
South Riana TAS 54 E6
South Springfield TAS 55 E11
South Stradbroke Island QLD 5 B11 7 H13
South Wellesley Islands QLD 10 D3
South West Island NT 87 J12 89 A12
South West Rocks NSW 25 J12
Southbank VIC 34 D1
Southend QLD 9 H11
Southend SA 63 C13
Southern Beekeepers Nat Res WA 76 H3
Southern Brook WA 72 C1
Southern Cross QLD 8 B4 11 J13
Southern Cross WA 75 B9 77 J8
Southern Moreton Bay Islands Nat Park QLD 5 B11
Southern River WA 71 K6
Southport QLD 5 B12 7 H13
Southport TAS 53 J9
Southwest Con Area TAS 52 E3
Southwest Nat Park TAS 52 H6
Southwood QLD 6 G7
Southwood Nat Park QLD 6 G7
Sovereign Island QLD 5 B11
Spalding SA 62 F3 65 F10
Spalford TAS 54 E6
Spargo Creek VIC 39 E11
Spearwood WA 71 K2
Speed VIC 28 J4 40 F6
Speewa VIC 28 H6 41 E9
Spencer NSW 20 D5
Spencer Gulf SA 62 J5 64 G7
Spencers Brook WA 72 D2
Spicers Creek NSW 22 C4
Spilsby Island SA 64 H6
Spinnaker Island ACT 32 B1
Sprent TAS 54 E6
Spreyton TAS 54 E7
Spring Beach TAS 53 E12
Spring Farm NSW 21 F11
Spring Hill NSW 22 F4
Spring Hill QLD 2 A2 3 E4
Spring Mount Con Park SA 61 G5
Spring Ridge NSW 22 A7 22 C5 24 K6
Springbank Island ACT 32 B1
Springbrook QLD 5 C14 7 H13 25 A13
Springbrook Nat Park QLD 5 C14 25 A13
Springcreek QLD 8 A3 11 H12
Springdale NSW 22 K1 29 F14 30 B6
Springfield QLD 3 K1 5 F9
Springfield SA 59 H5
Springfield TAS 55 E11
Springhurst VIC 30 G3 42 B7
Springsure QLD 8 J7
Springton SA 60 D7 62 E6 65 J10
Springvale VIC 35 G6 37 E8
Springwood NSW 21 H8 23 G8
Springwood QLD 3 J6 5 D9
St Agnes SA 59 D7
St Albans NSW 20 F3 23 F9
St Albans VIC 35 C1 36 C6
St Andrews VIC 37 B10
St Arnaud VIC 39 A8
St Bees Island QLD 9 D9
St Clair NSW 21 F9 23 D9
St Clair Island QLD 5 C9
St Fillans VIC 37 A12 42 J4 44 A4
St Francis Island SA 64 D2
St George QLD 6 H4
St Germains VIC 41 J14 42 C3
St Helena Island QLD 4 C7
St Helena Island Nat Park QLD 4 C7
St Helens TAS 55 F14
St Helens VIC 38 H5
St Helens Island TAS 55 F14
St Helens Point Con Area TAS 55 E14
St Helier VIC 37 J12
St Ives NSW 19 C5 20 C7
St Ives Chase NSW 20 C7
St Ives Mine WA 75 B13 77 J11 83 G1
St James VIC 42 C5
St Kilda SA 59 A3 60 D1 62 F6 65 J10
St Kilda VIC 36 D7 39 F14 42 K2 44 C1
St Kitts SA 62 E5 65 H11
St Lawrence QLD 9 F9
St Leonards NSW 21 C8
St Leonards TAS 55 F10 56 G6
St Leonards VIC 36 G5 39 G13
St Lucia QLD 3 F3 5 E8
St Margaret Island VIC 45 G9 46 H3
St Marys NSW 21 F8
St Marys SA 59 J4
St Marys TAS 55 G13
St Patricks River TAS 55 F11 56 F7
St Peter Island SA 64 D2
St Peters NSW 21 B9
St Peters SA 59 F5 60 F3
Staaten River Nat Park QLD 11 C8
Stacks Island TAS 54 B1
Stafford QLD 3 C3 4 E7
Stalker VIC 39 K9
Stamford QLD 13 B10
Stanage QLD 9 F9
Stanborough NSW 25 F8
Stanhope VIC 41 K14 42 D2
Stanley TAS 54 C3
Stanley VIC 43 C8
Stanley Island QLD 16 H5
Stanmore QLD 4 G3
Stannifer NSW 25 E8
Stannum NSW 25 D10
Stansbury SA 62 H7 65 J9
Stanthorpe QLD 7 J10 25 B10
Stanwell QLD 9 H10
Stanwell Park NSW 21 C12 23 J9 31 A13
Stapylton QLD 5 C10
Starcke Nat Park QLD 11 A12 16 J6
Starling Gap VIC 44 B5
Staughton Vale VIC 36 D2
Stavely VIC 38 E7
Staverton TAS 54 F6
Stawell VIC 38 C7
Steels Creek VIC 37 A10
Steep Island TAS 54 B1
Steiglitz QLD 5 C10
Steiglitz VIC 36 D1 39 F11
Steiglitz Historic Park VIC 36 D1
Stenhouse Bay SA 62 J7 64 K7
Stephens QLD 5 B13
Stephens Creek NSW 26 J2
Steppes TAS 53 C9 55 J9
Stevens Island NT 87 B12
Stieglitz TAS 55 F14
Stirling SA 59 J7 60 H4 61 B7 65 J10
Stirling VIC 43 H11 46 C6
Stirling WA 71 D3
Stirling North SA 62 G1 65 D9
Stirling Range Nat Park WA 74 H6
Stockdale VIC 43 K9 45 B11 46 D4
Stockinbingal NSW 22 K1 29 F14 30 B6
Stockleigh QLD 5 E10
Stockmans Reward VIC 42 J5 44 A6
Stockport SA 62 F5 65 H10
Stockton NSW 23 E11
Stockyard Gully Nat Park WA 76 H3
Stockyard Hill VIC 39 E9
Stockyard Point QLD 9 G11
Stokes Bay SA 63 J8 65 K8
Stokes Nat Park WA 75 G11
Stone Hut SA 62 F2 65 E9
Stonefield SA 62 D5 65 H11
Stonehaven VIC 36 G2
Stonehenge NSW 25 E9
Stonehenge QLD 13 G9
Stonehenge TAS 53 D11
Stoney Point NSW 29 F11 30 B3
Stoneyford VIC 39 H9
Stonor TAS 53 D11
Stony Creek VIC 44 G6
Stony Crossing NSW 28 H6 41 E9
Stony Point VIC 37 J9 44 F2
Stonyfell SA 59 G6 60 G3 61 A7
Stoodley TAS 54 F7
Store Creek NSW 22 E4
Storm Bay TAS 51 H9 53 H11
Stormlea TAS 51 J11 53 H12
Storys Creek TAS 55 G12
Stowport TAS 54 D5
Strachan WA 73 D14
Stradbroke VIC 45 E10 46 G4
Stradbroke West VIC 45 E10 46 F3
Strahan TAS 52 C3 54 K3
Stratford NSW 23 C11
Stratford VIC 45 C11 46 E4
Strath Creek VIC 42 G3
Strathalbyn SA 62 E7 65 K10
Stratham WA 73 H10 74 G2
Strathblane TAS 53 J9
Strathbogie NSW 25 D9
Strathbogie VIC 42 E4
Strathdownie VIC 38 F2
Stratherne WA 72 A6
Strathewen VIC 37 A10
Strathfield NSW 19 F3 21 C9
Strathfieldsaye VIC 39 B12
Strathgordon TAS 52 F6
Strathkellar VIC 38 F5
Strathmerton VIC 29 K10 30 F1 42 A4
Strathpine QLD 3 A3 4 F6 7 F13
Straughton Vale VIC 30 H2
Straun SA 38 C1
Streaky Bay SA 64 E3
Streatham VIC 39 E8
Stretton QLD 3 J5
Strickland TAS 53 D8
Stroud NSW 23 D11
Stroud Road NSW 23 D11
Struan SA 63 B12
Strzelecki VIC 37 J14 44 E5
Strzelecki Nat Park TAS 55 C9
Strzelecki Reg Res SA 14 K2 67 G12
Stuart QLD 8 A5 11 H14
Stuart Creek Opal Deposit SA 67 J8
Stuart Mill VIC 39 B9
Stuart Park NT 84 D2
Stuart Town NSW 22 E4
Stuarts Point NSW 25 H12
Stuarts Well NT 90 G7
Sturt Nat Park NSW 14 K5 26 C1 67 G14
Suarji Island QLD 16 A2
Subiaco WA 71 F3
Sugarloaf Reservoir VIC 37 B10
Suggan Buggan VIC 43 F14
Sulphur Creek TAS 54 D6
Summerfield VIC 39 A12
Summerholm QLD 5 K9
Summerland VIC 37 K9 39 J14 44 F2
Summerland Point NSW 20 A1
Summertown SA 59 H7 60 G4 61 A7
Sumner QLD 3 G2
Sunbury VIC 36 A5 39 E13 42 J1
Sunday Creek VIC 39 D14 42 G2
Sunday Island VIC 45 H8 46 H2
Sunday Island WA 80 E5
Sundown Nat Park QLD 7 K10 25 B9
Sunny Cliffs VIC 40 A5
Sunny Corner NSW 22 F6
Sunnybank QLD 3 H5
Sunnybank Hills QLD 3 H4
Sunnyside NSW 25 C10
Sunnyside TAS 54 F7
Sunrise Mine WA 77 F12 83 D2
Sunshine NSW 20 B1
Sunshine VIC 35 D1 36 C6
Sunshine Coast QLD 4 D1 7 E13
Surat QLD 6 F5
Surfers Paradise QLD 5 B12 7 H13
Surges Bay TAS 50 K1 53 H9
Surrey Downs SA 59 C7
Surveyor Generals Corner NT SA WA 68 A1 79 K14 83 B7 90 K1
Surveyors Bay TAS 53 H9
Sussex Inlet NSW 31 D12
Sussex Mill WA 73 G12
Sutherland NSW 19 J3 21 C10 23 H9 31 A13
Sutherland Creek VIC 36 F2
Sutherlands SA 62 D5 65 H11
Sutton NSW 31 D9
Sutton VIC 41 G8
Sutton Forest NSW 22 K7 31 B12
Sutton Grange VIC 39 C12
SW Vernon Island NT 85 B2 86 C3
Swain Reefs Nat Park QLD 9 E13
Swan Bay VIC 36 H5
Swan Hill VIC 28 J6 41 F9
Swan Island TAS 55 C13
Swan Island VIC 36 H5
Swan Marsh VIC 39 H9
Swan Reach SA 62 D6 65 H11
Swan Reach VIC 43 K12 45 C14 46 D7
Swan Reach Con Park SA 62 D6 65 H11
Swanbourne WA 71 G1
Swanpool VIC 30 H2 42 E5
Swansea NSW 23 F10
Swansea TAS 53 C13 55 K13
Sweers Island QLD 10 D3
Swifts Creek VIC 30 K6 43 H11 46 B6
Swim Creek Con Res NT 85 C4 86 D5
Sydenham NSW 19 G5 21 C9
Sydenham VIC 36 C6 39 F13 42 J1
Sydney NSW 19 F6 21 B8 23 H9
Sydney CBD NSW 18
Sydney Harbour Nat Park NSW 19 E7 21 B8 23 H9
Sydney Island QLD 10 D3
Sylvania NSW 19 J4 21 C10


# T


Tabbara VIC 43 K14 47 D9
Tabberabbera VIC 43 J10 45 A12 46 C5
Tabbita NSW 29 F10 30 A2
Tabby Tabby Island QLD 5 B10
Table Top NSW 29 K12 30 F4 43 A9
Tabor VIC 38 F5
Tabourie Lake NSW 31 E12
Tabulam NSW 25 C12
Tacoma NSW 20 B2
Taggerty VIC 30 K1 42 H4
Tahara VIC 38 F4
Tahara Bridge VIC 38 F4
Tahmoor NSW 21 F13 23 J8 31 A12
Taigum QLD 3 B4
Tailem Bend SA 62 D7 65 K11
Takone TAS 54 E4
Takone West TAS 54 E4
Talapa Con Park SA 63 B11
Talarm NSW 25 H12
Talawa TAS 55 E12
Talbingo NSW 30 E7
Talbot VIC 39 C10
Talbot Brook WA 72 C3
Talbotville (site) VIC 43 H9 46 B4
Taldra SA 28 F1 40 B1 62 A5 65 H13
Talgarno VIC 43 B10
Talia SA 64 F4
Talisker Con Park SA 61 K1
Tallageira VIC 38 B2
Tallai QLD 5 C13
Tallanalla WA 73 F8
Tallandoon VIC 30 G5 43 C10
Tallangatta VIC 29 K13 30 G5 43 C10
Tallangatta Valley VIC 43 C10
Tallaringa Con Park SA 66 F2 68 E7
Tallarook VIC 39 C14 42 G2
Tallebudgera QLD 5 B14
Tallebudgera Valley QLD 5 C14
Tallebung NSW 29 B12
Tallegalla QLD 5 J9
Tallimba NSW 29 E12
Tallong NSW 22 K6 31 C11
Tallygaroopna VIC 42 C3
Talmalmo NSW 29 K13 30 F5 43 A11
Talmo NSW 31 C8
Taloon NSW 24 J1
Talwood QLD 6 J6 24 A4
Tamarang NSW 22 A7 24 K5
Tambar Springs NSW 24 K5
Tambelin SA 60 C3
Tambellup WA 74 H6
Tambo QLD 8 K4 13 H13 15 A14
Tambo Crossing VIC 43 J12 45 A14 46 C7
Tambo Upper VIC 43 K12 45 B14 46 D7
Tamborine QLD 5 D11 7 H13
Tamborine Nat Park QLD 5 D11
Tamboy NSW 23 D12
Tamleugh VIC 42 D4
Tammin WA 74 C5 76 K6
Tampa WA 77 F11 83 E1
Tamrookum QLD 5 F14
Tamworth NSW 24 J7
Tanami Mine NT 88 H2
Tanara West VIC 38 F4
Tanawha QLD 4 E1
Tandarra VIC 41 K11
Tangalooma QLD 4 B5 7 F13
Tangambalanga VIC 43 C9
Tangmangaroo NSW 22 K3 31 B8
Tangorin QLD 8 E1 13 C10
Tanja NSW 31 H11
Tanjil Bren VIC 42 K6 44 B7 46 D1
Tankaanu SA 68 B2 90 K3
Tankerton VIC 37 J10 44 F3
Tannum Sands QLD 9 J11
Tansey QLD 7 D11
Tantanoola SA 63 B13
Tanunda SA 60 A6 62 E6 65 H10
Tanwood VIC 39 C9
Tanybryn VIC 39 J10
Taperoo SA 59 C2
Taplan SA 28 G1 40 C1 62 A6 65 H13
Tara NT 91 B8
Tara QLD 7 F8
Taradale VIC 39 C12
Tarago NSW 31 D10
Tarago VIC 37 F14
Tarago Reservoir VIC 44 C5
Taragoola QLD 9 J11
Taralga NSW 22 J6 31 B11
Tarana NSW 22 G6
Taranna TAS 51 G13 53 G12
Tarcoola SA 64 A4 66 K4
Tarcoon NSW 27 E12
Tarcowie SA 62 F2 65 E10
Tarcutta NSW 29 H14 30 D6
Tardun WA 76 F4
Taree NSW 23 B12
Taren Point NSW 19 J4 21 B10
Targa TAS 55 E11 56 F7
Tarin Rock Nat Res WA 74 F7
Taringa QLD 3 F3
Tarlee SA 62 E5 65 H10
Tarlo NSW 22 K6 31 B11
Tarlo River Nat Park NSW 22 K6 31 B11
Tarnagulla VIC 39 B10
Tarneit VIC 36 D5
Tarnma SA 62 E5 65 H10
Tarnook VIC 42 D5
Taroborah QLD 8 H6
Tarome QLD 5 K12
Taroom QLD 6 C7
Taroon VIC 38 H7
Taroona TAS 50 E6 53 G10
Tarpeena SA 38 F1 63 B13
Tarra-Bulga Nat Park VIC 45 F8 46 G2
Tarragal VIC 38 H3
Tarragindi QLD 3 F4
Tarraleah TAS 52 C7 54 K7
Tarrango VIC 28 G3 40 B3
Tarranyurk VIC 40 J5
Tarraville VIC 45 G9 46 H3
Tarrawarra VIC 37 B11
Tarrawingee VIC 42 C7
Tarrayoukyan VIC 38 D3
Tarrington VIC 38 F5
Tarvano QLD 13 B9
Tarwin VIC 44 G6
Tarwin Lower VIC 44 H5
Tarwin Meadows VIC 44 H5
Tarwin Middle VIC 44 G5
Tarzali QLD 11 E12
Tasman Island TAS 51 K14 53 H13
Tasman Nat Park TAS 51 J13 53 H12
Tasman Peninsula TAS 51 H12 53 H12
Tatham NSW 25 C13
Tathra NSW 31 H11
Tathra Nat Park WA 76 G4
Tatong VIC 42 E6
Tatura VIC 42 C3
Tatyoon VIC 39 E8
Tatyoon North VIC 39 E8
Taunton (Scientific) Nat Park QLD 9 H8
Tawonga VIC 43 E9
Tawonga South VIC 43 E9
Tayene TAS 55 F11
Tayetea Bridge TAS 54 D3
Taylor Island SA 64 J6
Taylors Arm NSW 25 H12
Taylors Flat NSW 22 J4 31 A9
Tchanning QLD 6 E6
Tea Gardens NSW 23 D11
Tea Tree TAS 53 F10
Tea Tree Gully SA 59 D7 60 E4
Teddywaddy VIC 41 J9
Teddywaddy West VIC 41 J8
Teds Beach TAS 52 F6
Teesdale VIC 39 G11
Teeta Bore SA 68 C5
Telangatuk VIC 38 C5
Telegraph Point NSW 23 A13 25 K12
Telfer Mine WA 79 F8
Telford SA 67 K10
Telford VIC 42 B5
Telita TAS 55 E12
Telopea Downs SA 40 J2 63 A10
Telowie Gorge Con Park SA 62 G2 65 E9
Temma TAS 54 E1
Temora NSW 22 J1 29 F13 30 B5
Tempe NSW 19 G5
Temple Island QLD 9 E9
Templer Island NT 86 B6
Templers SA 60 A4
Templestowe VIC 35 C6 37 C9
Templin QLD 5 H12
Tempy VIC 40 F6
Ten Mile Lake WA 78 J7
Tenby Point VIC 37 K11
Tenindewa WA 76 F4
Tennant Creek NT 89 G9
Tennyson NSW 19 E4 20 G6
Tennyson SA 59 F1 60 F1
Tennyson VIC 41 K12
Tent Hill NSW 25 D9
Tent Hill SA 62 H1 65 D8
Tent Island Nat Res WA 78 F2
Tenterfield NSW 7 K11 25 C10
Teodter O/P Mine WA 77 C8
Tepko SA 62 E7 65 J11
Terang VIC 39 H8

Teridgerie NSW 24 H2
Teringie SA 59 G7
Termeil NSW 31 E12
Terowie NSW 22 D1 27 K14 29 B14
Terowie SA 62 E2 65 F10
Terranora NSW 5 A14
Terrey Hills NSW 19 B6 20 C7
Terrick Terrick Nat Park VIC 41 J11
Terrigal NSW 20 B4 23 G10
Terry Hie Hie NSW 24 E6
Tetoora Road VIC 37 H14
Teutonic Bore WA 77 E10
Tevan NSW 7 K13 25 C14
Teviotville QLD 5 H12
Tewantin QLD 7 D13
Tewkesbury TAS 54 E5
Texas QLD 7 K9 25 B8
Thalaba NSW 22 J5 31 A10
Thalanga QLD 8 B3 11 K13
Thalia VIC 41 J8
Thallon QLD 6 J5 24 B3
Thangool QLD 9 K10
Tharbogang NSW 29 F10 30 A2
Thargomindah QLD 15 H9
Tharwa ACT 31 E9
The Banca TAS 55 D12
The Basin VIC 37 D10
The Bump VIC 37 D13
The Caves QLD 9 H12
The Channon NSW 25 B13
The Cove VIC 38 J7
The Dutchmans Stern Con Park SA 65 D9
The English Company's Islands NT 87 C12
The Entrance NSW 20 A3 23 F10
The Gap NSW 3 D2 4 F7
The Gap SA 62 H5 65 H8
The Gap VIC 36 A5
The Gardens NT 84 D1
The Gardens TAS 55 E14
The Glen TAS 55 D12
The Granites Mine NT 88 J3 90 A3
The Gums QLD 6 F7
The Gurdies VIC 37 J12
The Heart VIC 45 D11 46 F4
The Knoll Con Park SA 60 H3 61 B7
The Lakes NSW 72 E3 74 C3 76 E4
The Lakes Nat Park VIC 45 C14 46 E6
The Monument QLD 12 C4
The Narrows NT 84 C2
The Oaks NSW 21 G12 23 J8 31 A12
The Peak Goldmine NSW 27 H10
The Risk NSW 25 A13
The Rock NSW 29 H13 30 D4
The Sisters VIC 38 H7
The Triangle VIC 42 J6 44 A6 46 C1
The Vines WA 71 A7
Thebarton SA 59 G3 60 F2 61 A6
Theebine QLD 7 C12
Theodore QLD 6 A7 9 K9
Theresa Park NSW 21 G11
Thevenard SA 64 D2 68 K7
Thirlmere NSW 21 G13 23 J8 31 A12
Thirlmere Lakes Nat Park NSW 21 G13 22 J7 31 A12
Thirlstane TAS 55 E8
Thirroul NSW 21 C13 31 A13
Thistle Island SA 64 J6
Thologolong VIC 43 A10
Thomastown VIC 35 A4
Thooloora Island QLD 4 E3
Thoona VIC 42 C6
Thora NSW 25 G12
Thornbury VIC 35 C4
Thorneside QLD 3 E7
Thorngate SA 58 A2
Thornlands QLD 5 C9
Thornleigh NSW 19 C3 20 D7
Thornlie WA 71 J6
Thornton Beach QLD 11 C12
Thorpdale VIC 44 E7 46 F1
Thowgla VIC 43 C12
Thowgla Upper VIC 43 C12
Thredbo NSW 30 H7 43 D14
Three Bridges VIC 37 D13
Three Hummock Island TAS 54 A2
Three Moon QLD 7 A9 9 K11
Three Springs WA 76 G4
Three Ways NT 89 G9
Thrushton Nat Park QLD 6 G3
Thuddungra NSW 22 J2 29 F14 30 A7
Thule NSW 41 G12
Thulloo NSW 29 D12
Thurgoona NSW 29 K12 30 F4 43 B9
Thuringowa QLD 8 A5 11 H14
Thurla VIC 28 F3 40 B5
Thursday Island QLD 16 B2
Tia NSW 25 J9
Tiaro QLD 7 C12
Tibarri QLD 10 K6 12 A6
Tibbuc NSW 23 B11
Tibooburra NSW 26 C3
Tichborne NSW 22 F2 29 C14
Tickera SA 62 H4 65 G8
Tidal River VIC 44 K7 46 K1
Tieri QLD 8 G7
Tilba Tilba NSW 31 G11

Tilbuster NSW 25 G9
Tilmouth Roadhouse NT 90 D6
Tilpa NSW 27 F9
Timbarra VIC 43 H12 46 B7
Timber Creek NT 86 J3 88 A3
Timberoo VIC 28 H4 40 E5
Timberoo South VIC 28 H3 40 E5
Timbillica NSW 31 K10 47 C13
Timboon VIC 39 J8
Timor NSW 23 B9
Timor VIC 39 C10
Timor West VIC 39 C10
Tin Can Bay QLD 7 C13
Tin Kettle Island TAS 55 C9
Tinamba VIC 45 C10 46 E3
Tinaroo Falls QLD 11 D12
Tindal NT 85 J5 86 G6
Tinderbox TAS 50 G6 53 G10
Tinderry Nat Res NSW 31 E9
Tindo QLD 8 C1 13 A11
Tingalpa QLD 3 E6 5 D8
Tingalpa Reservoir QLD 3 G7
Tingaringy Nat Park VIC 31 J8 47 A9
Tingha NSW 25 F8
Tingiring NSW 31 J8
Tingoora QLD 7 D10
Tinonee NSW 23 B12
Tintaldra VIC 29 K14 30 F6 43 B12
Tintinara SA 63 C9
Tirranaville NSW 31 C10
Tirrawarra Oil & Gas Field SA 14 G2 67 D13
Titjikala NT 91 H8
Ti-Tree NT 90 C7
Tittybong VIC 41 G9
Tiwi NT 84 A3
Tjintalka SA 68 A2 79 K14 90 K2
Tjinturritjan WA 83 B6
Tjirrkarli WA 79 K11 83 A4
Tjukayirla Roadhouse WA 77 D14 83 C3
Tjukurla WA 79 J14 90 H1
Tjuninanta NT 79 J14 90 H1
Tjunti NT 79 J14
Tjuntjuntjarra WA 83 E5
Tjuwaliyn (Douglas Hot Springs Nature Park) NT 85 G3 86 F4
Tnorala Con Res NT 90 F6
Tocal QLD 13 F9
Tocumwal NSW 29 K10 30 F1 42 A4
Tods TAS 53 B8 55 J8
Togari TAS 54 C2
Togganoggera NSW 31 E10
Toilberry TAS 55 G9 56 J4
Tolga QLD 11 D12
Tolmie VIC 42 F6
Tolmies QLD 8 H7
Tom Groggin NSW 30 H7 43 D13
Tom Price WA 78 G5 82 F3
Tomahawk TAS 55 C12
Tomalla NSW 23 B10
Tomaree Nat Park NSW 23 E11
Tomboy NSW 31 D11
Tomerong NSW 31 D12
Tomingley NSW 22 D2
Tonebridge WA 73 C13
Tongala VIC 41 J14 42 C2
Tonganah TAS 55 E11
Tonghi Creek VIC 47 C11
Tongio VIC 30 K6 43 G11 46 A6
Tongio West VIC 43 G11 46 B6
Tonimbuk VIC 37 F13
Tooan VIC 38 B4
Tooan East VIC 38 B4
Toobanna QLD 11 G13
Toobeah QLD 6 J7 24 A5
Tooborac VIC 39 C13 42 F1
Toodyay WA 72 D1 74 B4 76 K5
Toogong NSW 22 F3
Toogoolawah QLD 7 F11
Toolakea QLD 11 H14
Toolamba VIC 42 D3
Toolangi VIC 37 A11 42 J4 44 A3
Toolern Vale VIC 36 B4 39 E13
Tooleybuc NSW 28 H6 41 E9
Toolondo VIC 38 C4
Toolong VIC 38 H5
Toolonga Nat Res WA 76 C3
Tooloom NSW 25 B11
Tooloom Nat Park NSW 7 J11 25 A11
Tooloombah QLD 9 G9
Tooma NSW 29 K14 30 F7 43 A13
Toombul QLD 3 C5
Toompine QLD 15 F10
Toomulla QLD 11 G14
Toongabbie NSW 19 D1 21 E8
Toongabbie VIC 45 D9 46 E2
Toongi NSW 22 D3
Toonpan QLD 8 A5 11 H14
Toonumbar NSW 25 B12
Toonumbar Nat Park NSW 7 J12 25 B12
Tooperang SA 61 G7
Toora VIC 44 G7 46 H1
Tooradin VIC 37 H10 44 E3
Toorak VIC 35 E4

Toorak Gardens SA 59 G5
Toorale East NSW 27 F9
Tooraweenah NSW 22 A4 24 K2
Toorbul QLD 4 E4
Toorloo Arm VIC 43 K12 46 D7
Toorongo VIC 42 K6 44 B6 46 D1
Toowong QLD 3 E3
Toowoomba QLD 7 G11
Toowoon Bay NSW 20 A3
Top Springs NT 88 B5
Topgallant Island SA 64 G4
Torbanlea QLD 7 B12
Tornakin NSW 31 F11
Torndirrup Nat Park WA 74 K6
Toronto NSW 23 G12
Torquay VIC 36 J2 39 H12
Torrens Creek QLD 8 C2 11 K12 13 A11
Torrens Island SA 59 C2 60 D1
Torrens Island Con Park SA 59 B2 60 D1
Torrens Park SA 59 H4
Torrens Vale SA 61 H4
Torrensville SA 59 G3
Torres Strait 16 A2
Torrilla Peninsula QLD 9 F10
Torrington NSW 25 D9
Torrita VIC 28 H3 40 E4
Torrumbarry VIC 41 J12
Tostaree VIC 43 K13 47 D8
Tottenham NSW 27 K13 29 A13
Tottington VIC 39 B8
Toukley NSW 20 A2
Towallum NSW 25 F12
Towamba NSW 31 J10 47 A13
Towaninny VIC 41 H9
Tower Hill TAS 55 G12
Townshend Island QLD 9 F10
Townsville QLD 8 A5 11 H14
Towong VIC 29 K14 30 G6 43 B12
Towra Point Nat Res NSW 19 J5
Towradgi NSW 21 C14
Towrang NSW 22 K6 31 D11
Trafalgar VIC 44 E7 46 F1
Tragowel VIC 41 H11
Trangie NSW 22 B2 27 J14 29 A14
Tranmere SA 59 F6
Traralgon VIC 45 E8 46 F2
Traralgon South VIC 45 E8 46 F2
Trawalla VIC 39 E9
Trawool VIC 39 C14 42 G3
Trayning WA 74 A6 76 J7
Trebonne QLD 11 G13
Treesville WA 73 E9
Treeton WA 73 J12
Trefoil Island TAS 54 B1
Tregole Nat Park QLD 6 D2
Trenah TAS 55 E12
Trentham VIC 39 D12
Trentham East VIC 39 D12
Trephina Gorge Nature Park NT 91 F9
Tresco VIC 41 F10
Trevallyn NSW 23 D10
Trevallyn State Rec Area TAS 56 G5
Trewalla VIC 38 H3
Trewilga VIC 22 E2
Triabunna TAS 53 E12
Trida NSW 29 C9
Trigg WA 71 D1
Trinity Bay QLD 11 C12
Trinity Beach QLD 11 D13
Trinity Gardens SA 59 F5
Troubridge Island Con Park SA 62 G7 65 J9
Troughton Island WA 81 A10
Trowutta TAS 54 D2
Truant Island NT 87 B13
Truganina VIC 36 D5
Trundle NSW 22 E1 29 C14
Trunkey Creek NSW 22 H5
Truro SA 62 D3 65 E12
Truslove Townsite Nat Res WA 75 F13 83 J1
Tryon Island QLD 9 G12
Tryphinia QLD 9 H9
Tuan QLD 7 C13
Tuart Forest Nat Park WA 73 H10 74 G2
Tuart Hill WA 71 E3
Tubbul NSW 22 J2 29 F14 30 A6
Tubbut VIC 43 G14 47 A9
Tucabia NSW 25 E13
Tuckanarra WA 76 C7
Tucklan NSW 22 C5
Tudor VIC 28 H5 41 E8
Tuena NSW 22 H5
Tugan QLD 5 A14
Tuggerah NSW 20 B2
Tuggerah Lake NSW 20 B2
Tuggeranong ACT 31 E9
Tuggerawong NSW 20 B2
Tulburrer Island QLD 10 D3
Tulendeena TAS 55 E12
Tulka SA 64 J5
Tullagri QLD 7 F8
Tullah TAS 52 A4 54 G4
Tullamarine VIC 35 B2 36 B6
Tullamore NSW 22 D1 29 B13
Tullibigeal NSW 29 D12
Tullich VIC 38 E2
Tully QLD 11 F13
Tully Gorge Nat Park QLD 11 E13

Tully Heads QLD 11 F13
Tumbarumba NSW 29 J14 30 F6 43 A13
Tumbi Umbi NSW 20 B3
Tumblong NSW 29 H14 30 D6
Tumbulgum NSW 25 A14
Tumby Bay SA 64 H6
Tumorrama NSW 30 D7
Tumoulin QLD 11 E12
Tumut NSW 29 H14 30 D7
Tunart VIC 28 G2 40 B2
Tunbridge TAS 53 C11 55 K11
Tuncurry NSW 23 C12
Tungamah VIC 42 B5
Tungkillo SA 60 E7 62 E6 65 J10
Tunnack TAS 53 D11
Tunnel TAS 55 D6
Tunnel Creek Nat Park WA 79 B11 81 H8
Tunney WA 73 A13
Tuppal NSW 29 J9
Tupul SA 68 A4 90 K4
Tura Beach NSW 31 J11
Turill NSW 22 C6
Turkey Beach QLD 9 J12
Turkey Creek WA 79 A14 81 G13
Turlinjah NSW 31 F11
Turners Beach TAS 54 E7
Turners Marsh TAS 55 E10 56 E5
Turondale NSW 22 C5
Tuross Head NSW 31 F11
Turramurra NSW 19 C4 20 D7
Turrawan NSW 24 G5
Turriff VIC 40 F6
Turrumbarry VIC 29 K8
Turtle Group Nat Park QLD 16 J6
Turtle Head Island QLD 16 B2
Tusmore SA 59 G5
Tutanning Nat Res WA 72 A6 74 D5
Tutunup WA 73 H11
Tutye VIC 28 H2 40 E3
Tweed Heads NSW 5 A14 7 J14 25 A14
Twelve Mile NSW 22 D5
Two Mile Flat NSW 22 D5
Two Peoples Bay Nat Res WA 74 K7
Two Rocks WA 72 H1 74 B2 76 K4
Two Wells SA 60 B1 62 F6 65 H10
Twyford QLD 11 C12
Tyaak VIC 39 D14 42 G2
Tyabb VIC 37 H9 39 H14 44 E2
Tyagong NSW 22 H2 30 A7
Tyalgum NSW 7 J13 25 A13
Tyalla VIC 28 H2 40 E3
Tycannah NSW 24 E5
Tyenna TAS 53 F8
Tyers VIC 45 D8 46 F2
Tylden VIC 39 D12
Tynong VIC 37 F12 44 D4
Tynong North VIC 37 F12
Tyntynder Central VIC 28 H6 41 E8
Tyntynder South VIC 28 H6 41 F9
Tyrendarra VIC 38 H4
Tyrendarra East VIC 38 H4
Tyringham NSW 25 G11
Tyrrell Downs VIC 28 J5 40 F7

## U

Uarbry NSW 22 B6
Ubobo QLD 9 J11
Ukatjupa NT 79 K14 90 K1
Uki NSW 7 J13 25 A13
Ulamambri NSW 24 K4
Ulan NSW 22 C6
Ulaypai SA 68 A4 90 K5
Uleybury SA 60 C4
Ulidia VIC 38 D2
Ulinda NSW 22 A5 24 K4
Ulladulla NSW 31 E12
Ullina VIC 39 D10
Ulmarra NSW 25 E13
Ulmina NSW 20 B5
Ulong NSW 25 G12
Ultima VIC 28 J5 41 F8
Ultimo NSW 18 D1
Uluru-Kata Tjuta Nat Park NT 90 J4
Ulverstone TAS 54 E6
Umagico QLD 16 B2
Umbakumba NT 87 F13
Umerina SA 66 C1 68 B6
Umpukulu SA 90 K3
Umuwa SA 68 B5
Unanderra NSW 21 D14
Undara Volcanic Nat Park QLD 11 F11
Undera VIC 42 C3
Underbool VIC 28 H3 40 E4
Underwood QLD 3 H5
Underwood TAS 55 E10 56 E6
Undina QLD 10 K6 12 A5
Ungarie NSW 29 D12
Ungarra SA 64 G6
Ungo QLD 8 K1 13 H10
Unicup Nat Res WA 73 C14 74 H4
Unley SA 58 D2 59 G4 60 G2 61 A6
Unnamed Con Park SA 68 E2 83 E7
Upper Bingara NSW 24 F7
Upper Blessington TAS 55 F11
Upper Bowman NSW 23 B11
Upper Caboolture QLD 4 F5
Upper Castra TAS 54 E6

Upper Colo NSW 20 H5
Upper Coomera QLD 5 C11
Upper Esk TAS 55 F12
Upper Ferntree Gully VIC 37 E10 42 K3 44 C3
Upper Hermitage SA 60 E4
Upper Horton NSW 24 F6
Upper Kedron QLD 3 D1
Upper Manilla NSW 24 H7
Upper McDonald NSW 20 F3
Upper Mount Gravatt QLD 3 G5
Upper Mount Hicks TAS 54 D5
Upper Myall NSW 23 C12
Upper Nariel VIC 30 H6 43 D12
Upper Natone TAS 54 E5
Upper Orara NSW 25 G12
Upper Plenty VIC 39 D14 42 H2
Upper Rollands Plains NSW 25 K11
Upper Scamander TAS 55 F14
Upper Stone QLD 11 G13
Upper Stowport TAS 54 E5
Upper Sturt SA 59 K6
Upper Swan WA 72 F2 74 C3 76 K5
Upper Tallebudgera QLD 5 C14
Upper Yarra Dam VIC 37 B14 42 J5 44 A5

Upstart Bay QLD 8 A6
Upukula SA 68 A3
Uraidla SA 59 H7 60 G4 62 F7 65 J7
Uralla NSW 25 F9
Urana NSW 29 H11 30 D3
Urandangi QLD 12 C2
Urangeline NSW 29 J12 30 E3
Urangeline East NSW 29 J12 30 E4
Urania SA 62 H6 65 H8
Uranquinty NSW 29 H13 30 D5
Urapunga NT 87 G9
Urapuntja (Utopia) NT 91 C9
Urawa Nat Res WA 76 E4
Urbenville NSW 7 J12 25 A12
Urilpila NT 90 J3
Urlampe NT 91 D14
Urrbrae SA 59 H5
Urunga NSW 25 G12
Useless Loop WA 76 B1 78 K1
Uxbridge TAS 53 F9

## V

Vacy NSW 23 D10
Valencia Island NT 86 B6
Valley Heights NSW 21 H8
Valley View SA 59 D5
Van Diemen Gulf NT 85 B4 86 C5
Vanderlin Island NT 87 J13 89 A13
Vansittart Island TAS 55 C10
Varley WA 75 E9
Vasey VIC 38 D4
Vasse WA 73 J11
Vaucluse NSW 19 F7 21 B8
Vectus VIC 38 D3
Veitch SA 62 B6 65 J13
Venman Bushland Nat Park QLD 3 J1 5 D9
Ventnor VIC 37 K9 39 J14 44 F2
Venus Bay SA 64 F4
Venus Bay VIC 44 H5
Venus Bay Con Park SA 64 F4
Verdun SA 60 H4
Veresdale QLD 5 F12
Vermont VIC 37 D9
Verona Sands TAS 53 H10
Verran SA 64 G6
Vervale VIC 37 G12
Victor Harbor SA 61 J6 63 F8 65 K14
Victoria Park WA 71 G4
Victoria Point SA 5 C9
Victoria River NT 86 J4 88 A4
Victoria Rock Nat Res WA 75 B11 77 J10
Victoria Valley TAS 53 D8 55 K8
Victoria Valley VIC 38 E6
Victory Well SA 68 C5
Villawood NSW 19 F2
Villeneuve QLD 4 J3
Vincentia NSW 31 D13
Vineyard NSW 20 F7
Vinifera VIC 28 H6 41 E9
Violet Town VIC 30 H1 42 D4
Virginia QLD 3 C5
Virginia SA 60 C2 62 F6 65 H10
Vista SA 60 E5
Vite Vite VIC 39 F8
Vite Vite North VIC 39 F8
Vivonne SA 63 J9
Vivonne Bay Con Park SA 63 J8
Vokes Hill Corner SA 68 E3

## W

Waaia VIC 42 B3
Waarre VIC 39 J8
Wabba VIC 30 G6
Wabba Wilderness Park VIC 30 G6 43 C11
Wacol QLD 3 H1 5 F9
Wadbilliga Nat Park NSW 31 G10
Waddamana TAS 53 C8 55 K8
Waddi NSW 29 G10 30 B2
Waddikee SA 64 F6
Wadeye NT 86 G1
Waeel WA 72 B2

Wagaman NT 84 B3
Wagant VIC 28 H4 40 E6
Wagerup WA 72 F7
Wagga Wagga NSW 29 H13 30 D5
Waggabundi QLD 10 H3
Waggarandall VIC 42 C5
Wagin WA 73 A9 74 F5
Wagonga NSW 31 G11
Wahgunyah VIC 42 B7
Wahgunyah Con Res SA 68 K5
Wahroonga NSW 19 C4 20 C7
Waikerie SA 62 C5 65 H12
Wail VIC 38 A5
Wairewa VIC 43 K13 47 D8
Waitchie VIC 28 J5 41 F8
Waite Creek Settlement NT 90 D3
Waitpinga SA 61 J5 63 F8 65 K10
Waitpinga Con Park SA 61 J3
Wakool NSW 28 J5
Walalkarra SA 68 C4
Walang NSW 22 G6
Walbundrie NSW 29 J12 30 E4
Walcha NSW 25 J8
Walcha Road NSW 25 J8
Waldegrave Island Con Park SA 64 F4
Walebing WA 74 A3 76 J5
Walga Gunya WA 77 C8
Walgett NSW 24 F1 27 E7
Walgoolan WA 74 B7 77 J8
Walhalla VIC 47 A8
Walitjara SA 68 A3 90 K3
Walka NT 79 J14 83 A7 90 H1
Walkaway WA 76 J4
Walkamin QLD 11 D12
Walker VIC 37 A14
Walker Bay VIC 38 B7
Walker Flat SA 62 D6 65 J11
Walker Island TAS 52 K7 54 B2
Walkers Crossing SA 67 D12
Walkerston QLD 9 D8
Walkerville SA 59 F4 60 F2
Walkerville North VIC 44 H6
Walkerville South VIC 44 H6
Wall SA 62 D7 65 J11
Walla Walla NSW 29 J12 30 F4
Wallabadah NSW 23 A8 24 K7
Wallabi Group WA 76 F2
Wallabrook SA 38 B1 63 B11
Wallaby Island QLD 10 A6 16 K1
Wallace VIC 39 E11
Wallace Rockhole NT 90 G7
Wallacedale VIC 38 G4
Wallacia NSW 21 G9 23 H8
Wallaga Lake Nat Park NSW 31 G11
Wallal QLD 15 E13
Wallaloo VIC 38 B7
Wallaloo East VIC 38 B7
Wallan VIC 39 D14 42 H2
Wallan East VIC 39 D14 42 H2
Wallangarra NSW 7 K10 25 C10
Wallangra NSW 24 D7
Wallany SA 90 K4
Wallaroo SA 62 H4 65 G8
Wallatinna SA 90 D2 68 C7
Wallaville QLD 7 A11
Wallendbeen NSW 22 K2 29 G14
30 B7
Wallerawang NSW 22 F6
Walleroobie NSW 29 F12 30 B4
Walli NSW 22 G4
Wallinduc VIC 39 F9
Wallington VIC 36 H4
Wallis Lake NSW 23 C12
Wallon QLD 5 H9
Wallpolla Island VIC 40 A3
Walls of Jerusalem Nat Park TAS
52 A6 54 H6
Wallsend NSW 23 E10
Wallumbilla QLD 6 E6
Wallundry NSW 22 J1 29 F14 30 A6
Wallup VIC 40 K5
Walmer NSW 22 D3
Walpa VIC 43 K10 45 B12 46 D5
Walpeup VIC 28 H3 40 E5
Walpole WA 74 J4
Walpole-Nornalup Nat Park WA 74 K4
Walsh Bay QLD 11 B12
Waltara NSW 20 D7
Walu NT 79 J14 90 H2
Walungurru (Kintore) NT 79 G14 90 E1
Walunuju WA 79 A9 80 F5
Walwa VIC 29 K14 30 F6 43 A12
Walyahmoning Nat Res WA 77 H8
Walyinynga SA 68 A4 90 K4
Walytjatjata NT 68 A1 79 K14 90 K2
Walyunga Nat Park WA 72 F2
Wamberal NSW 20 B4
Wamboota NSW 41 H13
Wamboyne NSW 29 D13
Wammuta QLD 4 G4 7 F12
Wamoon NSW 29 F11 30 B3
Wamuran QLD 4 G4 7 F12
Wamuran Basin QLD 4 G4
Wanaaring NSW 26 D7
Wanagarren Nat Res WA 74 A1 76 J4
Wanbi SA 65 J12
Wandana Nat Res WA 76 E4
Wandandian NSW 31 D9
Wandearah QLD 11 C13
Wandella NSW 31 G11
Wandering WA 72 C6 74 E4
Wandiligong VIC 43 E9
Wandilo SA 63 B13

Wandin North VIC 37 C11
Wando Bridge VIC 38 E3
Wando Vale VIC 38 E3
Wandoan QLD 6 D7
Wandong VIC 39 D14 42 H2
Wandoo Con Park WA 72 D4 74 D4 76
K5
Wandsworth NSW 25 F9
Wanganella NSW 29 H8 41 E13
Wangara WA 71 B3
Wangarabell VIC 47 C12
Wangaratta VIC 30 G3 42 C7
Wangary SA 64 H5
Wangerrip VIC 39 K9
Wangkatjungka (Christmas Creek) WA
79 C12 84 J6
Wangoom VIC 38 H7
Wanguri NT 84 A3
Wanilla SA 64 H5
Wanjari Nat Res WA 77 D10
Wankari NT 79 J14 83 A7 90 H1
Wanko QLD 15 E13
Wannamal WA 74 B2 76 J5
Wannarn WA 79 J13 83 A6
Wanneroo WA 71 A3 72 G2 74 C2
76 K4
Wannon VIC 38 F4
Wannoo Billabong Roadhouse WA
76 C3
Wanora QLD 5 H8
Wantabadgery NSW 29 H14 30 C6
Wanwin VIC 38 G2
Wapengo NSW 31 H11
Wapet Camp WA 78 E3
Wappinguy NSW 22 C7
Warakurna WA 79 J13 83 A7
Warakurna Roadhouse WA 79 J13
83 A7
Warana QLD 4 D1
Waranga VIC 39 A14 42 D2
Waratah TAS 54 F4
Waratah Bay VIC 44 H6
Waratah North VIC 44 H6
Warburn NSW 29 F10 30 A2
Warburton VIC 37 C13 42 K4 44 B5
Warburton WA 79 K12 83 B5
Warburton East VIC 37 C13
Warby Range State Park VIC 30 G2
42 C6
Ward Island SA 64 G3
Wardang Island SA 62 H6 65 H8
Wardell NSW 25 C14
Warden Head NSW 31 D12
Wards Mistake NSW 25 F10
Wards River NSW 23 C11
Warge Rock NSW 29 B14
Warginburra Peninsula QLD 9 F10
Warialda NSW 24 D7
Warianna QLD 13 B10
Warkton NSW 24 K3
Warkworth NSW 23 D9
Warmun WA 79 A14 81 G13
Warncoort VIC 39 H10
Warneet VIC 37 H10 44 E3
Warnertown SA 62 G3 65 F9
Warnervale NSW 20 B2
Warooka SA 62 H7 65 J8
Waroona WA 72 F7 74 E3
Warra QLD 7 E9
Warrabah Nat Park NSW 24 G7
Warrabillinna SA 68 B5 90 K6
Warrabkook VIC 38 G5
Warracknabeal VIC 40 K6
Warradale SA 59 J2
Warraderry NSW 22 G4
Warragamba NSW 21 G10 23 H8
Warragamba VIC 41 K12
Warragoon NSW 29 K11 30 F2 42 A6
Warragul VIC 37 G14 44 D6
Warrah Creek NSW 23 B8
Warrak VIC 39 D8
Warrambine VIC 39 G10
Warramboo SA 64 F5
Warrandyte VIC 35 C7 37 C9 42 K3
44 B2
Warrandyte State Park VIC 35 B7
37 C9 42 K3 44 B2
Warranmang VIC 39 C9
Warranulla NSW 23 C11
Warrapura WA 79 J14 83 A7
Warrawee VIC 20 C7
Warrayure VIC 38 F5
Warreah QLD 8 C2 11 K11 13 A11
Warrego Mine NT 89 G8
Warrell Creek NSW 25 H12
Warren NSW 27 J7 28 A5
Warren Con Park SA 60 D5
Warren Nat Park WA 73 F14 74 J3
Warrenbayne VIC 42 E5
Warrenben Con Park SA 62 J7 64 J7
Warrentinna TAS 55 D12
Warriewood NSW 20 B7
Warrigal QLD 8 C2 11 K12 13 A12
Warrill View SA 5 J11
Warrimoo NSW 21 H8
Warrina SA 66 E6
Warringa TAS 54 E6
Warrion VIC 39 H10
Warrnambool VIC 38 H6
Warrong VIC 38 H6
Waroo NSW 22 F1 29 D13
Warrow SA 64 H5
Warrumbungle NSW 24 J2
Warrumbungle Nat Park NSW 24 J3

Warrupura WA 90 H1
Warruwi NT 86 B7
Wartburg QLD 9 K12
Wartook VIC 38 C6
Warup WA 73 A9
Warwick QLD 7 H11 25 A10
Warwick WA 71 C2
Warwick Farm NSW 19 G1
Washpool Nat Park NSW 25 D11
Wasleys SA 60 A3 62 F6 65 H10
Watagan NSW 20 E1
Watanobbi NSW 20 B2
Watarrka Nat Park NT 90 G5
Watarru SA 68 C2
Watchem VIC 40 J7
Watchupga VIC 28 K4 40 H7
Waterfall NSW 21 C11 23 J8 31 A13
Waterfall Gully SA 59 H6
Waterford VIC 43 J10 45 A11 46 C4
Waterford TAS 71 H4
Waterhouse TAS 55 C12
Waterhouse Con Area TAS 55 C11
Waterhouse Island TAS 55 C11
Waterloo SA 62 E4 65 G10
Waterloo TAS 50 J1 53 H9
Waterloo VIC 39 D9
Waterloo WA 73 G9
Waterloo Corner SA 59 A3
Waterman WA 71 C1
Watervale SA 62 E4 65 G10
Watgania VIC 38 E7
Watheroo WA 76 H5
Watheroo Nat Park WA 76 H4
Watinuma SA 68 B5
Watson SA 68 H4
Watson Island NT 87 J13
Watsonia VIC 35 B5 37 C8
Watsons Creek NSW 25 H8
Watsons Bay NSW 19 E7 21 B8
Watsons Creek VIC 37 B9
Wattamolla NSW 21 B11
Wattamondara VIC 22 H3
Wattle Creek VIC 39 C8
Wattle Flat NSW 22 F6
Wattle Glen VIC 37 B9
Wattle Grove NSW 21 D10
Wattle Grove TAS 50 J2 53 H9
Wattle Grove WA 71 H7
Wattle Hill TAS 51 A10 53 F11
Wattle Island VIC 44 K7 46 K1
Wattle Park SA 59 G6
Wattle Park VIC 46 E6
Wattle Point VIC 45 C13
Wattle Range SA 63 B13
Wattle Vale VIC 39 B14 42 E2
Waubra VIC 39 D10
Wauchope NSW 23 A13 25 K12
Wauchope NT 89 J9 91 A9
Waukaringa SA 62 D1 65 D11
Wauraltee SA 62 H6 65 H8
Waurn Ponds VIC 36 H2 39 H12
Wave Hill NSW 27 F11
Wavell Heights QLD 3 C4
Waverley NSW 19 F7 21 B8
Wayatinah TAS 52 D7
Waychinicup Nat Park WA 74 J7
Waygara VIC 43 K13 47 D8
Wayville SA 58 D2 59 G4
Weabonga NSW 25 J8
Weary Bay QLD 11 B12
Weavers SA 62 H7 65 J8
Webbs NSW 22 C3
Webbs Creek NSW 20 F4
Wedderburn NSW 21 E12
Wedderburn VIC 41 K10
Wedderburn Junction VIC 41 K10
Weddin Mountains Nat Park NSW
22 H1 29 E14
Wedge Island SA 62 K7 64 J6
Wedge Island TAS 51 H10
Wedge Island WA 74 A1 76 J4
Wednesday Island QLD 16 B2
Wee Jasper NSW 31 D8
Wee Waa NSW 24 F4
Weegena TAS 54 F7
Weemelah NSW 24 C3
Weemol NT 87 F9
Weerangourt VIC 38 G4
Weerite VIC 39 H9
Weetah TAS 55 F8
Weetaliba NSW 22 A5 24 K4
Weethalle NSW 29 E13
Weetulta SA 62 H5 65 H8
Wee-Wee-Rup VIC 41 H12
Wehla VIC 39 A10
Weilmoringle NSW 6 K1 27 C12
Weimby NSW 28 G5 41 C8
Weipa QLD 16 E1
Weismantels NSW 23 C11
Weitalaba QLD 9 J11
Weja NSW 29 D12
Welaregang NSW 29 K14 30 F6
43 B12
Weldborough TAS 55 E12
Welford Lagoon QLD 13 H10 15 A8
Welford Nat Park QLD 13 H9 15 A8
Wellesley Islands QLD 10 C4
Wellingrove NSW 25 E9
Wellington NSW 22 D4
Wellington SA 63 D8 65 K11
Wellington Point QLD 5 C8
Wellsford VIC 39 A12

Wellstead WA 74 J7
Welshmans Reef VIC 39 C11
Welshpool VIC 45 G8 46 H2
Welshpool WA 71 G6
Wembley WA 71 F3
Wembley Downs WA 71 E2
Wemen VIC 28 G4 40 D6
Wentworth NSW 28 F3 40 A4
Wentworth Falls NSW 21 K9 22 G7
Weranga QLD 7 E9
Werneth VIC 39 G10
Werombi NSW 21 G11 23 H8
Werrap VIC 40 H4
Werribee VIC 36 E5 39 F13 42 K1
Werribee Gorge State Park VIC 36 B3
39 E12
Werribee South VIC 36 E5 39 G13
Werrikimbe Nat Park NSW 25 J10
Werrimull VIC 28 F2 40 B3
Werrington NSW 21 G8
Werris Creek NSW 24 K7
Wesburn VIC 37 C12
Wesley Vale TAS 54 E7
Wessel Islands NT 87 B12
West Beach SA 59 G2 60 G1 61 A5
West Bore No. 2 SA 68 B5
West Cape Howe Nat Park WA 74 K6
West End QLD 2 D1 3 E3 5 E8
West Frankford TAS 55 E8 56 F1
West Gosford NSW 20 C4
West Hill QLD 9 E8
West Hill Island QLD 9 E9
West Hill Nat Park QLD 9 E9
West Hobart TAS 49 C1
West Hoxton NSW 21 E10
West Island NT 87 J12 89 A12
West Island QLD 16 B1
West Island SA 61 K6
West Kentish TAS 54 F7
West Killara NSW 21 C8
West Lakes SA 59 E1 60 F1
West MacDonnell Nat Park NT 90 F7
West Pennant Hills NSW 19 C4
West Perth WA 70 A1 71 F3
West Pine TAS 54 E6
West Pymble NSW 19 D4 20 C7
West Ridgley TAS 54 E5
West Ryde NSW 19 E4
West Scottsdale TAS 55 E11
West Swan WA 71 C6
West Wyalong NSW 29 E13
Westbourne Park SA 59 H4
Westbury TAS 55 G9 56 H2
Westby NSW 29 J13 30 E5
Westby VIC 28 J2 41 G11
Westdale WA 72 D5
Western Creek TAS 54 G7
Western Flat SA 38 A1 63 B11
Western Junction TAS 55 G10 56 J6
Western Port VIC 37 H10
Western Port Bay VIC 44 E3
Western River SA 63 J8 64 K7
Western River Con Park SA 63 J8
64 K7
Westerway TAS 53 E8
Westfield WA 71 K7
Westgate QLD 15 D14
Westmar QLD 6 H6
Westmead NSW 19 E2
Westmeadows VIC 35 A2
Westmere VIC 39 F8
Westminster WA 71 D3
Westonia WA 74 B7 77 J8
Westwood QLD 9 H10
Westwood TAS 55 F9 56 H3
Wetherill Park NSW 17 J1
Weymouth TAS 55 D10 56 B5
Whale Beach NSW 20 B6
Wharminda SA 64 G6
Wharparilla VIC 41 J13 42 B1
Whealban NSW 29 E8
Wheelers Hill VIC 35 F6
Wheeo NSW 22 K5 31 B9
Wherrol Flat NSW 23 B12
Whetstone QLD 7 J9 25 A8
Whidbey Isles Con Park SA 64 J4
Whim Creek WA 78 E5 82 C3
Whiporie NSW 7 K12 25 D13
Whirily VIC 41 H8
White Beach TAS 51 H11 53 H12
White Cliffs NSW 26 G5
White Flat SA 64 H6
White Gum Valley WA 71 J2
White Hills TAS 55 G10 56 H6
White Hut SA 62 J3
White Mountains Nat Park QLD 8 C2
11 K12 13 A11
Whitefoord TAS 53 D11
Whiteheads Creek VIC 42 F3
Whiteman WA 71 C5
Whitemark TAS 55 C9
Whitemore TAS 55 G9 56 J3
Whitewood QLD 13 B9
Whitfield VIC 30 H3 42 E7
Whitsunday Island QLD 9 B8
Whitsunday Islands Nat Park QLD 9 B8

Whittlesea VIC 37 A8 39 E14 42
H2 44 A2
Whitton NSW 29 F11 30 B2
Whitwarta SA 62 F5 65 G9
Whoorel VIC 39 H10
Whorouly VIC 42 D7
Whorouly South VIC 42 D7
Whroo VIC 39 A14 42 D2
Whyalla SA 62 H2 65 E8
Whyalla Con Park SA 62 H2
Whyte Island SA 3 D7 4 D7
Whyte-Yarcowie SA 62 E3 65 F10
Wialki WA 76 H7
Wiangaree NSW 7 J12 25 B13
Wickepin WA 74 E6
Wickham WA 78 E4 82 C2
Wickliffe VIC 38 F7
Wide Bay QLD 7 C13
Widgelli NSW 29 F11 30 A2
Widgiemooltha WA 75 B12 77 K11
83 G1
Widgiewa NSW 29 H11 30 C2
Wigram Island NT 87 B12
Wigton Island QLD 9 C6
Wilban WA 83 F4
Wilberforce NSW 20 F6
Wilburville TAS 53 B9 55 J9
Wilby VIC 42 B6
Wilcannia NSW 26 H5
Wild Duck Island Nat Park QLD 9 E9
Wild Horse Plains SA 62 G5 65 H9
Wildcat Bore SA 68 C6
Wilga WA 73 C7
Wilgarup WA 73 E13
Wilgena SA 64 A4 66 K4
Wilkatana SA 65 D9
Wilkawatt SA 63 B8 65 K12
Wilki Island QLD 16 G4
Willa VIC 40 F5
Willalooka SA 63 C10
Willandra Lakes World Heritage Area
NSW 28 D5
Willandra Nat Park NSW 29 C8
Willangie VIC 40 G7
Willara Crossing NSW 15 K10 26 C7
Willare Bridge Roadhouse WA 79 B10
80 G5
Willatook VIC 38 H5
Willaura VIC 38 E7
Willawarrin NSW 25 J11
Willawong QLD 3 H3 5 E9
Willbriggie NSW 29 F11 30 B2
Willenabrina VIC 40 J5
Willetton WA 71 J4
Willi Willi VIC 68 B1 79 K14 90 K2
Willi Willi Nat Park NSW 25 J11
William Creek SA 66 G6
Williams WA 73 C8 74 F4
Williamsdale NSW 31 E9
Williamsford TAS 52 A4 54 H4
Williamstown SA 60 C5 62 E6 65 J10
Williamstown VIC 35 E2 36 D7 39 F14
42 K2 44 C1
Williamtown NSW 23 E11
Willis VIC 30 J7 43 F14
Willmot NSW 21 F8
Willochra SA 65 D9
Willow Crossing VIC 43 C12
Willow Grove VIC 44 D7 46 E1
Willow Springs WA 73 F12
Willow Tree NSW 23 A8
Willow Waters SA 65 C10
Willowbank QLD 5 H10
Willowie SA 62 F1 65 E9
Willowra NT 88 K6 90 B6
Willows QLD 8 H6
Willows Gemfield QLD 8 H6
Willowvale VIC 39 F9
Willung VIC 45 E9 46 F3
Willunga SA 61 E6 62 F7 65 K10
Willunga Hill SA 61 F6
Willyabrup WA 73 K11
Wilmington SA 62 G1 65 E9
Wilmot TAS 54 F6
Wilora NT 91 C8
Wilpena SA 65 B10
Wilson SA 65 C10
Wilson Island Q 9 H12
Wilsons Downfall NSW 25 B10
Wilsons Promontory VIC 44 J7 46 K1
Wilsons Promontory Nat Park VIC
44 J7 46 K1
Wilton NSW 21 F13
Wiltshire TAS 54 C3
Wiluna WA 77 C9 78 K7
Wimba VIC 39 J10
Wiminda NSW 24 E1
Winbin QLD 15 E11
Winburndale Nat Res NSW 22 F6
Winceby Island SA 64 H6
Winchelsea VIC 39 H11
Winchelsea Island NT 87 F12
Windarra NSW 77 E12 83 D1
Windellama NSW 31 C11
Windemere VIC 39 E10
Windera QLD 7 D11
Windermere TAS 55 E9

Windermere Dam NSW 22 E6
Windeyer NSW 22 E5
Windjana Gorge Nat Park WA 79 A11 81 G8
Windomal Landing NSW 41 C9
Windorah QLD 13 J8 14 B7
Windsor NSW 20 F7 23 G8
Windsor QLD 3 D4
Windsor SA 62 F5 65 H9
Windsor Downs NSW 20 F7
Windsor Gardens SA 59 E5
Windurong NSW 22 A3 24 K2
Windy Corner WA 79 G11
Windy Harbour WA 74 J3
Wingala NSW 19 D7
Wingarnie WA 75 C13 77 K11 83 G1
Wingeel VIC 39 G10
Wingellina (Irruntjtju) WA 68 A1 79 K14 83 B7 90 K1
Wingello NSW 22 K7 31 C11
Wingen NSW 23 B9
Wingen Maid Nat Res NSW 23 B8
Wingfield SA 59 D3 60 F2
Wingham NSW 23 B12
Winiam VIC 40 K3
Winiam South VIC 40 K4
Winjallock VIC 39 B8
Winkie SA 62 B5 65 H13
Winkleigh TAS 55 E9 56 E2
Winmalee NSW 21 H8
Winnaleah TAS 55 D12
Winnambool VIC 28 H5 40 D7
Winnap VIC 38 G3
Winnellie NT 84 D3
Wininnowie NSW 62 G1 65 E9
Wininnowie Con Park SA 62 G1 65 E9
Winnungra NSW 29 D12
Winslow VIC 38 H6
Winston Hills NSW 19 D2 21 D8
Wintawatu SA 68 A3 90 K4
Winthrop WA 71 J3
Winton QLD 13 D9
Winton VIC 30 H2 42 D6
Winulta SA 62 G5 65 H9
Winya QLD 4 J3
Wirha SA 62 B7 65 K13
Wirra Wirra QLD 11 G10
Wirrabara SA 62 G2 65 E9
Wirraminna SA 64 B6
Wirrega SA 63 B10
Wirrida SA 66 H4
Wirrimah NSW 22 J3 30 A7
Wirrinya NSW 22 G1 29 E14
Wirrulla SA 64 D4
Wisanger SA 63 H8 65 K8
Wisemans Ferry NSW 20 F4 23 G9
Wishart QLD 3 G5
Wistow SA 60 J5
Witchcliffe WA 73 J12 74 H2
Withersfield QLD 8 H6
Witjira Nat Park SA 66 B5 91 K11
Witta QLD 4 G1
Wittenbra NSW 24 J3
Wittenoom WA 78 F5 82 F4
Wivenhoe Pocket QLD 5 J8
Wodonga VIC 29 K12 30 G4 43 B9
Wokalup WA 73 G8 74 F3
Woko Nat Park NSW 23 B11
Wokurna SA 62 G4 65 G9
Wolfdene QLD 5 D11
Wolfe Creek Meteorite Crater Res WA 79 C13 81 K12
Wolfram QLD 11 D12
Wollar NSW 22 C6
Wollemi Nat Park NSW 20 K4 22 D7
Wollert VIC 37 A8
Wollombi NSW 23 E9
Wollomombi NSW 25 G10
Wollongong NSW 21 C14 23 K8 31 B13
Wollun NSW 25 H9
Wolseley SA 40 K1 63 A10
Wolumla NSW 31 J10
Wolvi QLD 7 D12
Wombarra NSW 21 C13
Wombat NSW 22 J2 30 B7
Wombelano VIC 38 B3
Womboota NSW 29 K8
Womikata SA 64 A5 90 K6
Won Wron VIC 45 F9 46 G3
Wonboyn Lake NSW 31 K11 47 B14
Wondai QLD 7 D11
Wondalga NSW 29 J14 30 D7
Wondul Range Nat Park QLD 7 H9
Wonga Beach QLD 11 C12
Wonga Park VIC 37 C10
Wongamine WA 72 J1
Wongan Hills WA 74 A4 76 J5
Wongarbon NSW 22 C3
Wongarra VIC 39 K10
Wongianna SA 67 H9
Wongoondy WA 76 F4
Wongwibinda NSW 25 G10
Wonnangatta Station VIC 43 G8 46 A3
Wonnerup WA 73 H11
Wonoka SA 65 C10

Wonthaggi VIC 44 G4
Wonwondah East VIC 38 B5
Wonwondah North VIC 38 B5
Wonyip VIC 45 G8 46 H2
Woobera QLD 12 B4
Wood Wood VIC 28 H6 41 E9
Woodanilling WA 74 G5
Woodbridge TAS 50 J4 53 H10
Woodburn NSW 7 K13 25 C13
Woodburne VIC 39 F11
Woodbury TAS 53 C11 55 K11
Woodchester SA 60 K6 62 E7 65 K10
Woodenbong NSW 7 J12 25 A12
Woodend NSW 29 J12 30 D4
Woodend VIC 39 D12
Woodford NSW 21 J9
Woodford QLD 4 G3 7 F12
Woodgate QLD 7 B12
Woodhill QLD 5 F12
Woodhouse QLD 8 B5
Woodhouselee NSW 22 K5 31 B10
Woodie Woodie Mine WA 79 E8
Woodlands WA 71 E2
Woodleigh VIC 37 K12 44 F4
Woodpark NSW 21 E9
Woodridge QLD 3 J5 5 C11
Woods Point VIC 42 J6 44 A7 46 C1
Woods Reef NSW 24 G7
Woods Well SA 63 D9
Woodsdale TAS 53 D11
Woodside SA 60 G5 62 E7 65 J10
Woodside VIC 45 G10 46 H3
Woodstock NSW 22 G4
Woodstock QLD 8 A5 11 H14
Woodstock SA 50 G2 53 G9
Woodstock VIC 37 A8 39 B11 39 E14 42 J2 44 A2
Woodvale WA 71 B2
Woodville NSW 23 D10
Woodville SA 59 E3 60 F2
Woodville South SA 59 E3
Woody Island QLD 7 B13
Woody Point QLD 4 D6
Woogoompah Island QLD 5 B11
Woohlpooer VIC 38 D5
Wool Bay SA 62 H7 65 J8
Wool Wool VIC 39 H9
Woolamai VIC 44 F4
Woolbrook NSW 25 J8
Woolgarlo NSW 31 C8
Woolgoolga NSW 25 F13
Wooli NSW 25 F13
Woollahra NSW 21 B8
Woolloomooloo NSW 18 C3
Woolomin NSW 25 K8
Woologoa QLD 7 D12
Woolooma NSW 23 B9
Wooloowin NSW 19 K4
Wooloware Bay NSW 21 B10
Woolshed Flat SA 62 G1 65 D9
Woolsthorpe VIC 38 H6
Woomargama NSW 29 K13 30 F5 43 A10
Woomelang VIC 28 J4 40 G7
Woomera SA 64 B7
Woonbye QLD 4 F1
Woongoolba QLD 5 C10
Woonigan QLD 12 B4
Woonona NSW 21 C13
Woorabinda QLD 9 J8
Wooragee VIC 30 G4 43 C8
Woorak VIC 40 K4
Wooramel Roadhouse WA 76 B2 78 K2
Wooreen VIC 44 F6
Woori Yallock NSW 37 C11 42 K4 44 B4
Woorim QLD 4 D4
Woorinen VIC 28 H6 41 F9
Woorinen North VIC 41 E9
Woornack VIC 28 H4 40 E6
Woorndoo VIC 38 F7
Wooroloo WA 72 E3 74 C3 76 K5
Woorooilin QLD 7 D11
Wooroonook VIC 41 K8
Wooroonooran Nat Park QLD 11 D13
Woosang VIC 41 K9
Wootha QLD 4 G2
Wootton NSW 23 C12
Woronara Reservoir NSW 21 D11
Worongary QLD 5 C13
Woronora NSW 19 J3
Worsley WA 73 F9
Wotto Nat Res WA 76 G4
Wowan QLD 9 J10
Woy Woy NSW 20 B5
Wreck Island QLD 9 H12
Wrens Flat VIC 42 H7 46 B2
Wright Island SA 61 J6
Wroxham VIC 31 K10 47 B12
Wubalawun NT 86 J7
Wubin WA 76 H5
Wudinna SA 64 E5
Wugullar (Beswick) NT 86 G7
Wujal Wujal QLD 11 B12
Wulgulmerang VIC 43 G13 47 A8
Wumalgi QLD 9 F9
Wundowie WA 72 E2 74 C3 76 K5
Wunghnu VIC 42 B3

Wungu WA 81 J12
Wunkar SA 62 B6 65 H12
Wurarga WA 76 E5
Wurdiboluc VIC 39 H11
Wurruk VIC 45 D10 46 F4
Wurtulla QLD 4 D1
Wutul QLD 7 F10
Wutunugurra NT 89 J10
Wy Yung VIC 43 K11 45 B13 46 D6
Wyalkatchem WA 74 B5 76 J6
Wyalong NSW 29 E13
Wyan NSW 25 C12
Wyandra QLD 15 F13
Wyanga NSW 22 D2 27 K14 29 B14
Wyangala NSW 22 H4
Wybong NSW 23 C8
Wycarbah QLD 9 H10
Wycheproof VIC 28 K5 41 J8
Wychitella VIC 41 K10
Wycliffe Well NT 89 J9 91 A9
Wye River VIC 39 J11
Wyee NSW 20 B1 23 F10
Wyee Bay NSW 20 B1
Wyee Point NSW 20 B1
Wyeebo VIC 43 C10
Wyelangta VIC 39 K9
Wyena TAS 56 D6
Wylie Creek NSW 25 B11
Wymah NSW 29 K13 30 F5 43 B10
Wymlet VIC 28 H3 40 D5
Wynarka SA 62 D7 65 J11
Wynbring SA 66 K2 68 H7
Wyndham NSW 31 J10
Wyndham WA 81 D13
Wynn Vale SA 59 C6
Wynnum QLD 3 D7 4 D7
Wynyard TAS 54 D5
Wyola WA 72 A2
Wyoming NSW 20 B4
Wyong NSW 20 B2 23 F10
Wyong Creek NSW 20 C3
Wyongah NSW 20 B2
Wyperfeld Nat Park VIC 28 J3 40 G4 65 K14
Wyrallah NSW 25 C13
Wyrrabalong Nat Park NSW 20 A2 23 F10
Wyuna VIC 41 J14 42 B2

## Y

Yaamba QLD 9 G10
Yaapeet VIC 40 H5
Yabba VIC 43 C10
Yabba North VIC 42 B4
Yabulu QLD 8 A4 11 H14
Yacka SA 62 F3 65 F10
Yackandandah VIC 43 C8
Yagga Yagga WA 79 E13
Yagoona NSW 21 D9
Yahl SA 38 G1 63 B14
Yakanara WA 79 C11 81 J8
Yalamurra QLD 15 E12
Yalata SA 68 J5
Yalata Roadhouse SA 68 J5
Yalboroo QLD 8 C7
Yalbraith NSW 22 J6 31 A10
Yalca VIC 42 A3
Yalca North VIC 42 A3
Yalgogrin NSW 29 E12
Yalgogrin South NSW 29 F12 30 A4
Yalgoo WA 76 E5
Yalgorup Nat Park WA 72 H7 74 E2
Yallakool WA 41 F12
Yallambie NSW 20 E1
Yallaroi NSW 7 K8 24 C6
Yalleroi QLD 8 J3 13 F13
Yallingup WA 73 K11 74 G1
Yallock VIC 37 H12
Yallook VIC 41 K11
Yallourn VIC 44 E7 46 F1
Yallourn North VIC 44 D7 46 F1
Yallunda Flat SA 64 H6
Yaloak VIC 36 B2
Yaloak Vale VIC 36 C2
Yalwal NSW 31 C12
Yam Island QLD 16 A3
Yamala QLD 8 H7
Yamanto QLD 5 H9
Yamba NSW 25 D13
Yamba SA 40 B1 62 A5 65 H13
Yambacoona TAS 54 A6
Yamboyna QLD 8 H7
Yambuk VIC 38 H5
Yan Yean VIC 37 A8 39 E14 42 J2 44 A2
Yan Yean Reservoir VIC 37 A9
Yanac VIC 40 J3
Yanac South VIC 40 K3
Yanakie VIC 44 H7 46 J1
Yanamah WA 73 F13
Yanchep WA 72 H1 74 C2 76 K4
Yanchep Nat Park WA 72 G1 74 B2 76 K4
Yanco NSW 29 G11 30 B3
Yanco Glen NSW 26 J2
Yandaran QLD 7 A11 9 K12
Yanderra NSW 21 F14
Yanderup WA 72 G6
Yandina QLD 7 E13
Yandoit VIC 39 C11
Yanga Nat Res NSW 28 G6

Yango NSW 20 F1
Yaninee SA 64 E5
Yankalilla SA 61 H3 63 F8 65 K9
Yanna Ridge QLD 15 E13
Yannathan VIC 37 H12 44 E4
Yantabulla NSW 27 C8
Yaouk NSW 31 F8
Yaraka QLD 8 K1 13 H10 15 A10
Yaraman NSW 22 A7 24 K5
Yarck VIC 30 K1 42 G4
Yardanogo Nat Res WA 76 G4
Yarloop WA 73 G8 74 E3
Yarra Creek TAS 54 C6
Yarra Glen VIC 37 B10 42 J3 44 A3
Yarra Junction VIC 37 C12 42 K3 44 B4
Yarra Ranges Nat Park VIC 37 B12 42 J5 44 A5 46 D1
Yarrabah QLD 11 D13
Yarrabandai NSW 22 F1 29 C13
Yarrabin NSW 22 D5
Yarragon VIC 44 E6
Yarralena WA 73 A14
Yarralin NT 86 K3 88 B3
Yarralumla ACT 32 C1
Yarram QLD 45 G9 46 H2
Yarramalong NSW 20 D2
Yarraman QLD 7 E11
Yarrambat VIC 37 B9
Yarramony WA 72 C1
Yarranderie NSW 21 K13
Yarranderie State Rec Park NSW 21 J13
Yarrangobilly NSW 31 E8
Yarrara VIC 28 G2 40 B2
Yarras NSW 23 A12 25 K11
Yarrawonga VIC 29 K10 30 F2 42 B5
Yarrock VIC 40 K2
Yarroweyah VIC 42 A4
Yarrowitch NSW 25 K10
Yarrowyck NSW 25 G8
Yarrunga WA 79 B13 81 H12
Yarto VIC 40 F5
Yarwun QLD 9 H11
Yass NSW 31 C9
Yatala QLD 5 D10
Yatala Vale SA 59 C7
Yatchaw VIC 38 F5
Yathalamarra NT 87 C10
Yathong Nat Res NSW 29 B10
Yatina SA 62 F2 65 E10
Yatpool VIC 28 F3 40 B5
Yattalunga SA 60 C4
Yatte Yattah NSW 31 D12
Yawalpa QLD 5 B11
Yea VIC 30 K1 42 G3
Yeal Nat Res WA 72 G1 74 B3 76 K4
Yealering WA 74 E6
Yearinan NSW 24 J3
Yearinga VIC 40 K2
Yednia QLD 4 K2 7 E12
Yeelanna SA 64 G5
Yelarbon QLD 7 J8 24 B7
Yeldulkenie Con Park SA 62 K3 64 F7
Yellabinna Reg Res SA 64 B2 66 K2 68 J7
Yellangip VIC 40 J5
Yellingbo VIC 37 D11
Yellowdine WA 75 B9 77 J9
Yellowdine Nat Res WA 75 B9 77 J9
Yelta VIC 28 F3 40 A4
Yelverton WA 73 J11
Yenda NSW 29 F11 30 A2
Yendon VIC 39 E11
Yengo Nat Park NSW 20 G1 23 E9
Yennora NSW 21 D9
Yenyening Lakes Nat Res WA 72 A4 74 D5
Yeo Lake WA 83 C3
Yeo Lake Nat Res WA 77 E14 83 C3
Yeo Yeo NSW 22 K2 29 F14 30 B6
Yeoval NSW 22 D3
Yeppoon QLD 9 G10
Yerilla WA 77 G11 83 E1
Yering VIC 37 B10
Yerong Creek NSW 29 J12 30 D4
Yeronga QLD 3 F3
Yerongpilly QLD 3 F3
Yerranderie NSW 22 J7 31 A12
Yerrinbool NSW 21 F14
Yetholme NSW 22 G6
Yetman NSW 24 B7
Yilliminning WA 72 A7
Yin Barun VIC 30 H2 42 E5
Yinkanie SA 62 B5 65 H12
Yinnar VIC 44 E7 46 G1
Yinnar South VIC 44 F7 46 G1
Yirrirra WA 79 J13
Yirrkala NT 87 C13
Yiyili WA 79 C12 81 J10
Yokine WA 71 E4
Yolla TAS 54 D5
Yongala SA 62 E2 65 E10
Yoogali NSW 29 F11 30 A2
Yoongarillup WA 73 H11
York WA 72 C3 74 C4 76 K6
York Plains TAS 53 C11 55 K11
Yorke Peninsula SA 62 H6
Yorketown SA 62 H7 65 J8
Yorkeys Knob QLD 11 D13
Yorklea NSW 25 C13
Yorktown TAS 55 E8 56 D2
Yornaning WA 72 B7 74 E5
Yornup WA 73 E12

You Yangs Reg Park VIC 36 E3 3[?]
Youanmite VIC 42 B4
Youndegin WA 72 A2
Young NSW 22 J2 30 A7
Younghusband Peninsula SA 63 [?]
Youngtown TAS 56 H5
Youraling WA 72 B5
Yowie Bay NSW 19 K4
Yowrie NSW 31 H9 1
Yuelamu NT 90 D6
Yuendumu NT 90 D5
Yukan QLD 9 E8
Yulara NT 90 J4
Yuleba QLD 6 E6
Yulecart VIC 38 F5
Yulte Con Park SA 61 G5
Yuluma NSW 29 H11 30 D3
Yumbarra Con Park SA 64 C2 68 K[?]
Yumbarra Con Res SA 68 K6
Yuna WA 76 E3
Yundaga WA 77 G10
Yundamindera WA 77 F11 83 E1[?]
Yunderup WA 74 E3
Yundi SA 61 F6
Yundool VIC 42 C5
Yungaburra QLD 11 D12
Yungera VIC 41 C8
Yungngura WA 79 C11 80 J7
Yunta SA 62 D1 65 E11
Yunyarinyi (Kenmore Park) SA 6[?] 90 K6
Yurangka SA 68 B4 90 K5
Yuraygir Nat Park NSW 25 E13
Yurgo SA 62 C7 65 K12
Yuroke VIC 39 E13 42 J1 44 A1
Yuulong VIC 39 K9

## Z

Zagai Island QLD 16 A3
Zanthus WA 77 J13 83 F2
Zeally Bay VIC 36 J3
Zeehan TAS 52 A3 54 H3
Zeerust VIC 42 C3
Zillmere QLD 3 B4
Zumsteins VIC 38 C6
Zuytdorp Nat Res WA 76 D2

## List of Abbreviations

CBD — Central Business Di[...]
Con Park — Conservation Park
Nat Park — National Park
Nat Res — Nature Reserve
Reg Res — Regional Reserve
Res — Reserve